UNIVERSITY PRESS OF FLORIDA

Florida A&M University, Tallahassee
Florida Atlantic University, Boca Raton
Florida Gulf Coast University, Ft. Myers
Florida International University, Miami
Florida State University, Tallahassee
New College of Florida, Sarasota
University of Central Florida, Orlando
University of Florida, Gainesville
University of North Florida, Jacksonville
University of South Florida, Tampa
University of West Florida, Pensacola

Freedom for Women

Forging the Women's Liberation Movement, 1953–1970

Carol Giardina

University Press of Florida
Gainesville
Tallahassee
Tampa
Boca Raton
Pensacola
Orlando
Miami
Jacksonville
Ft. Myers
Sarasota

First cloth printing, 2010
First paperback printing, 2010

Library of Congress Cataloging-in-Publication Data
Giardina, Carol.
Freedom for women: forging the women's liberation movement,
1953–1970/Carol Giardina.
p. cm.
Includes bibliographical references and index.
ISBN 978-0-8130-3456-0 (cloth)
ISBN 978-0-8130-3692-2 (paperback)
1. Feminism—United States—History—20th century. 2. Second-
wave feminism—United States. 3. Women's rights—United
States—History—20th century. I. Title.
HQ1421.G53 2010
305.420973'090469–dc22   2009042595

The University Press of Florida is the scholarly publishing agency
for the State University System of Florida, comprising Florida
A&M University, Florida Atlantic University, Florida Gulf Coast
University, Florida International University, Florida State University,
New College of Florida, University of Central Florida, University of
Florida, University of North Florida, University of South Florida,
and University of West Florida.

University Press of Florida
15 Northwest 15th Street
Gainesville, FL 32611-2079
http://www.upf.com

For Judith Benninger Brown, freedom fighter,
who patiently taught me how to make a life in
the struggle for Women's Liberation

Contents

Illustrations

Illustrations follow page 97.

1. Ruby Doris Smith Robinson with her son, Kenneth Toure Robinson, ca. 1966

2. Kathie Amatniek (Sarachild) leaving on the bus to Mississippi from the Freedom Summer orientation in Oxford, Ohio, 1964

3. Judith Benninger (Brown) with CORE coworkers, Gadsden County, Florida, August 1964

4. Patricia Murphy (Robinson) with fellow Bennett College students, April 1963

5. Carol Hanisch with parents in Bancroft, Iowa, summer 1970

6. Frances M. Beal carrying the Third World Women's Alliance banner at the Women's Strike for Equality March, New York City, 26 August 1970

Acknowledgments

This book would not exist had not Women's Liberation Movements past and present toppled barriers to women's learning, engaged me in a life's work of social change, and deepened my desire and capacity for useful scholarship. My gratitude to these sisters-in-struggle is boundless. Coming from the movement, I hope the book will, in turn, serve the movement with more of its history.

My largest debt is to the political collaboration in 1968–69 of Judith Brown, Carol Hanisch, and Kathie Sarachild, with me as a very junior partner, which hashed out many of the ideas that would soon be providing valuable fuel for the Women's Liberation Movement. I am grateful for access to the intensive political correspondence among us, made possible by Brown, Hanisch, and Sarachild making copies of the letters and even circulating them in the early years, then carefully collecting and saving the letters. When we began, Judith recruited me as her apprentice and I helped her organize Gainesville Women's Liberation. Carol and Kathie were members of New York Radical Women. Although death stole Judith from the movement in 1991, she left behind volumes of powerful analysis in her correspondence over decades, derived from her continuing study and her experience in the Black Freedom and Women's Liberation Movements.

The Redstockings Women's Liberation Archives for Action, founded as a tool both for activist Redstockings strategists and theoreticians and an increasingly wider public, provided me with invaluable primary source material from its collection of public materials from the Women's Liberation

Movement's rebirth years. The Archives are rich for further mining, and I trust that my work will be scrutinized against the source documents to correct mistakes or to find points I have missed.

I am also indebted to the collections at the Schomburg Center for Research in Black Culture and to the research staff there who were always at the ready, knowledgeable, and gracious. Women's Liberation founder and scholar Jo Freeman took time out of her busy writing schedule to open her own extensive personal collection of early movement documents and letters and even helped make copies while offering context and commentary as I scribbled notes.

Kathie Sarachild and Carol Hanisch, whose analysis of the early Women's Liberation Movement in Redstockings' 1975 book *Feminist Revolution* greatly influenced my work, read the manuscript in some of its stages and provided major criticism and contributions, even though they were not in agreement with aspects of my perspective. They were, in fact, surprised by the degree of their differences with my understanding of the common history we shared in those formative years. Although many of our differences remained unresolved, wrestling over the ideas in this book was as stimulating as our discussions decades ago.

Kathy Scarbrough, a Redstocking in the 1980s and close collaborator of Carol Hanisch, gave keen and tireless editorial assistance with the manuscript and participated in many of the spirited debates. Black Liberation feminist and Redstocking Myrna Hill provided endless hours to "get it right." Scholar of women's history and the Black Freedom Movement Christina Greene twice read the manuscript almost in its entirety. Her pointers, especially on African American women's leadership participation in the Women's Liberation Movement, taught me lesson after lesson and sent me back into the archives again and again. Nancy Hewitt also read the manuscript in one of its early stages and made invaluable, virtually page-by-page commentary.

As hard as I have applied myself to the criticism these sister truth tellers provided, I am sure they will still be unsatisfied. Their high expectations kept me at it. It has been life-changingly validating to be taken so seriously by people whose work I deeply respect. Judith Brown, who brought me into the movement, was the first to teach me this way of working, and I have had the great good fortune to spend most of my life in the "Judith Brown school."

This book was made better and more urgent by the work and leadership of a new generation of Women's Liberation sisters in and around Redstockings and Gainesville Women's Liberation, who, like Kathy Scarbrough, came up after the 1960s: Jenny Brown, Marisa Figueiredo, Allison Guttu, Alexandra Leader, and Erin Mahoney. Jenny Brown and Annie Tummino, especially, held up my share of Women's Liberation organizing along with their own as I was writing.

Many other scholars and activists read and responded to all or parts of this work, and contributed ideas, encouragement, archival documents, historical memory, and help finding people. Among them I am especially grateful to Pam Allen, Lujoye Barnes, Frances Beal, Patricia Stephens Due, Sara Evans, Joshua Freeman, Thomas Kessner, Colin Palmer, Zoharah Simmons, Marilyn Webb, Barbara Welter, and Naomi Weisstein.

My deepest gratitude, also, goes to Spanish Civil War veteran John Penrod (15th International Brigade), dear companion and stalwart encourager, whose devotion to my success as a scholar and teacher has been peerlessly motivating and whose death in 2008 leaves an unfillable hole in my heart. Finally, I thank my family, Eleanor and August Giardina and Carmela Verdi, whose love and support made this study and so much else possible.

Abbreviations

BPP	Black Panther Party
CORE	Congress of Racial Equality
CP	Communist Party
EEOC	Equal Employment Opportunity Commission
ERA	Equal Rights Amendment
FAMU	Florida Agricultural and Mechanical University
GWL	Gainesville Women's Liberation
JBE	Judith Brown Endowment
JFPF	Jo Freeman, Personal Files
MFDP	Mississippi Freedom Democratic Party
NAACP	National Association for the Advancement of Colored People
NAG	Nonviolent Action Group
NARAL	National Association for the Repeal of Abortion Laws
NCNP	National Conference for a New Politics
NCNW	National Council of Negro Women
NOW	National Organization for Women
NWRO	National Welfare Rights Organization
NYRW	New York Radical Women
RAM	Revolutionary Action Movement
RWLAA	Redstockings Women's Liberation Archives for Action
SCEF	Southern Conference Education Fund
SCLC	Southern Christian Leadership Conference
SDS	Students for a Democratic Society
SNCC	Student Nonviolent Coordinating Committee

SNYC	Southern Negro Youth Congress
SSOC	Southern Student Organizing Committee
TWWA	Third World Women's Alliance
VWLM	*Voice of the Women's Liberation Movement*
WLM	Women's Liberation Movement
WSG	West Side Group (Chicago)
YNCL	Young Negro Cooperative League

Introduction

THIS IS AN INVESTIGATION of how Women's Liberation pioneers gained the courage and consciousness to make a movement against male supremacy in the United States in the 1960s. It chronicles the gaining of that courage and consciousness. It is not about the particulars of the male domination the founding organizers experienced as individuals or their reaction to that domination. Their experience of the sexism rampant in the period, while important, has been told many times, and as activist-sociologist Jo Freeman said, "social strain does not create social movements," only the potential for them.[1]

The focus of this investigation reflects a change since the rebirth years of feminism. A weighing of past experience and insights of new experience and research clarify the importance of the positive contributions of the Black Freedom Movement and the Left, Old and New, to the emergence of the Women's Liberation Movement. Their unique positive influence played a more significant part in fueling the new feminism than did women's righteous anger at male chauvinism in these movements and in society as a whole.

This study begins in 1953, the year that *The Second Sex* arrived in the United States and provided the germinal source of feminist consciousness for a significant number of Women's Liberation founders.[2] It is the story of the making of the movement and how it became established. I argue that it was a 1960s movement very much established by 1970, which in no way suggests that momentous events and advances of the movement were over by 1970. The study closes in 1970, the year the movement was established in the United States and its spread around the world was well under way.[3]

The investigation seeks the impetus for the movement in the seeds of the new society that early Women's Liberation organizers wished to create—seeds that, as Karl Marx's concept has it, blossomed right there amidst the sexism in which the founders lived. I have focused on the sources instrumental to Women's Liberation in founders' families, in the Black Freedom Movement, in the Left, Old and New, and in the legacies of earlier feminists, from the "First Wave" of the 1820s through the 1920s to Simone de Beauvoir in the mid-twentieth century.

What does it take to make a social movement of such scope? Certainly consciousness that collective action is needed to overcome oppressive conditions is a necessary, if insufficient, ingredient in any radical struggle. Individuals realizing that what appear to be personal problems have a social basis is also critical. So is the related understanding that a liberation struggle is most effective and radical when waged by the oppressed themselves, not saviors from the outside, or when it organizes on the basis of the common stake of all concerned rather than on the noblesse oblige idea of helping the "less fortunate." In the 1950s and 1960s these essential insights came together for a handful of young women who pressed the ideas into service for themselves as members of an oppressed sex.

In the United States today millions benefit from achievements of the Second Wave of feminism, such as legal abortion and public awareness of sexism and gender equality. But the origins and founders of the Women's Liberation branch of the movement that brought about these changes are little known and even less well understood in comparison with the movement's moderate branch.[4]

Feminism resurfaced in the early 1960s in two distinct forms, a moderate branch, then consisting of mostly middle-aged women, and one mostly made up of young women who openly called themselves "radical women." The younger women used terms like Women's Liberation, Female Liberation, Radical Feminist, or Socialist Feminist to describe themselves. The founding organization of the moderate branch was the National Organization for Women (NOW). Emblematic of their political and age differences, and demonstrating the Civil Rights Movement's inspiring influence on both, NOW characterized itself as an NAACP for women, while Women's Liberation identified with the daring and militant young organizers in the South associated with the Student Nonviolent Coordinating Committee (SNCC).[5]

There is important recent literature reclaiming the erased history of the key role black women played in the development of the U.S. Second Wave, in first triggering the earliest of stirrings of feminism in SNCC and other flashpoints.[6] But the Women's Liberation Movement still has not dispelled its false image as the concern of white, affluent women. It continues to appear for the most part spontaneous and leaderless, and, as we shall see, its origins remain misunderstood.

This study closely examines the coming together of two of the several elements upon which the rebirth of the movement depended: understanding of collective oppression—that the unhappiness in one's life has a social cause— and readiness for collective action. Feminist scholar Sara Evans caught the centrality of these two ingredients in her comparison of black civil rights organizing in the South with the organizing by Students for a Democratic Society (SDS) of the inner-city poor in the North. In the South, she said, because of the visibility of segregation, "one could presume a consciousness of collective oppression and had only to generate the will to act." In the North, on the other hand, there was neither an understanding of the need for collective action nor even a consciousness of group oppression, and "organizing began a step back."[7]

In the United States—with women of all classes beset, as black feminist playwright Lorraine Hansberry observed in 1957, by the reign of "the most devastating anti-equality myth of all," the myth that women were already free—the process of organizing against women's subordination began more than a few steps back.[8]

But a few young women got a head start. They knew about the social and political existence of male supremacy before they experienced it in the movements of the 1960s. Rather than giving them their first taste of male domination, the 1960s movements gave them the first taste of a freedom movement and with it vital theory and strategy for solving the problem of sexism. Incipient Women's Liberation founders learned from socially conscious families and mentors and from reading *The Second Sex* as teenagers that, because women were suppressed as a group, their own lives too would be restricted. Yet they did not consider collective solutions to the "woman question" until they experienced the effectiveness of collective action in the Civil Rights Movement.[9] As black activist scholar Bernice Johnson Reagon said, the black-led Southern Civil Rights Movement was the "borning" movement."[10]

Other women learned collective protest in the New Left as they organized to stop the war in Vietnam, and yet others in the Black Power Movement. In some cases, both insights drew on traditions of family activism, mostly on the Left in families in or near the Communist Party. In this way and others, as we'll see, the "Old" Left was significant in the resurgence of feminism.[11]

The preceding First Wave of feminism in the United States also had an influence from within families. For example, Patricia Robinson, a black founder of Women's Liberation, had a father who had been on the national board of Planned Parenthood and brought the influence of the First Wave fight for birth control into Robinson's politics. Judith Brown and Pam Allen, white founders of Women's Liberation, grew up learning about the suffragists in their families. Whatever the order in which women understood they were oppressed because of their sex and that this called for collective action, once these two understandings combined, the powerful mix propelled Women's Liberation pioneers into organizing.

Feminist ideas and principles had been a continuous force in the lives of these women. Their feminism was not simply reactive. Many had been feminist as long as they could remember, well before they entered the movements of the 1960s.[12] As a result, these pioneers actively used and transformed the resources of the Black Freedom Movement and the Left, Old and New, in the collective interests of women. And yet the story of their relationship to these movements has often cast them only as victims of male chauvinism in these movements, and an allegedly extreme form at that.

Black and white women in the Black Freedom Movement and the Left, like their sisters in the larger society, did face treatment as second-class citizens within these movements, as elsewhere. But there were some paradoxes. While those who began organizing for Women's Liberation were no exception, most of them were also longtime leaders of local and even national movement projects. Like many of the leaders of anticolonial revolutions in Third World nations, they were among the least oppressed of their group. That is, they were those who had pushed through openings in an overall system that nevertheless oppressed them in many other ways.[13]

For a woman to take leadership in male-dominated movements took more courage and commitment than that of many of the males holding more advanced positions—not to mention outthinking and outworking male leaders. Importantly, in the Black Freedom Movement and the Left, compared to the rest of society, leadership was more possible for women. The margin of possibility was just wide enough to enable a critical mass of Women's Liberation organizers to develop.

The notion that the 1960s movements were a bit less, not more, sexist than the larger society has been circulating in the literature on the history of the Women's Liberation Movement since the earliest monographs.[14] The contribution of the Civil Rights Movement to Women's Liberation is routinely acknowledged, if insufficiently understood and explored, and awareness of the usable legacy from the Left, Old and New, has been growing.[15] However, the larger margin of opportunity for women in these movements continues to escape scholarly attention commensurate with the immensity of its significance, and it has escaped public attention even more. Women's Liberation pioneers in the Black Freedom Movement and the Left took action in their own interests as women despite the prevailing expectations and limitations governing women at that time. They took on nontraditional work for women, leading demonstrations and projects, confronting the authorities and serving jail time, making public speeches, and writing for movement newspapers.[16] They frequently held formal leadership over men in this work. African American women also had formal leadership over white men and white women.

Finally, in the collective interests of their sex, Women's Liberation pioneers redirected publishing opportunities, funds, and meeting space, and, most precious of all, their freedom movement acquired newfound knowledge, skills, and courage in the struggle. By 1970 they had men all across the various protest movements on the defensive. Although the men had hardly purged themselves of male chauvinism, many took the step of recognizing and opposing it. From the Black Panther Party (BPP) to various factions of the New Left came official positions and statements against male supremacy in the movement and in the larger society.[17]

Nevertheless, the longstanding explanation of the origin of the Women's Liberation Movement still prevails: that it was primarily a result of the conflict between women's rising expectations and frustration with male domination in the Black Freedom Movement, especially Black Power, and the New Left. While this observation does describe the experience of a number of women in those movements, it also obscures the active nature of these movements in the making of the Women's Liberation Movement. Why? First, our attention is typically focused on the women's frustrated reaction to sexism rather than on the reasons for their growing sense of power and possibility. Second, with today's heightened recognition and lower tolerance of male chauvinism, the things that men did in the 1960s to suppress feminist protest appear very striking and leave the strongest impression.

Yet it should be exactly the opposite. Women's greater expectations, not male domination and oppression, were the ignition spark and catalyst for the birth of the new movement. Women have been angry about and resisted male domination for centuries; that was a given. Rarely has resistance taken the form of a social movement or led to the development and public articulation of feminist politics. What was new and provocative in the Black Freedom Movement and the New Left was the experience of new ideas, bold deeds, the courage of one's convictions, and victory against great odds through collective action.

This taste of freedom and power to change things brought an insatiable desire for more. Simultaneously, the methods of these movements demonstrated the means to contend for it. For example, in 1964 Zoharah Simmons (then Gwendolyn Robinson) was a young African American woman effectively leading a Student Nonviolent Coordinating Committee project for a year and a half in Laurel, an especially dangerous small town in Mississippi. Her staff included white men, some older than she was. The project offices were repeatedly attacked and twice destroyed by firebombs. Simmons emerged from the experience a changed person because, as she said, "I had proven that a woman could run a SNCC project in Mississippi and succeed. I had faced my fear of Mississippi and overcome that too."[18]

A few years later, in the black nationalist Revolutionary Action Movement (RAM) she challenged attempts to impose requirements that women not speak in meetings. She recalls how she confidently protested this because "I'd been among the baddest organizers on the SNCC field staff in Mississippi— now *who* was telling *me* not to speak in a meeting?"[19] Being project director had prepared her to fight the male chauvinism she subsequently faced. What strikes us today is RAM requiring silence of its female members, while a woman leading a project does not have such attention-catching novelty. So we wrongly conclude that the male chauvinism was the catalytic influence.

When the particulars of women's new and liberatory experiences see the printed page they appear unremarkable and leave almost no impression as courageous firsts for women. A woman in SNCC came up with an important policy, a woman in SDS gave a public speech. Because we have become accustomed to women doing these things, our reaction, if we even notice, is "So what?" Thus the terrain of freedom that women seized in these movements, which held the seeds of Women's Liberation, has gone largely unnoticed. So have the women themselves.

Yet in the 1960s such actions—women giving public political speeches or leading demonstrations that took on the authorities—were rarely seen in the United States. Few people today reading black SNCC staff member Fannie

Lou Hamer's electrifying remarks at the National Democratic Convention in 1964 know that her behavior was utterly outside the gender conventions of the day for black or white women or that she had the admiration and support of all in SNCC, men as well as women. But today's readers are understandably vexed to learn that a male leader, an admiring coworker of Hamer, responded to discussion of women's position in the movement with a sexist joke.

The failure to absorb and appreciate such paradoxes results in the erasure of women's agency in the making of the Women's Liberation Movement, subordinating it to an exaggerated view of sexism in the other sixties movements. This disproportion was described by Martha Prescod Norman, former SNCC field secretary in Mississippi and in Selma, Alabama. In the 1980s Norman, who often spoke in college classes, found herself perpetually on the defensive because, as she put it, "there was a particular established view on the floor" already.[20] "People would ask, 'How did you deal with the sexism in SNCC?'"[21] These questions, Norman said, reflected "an extremely negative view of male/female relations within SNCC."[22] When she told audiences that "as a woman, I felt it [SNCC] was the singularly most liberating environment I've ever been in," she felt that her own gender consciousness was "being held in question."[23]

This study, then, enters the discussion of the origins of the Women's Liberation Movement and aims to focus attention on the instrumental part the nonfeminist social movements played—movements in which women held a contradictory position of more equal partnership and freedom for contribution and self-development than in the larger society within a context of other continuing inequalities.

My own learning process may help clarify this. When I began this study, Sara Evans's *Personal Politics* (1979) and Alice Echols's *Daring to Be Bad* (1989) were the preeminent books on Women's Liberation. I believed that the view of Women's Liberation as a reaction to male chauvinism in the Black Freedom Movement and the Left had been established by Evans and Echols.

Rereading *Personal Politics*, I was surprised to find that Evans repeatedly made observations such as "within these movements [the Civil Rights Movement and New Left] they [Women's Liberation founders] had learned to respect themselves and to know their own strength."[24] Similarly, Alice Echols, in a clear acknowledgment of Evans, argued that women in these movements "began to acquire political skills" and "felt themselves to be involved in socially meaningful work."[25]

I turned to an earlier work, Jo Freeman's *The Politics of Women's Liberation*

(1975), with the same result. Evans, Echols, and Freeman all explained the origins of the new movement by referring to a "threatened loss of new possibility," as Evans put it.[26] Indeed, Echols quoted Evans with approval, and Evans acknowledged Freeman. How, then, had the impression of male domination in the 1960s movements come to so overshadow all the positive things women found there?

One source of this misinterpretation is the vivid firsthand accounts of male chauvinism in the Black Freedom Movement and New Left given by incipient Women's Liberation founders.[27] Even as the founders' daringly aggressive and detailed criticism helped to reform those movements, it hung out their "dirty laundry" as no other institutions' was hung out. This public airing of sexism in the 1960s movements was followed in the 1980s by a body of secondary literature that reduced the experience of Women's Liberation founders in the Black Freedom Movement and the New Left to shock, outrage, and derision so intense that the creation of the Women's Liberation Movement appeared to have been little more than a withdrawal into a sequestered female community for self-preservation and healing.[28]

While pondering how the emphasis on sexism had preempted a deeper understanding of the relationship between Women's Liberation, the Black Freedom Movement, and the New Left, I began to notice other scholars making the same misinterpretation that I had. Claire G. Moses, the editor of the journal *Feminist Studies*, wrote to me saying that the interpretation that Sara Evans had established—namely, the notion that the Women's Liberation Movement resulted from women's spontaneous opposition to sexism in the Black Freedom Movement and the New Left—had been overturned by the newer literature, in particular Ruth Rosen's *The World Split Open*.[29] Historian and Women's Liberation veteran Barbara Winslow also saw Evans and Echols as the sources of this view. Winslow said, "Much has been written—for example, by Sara Evans and Alice Echols—about how the male chauvinism of the Civil Rights, antiwar, draft resistance, and student movements gave birth to the women's liberation movement."[30]

Close reading of the newer literature revealed little, if any, departure from the model Evans actually did establish: the birth of Women's Liberation out of the contradiction between the women's experience of male chauvinism in the movements of the 1960s and the new ideas and skills they developed there. For example, in their 1998 anthology Rachel Blau DuPlessis and Ann Snitow refer to the birth of Women's Liberation out of "contradictions between the radical ethos in such groups as SDS . . . and SNCC . . . and their proud, unthinking male chauvinism."[31]

Two years later veteran activist historians Rosalyn Baxandall and Linda Gordon wrote of the political roots of Women's Liberation in the movements of the 1950s and 1960s. There, they said, women were "valued participants who gained skills and self-confidence. At the same time, they have been treated as subordinates. . . . It is precisely this combination of raised aspirations and frustration that gives rise to rebellion."[32] Like DuPlessis and Snitow, Baxandall and Gordon gave examples of "identifiable legacies" of the Black Freedom Movement and the New Left for Women's Liberation including antiauthoritarianism and irreverence. They also noted: "Women in civil rights and the New Left were on the whole less victimized, more respected, and less romanticized than they were in the mainstream culture."[33]

This was similar to Evans's formulation in *Personal Politics* about the Civil Rights Movement being "strikingly egalitarian" in comparison to most of U.S. society and the New Left's being "marginally freer for women," as already noted.[34] Evans had also identified the indebtedness of Women's Liberation founders to the Civil Rights Movement for "language to name and describe oppression; a deep belief in freedom, equality, and community . . . a willingness to question and challenge any social institution that failed to meet human needs; and the ability to organize."[35] Given her reputation as the purveyor of the notion that Women's Liberation was a reaction to male chauvinism, it is ironic that of all the explanations of the birth of Women's Liberation, Evans provided foundational evidence, usually eloquent and inspiring description and clearer analysis of the ways in which the Civil Rights Movement and the New Left provided building blocks for Women's Liberation.

Like Evans and others, historian Ruth Rosen used what could be called a model of a contradiction when she spoke of a "painful collision" between the new "skills and confidence" women learned in the movements of the 1960s and their "lack of recognition" from male coworkers. She enumerated skills women gained in these movements, including exploring ideas and values, learning how to organize, and "thinking strategically and theoretically."[36] But most of Rosen's reviewers failed to see in her account the picture of these movements as "nurturing women's political and leadership skills" that Claire Moses of *Feminist Studies* had seen.[37] Indeed, the *New York Times* reviewer, Janny Scott, said Rosen had pinpointed the birth of Women's Liberation in the "disenchantment" of women who felt that SNCC and SDS had "subordinated them."[38]

Another reviewer said she had learned from Rosen's book that the movement began because of women's rage at men in the 1960s movements who "presumed them to be subordinates and sexual side dishes." Shocked by the "level of antipathy toward women" Rosen described in the New Left, the reviewer repeated in detail the often retold story of men yelling obscenities as Women's Liberation founder Marilyn Webb gave a feminist speech at an antiwar rally and Webb's "depression" at the men's "scorn."[39]

Baxandall and Gordon also did not find in Rosen's work the "nurture" of women's skills in the Black Freedom Movement and the New Left. Instead, they called Rosen's view of the New Left "lopsided hostility" because she did not "acknowledge adequately the role of SDS and SNCC in providing vital education, skills and theory for early feminism."[40] The descriptions of sexism simply trumped the instrumental legacy and relegated it to a minor, if even noticed, role.

However, historians of the movement are now beginning to recognize this problem. Baxandall and Gordon saw that Rosen had failed to give the impression she may have wished to give. Although Winslow wrongly held Evans and Echols responsible, she was critical of the position she attributed to them—that male chauvinism was the cause of Women's Liberation. Similarly, Moses found this idea inadequate to explain the birth of the movement. And so it is.

More recently, Evans offered a corrective to the view that sexism was the cause of Women's Liberation, a narrative that, she rightly points out, "continues to predominate."[41] Evans targets "jeremiads against the sexism on the left" in the founding Women's Liberation documents as the source of the erroneous idea that male chauvinism caused a rebirth of Women's Liberation. She distances herself and her early feminist coworkers from what she describes as the extremes of anger found in these documents.[42]

But the anger was there, and was hardly limited to a few early papers. It was widespread, and understandably so. Little wonder, after all, that people with just grievances were very angry about them. Many of us knew that anger well.

The main problem is neither that the anger of the founders has been exaggerated nor that the views of those who were less angry have been ignored. The problem is that the anger alone was impotent. It had been present for a long time and amounted to little.

The catalyst for Women's Liberation was something new that came along and shaped the anger into an instrument for social change. Anger at domination is a constant in the lives of subordinated people. The impetus for a movement comes from something else besides oppression, something that enables oppressed people to find an understanding of their experience that produces the courage to stand up collectively and fight.

There is a growing consciousness that the view of women's agency in explanations of the birth of the Women's Liberation Movement has been too narrow, sometimes to the point of eliminating it completely.[43] The emerging interpretation holds that the building blocks of the continuity of political heritage and the instrumentality of successful political experience must be better understood if we are to get the origins of the movement right. Evans's new active framing of Women's Liberation pioneers in the other 1960s movements shows this new interpretation when Evans says that, having gained skills and courage in these movements, they began to "turn these assets to their own use."[44]

This interpretation is more than a historiographical shift. Many of the historians involved in the revision, including this author, were early Women's Liberation activists.[45] So the shift represents a desire on the part of the activists for a deeper understanding of their own work.

For instance, my first sense of this shift came in 1985 from reading "The Civil Rights Movement: Lessons for Women's Liberation," a speech that powerfully demonstrated the causality of and gratitude due to SNCC. This speech was given in 1983 by white SNCC volunteer and Women's Liberation founder Kathie Sarachild at a conference about the movements of the 1960s.[46] Sarachild opened my eyes to the distinction between the debt feminists owed the Black Freedom Movement and the terrible reputation for sexism it continued to have in many feminist circles. Sarachild reflected on how much more important SNCC leader Stokely Carmichael's injunction to whites to "fight your own oppressor" was to her organizing for Women's Liberation than his sexism. She also emphasized learning ideas for mass organizing and gaining from experience a new certainty of belief in the reality and possibility of an oppressed people rising and uniting on its own behalf. She learned this from both the SNCC leaders and the everyday people on the Batesville Project in Mississippi where she worked.

This stirring appreciation expressed for SNCC, and particularly for Stokely Carmichael, was striking because in the politics of the early Women's Liberation Movement, and in historical accounts of it, Sarachild has a reputation for being a militant in the "antimale" camp (which was also at the time derided as "feminist"). I soon began to hear other renowned white "kick male chauvinist butt" pioneers such as Judith Brown and Carol Hanisch talk this way about their Civil Rights Movement experience in the Deep South.[47]

Black pioneers of Women's Liberation who fought male domination within the Black Freedom Movement also found the positive lessons of their struggle against white supremacy more important than their experiences with male supremacy. Former Black Panther Party communications secretary Kathleen Cleaver, an outspoken critic of male chauvinism in the Black Panther Party, referred to the "tremendous education" the Party gave her, citing "how to understand the world around us, how to think through the issues of what we could do on our own to advance our people's cause, how to organize our own people to change the world around us."[48] Cleaver questioned the political agenda of those "nowadays" who ask "what were the gender issues in the Black Panther Party?" Did they use the question to "deflect attention from confronting the revolutionary critique our organization made of the larger society?"[49]

Black activist and founding Women's Liberation organizer Frances M. Beal considered all her work against male supremacy, imperialism, and racism as taking place in and benefiting the "left wing of the revolutionary nationalist wing of Black Power."[50] Despite the views of their sources, however, most feminist scholars of the Black Freedom Movement who were not participants in it either condemn as male chauvinist the turn to nationalism and Black Power in the second half of the sixties or consider it (along with the racism of white feminists) the central cause of the rise of black feminism.[51]

The evidence offered in this study is, in part, an attempt to go deeper into the roots and rebirth of the Women's Liberation Movement. There is more at stake in understanding the origins of the Women's Liberation Movement. We should know, for example, that its founders' exposures of and "jeremiads" against male chauvinism on the Left did not result in the organization of Women's Liberation as an anti-Left movement.

While the Black Freedom Movement and the New Left were sometimes egregiously sexist, they were the first male-dominated formations of the 1960s to begin to make voluntary public self-criticism and change in their practice in response to ever greater pressure from Women's Liberation. Unlike schools, churches, unions, the sports world, the media, government, and most employers, they did this without being ordered to do so by the courts. Far from being the most sexist institutions of their day, these movements were, as Kathleen Cleaver observed, among the least sexist: "In 1970 the Black Panther Party took a formal position on the liberation of women. Did the U.S. Congress make any statement on the liberation of women? Did the Congress enable the Equal Rights Amendment to become part of the Constitution? Did the Oakland police issue a position against gender discrimination? It is in this context that gender relations . . . in the Black Panther Party should be examined."[52]

Again, the sexism in the movements of the 1960s is not the focus of this study. Its direction is guided by deeply held assumptions about women's agency and the power of continuity—as opposed to ignorance of male chauvinism in the 1960s movements or rose-colored glasses of nostalgia. Indeed, this writer, a participant in those movements, experienced the fury that Evans did not and the male chauvinism, in the egregious and diverse forms detailed in firsthand and secondary accounts of the genesis of the Women's Liberation Movement.[53] Instead, I hope to train a floodlight on the parts of the story of the Women's Liberation Movement that overemphasis on male chauvinism has repeatedly distracted attention from—the interdependence of freedom movements, and the gift of the legacy of freedom movement experience from generation to generation.

In addition, this study barely touches upon some other conditions needed to fully understand the resurgence of feminism. First, the broad economic and political context of the 1950s and 1960s was wind beneath the founders' wings. Throughout most of history, after all, there has been little or no organized feminist movement, although oppression always breeds resistance in one form or another. Pioneering women with radical knowledge and special skills have come into being across the ages but found themselves condemned or worse and, at least in their own time, unable to advance the collective interests of their sex. Under conditions less conducive to change than the 1960s, a rebel intellectual such as Women's Liberation organizer Shulamith Firestone, founder of influential 1960s radical feminist groups and author in 1970 of *The Dialectic of Sex: The Case for Feminist Revolution*, might have been a lone voice producing a classic statement whose influence would have to wait for the future. Or she might have been burned at the stake as a heretic, no trace of her dreams of freedom left behind.

The international context of Cold War competition between the superpowers, and the structural economic changes in the United States under way in the 1950s and 1960s, which saw Women's Liberation take off, bear much more investigation. So does the consciousness of the masses of women of the period, although radical and feminist activist and theoretician Selma James made a good start on it as early as 1957.[54] Why were so many diverse women so surprisingly ready to take up the struggle? The start of the movement depended on a particular mix of changing political and economic conditions, the readiness of large numbers of women for protest, and the work of other women whose influence I have not included.[55]

As may be already apparent, this study is what is sometimes called "engaged history." Like Sara Evans and others, I was a participant in the movements of the 1960s. The study was undertaken in part because, like Evans, I did not see my own experience in what seemed to be the common understanding of the movement's emergence. I had been angrier at male chauvinism than Evans and her coworkers, but there were times in the Black Freedom Movement and the New Left when I experienced appreciation as a peer that was unequaled in the larger society. In the Black Power Movement in our small southern town, I knew that men as well as women valued my work in a way that was far greater and felt different and better than at my paid job or in my college classes. I played on the sexually and racially integrated SDS softball team, where the guys often raced in front of me to catch balls that were clearly mine to catch. But I played ball on this team, nonetheless, at a time when sports at the university and in the city league were segregated by sex and by race.

I was a novice agitator then whose heart lay in the counterculture; I was not a longtime local movement leader. When I attended the first national meeting of the Women's Liberation Movement in 1968 in Sandy Springs, Maryland, the difference between me and the others there was palpable. The phrase "skills and confidence" utterly understates what they had that I did not. Their transcendent presence filled the meeting hall with sparkling energy and power I can feel today. Although the Women's Liberation branch of the Second Wave prided itself on "leaderlessness," there were leaders, women who showed this lucky new recruit how to participate in building a movement that would transform how both sexes lived their lives.[56]

I felt that even the anger of the powerful could not stop the women I met at that conference, because making the Women's Liberation Movement was not the first time they had acted upon strongly held convictions. What distinguished them was years of work in the Black Freedom Movement and the New Left, years in which many had risked everything they had, including their lives. They also had done the considerable intellectual homework necessary to create social change. I immediately aspired to understand and gain the sense of purposefulness and capability that emanated from these women. Far from suffering from exceptionally bad experiences in their lives as women, or in some other ways, as goes the common defense against the feminist critique, these young women were the strongest, most clearheaded people, full of hope and self-determined, that I had ever seen congregated in one place.

Toward a Female Liberation Movement

IN THE EARLY 1960s, male domination limited the participation of women in the life of the nation, the family, and the community, and interfered with women's ability to determine the course of their lives. Women struggled as best they could, but because of the reigning myth Lorraine Hansberry had referred to, the myth that women in the United States were already emancipated, few of them were aware that the boundaries of their freedom as women were anything more than the impositions of their own individual shortcomings. Winning the right to vote just a few decades earlier was what had set women free, cheerleaders for this myth often argued. There was no publicly held concept of sexism.

Yet by the close of the decade, a resurgent movement for the liberation of women challenged male domination in virtually every aspect of life. Simone de Beauvoir's prediction, in 1949, that the "myth of femininity" was "about to be dethroned" appeared to be coming true.[1] Women, heretofore burdened as individuals with an unacknowledged imbalance of power between the sexes, now began to understand what they were up against.

No great leader came. The forces of history alone had not liberated women. Nor did angry women, fed up with male chauvinism, spontaneously arise and fight. The change from the early to the late sixties was due, in large part, to the readiness of a small number of young women who dared to harness a wave of economic and demographic changes, fortuitous to their cause, that rose in the aftermath of World War II.

Although many women had been dismissed from paid employment to make way for returning veterans after the war, large numbers soon began to return to work. In contrast to war-related fluctuations in their job opportunities, women were able to find work in newly expanding sectors of the economy such as services and clerical. As early as 1950, women's presence in the paid labor force equaled its previous wartime peak.

During these years, as women returned to paid employment and the birthrate slowed, incipient Women's Liberation founders were growing up, many of them imbued with the values of socially conscious families, mothers who worked outside the home, and, as we will see, the feminism of Simone de Beauvoir. Far from merely coasting on changing conditions, these women tested the limits. Between 1964 and 1966, they took the first steps toward Women's Liberation. By 1968 they had started a mass, grassroots movement. By 1970 the movement was established in the United States and its spread around the world was under way.

Oppressive Conditions, Unconscious Women

Considering the restrictive conditions of the 1950s, the challenge of Women's Liberation appeared formidable. Abortion was illegal, birth control was harder to come by than it is now, and women's wages were just a little over half of men's. As the percentage of women in the paid labor force increased, so did the burden of the "double shift"—a paid job from nine to five and a second, unpaid one at home with no closing time.

In 1960, a woman was only half as likely to go to college as a man.[2] The percentage of women to men in college had been declining through the mid-1950s, as had the percentage of women who graduated from college.[3] Sixty percent of women dropped out of college to marry, and women were marrying at increasingly younger ages—the average was then twenty.[4] For those women who graduated, about half would take paid work, one out of three as clerical workers. As late as 1968, one-third of employed female college graduates were still clerical workers. While the percentage of women in clerical work increased in the 1950s, the proportion of women in professional fields had been decreasing since 1940.[5] It was lower in the United States than in many countries in Europe, as Betty Friedan's *Feminine Mystique* noted in 1963.[6]

Differences between black women and white women were considerable. In 1966, African American women's median earnings were 71 percent of white women's, and they were far more likely than white women to be employed as domestic workers. Indeed, more than one-third of all wage-earning African American women worked in private household employment, where they were not covered by workers' compensation, unemployment compensation, or wage and hour laws. All in all, compared with white women, African American women spent more time in the paid labor force, and as working wives they shouldered a greater share of responsibility for economic support of the family. They were more likely to head single-parent households, to be widowed, and to have completed fewer years of school.

There were numerically more college-educated African American women than African American men, but African American feminist scholar Pauli Murray attributed this to the numerical imbalance between the sexes for African Americans: ninety-four black males for every hundred black women. In other words, black women were not going to college at a greater rate than black men, there were simply more black women than black men in the population. Moreover, African American women were still on the bottom of the wage scale, earning 65 percent of the salaries of African American men. Ranked by income, white men were at the top, black men second, white women third, and African American women last. Concluding her study of income and education statistics, Murray observed, "The notion of the favored economic position of the black female in relation to the black male is a myth."[7]

In most newspapers, "help wanted" advertisements were segregated by sex as well as race. To purchase on credit, even a wage-earning woman was required to document her husband's permission. Women on many college campuses were subjected to curfews, and to dress codes banning slacks from nine to five. Repeated dress code violations were punished by weekend-long detention in the dormitory. Few campuses had comparable requirements or penalties for male students.

Women chafed against these boundaries as individuals, and some were risking their lives. From illegal abortions, for example, five to ten thousand died each year. According to African American feminist organizer Frances Beal, the death rate from illegal abortions was higher for black women than for white women.[8] Yet before the Women's Liberation Movement made the existence of sexism a publicly recognized injustice, women, while conscious of putting up a fight against unfair odds, could be unconscious of the political nature of that fight. Aptly characterizing the unconsciousness of the period, pioneer Women's Liberation organizer Jo Freeman reflected on her undergraduate years at the University of California at Berkeley in the early 1960s. "I not only never had a woman professor, I never even saw one," Freeman said. "Worse yet, I didn't notice."[9]

Although vastly dissatisfied with the conditions they faced, countless women were unaware that they were up against the socially imposed political and economic boundaries of male domination. Even those who were aware that they faced a system of sexism did not know what to do about it. Women in the United States were said to be already emancipated and the freest in the world; too free, according to some social commentators, for their own or anyone else's good. If women were already free, then must not the source of their unhappiness be personal rather than political?

As late as 1968, when first encountering feminism, a woman could emphatically assert, as I did, that women in the United States were not oppressed. She could argue this with conviction, as I did, despite having helped more than one friend get an illegal, expensive, and often life-threatening abortion; despite knowing that most men did not consider it their responsibility to help prevent unwanted pregnancy. Perhaps she was a student who, like me, had seen female classmates expelled from school for pregnancy or simply for being sexually active. She knew male students were not disciplined for these reasons.

Still, in her first encounter with the notion of women's liberation, her response was, as mine was, "Me, oppressed? I'm not oppressed!" And at the same time she may have been thinking, as I was, "Are these feminists just losers?" To me, and to many others I knew then, admission of female oppression was tantamount to admission of personal inadequacy.

As women posed such questions to themselves, they knew they were often disappointed. But so, after all, were men. Unhappiness and disappointment were part of the human condition or, as one widespread theory had it, the product of neurosis brought on by unenlightened child-rearing practices. Moreover, although men did not face the problems of unwanted pregnancy and its terrifying penalties, many women blamed themselves for letting this happen.

Often a woman thought she could find a way around the problem or seek a new way to overcome it. She could make a guy use a condom, couldn't she? If she was smart enough she could, or had enough self-respect. If she were more beautiful, then he would use one. Perhaps she should get a new outfit, a new hairstyle, new makeup, ditch her glasses for contact lenses, go on a new diet. Then she could make a new plan and find a new date—the Horatio Alger equivalent of "work hard and save" for women. There was not much else to do. Few women had a concept of sexism to protest or attribute a problem to, much less the idea of organizing a union that would give raising these issues a better chance of winning.

Changing Conditions

The decades between the close of World War II and the start of Women's Liberation in the mid-1960s were stultifyingly sexist. This was as true in the United States as in many other countries, and probably even more so. Yet under the surface, beneath women's roiling frustration, continuing changes were eroding some of the pillars of male domination. By the end of the 1960s, 40 percent of women over sixteen years of age were in the paid labor force, and one-third of married women were employed. This was a 400 percent increase since 1940 in the rate of employed married women.[10] Half of all women with school-age children were employed, including women whose husbands earned incomes well above the poverty level.[11] Although women were no longer hired into the better-paying jobs they had held during the war, they had been absorbed into the expanding "pink collar" and service sectors.

Beyond paid employment, the birth control pill, marketed in 1960, further decreased women's dependency on men. Women had already, in effect, decided three years earlier to end the "baby boom," the fifteen-year reversal of the century-long decline in the birthrate.[12] This had been a demonstration of combined, if not collectively planned and coordinated, action.

But the pill, 97 percent effective, tied childbearing even less inevitably to sex. This, combined with no longer having to marry or stay married to survive economically, made women more independent than perhaps ever before. As more and more married women joined the paid workforce, the percentage of women supported only by their husbands decreased. At the same time, divorce rates began rising in the 1950s and early 1960s—and would continue to climb more steeply.[13] Further, more and more women of marriageable age were remaining single.

Thus changes were under way that made greater self-determination for women increasingly possible. Despite the postwar ideology of domesticity described by Betty Friedan, women appeared to be voting with their feet against the "feminine mystique." Indeed, women voted against it with their whole bodies—just about every way but collectively through a feminist political movement.[14]

Conditions were changing, but unless women themselves were to actively challenge the limits, how much difference would it make? Men of high enough rank had underpaid secretaries in the workplace, and nearly all men had wives serving as unpaid housekeepers and child care workers at home. Almost half of these women had already put in a full day's paid work. Little more than this small measure of freedom could be expected.

Testing the Limits

The first direct public-action challenges to institutionalized sexism of the time came from individuals, only tangentially connected to the most visible and active social movement at the time, the Civil Rights Movement. They came from blue-collar, wage-earning women, not college-educated women. It was these women's actions that might be said to have directly precipitated the formation of the first new feminist organization of the Second Wave, the National Organization for Women (NOW).

The Civil Rights Act of 1964 was brought into being by the brave campaigns in the Deep South, and among the participants in these campaigns were many of the young women who would later begin Women's Liberation organizing. The Act contained a provision called Title VII that specifically prohibited sex discrimination in employment. It was included to the surprise and chagrin of most of the Civil Rights Act's framers and immediate enforcers.[15] Title VII was an opening in the barriers constraining women's lives, and blue-collar women came forward through this opening in droves.

They had long been frustrated by protective legislation that kept them out of higher-paying jobs. But the Equal Employment Opportunity Commission (EEOC), which had been created to enforce the Act, made no secret of its intention not to enforce it when it came to equal job opportunities for women. Indeed, the EEOC chair announced his opposition to Title VII in the press. Despite this, thousands of women filed charges of sex discrimination. More than one-third of the charges filed in 1965 were from women, and in some regions women's complaints made up almost half of those filed.[16] When the unions would not support them, the women sued their unions. And though it took years even to have a charge reviewed, women just kept them coming.

In 1966 NOW, which called itself a "civil rights movement" for women, was explicitly organized to pressure the EEOC to enforce Title VII by taking action on the charges of sex discrimination.[17] Thus when NOW called its first meetings, blue-collar women were already in revolt—aware and acting on the new weapon that Title VII provided.

The younger women whose work pioneered the radical Women's Liberation branch of the movement were also testing the limits of male supremacy. Ruby Doris Robinson, even before the passage of the Civil Rights Act and its sex discrimination provision, had led what would become a legendary "sit-in strike" by women of the Student Nonviolent Coordinating Committee for equal treatment in SNCC's Atlanta headquarters. Coming of age as a black teenager in the 1950s, she had been keenly aware of the bold female leaders of the Civil Rights Movement such as Rosa Parks in Montgomery, Alabama, and Daisy Bates in Little Rock, Arkansas, and as early as age thirteen was telling her sister of her willingness "to die for that cause."[18]

Zoharah Simmons grew up thinking that "a woman leading was normal."[19] Like Ruby Doris Robinson, Simmons, who was also African American, had been inspired in her teen years by female race leaders such as Daisy Bates. Before she was even twenty, and shortly after she joined the SNCC staff, Simmons would become one of the few female SNCC project directors during Mississippi Freedom Summer in 1964. In that capacity she supervised men and women, black and white, many of them older than she was, and pioneered a "non-negotiable edict . . . to ban all forms of sexual harassment . . . of course, we didn't even have this term for it then. . . . Boy did I learn a lot about white liberal racism and male sexism," Simmons said.[20]

Casey Hayden and Mary King were the two women whose early critique of sexism was the next link in the Women's Liberation chain in SNCC. White women, they both could trace the origins of their egalitarian views to their childhood experience with family members who defied traditions circumscribing women's lives. King said that her father, a liberal Methodist minister whose "view of social justice included women," gave her a special place near the pulpit while he preached on Sunday mornings. That he sought and took very seriously her views on the sermons made her feel "as good as any man," King said.[21] Her father read her Bible verses referring to women's equality that he explained had been purposely passed over by churchmen.

Casey Hayden was the child of a twice-divorced mother who was also the only divorced woman in Victoria, the small East Texas town where Casey grew up. Hayden went to college in Austin on her mother's salary as a secretary. The benefits rather than hardships of her mother's unusual social position in the community, and the strengths that enabled her mother to stand up for what she believed in, impressed themselves on Hayden's aspirations. There during the late 1950s, at a time when little else in the South was racially integrated, Hayden socialized and lived with black and white women at the University YWCA and the Christian Faith and Life Community. These experiences helped strengthen her commitment to gender and racial equality in the larger society.

Women's Liberation founder Frances M. Beal's mother was a feminist and a radical, and Beal rebelled against norms that valued straight hair, light skin, and subservient manners for women of all races and men of color.

Kathie Sarachild was encouraged by her parents to challenge a gender-based division of labor. Sarachild and her mother, who had been divorced for a while and who continued to work full time, conspired to change gender inequalities at the daughter's junior high school. Her mother's lobbying with the school principal led to shop and home economics becoming mandatory for both boys and girls. When a scholarship allowed Sarachild to attend Radcliffe College, she challenged gender barriers to become one of the few female editors on the Harvard *Crimson*. She also protested campus curfews for female students. She campaigned on this issue and was elected to the Student Council, seeing the end of these curfews before she graduated.

Curfews for female students were also targets of incipient Women's Liberation founders Pam Allen and Heather Booth. Like Sarachild, Allen began organizing against the curfew as an undergraduate, at Carleton College, and ran for representative to the National Student Association on that issue. Heather Booth participated in "sleep outs" at the University of Chicago to protest the curfews.

Black feminist Eleanor Holmes Norton, in junior high in 1949, saw the fighter for racial and gender equality Mary Church Terrell in action.[22] Terrell, then eighty-six, was leading a winning campaign picketing and sitting in to integrate the segregated restaurants of Washington, D.C. "That was a consciousness-raising moment for me as a child," Norton said. "I wanted to enlist in any movement a woman like that was running."[23] By 1963 Norton was in law school at Yale and had met longtime African American feminist Pauli Murray, who became her mentor. The same year that Norton began to "sit at the feet" of Murray, as her biographer Joan Lester put it, she courageously put her law school education and her life on the line by going to work with SNCC in Greenwood, Mississippi.

In SNCC Norton met Ella Baker, who Norton said "performed and acted as a feminist."[24] Until 1970 Baker opposed the formation of an independent Women's Liberation Movement and did not endorse feminism explicitly. But in SNCC, which she founded in 1960 and thereafter guided, she created an organization in which the feminism of Women's Liberation pioneers like Hayden and Norton would blossom into papers, policies, and organizing ideas for women's freedom.

SNCC leader Bob Moses called Ella Baker "Fundi," which in Swahili means master teacher. By 1960 Baker, then fifty-seven, had put in a lifetime's work breaking gender conventions in the fight for racial and economic justice.[25] As a child, Baker played baseball on a mixed team of boys and girls. "I would rather play baseball than eat," Baker reminisced.[26] Baker said she had been a "tomboy" who was "neither a girl nor a boy in certain ways."[27] Early on, Baker determined that she would lead her life according to her own dictates.

In adulthood Baker, as African American feminist scholar Barbara Ransby put it, "consciously violated most of the social conventions that dictated proper feminine behavior,"[28] including the imperative to have children. Baker said, "I wasn't interested in having children, per se," and poured her whole being into movements for progressive social change.[29]

White founder Judith Brown's belief in women's equality was influenced by two feminist aunts and nurtured by years of Girl Scouting. At fourteen she was selected to attend a national Girl Scout roundup with other highly qualified Scouts. There were no men at the roundup. Of this experience Brown observed that "watching self-sufficiency and order with 5,000 high school girls acting like women . . . was a millennial experience."[30] Later, Brown would recommend that women develop all-female communes on which to regroup when weary from the fight against male domination.

Carol Hanisch, also a white founder, was born and raised on a farm in rural Iowa. She traced her readiness for feminism to contradictions she experienced in her family. "My parents tried to 'raise me as a girl,'" Hanisch said. The necessity for help with the farm, however, often led to her doing the same work as her brothers. "I threw hay bales, shoveled animal shit, walked the beans hoeing out weeds, fed the animals." Hanisch said she liked "using my body outdoors more then I liked housework, which I did plenty of, too. I did lots of the work my brothers did, but didn't get the privileges they did." Hanisch also compared the work of her mother and father. "My mother worked longer hours than my father (she did a lot of farmwork, too, but my father never lifted a finger in the house), yet he controlled the money and had the final say in decision making; she even had to ask his permission to use the car to go to town for groceries or to visit a friend." Reflecting on her childhood, Hanisch said, "I knew there was something wrong with this picture even then."[31]

Shulamith Firestone, a rebel in her orthodox Jewish family, had sworn as a child never to marry. She got in trouble for peeking through holes in the curtain that divided men and women at prayer. In her teenage years Firestone, associating dissembling with subordination, refused to fake a smile.[32] And as a teenager in the early 1960s, she joined civil rights demonstrations with the Congress of Racial Equality (CORE) in St. Louis, where the family lived at the time.

Marilyn Webb also got an early start on breaking gender conventions. Daughter of a union organizer mother, Webb at age nine insisted on trying out for Little League baseball. Although a good ballplayer, Webb was rejected because she was a girl.[33] She smarted over her rejection until she saw a chance to do something about it beginning to take shape in 1965 at a national conference of Students for a Democratic Society.[34]

Variations of the stories of these women are repeated again and again in the lives of those who went on to pioneer the Women's Liberation Movement. Florynce Kennedy, an older African American radical feminist, said that she wasn't out of her teens before she began to see that "the attitude toward marriage made little sense," and by age thirty she concluded that she didn't believe in "marriage . . . or religion."[35]

Naomi Weisstein, a founder of the nation's first Women's Liberation group, also decided early on that marriage alone would not fulfill her. As a graduate student, when she encountered the males-only policy at Harvard's Lamont Library, she organized female students to enter the library with her while she loudly played the clarinet. Jo Freeman cofounded the first group and soon after edited the first Women's Liberation newsletter. As a child Jo, although she did not connect it to feminism, knew that, unlike many of her classmates, she preferred "learning, careers, politics" to boys and clothes.[36]

Thus as teenagers and young adults incipient Women's Liberation pioneers questioned and challenged the sexist limitations imposed upon women. They were doing this in the 1950s and early 1960s as the material conditions supporting sexism began to shift and decrease the extent to which women's subjugation could be enforced. Across the nation other women strained for freedom in constricting marriages and in "pink collar" and service jobs that were underpaid, boring, and repetitive.

Feminism or "Feminisms"

Should the varying views and constituencies within the Second Wave of feminism be characterized as "feminisms"?[37] Is there a black Women's Liberation Movement and a distinctly white one? This study takes the position that a single feminist movement, including women of color and white feminists, NOW and Women's Liberation, gathered momentum in the first half of the decade of the 1960s, established itself in the second half, and began to lose strength as the 1970s wore on. Within the movement, sharply divergent interpretations contended about causes of female oppression and what Women's Liberation might entail.

Although these schools of thought differed on the causes of male supremacy, how to fight it, and the centrality of capitalism, imperialism, and racism to Women's Liberation, all of the streams contained the core feminist element of putting an end to the systemic power imbalance between men and women that favored the male sex. This idea would eventually become so widespread and powerful that the women advancing it were able to significantly alter that imbalance in the interests of their sex.

In the first decade of that broad and sustained mass movement, from the mid-1960s through the first half of the 1970s, millions of women of different ages, social classes, races, ethnic groups, religions, and sexual orientations simultaneously fought sexism in the larger society and their own particular communities. Radical feminists, socialist feminists, cultural feminists, black feminists, and lesbian feminists, among other varieties too numerous to list, battled each other's interpretations, and were deeply subdivided even within those broad categories.

In this regard feminism is similar to Marxism, Black Nationalism, and other ideologies of social change which include contending interpretations. Yet we do not speak of socialisms, Black Powers, or Civil Rights Movements. What social movement follows a single monolithic political line? To speak of "feminisms" waters it down and admits nonsensical claims on it ranging from "power nails" to sadomasochism. When the concept is diluted, anything that a woman may feel "empowered by" can be considered feminist.

The erasure of African American women from the founding and leadership roles they played in Second Wave feminism—not to mention those in the rank and file—is a deep and ongoing problem of racism that carries social and historical ramifications. But speaking of "feminisms" is not the answer. Some African American women fought sexism by joining with other African American women in Women's Liberation groups such as Poor

Black Women, and with women of color from all over the world, as in the Third World Women's Alliance; some, like Florynce Kennedy and Cellestine Ware, worked in the predominantly white women's movement; others, like Angela Davis, worked mostly in the predominantly white Left; still others, like Kathleen Cleaver, worked in the Black Power Movement. Many of these women worked in several of these formations and movements at the same time. Others moved from one to another as their politics developed and changed. Black feminists could work in and lead mixed groups, black groups, or both at once and be attacking different aspects of the same oppression: male supremacy as it affects all women and as it uniquely affects black women. Similarly, they worked in male/female black nationalist groups as well as in black women's groups to attack white supremacy as it affects all blacks or as it uniquely affects black women.

Separating the antisexist work of women of color from the larger context of the Black Freedom Movement, the Left, and the Women's Liberation Movement into "feminisms" is neither a signal nor a guarantee that it receives the attention that it merits.

For black and white women alike, roughly two "branches" arose, one that older women with more moderate politics tended to identify with, and a second that attracted younger women with more radical politics. Black feminism had an older, moderate branch associated, in part, with the National Council of Negro Women (NCNW), the NAACP, and the YWCA. Sometimes the older branch overlapped the younger branch, which emerged in the mid-1960s in the Civil Rights Movement, most notably in SNCC.

There are several ramifications of conceptualizing the Second Wave as one broad movement instead of separate "feminisms." Looking at all feminist activity in the 1960s at once clarifies the catalytic role that black women played in raising the issue of "women's liberation" in SNCC, where the term first germinated in the context of the SNCC-led mass movement in the South, soon sparking ideas for a social movement. An anonymous paper that Hayden and King wrote for the November 1964 SNCC conference has generally been considered the opening salvo of the movement's young radical feminists. Important though it was in providing the solidity of a written formulation, this paper did not instigate but rather affirmed a ferment in SNCC that had already been bubbling around "women's liberation."

African American women organized feminist groups during the same years when white feminists organized groups. Poor Black Women and the SNCC Black Women's Liberation Committee were, in 1968, among the earliest, best known, and most influential. Like the early largely-white groups, these groups had roots in the Black Freedom Movement, the Old Left, the First Wave of feminism, and, more importantly for black women, the anti-colonial revolutions in the Third World. The SNCC Black Women's Libera-tion Committee—renamed the Black Women's Alliance and then the Third World Women's Alliance (TWWA)—and Poor Black Women interacted with white feminists and predominantly white feminist groups, and participated in predominantly white feminist demonstrations. But their work was orga-nizationally distinct from that of the mostly white groups.

As prominent as some of these black Women's Liberation groups became, however, they represent only the tip of the iceberg of the influence of black feminist pioneers in the making of the Women's Liberation Movement. Black feminists such as Shirley Chisholm and Eleanor Holmes Norton belonged to both black feminist groups and predominantly white feminist groups at the same time, but Chisholm and Norton most certainly made their greatest impact directly on the larger society.

Norton also participated in the TWWA,[38] while Chisholm was influential in the predominantly white National Organization for Women. Older, mod-erate black feminists such as Pauli Murray, Aileen Hernandez, and Anna Arnold Hedgeman were likewise among NOW's founders.

Moderate black feminists had an impact on groups such as the NAACP, which by 1970 adopted a women's rights platform at its annual convention. As early as 1963 they waged a sustained campaign to include female civil rights leaders in the program of the 1963 March on Washington. Together they took on the Council of United Civil Rights Leadership, which was com-prised of the important male-led black organizations of the day, including the NAACP, Southern Christian Leadership Conference, Urban League, Broth-erhood of Sleeping Car Porters, CORE, and SNCC. Dorothy Height, leader of the National Council of Negro Women, called the campaign, which was widely publicized in the black press, a "new awakening" for black women.[39]

Black feminist Angela Davis worked within and influenced the predomi-nantly white Left as well as the Black Freedom Movement. Black feminists such as Kathleen Cleaver and Zoharah Simmons fought sexism from within the Black Freedom Movement even as they fought white supremacy as lead-ers in the Black Panther Party (BPP) and the Revolutionary Action Move-ment (RAM).

As will be shown, the influence of black feminist pioneers in all the move-ments of the 1960s and in the larger society has been wider and deeper than can be seen by focusing on black Women's Liberation groups alone. More-over, black feminist organizing did not begin in 1966 as a reaction to what so-ciologist Benita Roth and others have called the "masculinist" turn allegedly ushered in by Black Power.[40] Indeed, SNCC had more black women in lead-ership positions after its 1966 turn to Black Power than during the previous six years of the "nonmasculinist" period.[41] Additionally, Second Wave collec-tive black feminist organizing began at least by 1963, as women campaigned for their rightful positions in the March on Washington program and called the men out on "Jane Crow," the term Pauli Murray used for sexism directed at black women, on analogy with the "Jim Crow" designation of racism di-rected at black people.

The male chauvinism of the men of the cloth and the black business class that made up much of the pre–Black Power leadership of the Civil Rights Movement would seem as "masculinist" as all but the most sexist of black cultural nationalists in the late sixties. As African American SNCC leader and clergywoman Prathia Hall Wynn put it, "there is no place where women are more subordinated than the church."[42] Ella Baker, referring to her years of getting the Southern Christian Leadership Conference (SCLC) off the ground in 1957–58, said, "I knew from the beginning that as a woman, an older woman, in a group of ministers who are accustomed to having women largely as supporters, there was no place for me to have come into a leader-ship role."[43] Septima Poinsette Clark, called the "grand lady of civil rights" and a protégé of black feminist W. E. B. DuBois, was the lone female on the SCLC board of directors. Clark, reflecting on her work with Martin Luther King Jr. in the early 1960s, said: "in those days I didn't criticize Dr. King. . . . the way I think about him now comes from my experience in the women's movement. . . . of course, in the Black church, men were always in charge."[44]

In 1962, even before black female civil rights leaders fought to keep themselves from being erased from their movement by the male leaders of the March on Washington, they had had to fight the NAACP to get Daisy Bates included in its prestigious Spingarn Award. Daisy Bates was Arkansas NAACP president and the heroine and leader of school desegregation in Little Rock in 1957. Bates was not submissive to racism or sexism; she had been a "tomboy who competed with neighborhood boys" and had gone to flying school.[45] She wrote to Pauli Murray, "while we are fighting for human dignity, and many times for survival, one forgets the contribution made by women."[46]

To speak of "feminisms" is misleading, further, because both black and white feminism shared at least as many common roots as different ones. If one woman can be singled out as the source of what became the vanguard of the Women's Liberation branch of the Second Wave of both black and white feminism, that woman is Ella Baker. Baker founded and guided SNCC, which, in addition to being the shock troops of the Civil Rights Movement, produced significant numbers of black and white feminist organizers. Baker had been well aware of the woman question since at least the late 1920s and was bitingly critical of male chauvinism in the Civil Rights Movement. She promoted leaders such as Daisy Bates and Rosa Parks, and developed a host of younger black and white women in SNCC who would become ardent feminists, among them Diane Nash and Casey Hayden. From 1970 forward, Baker was explicitly feminist and participated in TWWA meetings. As black feminist scholars Johnnetta Cole and Beverly Guy-Sheftall put it, "Black women activists, many of whom were SNCC . . . workers, helped to catalyze a women's movement. . . . Much of what we associate with the emergence of Black feminist activism during the sixties can be traced to the women of SNCC."[47]

The black women of the Harlem YWCA circle, including Ella Baker, Pauli Murray, Anna Arnold Hedgeman, and Dorothy Height, would influence both black and white organizers of the Second Wave and themselves stood on the shoulders of a long, unbroken line of black feminist organizers beginning in slavery and taking shape in the antislavery movement simultaneously with that of white feminist abolitionists.[48] In 1831 black abolitionist Maria Stewart was the first U.S.-born female antislavery lecturer to address sexually integrated audiences, with whom she pulled no punches about the oppression of women. "How long," Stewart wrote in the abolitionist newspaper the *Liberator*, "shall the fair daughters of Africa be compelled to bury their minds and talents beneath a load of iron pots? . . . I would have you possess the spirit of independence, the spirit of men, bold and enterprising. . . . Sue for your rights and privileges."[49]

At a lecture in Boston in 1832, Stewart called the black woman the "servant of servants." In the 1960s black Women's Liberation organizer Frances Beal similarly spoke of "slave of a slave" characterizing the oppression of black women.[50]

Sojourner Truth is the best known among the black feminist abolitionists, but race leader Harriet Tubman also worked for the ballot for women.[51]

Spanning the nation at the turn of the century were black women's suf-

frage organizations, most notably and earliest among them the Alpha Suffrage Club in Chicago, organized by black feminist, antilynching crusader,
and all-around race woman Ida B. Wells.[52] A leading black feminist of this
period, Anna Julia Cooper, was probably among the earliest organizers to explain what today has been called "intersectionality." Cooper held that because
black women occupied "a unique position in this country . . . confronted by
both a woman question and a race problem," they were uniquely qualified
and best positioned to take a leading role in both struggles.[53] Declaring that,
although black men may "seem thoroughly abreast of the times on almost
every other subject, when they strike the woman question they drop back
into sixteenth-century logic,"[54] Cooper sounded much like Frances Beal on
the black male of the 1960s: "he sees the system for what it really is for the
most part, but when it comes to women, he seems to take his guidelines from
the pages of the *Ladies' Home Journal*."[55]

In the Progressive Era, black nationalist and Pan-Africanist Amy Jacques
Garvey was a feminist voice in the Garvey Movement, the Universal Negro Improvement Association (UNIA) organized by her husband, Marcus
Garvey. Amy Garvey, among others, pioneered a mix of black nationalism
and feminism, showing that despite even her husband's antifeminist views,
the mix was not only possible but salutary.

Black feminists were also early birth-control activists. In 1921 the Wom-
en's Political Association of Harlem advocated birth control as a significant
choice for black women in the same year white birth-control advocate Margaret Sanger founded the American Birth Control League. Arguments in
the Black Freedom Movement in the 1960s about birth control and black
genocide had played out in the early twentieth century as W. E. B. DuBois
and Marcus Garvey clashed over the issue. Black community organizing for
birth control in Baltimore during the 1930s included the Murphy family and
would influence Patricia Murphy Robinson to take a hard line on reproductive freedom in the 1960s. In both eras, black feminists supported birth control even as they fought forced sterilization as genocidal white supremacy.

The black Left of 1930s and 1940s produced such notable black feminists as
the political organizers and theorists Esther Cooper Jackson and Trinidadian
Claudia Jones and the award-winning writer Alice Childress. Dorothy Burnham, an organizer with the first "SNCC," the Southern Negro Youth Congress (SNYC), was a black feminist scientist on the Left who contested sexist
and racist biological theories. The Burnham family had worked in SNYC in
the 1940s in Birmingham, Alabama, with Sallye Davis, the mother of Angela
Davis, who would carry the radical and feminist views of the Communist

Left into the Women's Liberation Movement, the Black Freedom Movement, and the New Left of the 1960s.

The origins of black feminism, and its influence on other movements of the 1960s and on the larger society directly, are best understood as a rich and particular stream of feminism. Evidence in chapters to come will support the idea that "feminism," not "feminisms," best describes the Second Wave.

First Steps for Women's Liberation

The first clear step in the development of the Women's Liberation branch of the Second Wave was a sit-in by women on the SNCC staff in SNCC's Atlanta headquarters office in the spring of 1964. By all accounts this was a feminist action.[56] For a long time, to white Women's Liberationists who would later begin organizing for an independent movement, the SNCC women's strike was only a vague but inspiring legend. By 1979 one of them, later to become the historian Sara Evans, would do yeoman's work in tracing the legend to some concrete sources.[57]

The strike protested women's unequal treatment and "limited role," in the words of Bernice Johnson Reagon, a black SNCC staffer and member of the Freedom Singers, now an activist scholar.[58] Women demanding equality in job assignments, among other things, "sat in" in the headquarters office and refused to resume work. According to black male SNCC staffer Stanley Wise, who also worked there, the women "issued a memorandum of agreements" detailing the "activities that women would no longer tolerate in the organization."[59] The strikers included black staff Ruby Doris Robinson, Judy Richardson, and Bobbi Yancy, and white staff members Mary King and Betty Garmen.

Yancy and Wise said Ruby Doris Robinson was the lead organizer and most forceful negotiator for the women. As Yancy said, "[Ruby's] influence has to be credited with playing a very important role because she was the figure [men] clearly back off [from]. And that certainly gave other women courage."[60] Yancy and Wise described the strike as a serious move on the women's part, although Mary King portrayed it lightheartedly and Wise focused more on the sexual harassment aspect of the issues. Wise did recall: "All of the women, every woman did absolutely nothing. They didn't speak; they didn't type any letters; they didn't answer any phones . . ."[61]

The second known marker of growing feminist consciousness and influence in SNCC came a few months later in June 1964 when African American SNCC project director Zoharah Simmons established what years later she would call a "sexual harassment policy" for her Mississippi Freedom Summer project in Laurel, Mississippi. The policy prohibited any form of unwanted sexual attention to female staff or volunteers, and between project staff and volunteers. Underage women in the town were completely off limits. In a case of unwanted sexual attention, the perpetrator would receive one warning, and if he repeated the offense, discharge from the project would follow. All incoming staff and volunteers received an orientation to the policy.

The project in Laurel was assigned twenty-three volunteers over the summer. All but two were white, about half were women, most were from the middle or upper middle class, and many were older than Simmons, who was then nineteen years old and herself a newcomer to the SNCC staff. "I was just a girl myself, and I had to grow up real fast," Simmons said. "I had to assume an air of authority, especially with the white male volunteers who could not believe that a black girl younger than themselves was the Project Director."[62] Simmons said that the policy effectively prevented sexual harassment and that she did not have to discharge anyone from the project. Her authority was taken seriously but took considerable effort on her part. Simmons called this "difficult but unbelievably rewarding."[63]

Simmons had not known about the strike in the Atlanta office when she came up with the policy. She said the idea arose because she had been sexually assaulted at one of the orientations for volunteers for Freedom Summer, the civil rights project that brought roughly a thousand mostly white volunteers into Mississippi for the summer of 1964.[64] When she reported the incident to the SNCC leadership, nothing was done. Though she was very disappointed, Simmons remained completely committed to SNCC principles and strategy, and resolved to protect volunteers and local women from any unwanted sexual attention on her project.

Simmons acquired the somewhat dubiously bestowed reputation of being an Amazon, and the Laurel project was called the Amazon Project. Many men did not want to be assigned to work there. "They did not want an 'uppity' woman boss," as Simmons quipped. Interestingly, local black male Mississippians were recruited to the project without objection to the hierarchy or the antiharassment policy. The Amazon Project was famous throughout SNCC. Simmons later said, "The 'Amazon Project' was a title that I was proud of. It meant that I had 'come through the fire' and was much the better for the experience."[65]

How could SNCC have been a positive experience for her, given her assault and the reaction of male leaders? "It was an incredible experience in spite of the sexism," Simmons said.

I learned to fight men, hold my own, develop my leadership capacities and skills. I cursed men out as well as loved them like my brothers. Plus, the women of Mississippi outnumbered the men in the community, and it was positive for them to see a woman at the helm of the project, even though it was difficult for some. *It was great, great, great and yes I fought, fought, sexism, male chauvinism, and misogyny.*[66]

The wake of the Amazon Project rippled outward. The following year black SNCC staff member Jimmy Garrett represented SNCC at the national conference of the Students for a Democratic Society. Garrett had been Simmons's right hand on the Laurel project. When he heard the white men at the conference objecting to women's feminist demands, he raised his voice to weigh in on the women's side.[67]

The "Borning" Movement

"The idea of doing something about it"

THE CIVIL RIGHTS MOVEMENT, particularly SNCC with its young band of shock troopers, was a breeding ground for feminists, black and white, radical and liberal. Although it is widely acknowledged as the birthplace of Women's Liberation, the consensus in the literature is that the birth was painful.[1] The evidence that supports this view includes stories about male chauvinism that have become infamous: idealistic women seeking a meaningful role relegated to office work; white women manipulated into sexual acquiescence by charges of racism and exposed to jokes about their position in the movement; black women manipulated into subordination by charges of emasculating black men.[2] The view that Women's Liberation was a spontaneous oppositional reaction to male chauvinism remains central to the origins story of the radical branch of feminism. Indeed, discussion of male chauvinism continues to mute elements of the Civil Rights Movement that were the actual building blocks of the Women's Liberation Movement.

Sexism was hardly new to Women's Liberation pioneers in the Civil Rights Movement. As Kathie Sarachild put it, "I had run into male chauvinism in radical men many times before. It was nothing new. What was new in the civil rights movement were the positive organizing ideas and concepts. What was new was the idea of *doing* something about it in a grass roots movement—along with some tools for beginning."[3]

The positive ideas of the Civil Rights Movement also stimulated the feminism of black civil rights activist Eleanor Holmes Norton. "As someone [who came] out of the Civil Rights Movement, the women's rights movement seemed, to me, the logical next step," said Norton.[4] As opposed to a painful reaction to male chauvinism, Norton held, "If you were associated with civil rights, labor rights, the analogies are intellectually compelled. The transition to feminism is easy."[5] "I also knew that the first feminist wave had grown out of the abolitionist movement," Norton said. "So there was that history there, too. I've always been proud that the women's rights movement grew out of the Civil Rights Movement."[6]

One of the most important positive influences for Women's Liberation in the Civil Rights Movement was experience with a new form of leadership. Black women like Zoharah Simmons formally led racially and sexually integrated campaigns under almost warlike conditions. They were changed by this work, as were the black and white women they led. On the cutting edge of change, where violence and the threat of violence—often perpetrated by law enforcement—were constant, women and men risked their lives following female leaders. Down back roads in Mississippi guarded by the Ku Klux Klan, on the floor of the Democratic National Convention in Atlantic City, through hostile white mobs, and into the jailhouse, educated middle-class men, black and white, followed black women, some younger than themselves, some poor and poorly educated. So did educated, sometimes well-to-do white women. The last had become first, and this was clear for all to see in political campaigns and rural civil rights projects.

Young black women such as Patricia Stephens Due of CORE and Diane Nash and Ruby Doris Robinson of SNCC were respected organizers and administrators. They headed demonstrations, managed the resources of whole organizations, dealt with the national press and government officials in the Justice Department, the FBI, and the IRS as well as local, state, and federal elected officials. Older black women such as Ella Baker and Fannie Lou Hamer of SNCC were leading theoreticians and political strategists.[7]

Some were ideologically feminist and some were not, but the work of these black female leaders broke the black and white gender conventions of the day and, in the process, set new ones. As SNCC Black Women's Liberation Committee founder Frances Beal summarizes, "Women in SNCC really did do things . . . that other women did not take on. . . . We began to turn our analytical, freedom-loving minds toward this question of what is the role of women—not only in the organization but in the world."[8]

Black Gender Conventions, White Gender Conventions

Was the work of women in SNCC really so new for black women? Was it outside the gender conventions of the black community or just outside the gender conventions for whites? "We all grew up watching black women activists," said former SNCC field secretary Martha Prescod Norman, reflecting on growing up in the 1950s and seeing women such as Rosa Parks and Daisy Bates. "We witnessed these women in the public spotlight fighting for equal rights. . . . Their actions made it clear that women could play pivotal, determinative roles of leadership."[9]

Nonetheless, gender conventions in the black community were not supportive of black female independence. Black scholar Barbara Ransby pointed out that "certain patriarchal family practices and restricted gender roles" predominated in the black middle class and "through school and church institutions, working class blacks also adhered . . . even when the realities of their everyday lives prevented black women from conforming to the idealized model of homemaker."[10] Daisy Bates and Rosa Parks had played high-profile leadership roles, but it took a feminist campaign to force male civil rights leaders to allow them to sit on the platform of the 1963 March on Washington.

Ella Baker spoke of her mother: "a very bright woman. . . . at the time, of course, . . . there were only certain things that women, especially black women, could do. And she taught. . . . she never worked after she married. . . . had she not been female, she probably would have gone on into something else."[11]

But were these limitations just "at that time"? Black feminist Myrna Hill's father had been a Tuskegee Airman and an Air Force officer in the 1940s and 1950s. Her mother, although college educated, did not work outside the home when Hill was growing up, for "everybody else was home in the fifties in my family and neighborhoods. . . . Middle-class black women . . . didn't have to work for whites." Hill related:

> When I was eight years old, my mother planned to get a teaching job, but changed her mind at the last minute. All my life, I thought she

had bowed to pressure from my father, as most 1950s black middle-class men felt that it was shameful if their wives "had to" work, because it meant they were not good providers for their families. After my mother died . . . I asked him about it. He said my mother had told him that if she worked full-time just like he did, he was going to have to share with her the burden of taking care of the house. He refused, they fought about it, and that was why she didn't go through with work as a teacher.[12]

Similarly, SNCC's Ivanhoe Donaldson said in the black New York community where he grew up, "we came from homes where dinner didn't start until [the father] sat down, and he determined the rules of the house."[13]

Even Ruby Doris Robinson, who "was widely perceived [in SNCC] as a woman who did not conform to contemporary notions of femininity," had made her debut in a white evening gown at a debutante ball for the daughters of Atlanta's prosperous black middle class.[14] In 1957, the year before she entered historically black Spelman College, Spelman women were addressed by neighboring Morehouse College president Dr. Benjamin Mays: "over and above business, politics and professions, you Spelman women will be called upon to be wives, mothers and homemakers. . . . The husband and father will make exacting demands of you . . . in spite of your training and degrees."[15]

Clearly, if African American women were more independent than white women of the period, they were not free of the male chauvinist standards of the prefeminist 1950s, which prevailed among African Americans as well as whites.

"Women who had demonstrated a kind of dedication . . ."

Among the civil rights organizations, SNCC and CORE far outstripped the others in training future Women's Liberation founders. Seventy percent of the women who volunteered in the largely SNCC-organized Mississippi Freedom Summer Project in 1964 were subsequently involved in the Women's Liberation Movement, including many of its founders.[16]

What loosened the bonds of the 1950s pressure for the "domestic containment" of women in SNCC?[17] Bernice Johnson Reagon explained:

I grew up in a church and women sat on one side . . . and men sat on the other . . . the pulpit was in the center, and the only time the women went up was on Women's Day. Now, the civil rights movement was one time I saw women going up into the pulpit because they were leaders of the civil rights movement. . . . Fannie Lou Hamer . . . was always in the pulpit. . . . it had to do with your willingness to put your life on the line and your courage and your character.[18]

For Reagon, leadership, influence, authority based upon credibility was able to break through sex roles because it was conferred based on courage— one of the most needed qualities under the conditions SNCC workers faced. Among SNCC's founding female leaders, Diane Nash and Ruby Doris Robinson led with their courage and commitment. SNCC's founder, Ella Baker, led with the political wisdom she brought to its young freedom fighters. Baker, fifty-seven years old when she formed SNCC by recruiting the student leaders of the sit-in movement that swept the nation in 1960, was more than twice the age of most of her recruits.

Baker was the person most responsible for SNCC's development of female leadership.[19] The legendary organizer, whose life in the black freedom struggle began in the late 1920s in Harlem, had been trained for leadership from her earliest years. Baker refused to be daunted by limitations on her activism because she was a woman. Married in 1940, she kept her maiden name and spent the first six years of married life traveling the country and organizing in the Deep South as field secretary and then director of branches for the NAACP.

Baker would recruit and develop some of the Black Freedom Movement and Women's Liberation Movement's most important organizers. Some of the women Baker worked with were already feminist, some became feminist, and others simply did exemplary movement work that was outside the gender norms of the period.[20]

In 1946, as director of branches of the NAACP, Baker gave a leadership-training workshop for activists that was attended by Rosa Parks, then an NAACP officer in Montgomery, Alabama.[21] This was a crucial point in Parks's deepening commitment to the movement, and the two women became lifelong allies. After Parks refused to give up her seat on the bus and set in motion the Montgomery Bus Boycott, Baker and Parks teamed up to conduct a fundraising tour throughout the Northeast to sustain it.

But Baker was critical of the male leadership of the boycott. She noted with irritation, "The[se] were women who had demonstrated a kind of dedication, and who had enough intelligence . . . and had enough contacts . . . to have found a role to help move people along."[22] Determined to use the momentum generated by the boycott to build a grassroots movement across the South, Baker, with longtime movement activists Bayard Rustin and Stanley Levison, launched the Southern Christian Leadership Conference, which would become the organizational base for Martin Luther King Jr. Baker and Rustin called the first meeting and drew up the founding proposals, and Baker became SCLC's first director. She hoped to make SCLC a place where women would have a "role to help move people along." Yet try as she did to democratize the NAACP and SCLC, Baker was unable to influence either to a point where women's abilities were fully appreciated. SNCC would be different—not free of male chauvinism, but well ahead of the others.

Ella Baker, Diane Nash, and Ruby Doris Robinson Lead SNCC

In SNCC, which she founded in 1960 and continued to guide throughout its organizational life, Baker forged an organization with many bold, effective female leaders. Referring to women's changing role in the Civil Rights Movement, Baker observed, "The movement . . . was carried largely by women. . . . Black women have had to carry this [supportive] role." However, the younger women were now "insisting on equal footing." And, she continued, "certainly the young people who are challenging this ought to be challenging it, and it ought to be changed."[23]

Among the challengers was Diane Nash, the young black woman who led SNCC's direct action wing and, next to Baker, was in 1960 the most influential person in the organization. Nash had been recruited by Baker and was the group's first paid field organizer. As chair of the Central Committee of the Nashville Student Movement, Nash was leading the sit-in campaign to desegregate lunch counters when she attended SNCC's first meeting in April 1960. This made her the acknowledged leader of the largest bloc of students who first formed the organization. Nash had organized two hundred students who were sitting in on a well-planned schedule. They had braved violent attacks by white mobs who beat them and ground lit cigarettes into their backs. Committed to nonviolence, they submitted to arrest and went to jail. Nash said, "The movement had a way of reaching inside me and bringing out things I never knew were there. Like courage and love for people . . . to love people that you work with enough that you would put your body between them and danger."[24]

Nash was elected to the first SNCC coordinating committee. Within the first year of the organization's life Nash and Ruby Doris Robinson (then Smith) traveled to Rock Hill, South Carolina, to support students there after they elected to serve jail sentences for sitting in. They were arrested in Rock Hill and served thirty-day sentences. Within a few months of her release, Nash withdrew from college to work full-time for SNCC.

CORE had embarked on the Freedom Rides, but the first ride encountered so much violence that CORE decided they could not continue.[25] The bus had been firebombed and the riders were violently attacked in Birmingham, Alabama. One rider was paralyzed for life, another's head wounds required fifty stitches. Nash called CORE leader James Farmer to say that SNCC would continue the rides. "If the Freedom Riders had been stopped as a result of violence, I strongly felt that the future of the movement was going to be cut short."[26] Nash chose the students who would continue the rides, warning them that they had to be ready to accept death.

Ruby Doris Robinson was among the SNCC volunteers to ride the bus from Birmingham to Montgomery. There a white mob of three hundred awaited them and assailed them as soon as they left the bus. Badly beaten, they sought refuge in the black community. As they rallied at a mass meeting in church that night, they were surrounded by a mob of several thousand whites, who even attacked the federal marshals sent in to protect the riders. Still they continued the ride into Jackson, Mississippi, where they were arrested and jailed. After two weeks in the local jail, Ruby Doris Robinson and the other students were driven at four A.M. to Parchman State Penitentiary, a prison with a reputation for brutal racism. During their weeks of incarceration at Parchman, the students refused to cooperate and sang freedom songs. Finally the sheer volume of Freedom Riders pouring into Mississippi led to their release.

Within days of her release from the Penitentiary, Robinson went to the Mississippi town of McComb, where SNCC was setting up project. She returned to college that fall but continued her activism, getting arrested in a campaign to integrate public facilities in Albany, Georgia. By early 1962, although she was not yet full-time on the SNCC staff, she devoted herself to administrative work in the Atlanta headquarters office. Reginald Robinson, a full-time SNCC worker, commented on her growing power in the organization: "you got your money from Ruby; you got your orders from Ruby."[27] In the spring of 1963, Ruby Doris went to work for SNCC full-time. "She seemed to run the place as far as I know," observed SNCC staffer Jean

Smith. "Ruby Doris dominated SNCC," said SNCC field secretary Joyce Ladner.[28] Her SNCC colleague Matt Jones said that "you could feel her power in SNCC on a daily basis."[29] In 1966 Robinson would be elected to SNCC's top position, which she held until she was hospitalized with terminal cancer in 1967.

Equally with the best-known male leaders of SNCC—James Forman, Stokely Carmichael, and Bob Moses—Ruby Doris Robinson, Diane Nash, and Ella Baker led the organization. Indeed, Nash had recruited Forman. She was "responsible for the organization of a lot of us, including myself," Forman said.[30] Carmichael called Nash and Robinson "generals."[31] Speaking of his entry into SNCC, Carmichael recalled his first meeting with Nash and Robinson: "anyone with Freedom Ride jail experience was considered a 'veteran.' So at nineteen years old I was a 'movement veteran.' . . . if I were a 'veteran' then the people I was meeting were 'generals.' People I really looked up to."[32]

Of Baker, Carmichael observed: "The most powerful person in the struggle of the sixties was Miss Ella Baker, not Martin Luther King."[33] He said she was "just so overwhelming and ubiquitous in SNCC that it seems as if she was always present."[34] Chuck McDew, SNCC's second chair, told black activist Joanne Grant, Baker's first biographer, that "Miss Baker made me chairman of SNCC, period."[35] The myth persists that Baker promoted leadership by consensus as opposed to a formally structured chain of command. But James Forman and Joanne Grant held that Baker firmly believed in formal organizational structure.[36]

Eleanor Holmes Norton began working with SNCC in 1963 when she was in her early twenties. She was impressed by Baker's refusal to "play dumb" for male approval. Baker, Norton said, "seemed unintimidated by the fact that she was a woman in a movement led by men. She was just very smart. And she wasn't afraid to be a smart woman."[37] This meant a good deal to Norton, a Yale law school student who had already experienced comments aimed at women who were "too smart."[38]

White SNCC staff members Mary King and Casey Hayden attributed to Baker the ideological influence that prompted the feminist position papers they wrote in 1964 and 1965. Both worked under Baker's supervision at the Atlanta YWCA before she recruited them to the SNCC staff. King said: "Through Ella Baker's influence on me, these principles"—that "the oppressed themselves [should] define their own freedom" and "individuals should make their own decisions"—"gave rise to the two documents on women."[39] Hayden said of Baker, "She seemed to know that however much we think and talk . . . it is action that makes social change happen."[40]

Hayden believed that what was important in SNCC was the "capacity to unlock people and situations into action."[41] Along with Baker, Hayden counted Diane Nash as a critical influence. Nash's courage and commitment had inspired her to participate in a Freedom Ride through Georgia. Hayden called Nash's brand of nonviolent direct action "existentialism carried to the streets."[42] Hayden thought it was key to women's liberation. "It took one out of the role of victim and put her in total command of her life. By acting in this clear, pure way," Hayden said, and "by risking all for it, we were broken open, released from old and lesser definitions of ourselves in terms of race, sex, class, into the larger self of the Beloved Community."[43]

Direct action, along with ideological tools such as the idea that the oppressed define their own freedom, became weapons against sexism. Also part of the arsenal was the leadership example of Baker and Nash, who taught Norton, Hayden, and King how to fight. SNCC executive secretary Ruby Doris Robinson put it this way: "Negro women can be pretty hard on a man. I mean, white women don't do so much of this as far as I know, but we *fight!*"[44]

The Lessons of Women's Militancy

Although Eleanor Holmes Norton was influenced by Ella Baker, Fannie Lou Hamer was the SNCC freedom fighter Norton called her "mentor."[45] Hamer became involved with SNCC in 1962 and was a founder and vice chair of SNCC's Mississippi Freedom Democratic Party (MFDP), which had been organized to challenge as undemocratic the seating of the traditional all-white delegation.

Baker had chosen Norton to direct the lobbying of the credentialed delegates at the 1964 Democratic National Convention in Atlantic City to vote to seat the MFDP. Norton, who had just graduated from Yale Law School, and Hamer, who had dropped out of school in sixth grade to work in the cotton fields, worked together closely. Norton also helped write the MFDP's legal challenge with Joseph Rauh, who had defended victims of political repression in the McCarthy era and was the MFDP delegation's chief counsel. Rauh was strongly linked to the liberal elites in the regular Democratic Party.

At the convention Hamer made her legendary "I question America" speech, describing her brutal beating by police for trying to register to vote in Mississippi.[46]

"When she appeared before the [credentials] committee the clock stopped in America," Norton said. With Hamer's power as a speaker, "an awesome combination of focused intelligence and vision, she alone was in a class with Martin Luther King, Jr."[47]

Hamer's speech was not the only thing that distinguished her leadership at the convention. The MFDP was offered a compromise. They would be given two seats, to be filled by delegation members handpicked by the Johnson administration: Edwin King, the white chaplain of Tougaloo, a historically black college in Jackson, Mississippi, and Aaron Henry, delegation chair and president of the Mississippi NAACP. Both of these delegates supported the compromise. Hamer, who led the opposition, told Henry, "If you go out there . . . and say that, . . . you stay there . . . in that convention hall . . . the balance of your life, 'cause if you come out I'm gon' cut your throat."[48] When the moment came, Henry announced that the delegation rejected the compromise.

In leading the opposition to the compromise, Hamer not only took on and won over the chair of the delegation, she led the delegation in a majority vote over the objection of its chair and its white chief counsel. The delegation followed the lead of Hamer, a poor black woman, not Henry, a well-educated black man, nor Rauh, a well-to-do, well-educated white man. Her opposition to the compromise was also against the advice of Martin Luther King Jr. Norton, though thrilled by the opportunity to work with Rauh, was even more taken by Hamer's effectively militant leadership.

Hamer, unlike Ruby Doris Robinson, would have been unlikely to strike for women's equality. Unlike Baker and Nash, Hamer did not come to see herself as feminist. Black scholar Chana Kai Lee said that Hamer "did not regard herself as a feminist, not by anybody's definition." But her "life and powerful presence had undeniably feminist consequences."[49] Years later civil rights leader Andrew Young, while ambassador to the United Nations, discussed the significance of Hamer's civil rights work for the rise of feminism worldwide: "Mrs. Hamer was special but she was also representative. Hundreds of women spoke up and took leadership . . . and from the civil rights movement learned the lessons that inspired the women's movement. It . . . is now a global upsurge."[50]

Judith Brown, a white founder of the Women's Liberation Movement, was taught how to "speak up" by African American CORE field secretary Patricia Stephens Due. Brown recalled that Due made her understand that speaking up was an "obligation of following" her.[51] In 1963 Brown, then twenty-two, joined CORE. "My first two movement experiences were in militant civil rights groups led by black women," Brown recalled. "I was used to seeing a woman lead, be outspoken, take risks, confront men on male supremacy and confront white people on racism."[52] Brown worked for a year as right hand to Due in a CORE voter registration project in Quincy, Florida, the county seat of a majority black county in the Florida Panhandle. Brown said Due taught "a very high degree of militancy—and I had seen her make it work. Pat transformed the scary stuff into winning and converting more and more people. . . . this was my best model."[53]

When Brown began working with Patricia Due, Due was twenty-three, a year older than Brown and already a veteran civil rights leader. She bore little resemblance to the local "mama" often referred to in Civil Rights Movement literature.[54] Nineteen when she began organizing, Due was called a "spark-plug" and was known for "boundless energy and remarkable poise."[55] In the fall of 1959, in her junior year, Due with her sister Priscilla had organized a CORE chapter at Florida Agricultural and Mechanical University (Florida A&M, or FAMU), a historically black college in Tallahassee.

Their organizing had been spurred by an attack on two black FAMU co-eds the previous May in which one of the women was gang-raped by four armed white men. Remarkably, in light of the history of unpunished sexual abuse and rape of black women by white men, the attackers were caught, brought to trial, and given life sentences.[56] The trial attracted national publicity, received public commentary from Martin Luther King Jr., and sparked a rise in black activism in Tallahassee, where FAMU students demonstrated and NAACP membership rose dramatically.[57]

Due described the impact of the incident on her and her sister. "I'd been so enraged about it . . . it might easily have been Priscilla or me. . . . Yes, Priscilla and I were ready to help make a change."[58] That summer of 1959, Due and her sister took training to become CORE organizers.

On 13 February 1960, twelve days after the Greensboro sit-ins ignited a national chain reaction, Due led a sit-in at the local Woolworth's lunch counter. This made Tallahassee the third town outside of North Carolina to stage sit-ins.[59] Faced with mobs armed with knives, ax handles, and guns, Tallahassee CORE continued the sit-ins for a month. "Fill the jails, if necessary," Due urged as marches grew to one thousand strong and students were beaten and arrested.[60]

At their trials, Due, her sister, and six others accepted jail sentences rather than pay fines. From her cell, Due wrote a widely circulated letter, "Through Jail to Freedom." In the letter Due said, "We could be out on appeal but we all strongly believe that Martin Luther King was right when he said, 'We've got to fill the jails in order to win our equal rights.'"[61]

The "jailbirds," as they called themselves, came to the attention of the national media and began to receive mail from all over the world.[62] Martin Luther King Jr. wrote to them: "Your valiant witness is one of the glowing epics of our time."[63] As pioneers of the "jail-in," the sisters and three others embarked on a national tour, were hosted by Eleanor Roosevelt and Jackie Robinson, and spoke at Adam Clayton Powell's Abyssinian Baptist Church in New York.[64]

In late 1963 Due initiated the CORE voter registration project in which Judith Brown became her right hand. A September night rally and the tumultuous months that followed had readied Brown for this work. At the rally Brown, along with coworker Dan Harmeling, joined five whites from Florida State University and hundreds of black students from FAMU. The Tallahassee students, under Due's leadership, had been working all spring to integrate the town's segregated movie theatres. Now Due asked the rallying students to march on the theatre. Singing at the top of their lungs, the students marched down the main street in Tallahassee directly into a large crowd of white men armed with ax handles and chains. Harmeling described what followed:

Judy and I were walking to the Florida Theatre. Judy squeezed my hand.... The vicious beating of a white civil rights worker in the Ocala jail had us worried. We were too far in front to turn back and ahead a jeering white mob. Judy stepped forward, lifted her sign, and began the picket. Three hundred and forty-eight people arrested, days in jail, a trial, guilty verdicts, more jail time, and Judy lost her financial aid for graduate school.[65]

This was Brown's first arrest. It was the eve of Birmingham Sunday, 15 September 1963. The next day the jailed civil rights workers learned that four black children, Denise McNair, Cynthia Wesley, Carole Robertson, and Addie Mae Collins, had been killed in Sunday school when the Sixteenth Street Baptist Church in Birmingham was dynamited. Reflecting on the arrest, Brown said:

When I saw her [Patricia Due] getting dragged and kicked to a police car, I instantly changed my mind about not being arrested, and spent my first full day in jail on Birmingham Sunday. When we heard about the bombing that day, I was filled with gratitude to be in jail....

I changed overnight. . . . I don't know if I would have followed a man
to jail.[66]

Though grateful to be in jail, Brown was badly frightened there. She and
three other female civil rights workers were taunted by nonpolitical inmates
who had been let out of their cells and who pushed broomsticks tipped with
razor blades through the bars. Brown and her comrades, huddling at the back
of the cell, barely escaped being cut. Although frightened, the demonstrators
adopted the "jail, no bail" strategy pioneered by Due and remained in jail for
weeks. FAMU students brought them food and massed in the streets outside
singing freedom songs and demanding their release.

As a result of the arrest, Brown's Ford Foundation Fellowship was taken
from her, and she was suspended from the University of Florida. But she had
already decided she wanted to work with Due on the voter registration project and immediately set about convincing Due that she could do it. "How
much effort and thought and change I had to go through to pursue her so
she would allow me to follow her," said Brown.[67]

At Due's request, Brown recruited out-of-town volunteers. The volunteers
received no salary but lived with local black families or in a Freedom House
in a black neighborhood. Five of Brown's recruits were men who came to live
in the Freedom House in Quincy, the new base of operations for the project.
Quincy was the county seat of Gadsden County, one of five in Florida listed
by the U.S. Civil Rights Commission for disfranchisement and violent repression of blacks.[68]

Brown was arrested at her first presentation on voter education in Gadsden County. For three days she and another white female civil rights worker
were locked into a cell and left alone with eight male inmates who had been
encouraged by the guards to rape them. Fortunately, the men refused to go
along with the jailers.

Civil rights work in Gadsden County was like "going into a lion's cage
without a weapon," recalled Patricia Due.[69] Volunteers were trained in nonviolence and pledged to maintain it. But the Freedom House was guarded
at night by black neighbors armed with shotguns. During the course of the
summer, the house was shot into by night riders. One of Brown's recruits,
a white Marine veteran, was seriously injured when the white attackers hit
him in the face with a rifle. Brown wrote about one night in the Freedom
House:

By night the dark draws down its awful curtain, and all the specters
begin to walk . . . grown men playing a game in the bushes . . . seven

rifles are aimed into my house. Scott runs into the house with his face laid raw. "I'm a Marine, you know . . . I was taught to disarm and kill a man with a rifle . . . I could do it blind and I let him hit me." God, oh God, they are still outside my house. The night is clear again, all of our people in the hundred-mile range are accounted for. The lights are turned off . . . 3 A.M. and I hear a shot . . . My God, Pat, they are shooting at us now.[70]

To provide even minimal protection, the project maintained a strict system for volunteers to check in at regular intervals, and Brown often found herself accounting for the whereabouts of volunteers before the Freedom House shut down for the night. For the male volunteers, some older than Brown, the experience of reporting to a woman was undoubtedly their first.

The project continued for more than a year and included eight counties in the Florida Panhandle, four in the Black Belt or Old South section bordering on Georgia and Alabama. In these areas many black families lived on large tobacco plantations under almost feudal conditions. In two of the counties, Lafayette and Liberty, there had never been a black person who successfully registered to vote.[71]

When the project ended in 1965, North Florida saw more newly registered black voters than any other region in the South.[72] But as black registration rose, so did the violence directed at the civil rights workers. Cars were firebombed, staff beaten and threatened with death over the phone, shots fired into the Freedom House, and crosses burned at the homes of African Americans. Brown later wrote, "I was not in the Civil Rights Movement as an office worker . . . I was in the field with Pat . . . in dangerous situations. It scared the shit out of me, but although we got pushed around, shot at, arrested a lot, we made it out alive and we accomplished our goals. So my experience was very positive."[73]

As Brown said, her first *two* movement experiences were in militant groups led by black women. Brown's work with Pat Due was the second of the two. The first had come in mid-1963 with a CORE chapter in Dunnellon, Florida, led by Bettie Wright, who was a year younger than Brown. Wright was a student at FAMU that Due had brought into Tallahassee CORE. Through Wright, Brown had been introduced to Due.

When FAMU adjourned for the summer, as Wright put it, "there was just too much momentum."[74] Wright returned home to Dunnellon, a small town south of Gainesville, and immediately organized a CORE chapter which began picketing a segregated theatre. A national CORE staffer sent in to assist was arrested and brutally beaten in jail. Pickets began at the jail, and students in Gainesville, Brown among them, came to join in. As the students drove back to Gainesville after demonstrations, they were often chased by carloads of armed white men. Wright would accompany the students back to their homes.

According to Dan Harmeling, who was part of the student group, Wright, then twenty-one, was respected as the CORE leader by older adults of both sexes in Dunnellon and also by the students from Gainesville. Brown admired Wright and spent the summer working with her. Harmeling called Wright "dynamic—clearly someone who would inspire people."[75]

Brown learned from Bettie Wright and Patricia Due the fundamental lesson of the effectiveness of powerful female leadership. Wright and Due led with their courage, and they directed political strategy for the campaigns they waged. Although they were about Brown's age, they led the groups they had organized, which included white women and men.

The Transformation of Women's Liberation Pioneers

Judith Brown would take her leadership lessons back into the New Left, where she led in the formation of an independent movement for Women's Liberation. Black feminists such as Zoharah Simmons and Frances Beal drew on theirs to contend for female equality within the Black Power Movement, while Eleanor Holmes Norton took hers into mainstream politics as she continued in Hamer's footsteps to confront the white male establishment in the Democratic Party. Taking leadership under conditions of extreme danger from unremitting white violence in the Black Belt South would prove sustaining as these women fought for Women's Liberation, which took a different kind of courage.

When Simmons battled the imposition of sexist limitations on women's participation in two black nationalist groups she had helped to found, she recalled having triumphed over the chauvinism of white males she supervised in SNCC on her Amazon Project in Laurel, Mississippi. Despite the total destruction of the project's office and library by firebombing—not once but twice—she reached her goals. Consequently, having proven herself, she later found herself unable to submit to sexism.

Frances Beal tried to "rev up enough nerve" as the lone feminist speaker among a large gathering of mostly male black militants who "preached that the demand for women's rights was a white plot" and that "abortion was genocide." Beal recalled: "I felt as if I was about to become the main attraction at a metaphorical lynching party." Remembering earlier days in SNCC, she chanted to herself, "Think about facing down those Alabama State cops," and the memory helped "carry me all the way to the speaker's stand."[76]

Eleanor Holmes Norton said that "life-changing experience" in Mississippi sealed "a lifetime commitment" to working for social justice. She felt that she owed her feminist work to her "radicalization" in the Civil Rights Movement, which had "given me a great deal."[77]

In the summer of 1963, Norton left Yale to volunteer for SNCC in Mississippi. "The fight is a revolution down here," she wrote of the Mississippi Delta to a friend back at school. "Just being a freedom fighter down here is risking death—& I've been scared ever since I got here."[78] Norton had been picked up at the airport in Jackson by Medgar Evers, field secretary for the NAACP in Mississippi. Trying to persuade her to work with him in Jackson instead of going on to the SNCC project in Greenwood, Evers took her around Jackson to meet civil rights workers and home to meet his family.

Still, Norton left for Greenwood. Only hours later Evers, coming home after a civil rights meeting, was murdered in his own driveway. She learned about his murder the following afternoon in Greenwood. Arriving at the SNCC office there only deepened her fear. A group of civil rights workers, Fannie Lou Hamer among them, had been returning from voter registration training and were arrested and jailed in nearby Winona.

Lawrence Guyot, who was leading the SNCC project in Greenwood, had gone to get them out of jail and was himself jailed and severely beaten. What to do now? Norton had just arrived that day. "I couldn't just say 'Let's wait till somebody who knows how to handle this gets here.'"[79] As a law student, she felt she had to take responsibility. She managed to persuade the Greenwood police chief to call ahead to the Winona jail on her behalf. She told him she was a Yale law student and that she'd told everyone where she was going. "I have done that to protect myself," she told him.[80]

She was not harmed at the Winona jail and was permitted to visit Guyot and Hamer. "What I saw, I'll never forget," Norton said.[81] Hamer had been beaten so viciously that she had to be hospitalized for a month; a kidney had been permanently damaged. She was swollen, bruised, and could hardly speak. Guyot was in terrible condition also. Norton was told that she did not have enough money to bail them out. But her strategy had shown the Winona police that others knew about the situation, and she herself was not jailed. Finally SCLC came up with more money, national attention was focused on Winona, and the prisoners were bonded out.

Within days Norton would find herself marching with SNCC headlong into lines of Mississippi State Police who had their guns drawn. The civil rights workers had attended Evers's funeral in Jackson, and as they left the church, they began a demonstration. Soon their numbers grew to more than a thousand. "We want the killer," shouted the marchers as police dogs were brought to stop them.[82] Somehow Norton managed to come away from the march unharmed.

She attributed her resolve to Hamer, saying that she regretted that "more women and girls were not exposed to Fannie Lou Hamer. For she had the singular capacity to impart courage and to chase timidity."[83] But Norton had been transformed into a lifetime freedom fighter by her own leadership as well as by following Hamer's. It would not be long before Norton would draw upon this experience to defy established civil rights leaders and the liberal male establishment at the Democratic National Convention on behalf of the Mississippi Freedom Democratic Party.

White SNCC women who would soon be organizing for Women's Liberation were also transformed by their own "risking all" work, which, like Brown's work in CORE, deepened their sense of historical mission. It was not that they imitated the black organizers but that, in time, particular aspects of the daily work began to make over the white activists. Facing constant violence had forced the white workers to act, as Casey Hayden had said, "in this clear, pure way" and gave them a kind of presence or "transcendence" they admired in the black organizers.[84]

Of necessity, the young white women began to take themselves very seriously. One night when the SNCC project director was away, Heather Booth and twenty other Mississippi Freedom Summer volunteers gathered in their project's community center. They learned that the center was threatened with bombing and that armed men lay in wait for the returning project director. But it was more dangerous to leave the building than to stay in it. They turned out the lights and spent the night "re-emphasizing their conviction that this summer is necessary and right."[85] They also maintained phone contact with local police, the FBI, newspapers, and project headquarters. Booth later wrote home that fear "almost paralyzed" her. To "still the tension," she said, she thought about what could be gained in the "larger scope of the whole Project."[86]

Judith Brown found that she could lead men in the CORE project despite (or perhaps because of) the violence that project workers routinely faced. Five of Brown's recruits were men who came to live in the Freedom House in Quincy, Florida, and this was the first time Brown led men.

Pam Allen also experienced new, more egalitarian relationships with men. Allen observed the way the men respected Barbara Walker, an African American woman who was the Freedom School director. To her surprise, Allen, a white volunteer, found herself treated in a similar manner. One memorable example came early in the summer in the form of encouragement from a black male coworker with whom she was romantically involved. This man, Allen said, "expected me to be a great Freedom School teacher" even when it meant that her work came ahead of his needs.[87] "No man I'd known would have thought a woman's teaching was more important than he was."[88] Summing up the summer, Allen described it as "one of expansion, not male chauvinism."[89]

Although Allen spent only a few months in Holly Springs, life after Freedom Summer was unsatisfying by comparison. The project became a standard by which she measured jobs she would hold, places she would live, and future relationships with men. Her last year in college, a social work job in New York City, and marriage to Robert Allen, African American leader in the black draft resistance movement, left her feeling isolated and purposeless. Trying to understand the difference between her sense of purpose with SNCC and how much less meaningful life had become, Allen said: "It seemed to me there was a connection between my dissatisfaction with my life and my being a woman."[90]

The dissatisfaction that Allen connected with being a woman resulted, in part, from her earlier "expansion." Like Brown, she had gotten "used to seeing a woman lead" and men taking women seriously. She now wanted these things in equal measure in the world outside the project. Women's Liberation founders in the Civil Rights Movement surpassed their own expectations for courage and persistence. They gained a new feeling of recognition and respect from male coworkers. They learned that women could prevail in debates, plan, execute, and win campaigns against men with far greater political and economic power than they had. Once they had experienced more nearly equal relationships with men, new goals came into view.

Booth said that there was something about the work in Mississippi that she wanted "for the rest of my life."[91] Led by local black activists, Booth had learned that to successfully do work of great significance, "you didn't have to know enough according to some white person's standard or some man's standard."[92] Indeed, her work in Mississippi had lacked establishment approval or protection. Brown had undergone a similar shift in perspective when, on her first day in jail, she found herself grateful to be there. Casey Hayden once quoted Henry David Thoreau, jailed for refusing to pay taxes because the government sanctioned slavery. When Ralph Waldo Emerson visited the jail, he is alleged to have said: "Henry David, what are you doing in there?" Thoreau had replied: "Ralph Waldo, what are you doing out there?"[93] So it appeared to Women's Liberation pioneers in the Civil Rights Movement: those who defied authority were on the right side, while the authorities were on the wrong one.

Elected officials, judges, police, and pillars of the community perpetrated injustice by enforcing segregation, withholding the franchise, and arresting, jailing, violently intimidating, and even murdering movement workers.[94] The Justice Department and the FBI usually did little to stop the injustice. Moreover, the authorities on the wrong side were predominantly male and white. At the same time, poor black people, many of them women, were leading incipient Women's Liberation founders in life-changing work they loved, teaching them and protecting them. These experiences produced profound changes that for some civil rights workers became permanent.

Together for a while on her SNCC Project in Batesville, Mississippi, with only the local people, mostly farmers, Kathie Sarachild, a Radcliffe graduate and one of few female *Harvard Crimson* editors, remembered worrying that she would be bored, because "if we couldn't talk about books, movies, heavy politics, what was there?"[95] To what she self-critically described as her "surprise," Sarachild found herself engaged in challenging, analytical political discussions with the local Batesville activists. The experience with the local people, Sarachild said, "totally changed" her "reference group."[96] The opinion of "Harvard intellectuals" no longer mattered as the "test of success for my life."[97] For this young woman and others like her who initiated the struggle for Women's Liberation, the approval of white male authorities and peers had lost its former significance. Combined with positive experiences the women had with female leaders, the shift in reference group helped prepare Women's Liberation pioneers to confront men on women's behalf, and to look to women as a potentially militant constituency.

When they went into the Civil Rights Movement, Brown, Sarachild, and Allen already knew that sexism was a political system. But they did not know what to do about it. In the movement they began to develop the idea of taking on male supremacy collectively. Whether to change a law, bring publicity to an issue, raise bail, or back down more powerful opponents, they saw the effectiveness of mass action and solidarity. They also understood that everyday people could and would organize together against conventional wisdom and great odds.

The Lesson of Collective Strategy

The idea of taking on sexism in a mass movement, the strategy "Sisterhood Is Powerful," as Sarachild later named it, was critical among the lessons for Women's Liberation learned in the Black Freedom Movement.[98] The effectiveness of this strategy depended on the collective power of women, as opposed to the individual approaches such as personal efforts at education and moral persuasion that Women's Liberation pioneers had already tried for so long.

The strike in the SNCC office in the spring of 1964 was the earliest application of a conscious, collective approach to women's equality in a movement setting, and it was all the more pathbreaking because it came before the big burst of organizing that took place during the Freedom Summer that followed. Its roots, then, are clearly in the 1960 student sit-in movement. Ruby Doris Robinson knew the sit-in tactics because she had been in a core leadership group of the Atlanta Committee on Appeal for Human Rights. She had been arrested during sit-ins in Atlanta in early 1960. The strike was also characterized by black and white women working together, apparently with considerable unity.

The idea of fighting male supremacy collectively was also put forth by Hayden and King in 1964 in their anonymous "SNCC Position Paper" and again in 1965 in "Sex and Caste: A Kind of Memo," the letter they would mail to other female activists.[99] In the "Position Paper," Hayden and King made analogies between sexism and racism "to bring forward the fact that sexism was comparable to racism—a novel idea at the time," Hayden later reflected.[100]

"What can be done?" they asked, and suggested a continuum of possibilities, beginning with "Probably nothing right away" because "most men . . . are . . . too threatened" and many women seek "to be accepted by men."[101] Nevertheless, they held out hope for the other end of the continuum, namely, that "the whole of the women in this movement" could "force the rest of the movement to stop the discrimination."[102] Strongly implied was that, in order to stop sexist treatment of women, the "force" of many unified women would be needed.

Hayden and King were more explicit about a collective approach to sexism in the document they mailed to "women in the peace and freedom movements" in 1965.[103] Again they pointed to similarities between racism and discrimination against women. To deal with what they termed a "sex caste system," they modestly dropped the bombshell about starting a movement, but then retreated: "the chances seem nil that we could start a movement."[104] Referring to their civil rights work, Hayden and King said: "we've learned a great deal in the movement and perhaps ... a determined attempt to apply ideas we've learned there can produce some new alternatives."[105]

Hayden and King raised the woman question as they had learned to raise other issues in SNCC—by calling for discussion and writing position papers. In such a context, however "nil" the chances, a movement against sexism would be, as Eleanor Holmes Norton had observed, the logical outcome of the analogy they drew between racism and the "sex caste" system. After all, if a movement was the best strategy for fighting racism, even if a movement against sex-caste discrimination was unlikely, would it not be the appropriate strategy?

Sarachild first thought of taking on male supremacy in a movement when working with SNCC. She had learned about the woman question in her family. Reading *The Second Sex* as a teenager further raised her consciousness. But, as she said, "When I read *The Second Sex* I became a personal feminist ... the only thing possible before organized ... feminism began."[106]

Sarachild had returned to Batesville, Mississippi, in March 1965 to work on a filmstrip project associated with SNCC when she heard about the "women's liberation" ferment at SNCC's recent Waveland conference. "I didn't think about women's liberation as a possible movement until I came back down in March," she said. "Another volunteer ... came running up to me," she remembered, "and he said, 'Oh Kathie, you'll be so excited to know that there's something going on called 'women's liberation.'"[107] He reported that there had been a women's sit-in at the SNCC office, a feminist position paper at a conference, and that African American SNCC staff member Dona Moses, the wife of Bob Moses, the Mississippi project director, had reclaimed her maiden name.[108]

"A movement was starting on this issue, a movement like SNCC," Sarachild recalled thinking. She had "always known the issue," as she put it, "but the positive thing of ... a grass-roots movement, such as had been spreading through the South but in this case of women . . . It was the possibility of a *movement* . . . that I don't think any of us had conceived of . . . that it was possible to have a movement about it even though it was an old issue."[109]

According to Sarachild, hearing about "women's liberation" in the context of "a dynamic grass-roots movement in the wilds of Mississippi ignited the feminist part of my brain in new ways. . . . I remember . . . being thrilled with the sense of new possibilities."[110] "We saw that it was necessary to put the major part of our energy and resources into reaching women. . . . we saw that our *own* liberation depended on our reaching the masses of women—or else women would continue to be played off against one another."[111]

Heather Booth was beginning to get the same idea. In 1964, however, Booth had little background in feminism. Her family had not taught her about male chauvinism, nor had she read *The Second Sex*. Her mother recommended *The Feminine Mystique* to her. But as a high school student, Booth "did not really understand it when I read it then."[112]

In 1963 Booth, at the University of Chicago, knew that curfews discriminated against women. But she did not organize against sexism collectively until 1964 when she returned from her summer in Mississippi. Then she applied to sexism the tactics of the Civil Rights Movement, organizing "sleep outs" of women dorm residents to protest the curfews. In 1966 a friend was raped and treated in a sexist manner at the student health center. Booth organized a sit-in until the friend received proper care.[113] This trajectory of collective protest against male chauvinism culminated in 1967; Booth with others organized the West Side Group, the first group in the Women's Liberation Movement.

3

"Something had to be there already"

POWERFUL FORCES FRAMED the feminism of the women who first raised its banners in the Black Freedom Movement and the New Left. Their feminism, as Judith Brown observed, was fueled by "common movement and life experiences."[1] What were the common life experiences of the women to which Brown referred?

As has been said, most Women's Liberation pioneers had a head start. They were feminists well before they encountered sexism in the Black Freedom Movement and the Left. Their families and mentors taught them that there was a power imbalance in the world that favored men. Thus they could identify female oppression as a political problem rather than a personal one. Having come upon feminist political ideas before most other women helped the founders to go first in organizing the movement.

From the "SNCC Position Paper" in Mississippi to Poor Black Women in Mount Vernon and New Rochelle, New York, from "the Florida Paper" out of Gainesville to New York Radical Women and points in between, the roots of Women's Liberation drew upon feminist ideas that the movement's organizers learned early on.

Feminism in the Family

Judith Brown

Judith Brown's first mentor in the southern Civil Rights Movement, Bettie Wright, knew that Brown's commitment to fighting injustice was sown in well-prepared soil. Wright said, "Something had to be there already, for her to even be there with me."[2]

Julian Brown knew this too. Julian, a civil rights and antiwar activist, and Judith were married in 1966. Reflecting on how they came to be in the movement that brought them together, Brownie, as he was known, recalled with shameless male chauvinist adoration: "she was a queen, with truly royal bearing—tall, straight, blond, aloof. She also had the finest legs I'd ever seen on a woman. I loved walking behind her on a picket line."[3] But, he said, the combination of physical presence and acute awareness of "anything that was unfair" intimidated men.[4]

Of his wife's perception of unfairness Brownie said, "She would see this in men. And see the specifics in perspective, in the bigger picture." According to Brownie, Judith learned the "bigger picture" from her family. "It's in my genes," Judith exclaimed, retelling an incident from her teenage years.[5] Her mother, Ernestine Benninger, ironing clothes while watching the McCarthy hearings on television, had hurled her iron at the set. Not long after Judith witnessed her mother's reaction to McCarthyism, her family was subjected to its southern variety. Her father, Lawrence Benninger, a professor at the then segregated University of Alabama in Tuscaloosa, was fired for supporting the admission of Autherine Lucy, the first black student to enroll. "My father," Judith remembered, "got up in the faculty senate and suggested that her admission be based on her qualifications which seemed rather good."[6]

Lucy was admitted to the University of Alabama in 1956 under a court order resulting from an NAACP lawsuit. During her brief attendance she faced hostile white mobs who threatened her life and assaulted her.[7] Mrs. Benninger took Judith, then fifteen, and her younger brother Christopher to see the brave young woman make her way onto the campus. As they watched tensely from the sidelines, Judith's mother told them this was "like fascism."[8]

Despite his support for Autherine Lucy, Professor Benninger feared that his daughter's career would be jeopardized as his had been, and he opposed Judith's participation in the Civil Rights Movement. On her mother's side of the family, however, she was encouraged by her aunts, Roxane and Jane Eberlein, whom she had known since childhood as opponents of white supremacy and male supremacy. Indeed, her aunt Jane was a contemporary in the Civil Rights Movement. She blocked streets around the 1964 Democratic National Convention hall to protest the failure to seat the Mississippi Freedom Democratic Party.

Neither Roxane nor Jane had children of her own, and Judith and her brother were the only children in the extended family. Roxane, who took a particular interest in her niece, wrote, "How I would like to have her where I could . . . submit her to the most rigorous training."[9] As a child, Roxane herself had been trained by some of the leading activists of her day. She would pass on her activism and feminism to her niece.

The Eberlein sisters grew up in Free Acres, a Single Tax colony in New Jersey based on principles of racial and sexual equality. Years before the passage of the Nineteenth Amendment, women had full voting rights in colony affairs.[10] Established in 1910 by Bolton Hall, attorney for radical feminist and anarchist Emma Goldman, Free Acres attracted radicals and artists such as legendary black freedom fighter Paul Robeson. Hall, a friend of the Eberlein family, had been arrested for distributing birth control leaflets with Margaret Sanger. Roxane and Jane maintained the family home well into Judith's adulthood. Immersed in her family's political history, Judith was a frequent guest at Free Acres and honeymooned there.

Judith's maternal grandparents, Ernest and Undena Eberlein, were lifelong activists. Ernest was membership chair of the Socialist Party branch to which Undena also belonged. The couple held Party meetings in their home. As children, the Eberlein sisters learned feminism from their mother Undena, an ardent reader of Charlotte Perkins Gilman and an active suffragist. The sisters were jailed with Undena when she tried to vote. Their father, Ernest, also a suffrage supporter, came to get the family out of jail.

Free Acres administrator Ami Mali Hicks was a member of the Women's Political Union, a militant suffrage group modeled on the tactics of the British movement and organized in the United States by Harriet Stanton Blatch, Elizabeth Cady Stanton's daughter.[11] Hicks was influential with Judith's aunt Roxane, who in turn helped to "train" Judith. As suffrage agitation peaked in 1920, Roxane, then only ten, lived in New York City with Hicks. Theirs was a lifelong friendship. When Hicks became elderly and could no longer work, Roxane gave financial support.

Judith's brother Christopher said Roxane had imbued in niece and nephew alike the idea that they "could change the future."[12] Thus Judith's activist family was the "something" that, as Bettie Wright noted, was "there already" when Judith went to work with her in the Civil Rights Movement. Brown's experience was not exceptional among Women's Liberation pioneers.

Pam Allen

Pam Allen, cofounder of New York Radical Women (NYRW), was raised in Pennsylvania in a deeply religious Episcopal family. As a child she learned about the Women's Rights Movement from her suffragist great-grandmother. Allen's family claimed as a relative Lucretia Mott, the militant feminist and abolitionist Quaker. As a youngster, Allen was given books about the feminist and abolitionist work in which her family members had participated.

These feminist predecessors were honored in Allen's family. In 1963 when Allen became a civil rights activist, her grandfather and his brothers remarked that she was "just like mother."[13] Allen took on women's rights that same year. In 1966 Allen left the Episcopal Church because it would not ordain women.

Allen's family was Republican, and engaged in social reform through association with a liberal tradition in the Episcopal Church. Allen understood and was proud of family traditions of Christian pacifism and feminism before she went to work in the Civil Rights Movement.

Pauli Murray

Black feminist Pauli Murray was also influenced by First Wave feminism. Murray, in addition to other feminist activity, worked for inclusion of black female civil rights leaders on the program of the 1963 March on Washington (MOW), helped to pass Title VII of the 1964 Civil Rights Act banning discrimination against women in employment, mentored black feminist Eleanor Holmes Norton, and was a key force in founding the National Organization for Women (NOW). She was a sharp, early critic of the myth of the black matriarchy and urged black women to "assert a leadership role in the growing feminist movement . . . to help to keep it allied to the objectives of black liberation."[14] Murray's cutting-edge feminist influence was felt broadly, in law, national legislation, and religion—where she effectively challenged barriers to women's ordination.

In 1928, at age eighteen, Murray joined a circle of black female activists at the Harlem YWCA that she said "foreshadowed the revival of the feminist movement of the 1960s."[15] At the YWCA she engaged in lively analytical discussions of politics with future feminists including Ella Baker, Anna Arnold Hedgeman (the only official female organizer for the MOW), and Dorothy Height (future president of the National Council of Negro Women). These women would, as Murray said, engage in "concerted efforts to rise above the limitations of race and sex and to help younger women to do the same."[16]

Murray worked for the New Deal Workers' Education Project teaching black and white union members, and organized for the Workers Defense League on behalf of sharecroppers. She said that her union work made her aware of class oppression.

> I had never thought of white people as victims of oppression, but now I heard echoes of the black experience when I listened to white workers tell their personal stories of being evicted, starved out, beaten, and jailed when they tried to organize a union. . . . The study of economic oppression led me to realize that Negroes were not alone but were part of an unending struggle for human dignity the world over.[17]

Murray dated her feminist consciousness to her years at Howard Law School, which she entered on a scholarship in 1941. Murray began to understand male supremacy there, because at a historically black university "the race factor was removed . . . and the factor of gender was fully exposed."[18] She was excluded from the legal fraternity. Often the only female in her classes, she found herself passed over in class by male professors.

What Murray later called "an incipient feminism" would become full-fledged feminist consciousness through discussions with National Woman's Party veteran Betsy Graves Reyneau who, Murray said, "nourished my budding feminism."[19] Reyneau, who was white, was an internationally acclaimed portrait painter. She saw racism as an American version of fascism and fought it with her art, painting striking portraits of leading African Americans, particularly those in the fight for civil rights. Her political art brought her to Howard, where Murray met her.

Murray learned of Reyneau's suffrage militancy—that she had been jailed in the infamous Occoquan Workhouse with the 1917 Woman's Party White House pickets and subjected to force-feeding and rough treatment. Murray found that they shared a family history of abolitionism as Reyneau recounted her grandmother's work operating a station of the Underground Railroad and her friendship with the abolitionist and feminist Sojourner Truth. Murray's grandfather had also housed an Underground Railroad station, and Murray now saw his stories of sharing a platform with Susan B. Anthony in a new way. "My discovery of links between the struggles for the abolition of slavery and the rights of women gave me a new perspective that helped me balance the tensions created by the double burden of race and sex."[20]

Murray called Reyneau "a living link with an earlier phase of a struggle that had faded into obscurity by the time I grew up."[21] When Reyneau died, she left Murray her silver pin replica of a prison door, sixteen of which had been made by the Woman's Party when, after a sixty-day stay, the first sixteen pickets were released from prison.

From then on, Murray took up the struggle of the "double burden of race and sex" consciously and often simultaneously. She led sit-ins at segregated eating places in the District of Columbia in 1943–44, picketing with placards such as "Are You for Hitler's Way (Race Supremacy) or the AMERICAN WAY (Equality)? Make Up Your Mind!"[22] At the same time, she waged a high-profile losing campaign to sexually integrate Harvard Law School.[23]

Murray eventually went on to serve on the Committee on Civil and Political Rights of the President's Commission on the Status of Women, which had been initiated in 1961.[24] She called the commission "an intensive consciousness-raising process leading directly to my involvement in the new women's movement that surfaced a few years later."[25]

Eleanor Holmes Norton

Like Murray, her mentor at Yale Law School, Eleanor Holmes Norton was influenced by feminism's First Wave. She was just thirteen when she witnessed black First Wave leader Mary Church Terrell, then eighty-seven, leading a militant sit-in campaign near Norton's junior high school in Washington, D.C. This encounter was a lifelong inspiration for Norton. It would also draw her to Murray, of whom she said, "Her feminism seemed way out to us then. . . . I believed I had to catch up with her."[26]

At Yale, Norton learned of Murray's own 1943–44 sit-in campaign and wrote her major paper "World War II and the Beginning of Non-Violent Action in Civil Rights" on it. Murray's sit-in campaign had been revived six years later in 1950 by Mary Church Terrell, Norton's "most admired" woman. Terrell led the campaign to victory in 1953, defending herself on the basis of Reconstruction era laws that Murray had researched and publicized.[27] Norton said she was "thrilled to have a real-live original source" of this key civil rights strategy.[28]

In 1963 Norton was working in Mississippi in SNCC with Fannie Lou Hamer and soon came under the influence of Ella Baker, who appointed her to direct the lobbying for the Mississippi Freedom delegation at the Democratic National Convention.

In 1966 Norton worked with feminist attorney and future Supreme Court justice Ruth Bader Ginsberg, whom she called "the Thurgood Marshall of the women's movement."[29] Norton was legal advisor to the SNCC Women's Liberation Committee and part of the influential black Women's Liberation group, the Third World Women's Alliance. Like Murray's, her influence was not as an organizer of Women's Liberation groups but rather as a national voice for Women's Liberation.

Influences from the Left

Ella Baker

Ella Baker became conscious of the woman question in Depression-era Harlem in the Left, black nationalist, and Pan-Africanist circles to which she attributed her political development. She was part of the hotbed of female activism at the Harlem YWCA, where she met Pauli Murray, later a lifelong friend.

"The Bronx Slave Market," which Baker coauthored with black Communist Marvel Cooke in 1935, highlighted the ways in which race, sex, and class combined to exponentially oppress and exploit the black women who sold their "human labor" and "human love" for a "slave wage" to white buyers on the Simpson Avenue block in Harlem. The article, published in the NAACP's *Crisis*, opposed the "triple jeopardy" of African American women.

From 1930 through the mid-1930s Baker and George Schuyler organized the Young Negro Cooperative League (YNCL), an alliance of cooperative consumer groups. They saw the YNCL as a step into a socialist future that included equality for women. The YNCL's founding statement explicitly provided for women's participation as full members of the organization, a position that was considerably ahead of most other groups during that time.[30]

In 1969 Baker gave a speech titled "The Black Woman in the Civil Rights Struggle" in Atlanta at the Institute for the Black World. She recounted that in 1946 she and Pauli Murray had been excluded from the first Freedom Ride to oppose Jim Crow in interstate travel, organized by the Fellowship of Reconciliation, because "the decision was made that only the men could go."[31] This was particularly unjust in that Murray, Baker said, had been "one of the young persons who was part of the first efforts" to contest segregated travel.[32]

Indeed, Murray and another female student, Adeline McBean, had been jailed in 1940 in Petersburg, Virginia, in one of the earliest test cases. They were represented by NAACP lawyers, including Thurgood Marshall. Eleanor Roosevelt telephoned the governor of Virginia about their jailing. Their case was widely publicized in the black and white press. The *Carolina Times* wrote: "Perhaps Miss Murray and Miss McBean are the beginning of a new type of leadership—a leadership that will not cringe and crawl on its belly merely because it happens to be faced with prison bars in its fight for the right."[33]

Moreover, it is unlikely that the men who were chosen for the Freedom Ride had any more Jim Crow travel experience than Baker. Baker "had just finished a tour of duty with the NAACP and had ridden a lot of Jim Crow buses and wanted very much to go, but I guess it was decided that I was too frail to make such a journey."[34] Baker's "tour of duty" ran from 1940 to 1946, grueling Jim Crow travel on buses and trains, usually alone, through the Deep South, as director of branches for the NAACP. She suffered countless indignities and worse, including, in 1943 in Florida, being manhandled and bruised by military police who forcefully pulled her from her seat. "The travel was bum," said Baker.[35]

Little wonder that there was rancor in Baker's speech in 1969, even though the experience of sexist exclusion she discussed had taken place more than twenty years ago. Nonetheless, Baker said in the same speech, "I have never been one to feel great needs in the direction of setting myself apart as a woman. I've always thought first and foremost of people as individuals."[36] Baker effectively promoted equality for women throughout her life, but there is no evidence that she thought an independent Women's Liberation Movement could help achieve it.

Patricia Robinson

Unlike Baker, Patricia Murphy Robinson, who organized the black Women's Liberation group Poor Black Women, was in favor of organizing women independently of men when it came to fighting for Women's Liberation. For Robinson the politics of Women's Liberation and in particular black Women's Liberation were, as she put it, "up front" as a political priority.[37]

Robinson was close to the black Left in and around the Communist Party (CP), nationally and internationally.[38] She frequently spoke of "male chauvinism" and "male supremacy," which were Communist terms from earlier traditions of naming sexism.[39] Growing up, Robinson had an uncle in the CP; Paul Robeson was a family visitor, and W. E. B. DuBois a neighbor.

Robinson's family, the Murphys, founded, edited, and published the *Afro-American*, which serves the Baltimore-Washington area and is the longest-running family-owned African American newspaper in the United States. The *Afro-American* defended DuBois and Robeson when they were subjected to political repression during the McCarthy era. Robinson was in her mid-twenties when her family stood up to these anti-Communist attacks.

The paper had a tradition of challenging racism and sexism. It campaigned against Jim Crow railroad cars, collaborated with the NAACP on civil rights cases, and published articles in support of birth control. In the mid-1930s it employed women sportswriters, and in the 1940s had a woman war correspondent.

Robinson's family introduced her to the fight for reproductive freedom. Her father was on the national board of Planned Parenthood. He was also president of the Social Services Advisory Board of Maryland, where he blazed a trail of policies that stopped nighttime searches of welfare recipients' homes and ensured that they not be excluded from family planning because they were single. He called this work his "greatest accomplishment."[40] Poor Black Women got off the ground in 1960 when Robinson, a Planned Parenthood volunteer, undertook to lower the rising pregnancy rate among black teenagers by bringing birth control into the poor black neighborhoods of Mount Vernon, New York. She had not been planning to organize a Women's Liberation group, she was simply hoping to introduce a tool the women could use to gain a more self-determined life.[41]

Black women had a tradition of support for birth control nationally that was particularly evident in Baltimore when Robinson was growing up. She was twelve in 1938 when black organizations in Baltimore opened the Northwest Health Center, which continued to be black financed, sponsored, and staffed. At the Northwest Health Center the black community received birth control and maternal health services provided by black nurses, social workers, and physicians, without fear of sterilization.[42]

Robinson was no doubt well aware of all of this, given the Murphy family's advocacy for birth control and the views of neighbor DuBois. "The future woman must have a life work and future independence. . . . She must have knowledge . . . she must have the right of motherhood at her own discretion," DuBois had written.[43] His eloquent arguments that reproductive freedom was a cornerstone of women's freedom came with condemnations of sterilization, several of which were published while the Northwest Health Center was being organized.[44] Robinson's Women's Liberation organizing developed out of a strong foundation of reproductive freedom and Left politics. These influences would later distinguish the feminism of Poor Black Women.

Frances Beal

Frances Beal, cofounder of SNCC's Black Women's Liberation Committee and later the Third World Women's Alliance, had also been influenced by the Old Left. She was a "red diaper baby" (as the children of radicals were called), the daughter of a Jewish Communist mother, Charlotte Berman, and Ernest Yates, who was African American. Beal's maternal grandfather had been a Bolshevik in Russia. Berman and some of her siblings were in the U.S. Communist Party.

Beal, born in 1940, was raised in Binghamton, New York, and recalled her embarrassment as a child when her mother was red-baited by name on the front page of the local newspaper. Beal attended radical summer camps Wo-chi-ca (the Workers' Children's Camp) and Camp Kinderland, where she experienced integrated play activities. This was quite different from childhood play in Binghamton, where as a self-proclaimed "tomboy" Beal "plowed into a white crowd" and fought "to defend the family honor" when a bigger white youngster called her older brother racial epithets. Beal said her father explained racism to her and held the view that "if someone called you that [nigger] they should be beaten up so bad." Her mother counseled that if she encountered racist and anti-Semitic people she should "talk to them, educate them." Her mother imparted to her the belief that "things weren't right in the world and you were supposed to do something about it."[45]

Beal completed her undergraduate program at the Sorbonne in Paris, where she met black expatriates like Richard Wright and students from the anticolonial movements in Africa. She was influenced by the writings of Frantz Fanon and other intellectuals associated with *Presence Africaine*, a Pan-Africanist journal. Beal also embraced revolutionary ideas from the Movimento Popular de Libertação de Angola (MPLA), the Frente de Libertação de Moçambique (FRELIMO), and other struggles for national liberation. She worked in the United States in SNCC for several summers and returned to the States with her family in 1966 to work with SNCC's International Affairs Commission in New York City. Beal's internationalism has remained a source of political education throughout her life. She was, she said, "influenced by revolutionary ideas" from national liberation struggles, "some of these views of women [that] were challenging the mores."[46]

Naomi Weisstein

White feminist Naomi Weisstein acknowledged an upbringing on the Left as the taproot of her feminism. Weisstein said, "I grew up in the church of socialism." Speaking of the years from age ten to twenty, she reflected, "I was in the closet most of the time on two accounts . . . my socialism and my feminism."[47] Her maternal grandfather, an immigrant from Russia at the turn of the century, was an anarchist and a union organizer. The "legacy of resistance went from Grandpa, to Mary, to Naomi," Weisstein said, referring to her mother, Mary Menk Weisstein, who treasured her life on the Left.[48] "My mother talked about 'male chauvinism' quite a bit," Naomi said, and Mary taught her daughter not to submit to it.[49]

Naomi Weisstein became active in CORE in 1963, and later joined SDS protests against the war in Vietnam. There, along with male chauvinism from movement coworkers, Weisstein encountered feminist-minded women like herself and came joyously out of the "closet" for Women's Liberation.

Kathie Sarachild

Kathie Sarachild often named *The Second Sex* as the source of her feminist views. However, Sarachild said, "It's funny . . . in a certain sense I was already a feminist . . . I was a 'red diaper baby' and as a result I knew there was discrimination against women, male chauvinism, a woman question."[50] In 1964 Sarachild joined other volunteers in Mississippi for the SNCC Mississippi Freedom Summer Project. At first Sarachild hesitated about going, thinking it meant "absolutely certain death."[51] But when, despite her begging him not to go, Claude Weaver, an African American friend at Harvard, survived civil rights work in Mississippi in 1963, Sarachild decided that while there was a risk of death, it was "not certain."[52]

Sarachild's father by adoption, Ernest Amatniek, had been among the volunteers of his own generation who put their lives on the line to defend the Spanish Republic against the assault of Franco, Hitler, and Mussolini in 1936. One of some three thousand young men and women who joined the volunteer soldiers of the Abraham Lincoln Brigade, Ernest too must have wondered if he would make it back alive. Kathie felt pride in her father's participation in this, but she was equally aware and proud of something else about him. He did a great share of family household chores. Their family commented when the men in other Left households didn't share housework with the women. In the culture of the families Sarachild grew up with, "struggle on the woman question," as longtime African American freedom fighter Esther Cooper Jackson said—fathers sharing child care and housework, women pursuing public political lives, sexism eliminated in both personal and political life—was seen as a hallmark of a good home.[53]

Thus Sarachild considered herself both a radical and a feminist long before she went to Mississippi for Freedom Summer in 1964. Her family had sent Sarachild on a scholarship to the Little Red School House in Greenwich Village, a school that had become something of a refuge for progressive teachers and children of Left and Left-leaning parents persecuted by McCarthyism. There, girls wore blue jeans and took shop along with the boys. "A brand of feminist consciousness and reading had been an important part of my life—of my energy and enthusiasm—before the civil rights movement," Sarachild said.[54]

The "red" in Little Red School House had originally referred to the red bricks with which it was built, not the politics of its students or their families. The school was a product of the First Wave of feminism and the progressive education movement of that period. Its founder, Elisabeth Irwin, after whom its high school was named, was, with her lifetime partner Katharine Anthony, a member of the renowned circle of New Women of the period that called itself Heterodoxy.[55] Heterodoxy member Elizabeth Gurley Flynn, then a labor organizer in the Industrial Workers of the World, called Heterodoxy "a glimpse of the women of the future."[56] Feminist historian Nancy Cott said it "epitomized the Feminism of the time."[57]

Angela Davis

Black feminist Angela Davis also attended the Little Red School House. In her history classes there she learned about socialism, and "a whole new world opened up before my eyes," Davis said.[58] She also attended meetings of Advance, a Marxist-Leninist youth group that was close to the CP and participated in demonstrations for peace and in support of the sit-in movement that was sweeping the South.

But these were not Davis's first exposures to radical ideas. Davis was born in 1944 in Birmingham, where her mother, Sallye Davis, was a leader in the local chapter of the Southern Negro Youth Congress. SNYC had been organized by African American Communists to fight white supremacy in the South. Although Sallye Davis had not joined the Party, she worked within the African American Communist circle of Esther and James Jackson and Dorothy and Louis Burnham, the people to whom Esther Jackson was referring when she spoke of "struggle on the woman question" being a hallmark of a good Communist home. Dorothy Burnham, a black feminist scientist, said she had been a "Black feminist" since her student years in the 1930s.[59] Angela Davis was playmates with the Burnham and Jackson children when she grew up in Birmingham. Like Patricia Robinson, Davis used phrases like "male chauvinism."

Angela Davis was not a Women's Liberation founder, and not supportive of an independent movement for Women's Liberation. But she opposed the oppression of women and was critical of male chauvinism in the movement and in the larger society. Her article "Reflections on the Black Woman's Role in the Community of Slaves" brought attention to the woman question when it was published in the *Black Scholar* in 1971. At the time there was a high-profile worldwide Free Angela Davis movement engaging in ongoing public protest.[60] Davis wrote the article in prison and was still there when it came out.[61]

Her capture and incarceration, after months on the FBI's most-wanted list, garnered international attention. When she critiqued the Moynihan Report, calling it "a dastardly ideological weapon designed to impair our capacity for resistance today by foisting upon us the ideal of male supremacy," her words spread the concept of male supremacy widely to the general public.[62] So did her feminist courtroom defense at her trial. The prosecutor, seeking to convince the jury that Davis had manipulated a crime from behind the scenes, invoked Moynihan's stereotype of the black matriarch. As scholar and activist Bettina Aptheker said, "the Moynihan doctrine became the cornerstone of the prosecution's trial strategy."[63] In response, Davis told the jury that the prosecutor "would like to take advantage of the fact that I am a woman, for in this society women are supposed to act only in accordance with the dictates of their emotions. . . . this is clearly a symptom of the male chauvinism that prevails in our society."[64] Jury foreperson Mary Timothy later told Aptheker that the eight female jurors weren't buying the "matriarchal mirage."[65]

Florynce Kennedy

Black feminist Florynce Kennedy was an important leader of the predominantly white Women's Liberation Movement. Kennedy too was introduced to the concept of male supremacy through the Old Left.

In 1946, studying law at Columbia University, she took a sociology course with Bernhard Stern, who was a member of the Communist Party and the editor of the pro-Communist scholarly journal *Science and Society*. She called his course "a real turning point" in her political development.[66] Kennedy wrote a paper for the class, "A Comparative Study: Accentuating the Similarities of the Societal Position of Women and Negroes," which held: "The majority of both groups are generally dependent economically upon the dominant group. . . . More than any other aspect of culture, the economic factor determines cultural development and direction. . . . The far-reaching effects of their economic incompetencies leave not the minutest detail of their lives unaffected."[67]

Kennedy was active on all fronts. She was in NOW in 1966. That same year, she organized the Media Workshop to fight racism in media and advertising. Media Workshop picketed advertising agencies on Madison Avenue with signs such as "Jim Crow Lives on Madison Avenue" and demanded equal time on radio and TV networks when racist remarks were broadcast.[68] Kennedy also organized against the war in Vietnam, attended all four national Black Power conferences, and had a prominent role in the protest of the Miss America beauty pageant in 1968. She was on the team of attorneys who, in 1969, brought the class action lawsuit *Abramowicz v. Lefkowitz*, which helped make abortion legal in New York in 1970.

Carol Hanisch

Like Kennedy, founding white feminist Carol Hanisch did not encounter Left ideas until college. Hanisch had been born and raised in rural Iowa with no family history of exposure to the Left. Life wasn't easy for many small farmers in the early 1950s. In fact, Hanisch never lived in a house with an indoor toilet until she was a college student. This modest upbringing provided fertile ground for a gut-level understanding of class and a desire to work on eliminating poverty. When Carol read *The Communist Manifesto* in a college course titled "Democracy and Its Enemies," taught by a faculty member who was a former employee of the CIA, she saw some of her family's economic struggles reflected in the language of the *Manifesto*.

At Drake University in the early 1960s, she heard Carl Braden speak about resisting the House UnAmerican Activities Committee and being jailed for contempt for refusing to name names. Far from being put off by the red-baiting, she wanted to learn more. However, she was unable to stay for the discussion that followed the speech because she had to keep the early dorm hours imposed upon female students. Like many of her contemporaries,

Hanisch was stung by this injustice. Men could stay out as long as necessary to discuss the issues of the day, but women were not allowed to do the
same.

After graduation, Hanisch became the only female UPI reporter at the
wire service's bureau in Des Moines, Iowa, where she experienced sex discrimination in the type of news she was assigned to cover. Hanisch attributed
"greater exposure to theory about class and sexism as well as race" to the
Civil Rights Movement in Mississippi, where she went to work in the spring
of 1965.[69]

Shirley Chisholm

Shirley Chisholm was influenced by her father's black nationalist politics and
traced her feminist politics to one of her college professors. Chisholm called
Marcus Garvey her father's "idol" upon whom he would "hold forth."[70] He
took her to events in tribute to Garvey, where she first heard "black nationalist oratory—talk of race pride and the need for unity," Chisholm recalled.[71]
At Hunter College, Chisholm was mentored by a blind, white political science professor, Louis Warsoff, with whom she had long talks. Warsoff was
the first to suggest that she go into politics, and he encouraged her despite
her initial reaction that she would never make it because "I'm black—and I'm
a woman."[72] Warsoff and Chisholm discussed these barriers, and Chisholm
threw herself into campus politics, where she campaigned for female office
seekers and organized a black women's society, Ipothia, which meant "in
pursuit of the highest of all."[73]

In 1964 Chisholm won a seat in the New York State Assembly, the first African American there. As a freshman legislator she introduced bills (and got
them passed) preserving the tenure rights of pregnant public school teachers,
and establishing unemployment compensation for domestic workers. She
later got legislation passed that supported day care centers. In 1968 she ran
for Congress. Her Republican political opponent, black CORE leader James
Farmer, attacked her with the Moynihan stereotype "running me down as a
bossy female, a would-be matriarch," said Chisholm. However, like Angela
Davis with her jury, Chisholm was able to "turn the tables on him," because
female voters were registered in more than double the numbers of men.
Many of these women were working single mothers who must have been
as offended by the myth of the black matriarch as Chisholm. Chisholm was
the first African American woman to be elected to Congress. She had run an
unabashedly feminist and antiracist campaign.

Conclusion

Sara Evans was the first to point out that many early women's liberation organizers had Old Left family backgrounds. "I did not seek out 'red diaper babies,'" Evans said.[74] But as she studied founding Women's Liberation organizers, she noted, "Again and again I was surprised to discover a radical family background."[75] As Evans put it, "the specific connections are very important." But she had promised confidentiality and did not reveal their identities. "Many parents . . . [whose] daughters emerged as leading figures in the revival of the 'woman question'" did not wish their association with radicalism to be revealed. Evans called the necessity for discretion a "tragedy of the McCarthy era."[76] Since then, a number of the women Evans interviewed have spoken openly of the radical roots of their feminist ideas.

"Red diaper babies" were a sizable minority on the cutting edge of Women's Liberation. But most did not support it, seeing it as divisive or a distraction from larger issues. Still, the prevalence of founders learning feminist ideas from family suggests that this phenomenon is attributable to continuity rather than coincidence. More significant than their numbers, Sara Evans pointed out, these women "provided much of the key leadership."[77]

Indeed, Naomi Weisstein and Pam Allen helped to cofound, respectively, the nation's first and second Women's Liberation groups. The groups were important not only because they were the first but because they were the seedbed for most of the organizing, ideas, and actions that by 1968 had laid the base for a mass national movement. Frances Beal, Judith Brown, and Patricia Robinson also organized early Women's Liberation groups. The critical leadership Brown provided was her work on the Florida Paper. Kathie Sarachild was the lead developer of consciousness-raising, the movement's first program. Robinson's leadership in countering arguments that abortion was genocide and her brilliant analysis were beacons for the movement. Beal went first to organize women of color nationally for Women's Liberation.

Several historians have pointed out that a feminist conceptual framework among movement founders included the "words to name" sexist encounters.[78] "Male chauvinism" and "male supremacy" were familiar terms to those with Left backgrounds. Naomi Weisstein put it this way: "it was vitally important that I knew how to say 'male chauvinism' . . . otherwise, I would have thought—if I were just sexier, smarter, cooler," meaning that she'd have blamed herself for sexist treatment.[79]

Unlike contemporaries who did not have radical or feminist family backgrounds, these women also knew that fighting political injustice was something that people like them did. Pam Allen's mother told her daughter approvingly that she was following in the family tradition. Family support provided the security and power of continuity. Brown wrote to Sarachild, "My essential radicalism/feminism had their genesis in my childhood."[80]

That so many Women's Liberation pioneers had an understanding of the woman question before they entered the other 1960s movements indicates that their feminist organizing was not simply a product of their encounters with male chauvinism in these movements. A deep and compelling continuity of organizing against injustice mediated the founders' experience in the Black Freedom Movement and the Left.

4   The Influence of Simone de Beauvoir

BEAUVOIR RAISED Women's Liberation founders' consciousness that male domination, including everyday male behavior, imposed arbitrary limits on woman's achievement of her human potential. Moreover, Beauvoir clarified to radical women, those who opposed exploitation and oppression root and branch, that socialism, while necessary for Women's Liberation, would not automatically or by itself resolve the "woman question."

For some founders of the Women's Liberation Movement, Beauvoir provided a code for living, both as individuals and for a movement vanguard. Leading Women's Liberation organizers took feminist consciousness, ideology, and example from Beauvoir. She even gave the movement they would organize its name; "women's liberation" is a phrase repeated throughout *The Second Sex*.[1] Like the founders with feminism in the family, those who counted Beauvoir as their feminist source were distinguished by the impact of their work.

In 1953, when *The Second Sex* was published in the United States, Patricia Robinson and her husband and young children were living in New Rochelle, New York. The first to get the book from her local library, Robinson held on to *The Second Sex* long enough to pay a heavy fine. But unlike a number of white feminists, Robinson said she "had trouble with de Beauvoir as a model." Robinson believed that because she was black, she and her family had been denied privileges that made achievement possible for Beauvoir despite her unconventional ways. Indeed, Robinson found *The Second Sex* "so deeply subversive" that she did not feel it was "safe" for her daughters to read until they had children.[2]

While rejecting Beauvoir as a personal model, Robinson said she agreed with "everything" in *The Second Sex* because she was already an "unreconstructed *socialist*-feminist." For Robinson, Beauvoir had rightly put "women rights . . . up front in the fight for a more just society."[3] As opposed to a model for ridding one's individual life of sex role restrictions, Robinson found in Beauvoir a guide to organizing. In any struggle against injustice, Robinson would place women's rights "up front." Thus Poor Black Women fought male chauvinism in the black movement while opposing racism and capitalism as oppressive to black women and men.

Second Wave progenitor Lorraine Hansberry not only counted *The Second Sex* as important, she said it "may well be the most important work of this century" and "the world will never be the same again."[4] Hansberry said she read the book in 1953, the year it was published in the United States.[5] She was then twenty-three years old, an associate editor of Paul Robeson's journal *Freedom*, and active against House UnAmerican Activities Committee political repression. She described her reaction upon finishing the book: "after months of study . . . placing it in the most available spot on her 'reference' shelf, her fingers sensitive with awe . . . mind afire at last with ideas from France once again in history, *égalité, fraternité, liberté—pour tout le monde!*"[6]

Hansberry penned the commentary on *The Second Sex* in 1957 as she was working on *A Raisin in the Sun*, the play that propelled her into national critical acclaim. Black scholar Margaret Wilkerson said of the play that her introduction of abortion and her portrayal of Beneatha, the bright, political, and intellectually sophisticated daughter in *Raisin* who plans a career as a doctor "signaled early on Hansberry's feminist attitudes."[7] "Woman, like the Negro, the Jew, like colonial peoples, even in ignorance," Hansberry wrote in the commentary, "is *incapable of accepting the role* with harmony."[8] Beneatha, in *Raisin*, fully meets that description. Since Hansberry had a close association with the Left, including Robeson and W. E. B. DuBois, and was director of special events at Camp Unity, a Communist camp in upstate New York, she was undoubtedly already acquainted with the woman question when she read Beauvoir. But *The Second Sex* was clearly a decisive feminist source, if not her earliest encounter with feminism. Hansberry would surely have become even more of a feminist freedom fighter had she not died of cancer in 1965, at only thirty-four years of age.

Eleanor Holmes Norton and Frances Beal read *The Second Sex* in the mid-1960s. Norton gave it out to friends and commented on its influence on others. But neither Norton nor Beal refer to it as a feminist source.

At age fourteen Kathie Sarachild found Simone de Beauvoir's *The Second Sex* on her mother's bookshelf and, thinking it was about sex, picked it out. "I was one of the early radical feminists who considers that it was *The Second Sex* that made her a radical feminist," Sarachild said.[9] Struggling to distinguish what Beauvoir added to the views she already held, Sarachild described the book's impact:

> The thing that *The Second Sex* did for me that was new, was that . . . it gave me an incredibly strong commitment because it showed how it [male supremacy] affected everything. . . . though I was only a teenager . . . I was worried about how I looked. . . . it described the enormous amount of time that women have to put into making themselves look presentable in the world . . . that men didn't have to spend. . . . the book compared high heels to bound feet.[10]

Beauvoir had raised Sarachild's consciousness. "I felt literally, physically, as if my eyes were being opened. . . . It seared me with a consciousness so strong," she said.[11] After reading *The Second Sex* Sarachild said she could never stop thinking about the problem of male supremacy and could never stop trying to fight it.[12] Sarachild wrote a book report on *The Second Sex* for her ninth-grade class. Seventeen years later *Feminist Revolution*, published by Redstockings under Sarachild's editorial leadership, called Beauvoir "The French woman who exposed male supremacy for this era and gave us our feminism."[13]

Shulamith Firestone exemplifies these founders both for inspiration from Beauvoir and for unparalleled leadership of the movement in its formative period. Among a handful of feminists in 1967, Firestone, together with Jo Freeman, formed the nation's first Women's Liberation group. A few months later she organized the nation's second group, New York Radical Women, with Pam Allen. Then she cofounded Redstockings and New York Radical Feminists, which were among the new movement's most influential groups.

Firestone's pioneering organizing went hand in hand with pioneering work in theory, including editorship of the first radical feminist journal,

Notes from the First Year, which took on the vital issues of the emerging movement. Before Women's Liberation, many young activists in the 1960s had considered the First Wave of feminism a failure and its leaders an embarrassing collection of embattled old crones. In *Notes*, Firestone restored the First Wave to a position of prominence as a radical fighting force of which women could be proud and from which they could learn, and she exhorted women: "Put your own interests first."[14] Firestone coedited *Notes from the Second Year*, which first published much of the theoretical work that had established the base of the movement, including Carol Hanisch's "The Personal Is Political" and Sarachild's "A Program for Feminist Consciousness Raising."[15] Within the movement and academia as well, Firestone's seminal study *The Dialectic of Sex* is cited as a "founding text of radical feminism" with its analysis of women's situation as victims of "sex class" oppression and its call for feminist revolution.[16]

Beauvoir was Firestone's guiding spirit. Firestone rushed out *Notes from the First Year* to give to Beauvoir personally on a trip to France. She dedicated *The Dialectic of Sex* to Beauvoir as one who "kept her integrity" and "endured."[17] Firestone referred to *The Second Sex* as the "definitive analysis" on the woman question, opening sections of *The Dialectic of Sex* with quotations from *The Second Sex*.[18] Beauvoir, Firestone said, "related feminism to the best ideas in our culture."[19] In turn, Firestone related her own best ideas to Beauvoir. If for Beauvoir the handicap of maternity could be managed by women through control over reproduction, Firestone proposed to eliminate reproduction from women's sphere of responsibility through science. If for Beauvoir socialism was the starting point for Women's Liberation, Firestone saw Women's Liberation as paving the way for socialism. Beauvoir held that male supremacy created castes that crossed economic class. Firestone found divisions between men and women the basis of class—hence her phrase "sex class." Seeing herself as building on Beauvoir, at seemingly every turn Firestone honored Beauvoir as her springboard.

For Firestone, the foremost radical feminist theoretician and organizer, there had been no other radical or feminist mentor. Born in Canada, Firestone grew up in the Midwest in an orthodox Jewish family, went to the girls' division of the yeshiva, and broke with her family as her life assumed a secular bohemian style while she was on scholarship at the Art Institute of Chicago. Tiny, bespectacled, with a thick mane of long black hair, Firestone was the consummate "beat" intellectual. She spent many hours alone with books, reading and dreaming.

Beauvoir, she said, "fired my youthful ambitions at age sixteen."[20] Firestone had embarked on a painting and writing career, but in 1967 she found it "nearly impossible at that time for a woman to 'make it' legitimately" in the art world.[21] Firestone drew upon Beauvoir for spiritual and intellectual vision and support and said of her, "When the struggle seemed most hopeless, [Beauvoir] . . . gave us hope and strength of valor."[22]

Like Shulamith Firestone, Women's Liberation founder Ti-Grace Atkinson came to feminism through Beauvoir. Atkinson had grown up in Louisiana in a wealthy Republican family, and Beauvoir provided her first experience with antiestablishment politics. Married at seventeen and divorced at twenty-one, Atkinson read *The Second Sex* the year after her divorce and was deeply affected by it. She began to search for like-minded women. But it was 1962 and there was no feminist movement. Frustrated, Atkinson finally wrote Beauvoir in France. Beauvoir told her to contact Betty Friedan, which Atkinson did. Beauvoir and Atkinson began a lifelong collaboration, and Atkinson went to visit Beauvoir in France on a number of occasions.

In 1966 Friedan organized NOW and in February 1967 she recruited Atkinson to the New York City chapter, where Atkinson became president. But Atkinson soon left NOW to organize a radical feminist group. Atkinson came out for repeal of all laws against abortion and publicly committed herself to the defense of Valerie Solanas, the *SCUM Manifesto* (Society for Cutting Up Men) author who had just shot artist Andy Warhol. These and other bold positions alienated much of NOW, and Atkinson fomented a walkout to found what eventually became the Feminists, known even in the radical feminist branch of the movement for avant-garde politics and actions.

Militant among the militants, Atkinson and the Feminists believed they would "annihilate" sex roles by setting a standard for breaking out of them. Thus members of the Feminists rejected male domination in the way they lived their lives. For starters, no more than one-third of the group could marry or live with a man. The Feminists wrote influential papers condemning motherhood, sex, and love as reinforcing women's oppression, and conducted actions such as picketing the marriage bureau demanding that women "destroy marriage."[23] The group's no-holds-barred, public attack on male supremacy, its walk-the-walk-if-you-talk-the-talk approach to feminism, especially when combined with Atkinson's intensity and striking, classical appearance, projected the politics of the Feminists into the national media. Atkinson became a sought-after speaker and lectured across the country.

The Feminists exemplified the life of Beauvoir writ large. Beauvoir, after all, had exposed male supremacy with her writing and had rejected marriage and motherhood. Although she and Jean Paul Sartre were lovers and partners, they rarely lived together. Beauvoir wanted to write. She wanted, as she told her American lover, novelist Nelson Algren, to "give my life meaning by working . . . to write good books, and by writing them to help the world to be a little better."[24] Consequently, despite Algren's fervent entreaties, Beauvoir had little choice but to reject the traditional role of woman, because, as the Feminists pointed out, it reinforced dependency and subjugation. Part of Beauvoir's appeal was that of a woman who "practiced [her] own ideals"— "the spectacle of conscience in action," as one put it.[25] "Anything she did I wanted to copy," Atkinson said of Beauvoir. "I became a feminist because of her. I went into philosophy because of her."[26] Beauvoir set a standard Atkinson "copied" not only as she led her life but in organizing the Feminists as a Women's Liberation vanguard.

Roxanne Dunbar was also among the early movement organizers who counted Beauvoir as a transformative influence. Strikingly different from Atkinson, Dunbar grew up in poverty in a sharecropping family in Oklahoma. Marrying into the upper middle class, she moved to California and hid her background in shame. In 1963, with a nine-month-old daughter, she read *The Second Sex.* "The book affected me powerfully, with its analysis of marriage and the family as the seed of female bondage," she said. "Three months after I read the book, I left my husband."[27] In the divorce, her husband won custody of their child.

Dunbar, intent on "finding—or founding" a Women's Liberation Movement,[28] moved in 1968 to Boston and organized Cell 16, a militant radical feminist group. "At our first meeting, I read aloud the parts about the family in *The Second Sex*," Dunbar said. "I explained that I could trace my rejection of marriage in a straight line back to reading *The Second Sex* in the summer of 1963."[29]

Cell 16 became widely known for introducing karate into the movement, advocating celibacy, and cutting off its members' long hair in public demonstrations of feminist commitment. The group's journal, *No More Fun and Games*, called *The Second Sex* the book that "changed our lives."[30] Like the Feminists, Cell 16 saw itself as a vanguard whose members would refuse any form of collaboration with the enemy (men) in their personal lives. Going beyond the call for a Women's Liberation Movement independent from the New Left, Cell 16 advocated that radical feminists take over and lead the Left in feminist and socialist revolution.

Poor Black Women, Cell 16, and the Feminists, along with Robinson, Dunbar, and Atkinson individually, had an impact on the movement far beyond their numbers. For example, Pam Allen soon began consulting with Robinson on feminist organizing. In 1967 and 1968, Robinson also advised Roxanne Dunbar and other white Women's Liberation organizers.[31] The position papers and letters of Poor Black Women were widely circulated in early Women's Liberation publications, and the stands they took stimulated others to organize. One white contemporary later thanked Poor Black Women for work on birth control and abortion which "broke the chains of silence."[32] Poor Black Women's critique of some black nationalist groups' position on birth control was a predecessor of black feminist criticism and emboldened white feminists as well.

Whether as ideological guide, feminist model of noncollaboration with the enemy, source of hope and courage and consciousness-raising commitment, or some combination of all of these, Beauvoir had brought feminism into the founders' lives for the first time or added a decisive element to the feminist views they already held. These radical feminists were the movement's founding organizers and most influential theoreticians. Beauvoir was also a key influence on Betty Friedan, and *The Second Sex* was a precursor of feminist literary criticism.

Radical feminist writer Kate Millett, whose best-selling *Sexual Politics* is credited with beginning, in 1970, the then new field of feminist literary criticism, relied heavily on Beauvoir.[33] When *Sexual Politics* came out, Frank Prial of the *New York Times* called Millett the "principal theoretician . . . of the feminist wave."[34] But critic Irving Howe said that the "central ideas and sentiments" of Millett's book were "simply appropriated in vulgarized form from *The Second Sex*."[35] Beauvoir, on the other hand, called *Sexual Politics* a "very good book."[36] She agreed with Howe, however, about the appropriation of *The Second Sex*. Millett, Beauvoir said, "got it all, the form, the idea, everything from me."[37] A comparison of *The Second Sex* and *Sexual Politics* supports the view of Howe and Beauvoir.

In 1967, while writing the dissertation that became *Sexual Politics*, Millett, like Atkinson, began attending the first meetings of the New York City chapter of NOW. Also like Atkinson, Millett moved into the radical feminist branch of the movement that was taking shape that same year. Millett was well versed in Beauvoir's feminism before she attended her first feminist meeting, and also before she wrote the book for which the *New York Times* named her the movement's "principal theoretician." Although Millett never directly acknowledged a debt to Beauvoir for the ideas in *Sexual Politics*, in later years, speaking for her generation of young feminists, she said it was *The Second Sex* that "taught us . . . how to think" and that Beauvoir, "by the very conduct of her life, has been our model."[38]

Beauvoir lived separately from Sartre, declined marriage and motherhood, and was self-supporting. But Beauvoir herself did not organize a feminist movement, nor did she advocate doing so in *The Second Sex*. When she participated in collective activism in the 1960s, it was against colonialism or in support of the radical French students.

Betty Friedan never identified herself as a radical feminist. Although Friedan was an activist on the Left in the 1940s and early 1950s, in 1966 when she founded NOW she apparently wished to shield the organization from association with her earlier radicalism. NOW's founding documents stated that the goal of the organization was to bring women into the "mainstream of society."[39] But radical feminists such as Beauvoir (and many others following her) proposed to transform the "mainstream" as socialists as well as feminists—to make feminist claims "at the same time as carrying on the class-war," as Beauvoir put it.[40]

Friedan publicly acknowledged the openly radical Beauvoir as the source of *The Feminine Mystique*. "When I first read *The Second Sex* in the early fifties," she said, "I was writing 'housewife' on the census blanks." The book, Friedan said, "led me to whatever original analysis of women's existence I have been able to contribute to the Women's Movement and to its unique politics."[41] She continued to view Beauvoir as an advisor throughout at least 1975 when she visited her in France to confer over the direction of the women's movement in the United States.

While women soon to form the ranks of NOW devoured *The Feminine Mystique*, Casey Hayden and Mary King consumed *The Second Sex* just as Friedan had several years before them.

Mary King first learned of Beauvoir from Miriam Willey, the professor who introduced her to SNCC. Willey gave her Beauvoir to read and talked with her "candidly about the discrimination and condescension she faced as a woman professor."[42] As a result, King had "become conscious of double standards all about me, one standard for men and another for women."[43]

Mary King and Casey Hayden spent many evenings studying Beauvoir together. King described their copy of *The Second Sex* as "underlined, creased, marked up, and finally coverless from our study of it."[44] King called their interest in Beauvoir and in Doris Lessing, the white, Leftist British-Zimbabwean novelist, an "insatiable appetite . . . especially for Beauvoir's global perspective."[45] They urged female associates in SNCC to read Beauvoir and circulated their own copy of *The Second Sex*.

When they anonymously coauthored their first critique of sexism (the position paper for the Waveland SNCC conference), King said they decided not to include in the paper the "profound implications of the worldwide second-class status of women which Simone de Beauvoir had sharpened for us."[46] They instead restricted examples of male chauvinism to those ready at hand, "because we thought the points would be better understood."[47] Hayden and King, pioneers of Women's Liberation, had been influenced by Beauvoir as had many others.

Conclusion

As they came of age in the early 1960s, the founders of the Women's Liberation Movement understood that they were oppressed as women. But instead of moving directly to organize a feminist movement, they became activists in the Black Freedom Movement and the Left. As individuals, they expressed an intense feminist reaction to Beauvoir. Why had they not immediately organized a feminist movement?

Did they perceive a woman's feminism and liberation as an individual action qualitatively different from the civil rights struggle? The political development of British radical feminist Judith Okely, whose youthful reaction to Beauvoir was similar to the U.S. women's, points in that direction. Okely quoted an observation made by her friend Sheila Rowbotham, a founder of Second Wave feminism in England. In their college years, Rowbotham said, "Judith was always talking about Simone de Beauvoir. . . . I didn't really understand why she was getting so worked up. My emancipation still seemed to me to be a matter of individual choice, though I was beginning to understand that the emancipation of the working class was not."[48] According to Okely, Beauvoir's "emphasis on individual choice" reinforced her view that women were individually responsible for their freedom.[49]

If this was the case with their U.S. counterparts, it is not surprising that feminist reaction to Beauvoir was not initially expressed in a collective form. As committed feminists, they would make feminist life choices. If feminism was interpreted as a series of individual choices, it was not inconsistent to "be" a feminist without being in a feminist movement. There was no contradiction between living a feminist life and organizing collectively for other causes such the Left and the Black Freedom Movement. Beauvoir's feminism was, at least for a time, a "guide to the art of living," as one young activist put it, rather than a cause to build a movement around.[50]

Perhaps the more appropriate question might be, what was it that prompted these already committed feminists to begin to express feminist views in the form of a movement? What was it about the Black Freedom Movement and the Left that provoked a collective approach to feminism? Did it stem from male chauvinism, ever present in these movements and reflective of the larger culture? Most Women's Liberation founders were already feminists well before they experienced male chauvinism in the Black Freedom Movement and the Left. The young women in the United States who were inspired by Beauvoir did not begin to organize an independent movement for Women's Liberation until 1967 because the idea of a collective approach to feminism was the necessary lesson of the Black Freedom Movement and the Left. This essential lesson was not learned simply from experiencing male chauvinism or from reading about it in *The Second Sex*. Rather, for many of the young founders of the more radical branch of the movement, activism in the Black Freedom Movement taught them how to put feminist ideas into collective practice.

In 1972 Beauvoir observed, "NOW, a liberal, reforming feminist organization . . . was soon outstripped by more radical movements set up by younger women. . . . I have corresponded with their militants . . . met some of them, and learnt with great pleasure the new American feminism quotes *The Second Sex* as its authority."[51]

Next Steps to Women's Liberation

THE "SNCC Position Paper (Women in the Movement)" has long been considered the beginning of the Women's Liberation branch of the Second Wave.[1] It was submitted anonymously for consideration at the November 1964 SNCC Conference at Waveland, Mississippi. For years its authorship was attributed to Ruby Doris Robinson, who has also been described as having presented it at the conference.[2] Now most attribute the paper to white SNCC staff members Casey Hayden and Mary King, who worked in the headquarters office with Robinson.

The Origins of the Anonymous SNCC Position Paper on Women

Perhaps most important to the narrative of the origins of the Women's Liberation Movement is that the 1964 SNCC position paper appears to have had its beginnings in a feminist discussion group meeting (or meetings) on sexism in the movement. The meetings took place in the SNCC headquarters office in 1964 during the summer following the SNCC women's strike. They were called and led by Robinson and attended by women in the headquarters office including Hayden and King.[3]

The position paper, which presented a detailed critique of sexism within SNCC and recommended that movement women confront it collectively, was one of thirty-seven submitted for the Waveland conference. It began with a list of familiar incidents of discriminatory treatment of female co-workers by SNCC men. The paper then compared the treatment of women with the racist treatment of blacks by whites, and called it "as widespread and deep rooted and every much as crippling to women as the assumptions of white supremacy are to the Negro."[4] They submitted the paper anonymously, King said, because they did not want to face "the kinds of things which are killing to the insides—insinuations, ridicule, over-exaggerated compensations."[5]

The paper both attested and contributed to the rising feminist consciousness in SNCC. Looking in sequence at the women's strike that spring, the feminist discussion group over the summer, and then the anonymous paper in the fall—these built on each other, and Robinson was clearly the spearhead. The progression clarifies her leadership and leaves a very different impression than accounts that begin the stirrings of Women's Liberation with an anonymous paper that appeared out of the blue written by two white SNCC staff.[6] Little wonder that the anonymous paper was attributed to Robinson. Casey Hayden said, "our writing was generally attributed to . . . the driven, stalwart Ruby Doris Smith Robinson. She did not disown it. No one was going to tangle with Ruby Doris, or with the other strong black women of SNCC. The paper hardly caused a ripple."[7]

Hayden remembered typing the paper in the middle of a group of women, "pull[ing] the commentary together" from the "things the women were saying to me."[8] She recalled the group as white, but Zoharah Simmons said that she had been present at the meeting, along with other African American women, in particular Dona Richards, who Simmons said called the meeting along with Hayden and King. Dona Richards, on the SNCC staff in Mississippi, was already widely known for feminist views because of her then controversial decision to use her maiden name after she married SNCC leader Bob Moses.

According to Simmons, black SNCC staff in the meeting also included women's strike participant Judy Richardson, project director Muriel Tillinghast from Greenville, Mississippi, and field organizers Dorie Ladner and Jean Smith. For her, Simmons said, the meeting was the "first time the bigger picture came into view" and the discussion gave her a "context in which to place my awareness of male power."[9]

The paper was consciousness-raising. But it is unlikely that it would have been isolated by historians and others from the progression of black-led feminist activity leading up to it—and singled out as the origin of Women's Liberation—had not SNCC leader Stokely Carmichael repeatedly joked about it in the years to come. Mary King described an informal gathering after the Waveland conference ended for the day. There Carmichael, who would later regret it, satirized the sexual activity of SNCC's youthful staff and volunteers with the now notorious quip that the position of women in SNCC was "prone."[10] Hayden and King said that neither of them had been offended by what they understood as a joke and in fact had laughed with the others who were relaxing together with some wine.

Black SNCC project director Cynthia Washington heard the joke in a meeting at which Carmichael embellished it with the addition that "women who either dressed or looked like men" would not be among the "prone." Washington said that she and Muriel Tillinghast, who was also present, "were not pleased."[11] Neither was white British feminist Sheila Rowbotham when Carmichael repeated the joke at a Dialectics of Liberation Congress in 1967 in London. Rowbotham called it "sneering."[12]

Others who had heard the joke or heard about it also repeated it, often at their own risk. According to black SNCC staff member Stanley Wise, Ruby Doris Robinson, upon overhearing the quip repeated in the hallway outside her office and thinking Wise had said it, emerged from her office and "just knocked me right across my face."[13]

The problem with the joke was not its obvious sexist inaccuracy. Insiders knew that SNCC, probably more than any other place in the nation in prefeminist 1964, had influential female leaders who, like black project director Martha Prescod Norman, found it the "singularly most liberating experience in my life."[14] The problem was that the joke—for its time a rather run-of-the-mill sexist joke—has been misinterpreted as a symptom of SNCC's extreme misogyny, and this misogyny has come to be understood as the reason that Women's Liberation was born and raised in SNCC. In other words, the wrongheaded view goes that SNCC was so sexist the women there had to fight for liberation because they just could not stand it anymore. Mississippi SNCC staff member Joyce Ladner tried to correct this by explaining, "what the analysts, the scholars have gotten wrong . . . I don't think that we were oppressed women who got angry because Stokely . . . said that our position was prone. For a movement to use that as a rallying cry is . . . more pathetic than ridiculous."[15]

The immense attention to Carmichael's quip not only grossly exaggerated its importance to the rebirth of feminism but has overshadowed the significant progression of feminist activity that began with the women's strike. Attention to the quip has also overshadowed the authentic causes of the rise of feminism in SNCC, such as the influence of Ella Baker and the already existing feminist consciousness of so many of the women there, which in the context of a grassroots movement were the central reasons for the genesis of Women's Liberation in SNCC. If stupid sexist jokes could provoke a feminist movement, the routines of the stand-up comedians of the period would have initiated one long before Carmichael's remark. The fixation on it has also distracted secondary commentary from the Moynihan Report, which by comparison had a devastating impact.

The Moynihan Report as Backlash

Four months after the SNCC position paper at the Waveland conference, in March 1965, the U.S. government published *The Negro Family: The Case for National Action*, by Daniel Patrick Moynihan, a Harvard professor and former Kennedy administration official.[16] Commonly known as the Moynihan Report, the 78-page document was one of the most powerful and damaging racist, antiwoman, and antifeminist blows of the decade. It blamed black poverty and a host of seemingly obvious outcomes of racism on an alleged black matriarchy in which overly strong black women emasculated black men and rendered them unfit competitors in the capitalist marketplace and irresponsible heads of household. The solutions Moynihan proposed included women (but not white men) turning over some jobs to black men and black women allowing their men to take their allegedly rightful patriarchal position.

Black feminist scholar Paula Giddings declared that the Moynihan Report was "not so much racist as it was sexist."[17] White activist scholar Bettina Aptheker held that the report was backlash against the militancy of black female activists, a warning to white women, and a device to weaken the Black Freedom Movement by holding back what amounted to more than half its troops.[18]

Aptheker argued that shifts in the post-WWII workforce brought the overwhelming majority of black women out of agricultural work and the informal economy of domestic service and into the mainstream paid labor force. The resulting difference, Aptheker noted, "has not been in their subjective desire to fight [for equality] but in their objective capacity to deliver significant blows."[19] Aptheker was right. In the 1950s, southern white segregationists found themselves facing the "significant blows" of Rosa Parks in Montgomery, Alabama, and Daisy Bates in Little Rock, Arkansas. But in the early 1960s in the years immediately preceding the Moynihan Report, not only were southern segregationists having problems with black women who refused to defer to white male authority, liberal Democrats were having problems as well.

In May 1963 the Kennedy administration was more concerned than ever about the reputation of the United States as racist in the Cold War competition with the Soviet Union to attract the new nations in Asia and Africa emerging from colonial domination.

An upsurge in civil rights protest in the spring of 1963, including the high-pressure hoses and attacking police dogs that were turned on demonstrators in Birmingham, Alabama, was being reported on camera and in headlines worldwide.[20] In reaction, Attorney General Robert Kennedy asked noted radical black essayist and novelist James Baldwin to put together a meeting to open a dialogue with leading African Americans. Baldwin recruited a star-studded group including black sociologist Kenneth Clark, whose research had helped win *Brown v. Board of Education*, the school integration ruling; Lena Horne, the legendary black singer and Hollywood star; Harry Belafonte, also a film star, popular singer, and stalwart movement supporter; and Lorraine Hansberry, award-winning feminist playwright of *A Raisin in the Sun*.

At the meeting in Kennedy's New York City apartment, discussion centered on the government's role (and lack of a role) in stopping violent white reaction to the Civil Rights Movement. Kennedy was confronted repeatedly and bested by Hansberry, who was profound and brilliantly irreverent. Baldwin said Kennedy looked "insulted" because he was unable to hold his own with her in a room full of black intellectuals and celebrities and liberal white officials. Finally Hansberry said that she was worried about "the state of the civilization which produced that photograph of the white cop standing on that Negro woman's neck in Birmingham."[21] With those words Hansberry rose, turned away, and walked out of the room, and, Baldwin said, "We followed her."[22]

That same spring and summer, Robert Kennedy found himself in a public confrontation with another uncompromising black woman, Gloria Richardson, head of the Cambridge (Maryland) Nonviolent Action Committee (CNAC), soon to become a SNCC project. CNAC was demonstrating for integration of schools and public accommodations. There were mass arrests and jailings and the demonstrators were violently attacked by whites again and again. Because of Cambridge's proximity to the capital, the protests received national attention and the Kennedy administration intervened. Richardson was featured in the national media in face-to-face negotiations and press conferences with the attorney general.

Richardson's refusal to compromise on CNAC's demands "flummoxed" Kennedy, and the meetings were described as "loud" and "confrontational."[23] In the *New Republic*, journalist Murray Kempton quoted government officials' observations that with "a woman like Gloria Richardson . . . we can't deal with her and we can't deal without her."[24] The National Guard could not quell the white violence in Cambridge, and the attorney general could not back Richardson into a compromise. Seated between Richardson and Cambridge city officials, Robert Kennedy's face glowered in frustration in photographs released by the wire services to newspapers around the nation.[25] It appeared that the Kennedy administration was having trouble managing the country.

The following year, Title VII of the 1964 Civil Rights Act banned discrimination against women in employment. Fiercely debated in Congress, Title VII was opposed by leading establishment liberals such as Franklin D. Roosevelt Jr. and Emanuel Celler, longtime Democratic congressman from New York, who joked that in his household the women already had power over the men.[26] Lobbying for Title VII in the Senate was effectively organized by African-American feminist attorney Pauli Murray, among others.

Also in the summer of 1964, another high-profile confrontation between a militant black woman and the white liberal establishment took place at the Democratic National Convention in Atlantic City, some of it on national television. The Mississippi Freedom Democratic Party, an integrated grassroots group of largely disenfranchised Mississippians who had conducted an election for convention delegates, challenged the seating of the lily-white official delegation chosen by voter rolls kept lily-white by discrimination and intimidation. The MFDP challenge threatened what liberal officials feared could be an upset of national dimensions, since it could cause the southern wing of the party to block the presidential nomination of Lyndon Johnson.

FBI personnel tracked the Freedom Democrats with wiretaps and informants posing as journalists.[27] Liberal leaders of the Democratic Party enlisted an array of influential men including Martin Luther King Jr., vice presidential contender Hubert Humphrey, civil rights leader Bayard Rustin, NAACP president Roy Wilkins, and labor leader Walter Reuther to persuade

the Freedom Democrats to compromise and allow the seating of two members of the delegation picked by the Johnson administration. But thanks to
the leadership of black female militants Ella Baker, Annie Devine, Victoria Gray, and Fannie Lou Hamer, the Freedom Democrats refused to back
down.

Hubert Humphrey told the Freedom Democrats that their refusal to compromise could cost him the vice presidency. Fannie Lou Hamer, deputy director of the MFDP delegation, responded, "You're afraid to do what you
know is right . . . you just want this job. I lost my job and I know a lot of
people have lost their jobs. . . . Humphrey, if you take this job you won't be
worth anything."[28] Remarkably, Humphrey began to cry. When it came to
whether Hamer might be one of the two delegates if the two-seat compromise should prevail, Humphrey later said, "the President will not allow that
illiterate woman to speak from the floor of the convention."[29] But Hamer
did speak from the convention floor and was covered live on television. The
speech brought attention to White House support for the failure of democracy in Mississippi because, when presented with an opportunity to seat a
delegation elected with scrupulous fairness,[30] the president and his party
refused to do so.

The MFDP's challenge to the Mississippi delegation continued through
early 1965 and coincided with the Moynihan Report's publication that March.
Piggybacking on the portrayal of black women in the report, that April the
national media described Hamer as "disturbingly demagogic."[31]

Silencing uncompromising African American women such as Hamer,
Richardson, and Hansberry would serve the interests of the liberal white
establishment. A report blaming the "emasculating" independence and
strength of such women for their race's poverty and unemployment might
help to dampen black women's militancy and keep them out of the black
freedom struggle.

African American Women Fight the Influence of the Moynihan Report

The Moynihan Report stimulated black feminism and at the same time dealt
a blow to black women's struggle for equality—even within the Black Freedom Movement. Black scholar Paula Giddings said that "the report helped
shape black attitudes."[32]

In August 1966 the mainstream black magazine *Ebony* spread Moynihan's
indictment. In a special issue on black women, *Ebony* celebrated their con-

tributions in public life, including their leadership in the Civil Rights Movement. But *Ebony* editorialized that now "the past is behind us." For black women the "immediate goal today should be the establishment of a strong family unit in which the father is the dominant person."[33]

Angela Davis said the myth of the matriarchal black woman had been in the literature for some time. "When the Moynihan Report consecrated this myth with Washington's stamp of approval," Davis said, "its spurious content and propagandistic mission should have become apparent."[34] Implicit in her use of "should" was that "Washington's stamp" had not turned African Americans away from the myth. Black men, Davis said, could be "unconsciously lunging at the woman, equating her with the myth."[35] Davis noted that Black Panther George Jackson, to whom she dedicated her article refuting the Moynihan Report, had traced the roots of his "past misconceptions about black women" to "the ideology of the established order. He wanted to appeal to other black men, still similarly disoriented, to likewise correct themselves through self-criticism."[36]

Indeed, it was to the Moynihan Report, not Carmichael's sexist joke or the rise of Black Power, that many black feminists traced the rise of a new call by some black men that black women should become submissive. Gwen Patton in the SNCC Black Women's Liberation Committee and Jean Carey Bond, on the board of the black journal *Freedomways*, elaborated on the Report's "propagandistic mission." Patton called it "partly responsible for dividing black men and women" who had been a "unifying force that would march side by side . . . in order to combat racism." Now, Patton said, "Moynihan stopped that force and Black men began to look upon their women as . . . against them and trying to make them weak." She called the report "very successful because it invisibly became the guideline under the guise of Black Power."[37] Bond said the Moynihan Report was "so successfully popularized that even Blacks have swallowed his assumptions and conclusions hook, line, and sinker" and it was "ironic" that just when African Americans had begun "perceiving and denouncing the shallowness of white analyses of the Black experience, many members of the avant-garde are still capable of being mesmerized by racist social scientific thought."[38] Many black feminists echoed the perception by Davis, Patton, and Bond that some black men, while not openly citing it, had been influenced by the Moynihan Report.[39]

Eleanor Holmes Norton, who agreed, at least in part, with Moynihan, explained why blacks would not openly state agreement with the report. Although Moynihan "was absolutely right . . . the problem was that a white person simply could not say that. . . . What did I do? Get up and say to black people 'See, Moynihan was right!' No, that's no way to bring people to an understanding." Instead, Norton couched the message in the form of a love letter from a black woman to a black man and read it as part of a speech. Norton said her speech was very well received because "It was as if, thank God, somebody who we can listen to has said it."[40] No black militant would claim a white establishment figure as an authority. Looking for sources "we can listen to," some black men turned to the "manhood" rhetoric of Black Power and a glorification of oppressive aspects of a mythical African past as justification for male chauvinism.

The Moynihan Report was pernicious. As Bond pointed out, the theory of black emasculation erased centuries of black struggle and increased the negative consequences of black women taking feminist positions. Now they would be blamed for weakening the race, betraying the black man, and dividing the movement. Further, as Aptheker argued, when black inequality was blamed on black women's strengths, the implication was clear for white women. If the playing field leveled, might this not cause white men to drop out of the family and the economy, just as Moynihan claimed black women's strength had caused black men to do?

"The chances seem nil that we could start a movement"

In November 1965 Casey Hayden and Mary King, still on the SNCC staff, wrote a second feminist paper, "Sex and Caste" (also referred to as "A Kind of Memo").[41] They worked on the paper, King said, "from notes from conversations we had had with Dona Richards."[42]

The paper described the "sex caste system" which exploited women at work, in personal relations with men, in the family, the media, and the movement. Hayden and King took men to task for failing to consider the issue seriously. Women in the movement, the paper warned, had learned their own worth from movement ideas and activism and were now applying a higher standard to other areas of their lives. Could it be, as they said, that "a determined attempt to apply ideas . . . learned there can produce some new alternatives"?[43]

This time, Hayden and King signed the paper and sent it to forty women in the New Left, labor, peace, and Civil Rights movements. Although they sent the paper out, they said they thought the chances "nil" that a feminist movement would start.[44] "Even in our fantasies," King reflected, "we had no hope that a movement would develop."[45]

Hayden and King did not call for a new movement for Women's Liberation. Although they had a major part in instigating it, they did not join it when it came. They believed that educating their movement brothers would stop sexism in the New Left and Black Freedom movements. Thus "Sex and Caste" called for women in the "peace and freedom movements" to "open up dialogue" and "create a community of support" for each other while working "full time on problems such as war, poverty, race."[46]

Hayden and King were unable to create a community of support among women within their beloved SNCC and soon, with aching hearts, would leave it. King said that, when it came to the second paper, only Dona Richards and black SNCC field organizer Jean Smith were supportive.[47] In the next two years, however, an ever-widening circle of women outside SNCC heard the call of "Sex and Caste."

Within a month, the memo would land in fertile soil in the New Left in Gainesville, a small college town in rural North Florida, and in Champaign-Urbana, Illinois, at a workshop on women in the movement at a national conference of the premier New Left group, the Students for a Democratic Society. The SDS workshop would be a stepping-stone in the formation of the first Women's Liberation group in the nation, the West Side Group, in Chicago in September 1967.

Out of Gainesville in June 1968 would come the pamphlet "Toward a Female Liberation Movement," a powerful attack on male supremacy known as the Florida Paper, by Beverly Jones and Judith Brown.[48] The pamphlet went beyond the idea of stopping male supremacy in the Black Freedom Movement and the New Left. It named all men the enemy of women, at least as things then stood, and gave the first call for a new, independent mass movement to eliminate male domination in the larger society. Brown's search for coworkers with whom she might build such a movement led to the first national meeting of its organizers in Sandy Springs, Maryland, in August 1968.

The Florida Paper

Judith Brown learned about "Sex and Caste" from her soon-to-be husband Brownie, who was working with the Southern Christian Leadership Conference in Chicago. There Brownie had encountered the memo, sensed its importance, and called his fiancée in Gainesville to read it to her over the telephone.

Jones and Brown were local Civil Rights Movement and New Left leaders. Outspoken, direct, successful organizers, the two women, along with their husbands who were also local movement leaders, inhabited an inner movement circle known to participants as the Gainesville Band. Since 1963 the Band—black and white students, several older white professors, and activist women married to male faculty—had organized together against segregation, against the war in Vietnam, for reform of the university, and in support of Black Power. Many of them had been kicked out of school and fired from jobs together, arrested and jailed together, and then solaced and renewed one another for the next round. Loving each other's courage, they held together proudly with a bond that sometimes felt like "us against the world."

In 1966 the Band, under the auspices of SDS, undertook a series of internal study sessions. Ed Richer, a humanities instructor at the University of Florida (soon to be denied tenure because of his activism), conducted a session on Simone de Beauvoir's *The Second Sex*. Richer, the SDS faculty advisor, was, as Jones said later, a "dead serious" feminist who hoped to inspire a revolt against male domination.[49] In the workshop, he cited Hayden and King's "Sex and Caste" as evidence that the revolt had begun, and he made a hard-hitting case for Women's Liberation based on *The Second Sex*.

Neither Jones nor Brown had read Beauvoir. Jones thought that Richer must be exaggerating men's low opinion of women. If this was what Beauvoir had said, though, then Beauvoir too was wrong. A heated argument broke out. The women moved away from the men to one side of the room. Brown went to sit near Jones and put her arm around her shoulders in a gesture of support.

After the meeting, Jones asked her husband Marshall for the truth. To her complete surprise, Marshall Jones replied that Richer and Beauvoir were right: women were not respected by men, even in the freedom movement.

Incredulous, humiliated, and angry, Beverly Jones began to study feminism. She read Beauvoir, Betty Friedan's *The Feminine Mystique*, and everything else she could get her hands on. She began writing the Florida Paper in secrecy but finally showed some of her work to Brown. Brown asked if she could work with her. In the paper Jones, who had two children, demonstrated in powerful personal detail her subjugation as a housewife and mother. "There is something horribly repugnant," Jones wrote, "in the picture of women performing the same menial chores all day, having almost

interchangeable conversations with their children, engaging in standard television arguments with their husbands, and then . . . each agonizing over what
is considered her personal lot." Women were in a class struggle with men,
according to Jones, in which the "relationship between a man and a woman
is no more or less personal a relationship than the relationship between a
woman and her maid, a master and his slave, a teacher and his student." She
called upon women who would "begin new lives, new movements, and new
worlds" to reject romance, which she compared to the "rabbit at the dog
track . . . illusive, fake, and never-attained reward which for the benefit and
amusement of our masters keeps us running and thinking in safe circles."[50]

Judith Brown, younger and childless, wrote about sexism in the New Left.
She contended that the men "expect and require that women . . . function as
black troops—kitchen soldiers."[51] Unless women formed a movement to take
men on, this would not improve. Education and persuasion would not bring
men around because, without a struggle, men would not "relinquish . . . the
power their sex knows and takes for granted."[52]

The charges of male chauvinism brought by Jones and Brown led them to
propose a new movement with the potential to upset tightly knit political,
social, and intimate relationships, including their own. They knew from the
start that men were not going to forgo the pleasures and privileges of male
supremacy simply because the problem was brought to their attention. Thus
Jones and Brown worked on the paper in isolation until 1967.

Jones and Brown, like Hayden and King, had risked their lives in the freedom movement in the South. They too feared being treated as an "eccentric-
ity" by movement colleagues.[53] They were, Brown said, "so freaked about
what we were thinking" that they told no one about the Florida Paper until
a few months before they finished.[54] Then, in the Left press, they began to
read about the protest against sexism stirred by Hayden and King's "Sex and
Caste."

The Rise of Feminism in SDS

In the summer of 1965, before the writing of the second memo, Casey Hayden
went to Chicago to organize women in SDS's Economic Research and Action Project, the white side of a planned interracial movement of the poor.
Hayden said that in organizing white women, the need for feminist consciousness was greater than in SNCC. Hoping to raise that consciousness,
Hayden wrote a draft of the paper that became "Sex and Caste."

Female SDS activists to whom "Sex and Caste" was mailed planned a workshop on it at a national SDS conference in Champaign-Urbana in December 1965. Called "the real embryo" of the incipient Women's Liberation Movement, the workshop was attended by a number of the women who would go on to organize some of the early Women's Liberation groups.[55] This was the first time the woman question had been officially raised in SDS, and the women's public criticism of their subordinate position in the movement was met with male chauvinist derision.

Some men denied the existence of discrimination against women in SDS. Catcalls of "She's a castrating female" greeted the women, who found they had to put up a struggle simply to raise the issue.[56] When the women decided they would have to meet without men present in order to get their concerns out on the floor, men insisted on their right to participate. Black SNCC organizer Jimmy Garrett, who was a SNCC representative at the conference (and had been Zoharah Simmons's right hand on the Amazon Project), enjoyed the white men's discomfort with talk that was no longer controversial in SNCC. He defended the women's right to meet without the men. In what has been described as a walkout, the women finally excluded the men and, in a separate meeting, began to air their complaints.[57]

They found they had much to talk about. Lack of respect from men, being ignored or found threatening, being treated as sexual objects—all this and more came out, and was repeated by woman after woman. The discussion was wide ranging and included sexism in the larger society as well as in SDS. They discussed their backgrounds—expectations of them as girls when they were growing up. Many realized for the first time that they were not alone in their complaints and that the barriers they faced as women had a cause that lay outside their personal lives.

Heather Booth, who had been recruited by Casey Hayden to work in Mississippi Freedom Summer in 1964, had come to the conference specifically for the discussion of Hayden and King's memo. Reading it, she had thought, "Oh boy, this is really true. We're going to have to find some way to work this out."[58] She wanted the women and men to meet together, and tried to hold the group together. Finally, appalled at the men's behavior, she ended up leading a walkout of some of the women. But she was not yet ready for an independent Women's Liberation Movement.

The women called the workshop a "women's caucus." It lasted three days. Marilyn Webb said the discussion was the "first time we applied politics to ourselves."[59] Indeed, a postconference analysis listed women's relegation to "dish washing, cooking, cleaning, clerical work" as evidence that within SDS women were "an oppressed class."[60] The lesson of a women-only meeting endured. When the first Women's Liberation groups began meeting, they took the highly controversial stand of excluding men.

Momentum was an important outcome of the workshop. The women wanted to learn more. Some of them were unable to resume activism "as usual" when they got home. Cathy Barrett, an organizer with the Southern Student Organizing Committee, returned home and developed a course on women at the New Orleans Free School. Heather Booth initiated a course on women at the organizers' school in Chicago. From this point forward the woman question remained foremost in Booth's organizing. Not long after the workshop, she started Jane, the underground feminist abortion network that radiated out of Chicago.

Webb could not stop, either. She wanted to continue the workshop discussion. In Chicago she brought together a number of the women who would later found the nation's first Women's Liberation group. Webb's group met from January 1966 through the spring of 1967, readied Webb to organize a Women's Liberation group in Washington, D.C., and helped prepare Paula Goldsmidt for Women's Liberation organizing in Durham, North Carolina, when she and Sara Evans moved there in 1968.

Meanwhile in Gainesville, Jones and Brown worked in isolation on the Florida Paper. "Sex and Caste" circulated throughout the movement and in April 1966 was published in *Liberation*, a monthly magazine of the pacifist Left. As Hayden and King had hoped, feminist dialogue did open among women organizing against the war, poverty, and racism—a dialogue that continued to grow in militancy. More and more women spoke up and talked with one another about the politics of their treatment by men. The momentum begun at the 1965 SDS workshop escalated.

In June 1967 the call for ending sexism that had begun with the women's strike for equality in the Atlanta SNCC headquarters in early 1964 reached the floor of the national SDS conference in Ann Arbor, Michigan. At this conference a women's workshop brought a report to the floor of the convention. The women demanded that Women's Liberation be fully included in all aspects of SDS, and that shared housework and child care, and support for abortion and birth control, be added to its agenda. This would free women to fight the issues of the day as men's equals. The report also called for an internal education program that would study the position of women under capitalism, which the women said put them in a "colonial" relationship with men.[61] Amidst sexist catcalls from men, the report was approved. While the men were obviously not looking forward to having their privileges educated away, SDS had resolved, at least formally, to confront male chauvinism within its ranks.

Eventually the Women's Liberation Movement made the idea of women organizing for a feminist agenda appear self-evident. Looking back to the prefeminist mid-1960s, as men were drafted for the war in Vietnam and civil rights workers were murdered in the South, the concept of women prioritizing their own agenda seemed selfish, irresponsible, and trivial. Or so thought many social-justice-minded people, including many feminists, until 1966 when the application of Black Power to the woman question emboldened them to fight in the interests of their sex.

1. Ruby Doris Smith Robinson with her son, Kenneth Toure Robinson, ca. 1966. (Photo courtesy of Cynthia Griggs Fleming.)

2. Kathie Amatniek (Sarachild) leaving on the bus to Mississippi from the Freedom Summer orientation session in Oxford, Ohio, 1964. (Photo by Steve Schapiro, courtesy of Redstockings Women's Liberation Archives for Action.)

3. *Left to right:* Congress of Racial Equality (CORE) workers Doris Rutledge, Gene Pinkston, Judith Benninger (Brown), and Ira Simmons, Gadsden County, Florida, August 1964. (Judith Brown Endowment.)

4. Patricia Murphy (Robinson) (*left front*) with fellow Bennett College students, 23 April 1963. (Photo courtesy of Afro-American Newspapers Archives and Research Center, Baltimore.)

5. Carol Hanisch (*right*) at home with parents Mildred and Elmer Hanisch, Bancroft, Iowa, summer 1970. (Photo by Kathie Sarachild, courtesy of Redstockings Women's Liberation Archives for Action.)

6. Frances M. Beal carrying the Third World Women's Alliance banner at the Women's Strike for Equality March, New York City, 26 August 1970. (Photo courtesy of Frances Beal.)

6

The Influence of Black Power on the Rise of Women's Liberation

What we're gonna' start saying now is Black Power.
Stokely Carmichael

ON 16 JUNE 1966, chants of "Black Power" thundered out of Greenwood, Mississippi, as civil rights marchers in the Meredith March against Fear rallied there. "What do you want?" SNCC leaders Stokely Carmichael and Willie Ricks asked repeatedly. "Black Power," shouted back approximately six hundred angry, mostly black marchers who had just hours earlier watched Carmichael experience his twenty-seventh civil rights arrest and were marching because James Meredith, the first African American student admitted to the University of Mississippi, had been shot by a sniper and badly wounded as he marched against fear.

Black Power, as Carmichael explained it, was the winning of sufficient political power by poor black people to "make or participate in making the decisions which govern their destinies, and thus create basic change in their everyday lives."[1] Black people, Carmichael said, instead of invoking a call to white conscience, "must work to provide that [black] community with a position of strength from which to make its voice heard."[2] Thus, he argued, instead of seeking integration, black people should stick together to "struggle for the right to create our own terms to define ourselves and our relationship to society and to have these terms recognized."[3] In addition to economic exploitation, Carmichael held that black people were stripped of their "culture, their values, their language, their entire way of life . . . and forced to identify with the oppressor."[4] He likened the struggle of African Americans in the

United States to anticolonial revolutions for nationhood then being effectively waged throughout the Third World.

Although Black Power was not a new idea, the presence of the national
media in Greenwood on June 16, and all along the march route during the
almost two weeks of the Meredith March, made this the first high-profile
articulation of the concept in the post-WWII United States.[5] The call for
Black Power spread across the nation and was immediately and publicly controversial. It attracted mass black support, was adopted by other civil rights
organizations such as CORE, and alienated the NAACP, SCLC, and many
liberal white civil rights supporters. It provided the conceptual guide for the
student movement taking on the draft and university reform, and for black
and white founders of Women's Liberation.

Black Power and the Liberation of Black Feminism

Black Power was a powerful, definitive, positive, and liberating influence on
the rise of black feminism. It helped to free black women from the white suburban model of dependent, submissive womanhood implicit in the goal of
integration that, as Frances Beal put it, was being "beaten over [their] heads"
by the Moynihan Report.[6] Black Power helped to release African Americans
from the standards of the dominant white culture, thus loosening the hold of
the 1950s version of the cult of true womanhood that for most black women,
as Beal said, was "idle dreaming." Beal argued that this dream was not only
idle but a nightmare, because the woman in the model was "estranged from
all real work" and led an "extremely sterile existence . . . as a satellite to her
mate . . . reduced to only a biological function."[7]

From the start, Black Power attracted the same black women in the Civil
Rights Movement who would strike the early blows for Women's Liberation—women such as Ruby Doris Robinson and Zoharah Simmons, as well
as Patricia Robinson and Frances Beal who would later lead black Women's
Liberation groups.

SNCC founder Ella Baker shaped the organization from her own version
of Black Power. Baker believed that blacks should seek "liberation" from the
"physical, psychological, and spiritual destruction" of the "decadent values
of 'the American way of life,'"[8] and that society "need[ed] radical change to
provide for the masses of people."[9] Baker also helped to steer SNCC toward
learning the politics of self-determination from Third World revolutionaries.[10]

Ruby Doris Robinson was an ardent Black Power advocate. She had been among those who raised a clenched fist in the Black Power salute and led the crowd in the Black Power call and response at the rally in Greenwood. Also in 1966, Zoharah Simmons went to work in SNCC's Atlanta Project, which by then was a hotbed of Black Power and black separatism. Simmons would go on to help found and subsequently quit or be expelled from several black nationalist organizations that attempted to restrict women's participation.

Male Chauvinism of a New Type

It is important to distinguish between the left wing of black nationalism, whose male chauvinism could be challenged on the basis of commitment to revolutionary ideals and standards of behavior, and other nationalists for whom, as Beal put it, "'manhood' had replaced the achievement of racial justice."[11] "Certain black men," Beal said, "are maintaining that they have been castrated . . . that black women somehow escaped this persecution and even contributed to this emasculation."[12]

Beal did not hold that there was no male chauvinism in the black nationalist Left. She was simply saying that this sector of the movement contained within itself agreed-upon principles of freedom, justice, and equality that women could invoke to challenge sexist behavior.

How could the black nationalist Left be male chauvinist and at the same time provide women with tools with which they could fight male power? It is important to bear in mind that, for the most part, the male chauvinism in movement life did not arise from particular movement structures or precepts but from the same economic and political sources that produced sexism against women everywhere else in the United States in the 1960s. Readers of a later period have difficulty grasping the ubiquitous "everyday" character of male chauvinism and the extent to which it beset women then. Just like the larger society from which the movements of the 1960s arose, all sectors of all the movements had a plentiful share of run-of-the-mill, ever-present male chauvinist ideas and behavior. Double standards in the workplace, in relationships, and in family life, male chauvinist humor, sexual harassment of women—all of this and more was part of life in the movement and an even greater part of life outside the movement.

After the Moynihan Report, male chauvinism of a new type faced black women in the second half of the 1960s. Was it "worse" than the male chauvinism that in 1963 limited—and would have banned altogether, if women had not protested—female civil rights leaders' participation in the program of the March on Washington or in 1962 tried to omit Daisy Bates from the NAACP award for school desegregation in Little Rock? Probably not, given that women in the first half of the decade had far less feminist ammunition to muster than they did in the second half. In any case, it was new—a reaction to the Moynihan Report combined with and fueled by the credibility and appeal of Black Power ideas of the importance of black history, and of blacks setting their own terms for their lives. As Gwen Patton said, the Report "invisibly" provided "the guideline under the guise of Black Power."[13]

Basically, to prove that they were not emasculated, black men set about trying to control black women even better than white men controlled white women—and in a uniquely black way, a tradition straight out of an alleged golden age in precolonial Africa. Three men—activist and writer Imamu Amiri Baraka, formerly LeRoi Jones; Eldridge Cleaver, Black Panther leader and author of the 1968 bestseller *Soul on Ice*; and Maulana Ron Karenga, founder of Kwanzaa and US[14]—were probably the most influential black leaders of the period who promulgated some variation of this position. The Nation of Islam (NOI) had long placed women in an officially subservient position, but NOI was not a political social-change movement, and by late 1964 Malcolm X had left the NOI and repudiated this view of women.[15]

Often referred to as cultural nationalism, the positions that men like Karenga and their organizations espoused were consciously, purposefully, ideologically, and explicitly male chauvinist, unlike what has been referred to earlier as run-of-the-mill or everyday male chauvinism.[16] Karenga, for example, held: "What makes a woman appealing is femininity and she can't be feminine without being submissive. . . . male supremacy is based on three things: tradition, acceptance, and reason. Equality is false; it is the devil's concept."[17] This view was not a sexist wish or a joke but the official program of Karenga's US, which had written rules limiting women's participation in the organization. According to Eldridge Cleaver, by Karenga's precepts, black women were "subfeminine."[18] Baraka stated that "We do not believe in 'equality' of men and women. . . . a black woman must first be able to inspire her man."[19]

There were variations of this new strain of male chauvinism. All of them featured black women submitting to black men in the movement and in the larger society, and forgoing birth control so as to produce babies for the revolution in defiance of white attempts at genocide against blacks. In return, black women were to be supported, protected, and honored as queen mothers—put on an African-style pedestal—in reality, a pedestal not unlike the one white women allegedly occupied. In these men's distortion of Black Power, black women were to embrace a truly new subservience that, as black feminist Myrna Hill put it, "resembled the relationship between masters and slaves."[20]

Black nationalist feminists took sharp issue with these views and produced a body of Women's Liberation literature opposing them. Hill, for example, blasted as "blurred romanticism" the plan to reclaim "black Africa's pre-colonial, feudal past that is urged by some nationalists." Hill pointed to the diversity of Africa's cultural heritage, contrasting the subordination of Zulu women with the practices of the Balonda, in which a man left his village to live in his wife's village, and women "held a position economically superior to that of men."[21] Recounting some of the difficulties women faced in Africa's feudal past, Hill warned, "FUTURE BLACK QUEENS OF THE EARTH, BEWARE."[22]

Patricia Robinson also exposed the myth of an African golden age. She pointed out that "before the white European ever appeared off the African shores . . . the black woman of Africa . . . had been betrayed by the black men who lusted for high position and its gold and money symbols."[23] Robinson backed up her point with a quote from Ghana's then president Kwame Nkrumah: "All available evidence from the history of Africa, up to the eve of the European colonization, shows that African society was neither classless nor devoid of a social hierarchy. . . . Colonialism deserves to be blamed for many evils in Africa, but surely it was not preceded by an African golden age or paradise."[24]

Some black feminists saw evidence that precolonial African societies had been more egalitarian. According to Toni Cade, in some cultures African women "built dams, . . . engaged in international commerce . . . donned armor to wage battle," yet there was no evidence that these activities resulted in the emasculation of African males.[25]

Black nationalist feminists opposed the argument that black women should abandon birth control and have babies to aid the revolution and to oppose white-engineered genocide of African Americans. In the summer of 1968 the Mount Vernon, New York, branch of Poor Black Women, calling itself Black Women's Liberation Group, came out with what would soon become a classic statement of Women's Liberation on the reproductive work of women. The group had been studying critically the anti–birth control views of the NOI when they came across a statement from a local Black Power group, the Black Unity Party, which said: "to take the pill means contributing to our own GENOCIDE ... when we produce children we are also aiding the REVOLUTION in the form of NATION building."[26] In response, Poor Black Women declared:

> Poor black sisters decide for themselves whether to have a baby or not to have a baby. . . . Black women are being asked by militant black brothers not to practice birth control because it's a form of ... genocide on black people. . . . For us, birth control is the freedom to *fight* genocide of black women and children. . . . Having too many babies stops us from supporting our children, teaching them the truth, ... and from fighting black men who still want to use and exploit us.[27]

This position was also publicized by the Black Women's Alliance, formerly the SNCC Black Women's Liberation Committee, in another classic position paper of the period written by Frances Beal, "Double Jeopardy: To Be Black and Female."[28] This paper exposed and condemned the forced sterilization of women of color as genocide and also supported birth control and legalization of abortion.

Even black nationalist women who were not feminist but were active in the movement for black self-determination publicly opposed the positions of the very organizations they were in. For example, Dara Abubakari, who then bore the title Vice President, South, Republic of New Africa, said, "Women ... should be free to decide if and when they want children. Maybe ... we feel that we don't need any children because we have to fight the liberation struggle. . . . We should have the right to say so. Men shouldn't tell us. Nobody should tell us."[29]

As black nationalist feminist Myrna Hill put it,

> nationalist brothers who counsel Black women to concern themselves solely with bearing ... children to build our nation forget that ... Black women ... have been having babies for quite a while. What we want is not just more Black babies but a new Black nation that is free. . . . Black women can't do anything about changing this situation by cooking greens and getting pregnant.[30]

Some scholars argue that Black Power was responsible for an increase in sexist restrictions on black women.[31] Cynthia Griggs Fleming, for example, held: "One of the distinctive tenets of the black power philosophy was the belief in black male dominance."[32] Without even mentioning the Moynihan

Report, Fleming fell into the trap Patton warned of and did not see the report as an "invisible guideline." Thus Fleming attributed to Black Power the "fallacious assessment [that] blamed black women for emasculating their men through their willingness to assume dominant roles."[33] But it was the white power of the Moynihan Report, issued, backed, and spread by the U.S. government, that in 1965 insisted that African American women follow a white model of submissive womanhood, and even proposed that black men reclaim their manhood by serving in the U.S. military (this in the very month that ground troops were deployed to Vietnam).

Ella Baker dated to "around 1965" the rise of a concept she said she "personally [had] never thought of . . . as being valid . . . that . . . the black male had been . . . emasculated . . . because the female was the head of the household."[34] March of 1965 is, of course, when the Moynihan Report came out, while Black Power began to be publicly debated only in June 1966, more than a year later.

Black Power: A Basis on Which to Challenge Male Chauvinism

Cultural nationalism was very different from Black Power, and the differences between them provoked fierce debate during the period. Leading black feminists argued that Black Power gave black women the tools for a radical critique of white America, including its sexist treatment of women. Black Women's Liberation pioneer Frances Beal did not find male chauvinism intrinsic to the tenets of Black Power. On the contrary, Beal held that "with Black Power men had a revolutionary perspective so women could challenge them on that basis."[35] With integration as a goal of the movement, black men might, as Moynihan urged, seek greater authority and privilege over black women similar to white men's over white women. But with Black Power, black Women's Liberation founders could, as Beal did, challenge male chauvinism in radical male militants on a new basis. As Eleanor Holmes Norton, also a Black Power supporter, asked, "Do black women want to enter suburban split levels just as white women are fleeing them?"[36]

Thus a radical black man who wanted women to be submissive and stay out of politics faced the charge that his view was "adopted from a bourgeois white model." Further, men "exerting their 'manhood' by telling black women to step back into a submissive role" were, as Beal accused, "assuming a counterrevolutionary position" because "we need our whole army out there dealing with the enemy, and not half an army."[37]

"Radical Black women," Beal said, "placed the question of women's liberation squarely under the revolutionary arm of the Black Movement which in
turn saw itself linked to the international struggle against colonialism and
imperialism."[38] As women challenged male chauvinism in the Black Freedom Movement, black Women's Liberation found ammunition in the struggles of women of color in the Third World, whose unimpeachable credentials
as guerrilla fighters gave authority to their feminist politics, particularly in
men's eyes.

Black Power militants such as Malcolm X, Stokely Carmichael (Kwame
Ture), and Black Panther Party leader Huey Newton publicly and repeatedly
praised the courage, strategy, and inspiration of the revolutionary female
guerrilla in Vietnam and in the newly independent African nations. So now
how could adherents of Black Power who praised their efforts not acknowledge that as people of color in the newly emerging nations struggled for
self-determination, women were moving toward a position of equality with
men? As Malcolm X said in the closing months of 1964 after traveling in
Africa and the Middle East, "In every country you go to, usually the degree
of progress can never be separated from the woman. If you're in a country
that's progressive, the woman is progressive."[39]

In the United States, popular knowledge of what Malcolm had witnessed
was growing and provided increasing firepower to black Women's Liberation.
After 1964 direct communication and visiting increased between radicals in
Third World countries and U.S. movement activists, black and white.[40] Between 1966 and 1968 opposition to the war in Vietnam escalated and was
very much in the news. Female guerrilla fighters of the National Liberation
Front of South Vietnam, or Viet Cong, made front-page headlines in the *New
York Times*, as did Madame Nguyen Thi Binh, herself a former guerrilla and
the leader of the Front's delegation to the Paris peace talks.[41]

"Women have fought with men, and we have died with men, in every
revolution, more timely in Cuba, Algeria, China, now in Viet Nam. If you
notice, it is a woman heading the 'Peace Talks' in Paris for the NLF [Na-
tional Liberation Front]," wrote black feminist Mary Ann Weathers. "What
is wrong with black women?" she demanded. Faced with the myth of black
matriarchy, "we must not allow ourselves to be sledgehammered by it any
longer."[42]

After Vietnam gained independence from the French and was parti-
tioned, North Vietnam's Five Equals Plan worked explicitly toward equality between men and women "in fighting, in labor, in party leadership, in

management of society, and in the family."[43] In July 1969, black feminists from Poor Black Women led by Patricia Robinson went to Canada for a conference with revolutionary Vietnamese women. One of the group said that Robinson wanted them to go because "she wanted us . . . to find out how did they get from underneath the man."[44] The Poor Black Women attended a women-of-color caucus with the Vietnamese women and later wrote to them that they were "smashing the myths supporting white supremacy and male supremacy . . . beginning to see their oppressors as those who mean to keep them barefoot, pregnant, and ignorant of male oppression. . . . some have begun to move toward smashing the myth of Black female social and economic dominance over the Black male." The women ended their letter saying "Onward to the world revolution."[45]

The progress of Women's Liberation in revolutionary Algeria during the struggle for independence (won in 1962) was widely discussed within black (and white) women's liberation circles in the United States. Radicals inhaled material about this struggle from the film *The Battle of Algiers*, and also from *The Wretched of the Earth* and *A Dying Colonialism* by radical black psychiatrist Frantz Fanon, who had participated in the independence struggle.[46] "The men's words were no longer law. The women were no longer silent" were Fanon's often quoted words about women's increasing independence during Algeria's war of national liberation.[47]

Using the experiences of revolutionary Algerian women, black feminist Toni Cade challenged black men who, "in the name of the revolution, no less," encouraged women "to cultivate 'virtues' that if listed would sound like the personality traits of slaves." Cade said that, like their sisters in Algeria, black women in the United States "tend to think of a Man in terms of his commitment to the Struggle" and urged black men to apply the same standard to black women.[48] Cade described the ways in which the Algerian woman, who once led a "mute existence . . . in her father's . . . or . . . husband's household, found through involvement with the struggle . . . she was no longer simply an item in a marriage contract or a business deal but a revolutionary . . . [who] tended to see men in a new light: not as benevolent protectors or tyrants, but in terms of their preparedness to join the FLN"—the National Liberation Front.[49] Frances Beal called for a similar transformation of male-female relations, saying, "to live for the revolution means taking on the more difficult commitment of changing our day-to-day patterns. . . . To assign women the role of housekeeper and mother while men go forth into battle is a highly questionable doctrine for a revolutionary to maintain."[50]

Beal applauded the militancy and leadership of black male movement coworkers: "Since the advent of Black Power, the black male has exerted a more prominent leadership role in our struggle for justice. . . . black women are not resentful of the rise to power of black men."[51]

For Beal, Black Power did not mean male dominance over black women, but rather a refusal to submit to white supremacy. It also meant revolutionary black nationalism, the understanding that black communities in the United States were dominated and exploited much like Third World colonies and that some form of self-determination was the solution.

Black Feminism Continues to Rise in SNCC

SNCC, the birthplace of Black Power in the 1960s, was not among the organizations in the Black Freedom Movement that endorsed or promulgated male chauvinist cultural nationalist views. Between 1966 and 1968, as SNCC became more nationalist, more militant, and more radical, black feminist influence within the organization continued to grow. By 1968 SNCC had formally and organizationally endorsed black Women's Liberation.

Did Black Power produce black feminism because it was so very sexist that women got fed up, could not take it anymore, and just had to rebel? Or did it encourage feminism because Black Power contained within it tools and concepts that black feminists could use to advance their freedom? The growth of black feminism from Black Power was not a coincidence. As Frances Beal reflected, "the radical perspective in SNCC was the birth bed from which the SNCC Black Women's Liberation Committee flowered."[52]

The view that black men were emasculated was unacceptable to people seeking self-determination through a social movement because it denied and erased the centuries-long black freedom struggle that reached a peak of power in the United States in the late 1960s. The myth of black matriarchy was antithetical to the whole idea of a movement because it saw black people as the source of their own oppression, instead of racism. Such a view took responsibility for solutions off the system of white supremacy. Moreover, from 1966 to 1968 the demand for black history accelerated. The Black Freedom Movement studied slave revolts, black abolitionists, Garveyism, and more. This history contradicted the theory of black male emasculation.

Patricia Peery, who organized black women's study groups, and Jean Carey Bond, a longtime editor of *Freedomways*, the acclaimed literary and political journal founded by W. E. B. DuBois, held that the "companion myths" of black male emasculation and black female matriarchy were patently false because "Sojourner Truth and Harriet Tubman not withstanding, Black men hold the majority among our political (and cultural) heroes."[53]

After naming an impressive list from Nat Turner to Frederick Douglass to Muhammad Ali, Bond and Peery said, "Indeed the Black man always surfaces with his manhood not only intact, but with his manhood more intact than that of his oppressor." After all, Bond and Peery argued, "any fool knows that eunuchs . . . do not lead slave revolts," a reference to Turner and, invoking Ali, whose challenge to the Vietnam War had stripped him of his heavyweight championship, they "do not refuse to fight in unholy wars, thumbing their noses at trophies and fame. . . . We contend that as a whole people, Afro-Americans lack neither spirit nor strength nor vigor."[54]

Within SNCC, male leaders such as James Forman, Bob Moses, and Stokely Carmichael rejected the "companion myths" of emasculation and matriarchy. Forman, in a speech in Los Angeles in 1967, said, "I do not view much of the history of our people as accommodation. . . . our basic history is one of resistance."[55] Far from agreeing that women should become submissive, Forman held that "women should begin to become more militant in their demands."[56] He applauded SNCC's bold female leaders, in particular Ruby Doris Robinson, saying of her, "Ruby was one of the few genuine revolutionaries in the black liberation movement."[57]

Bob Moses did not agree that women should step back. He had supported the Women's Liberation declaration of Hayden and King in 1964. He had married Dona Richards, a black feminist who also supported it, and who kept her own name. Stokely Carmichael celebrated the strength and courage of black people. In a 1968 speech at a Black Panther rally in Oakland, California, Carmichael said, "Our people have resisted for 413 years in this wilderness. . . . we cannot fail our ancestors."[58] Carmichael also admired the strength of Ruby Doris Robinson despite her injunction that he stop publicly representing his own positions as those of SNCC.[59] Reflecting on Robinson as a woman who "was convinced that there was nothing that she could not do," Carmichael observed, "when you consider the battering that especially African women have to take on the question of self-confidence . . . she was a tower of strength."[60]

In May 1966, a month before Carmichael led the marchers in Greenwood in chants of "Black Power," Robinson was elected executive secretary, the position vacated by James Forman. She had gone from leading the strike for women's equality in the Atlanta SNCC office in the spring of 1964 to leading the whole organization in just two years. Robinson was not a leader simply because she was hardworking and risk-taking. She rose to leadership through a structured democratic process in which slates of officers were nominated and voted on. She and Carmichael were elected to office at the SNCC conference at Kingston Springs at which the organization adopted Black Power politics.

Yet black scholar Belinda Robnett wrongly held that SNCC's "change to a Black Power philosophy brought fewer free spaces for women's leadership."[61] She backed this up with a quote from SNCC staffer Prathia Hall to the effect that after 1965 SNCC reflected "all of the Black macho rhetoric" including women "having babies for the movement" and "walking . . . behind."[62] Hall left SNCC in 1965 and joined the staff of the National Council of Negro Women. On the other hand, as has been pointed out, the second half of the decade saw proportionally more women as SNCC project directors than the first five years had.[63]

Robinson's base of support in SNCC was the largely male and working-class field staff. SNCC staffer Curtis Hayes said that "by the time she was elected, she had a tremendous power base—what we call field organizers."[64] Had these men endorsed female subordination, even unconsciously, they would hardly have backed Robinson. Indeed, they voted for her precisely because of her effectiveness.

Robinson's leadership in the women's strike clearly demonstrated that she would advance a policy of treating men and women equally. Moreover, she was known to engage in activities not typical of feminine, submissive women, such as target shooting with a pistol and playing quarterback in SNCC's touch football games.[65]

Robnett did not see Robinson's election as the remarkable sign of rising egalitarianism in SNCC that it was. As evidence that after the adoption of Black Power "SNCC embraced patriarchy," Robnett cited James Forman's observation that Robinson "endured vicious attacks" that "embodied male chauvinism in fighting her attempts as executive secretary to impose a sense of organizational responsibility" with men "trying to justify themselves by the fact that their critic was a woman."[66]

But in few, if any, other organizations in 1966–67 would one find a young woman elected by men to a position of authority over them, much less find it happening without male chauvinist reactions to following a woman's directives. That some of the men used "the fact that their critic was a woman" to dodge following directives they did not wish to follow can surprise only

those who imagine that a sexism-free utopia is possible within a sexist society. To mistake scattered male resistance to female authority as an organizational "embrace of patriarchy" leaves us with an upside-down view of the
rise of feminism in SNCC and the role the organization played in feminism's
rise in the larger society.

While remarks such as Carmichael's joke about the position of women
or Forman's observation that Robinson faced male chauvinist resistance are
evidence of the presence of sexism in SNCC, they did not represent its policy
or even a contending point of view.[67] One need not gloss over or condone
the run-of-the-mill male chauvinism in SNCC to see that it was qualitatively
different from the officially sexist policies of the NOI or of US and Amiri
Baraka's Spirit House in Newark. As Barbara Ransby put it, "this does not
mean that sexism did not exist [in SNCC]—but that it was not institutionally
supported or encouraged."[68]

Robinson's election as executive secretary was but one among growing
signs that SNCC was becoming even more egalitarian than it had been. By
1966 the density of feminist-minded African American women concentrated
in SNCC's Atlanta project and headquarters offices and in its New York office
was increasing. The New York office counted Frances Beal along with Mae
Jackson, Gwen Patton, and Diane Watson, who would be Beal's collaborators
in organizing the SNCC Black Women's Liberation Committee. Kathleen
Cleaver went to work in SNCC's New York office in 1966 before leaving for
the Atlanta Project, as did Zoharah Simmons. Eleanor Holmes Norton was
in and out of the New York office between 1966 and 1968. Several women
who had participated in the 1964 strike, including Freddie Greene Biddle
and Judy Richardson, were in the headquarters office.

Also in 1966, Fay Bellamy and three other SNCC staff visited the Soviet
Union as guests of Komsomol, the Communist Party youth group. When
they returned they wrote a report on their meetings and impressions. Bellamy wasn't particularly impressed that the Soviet Union was a racism-free
environment. But she reported on the higher status Soviet women enjoyed
compared with U.S. women.[69] In 1967 former SNCC leader Diane Nash visited Hanoi at the invitation of the North Vietnamese women's union and was
attracted to their feminist politics. Although Nash was no longer in SNCC,
her views continued to have currency in the organization. Beal too had been
influenced by revolutionary women of color from Third World nations and
liberation movements.

By 1968 black Women's Liberation, which had been on the rise since

SNCC's earliest days, had reached critical mass. Beal and Patton collaborated on a paper titled "Soul on Fire," a critique of Eldridge Cleaver's bestseller *Soul on Ice*, which challenged some SNCC men who were promoting Cleaver's book. "Soul on Fire" denounced Cleaver's book as misogynist as well as male chauvinist.[70] Feminism, especially in the New York office, was far stronger, clearer, and more united than the disparate force of run-of-the-mill sexism. The formation of the SNCC Black Women's Liberation Committee was its high point and most conscious expression.

Beal, Patton, and Jackson wrote a formal proposal for such a committee for consideration at the national SNCC staff meeting, which was attended by approximately sixty people. Their purpose was threefold: to add black Women's Liberation to SNCC's agenda and to the agenda of the Black Freedom Movement; as SNCC staff members, to engage in study, analysis, and organizing of black women for Women's Liberation; and to deal with sexism within SNCC. Beal presented the proposal, and it was debated on the floor and voted on. Although most of those present at the meeting were men, the proposal was approved by a majority vote. According to Beal, former executive secretary James Forman had "thrown his weight behind it," and H. Rap Brown, then SNCC's chair, also voted for it.[71]

Thus the committee was established as an official body of the organization. SNCC accepted the fight for black Women's Liberation as its own and the work of the members of its Black Women's Liberation Committee as a legitimate aspect of the struggle for black self-determination. When the Third World Women's Alliance evolved from the SNCC Black Women's Liberation Committee and the Black Women's Alliance, Forman developed a series of workshops on revolutionary theory that he taught to the group, which they used as a foundation to add a women's perspective and theoretical and political principles.

In 1964, when Zoharah Simmons reported that she had been sexually assaulted, the organization had ignored it. The paper on women at the Waveland conference was blown off as a joke—at least by some. Now, after four years of struggle, SNCC voted to approve a formidable Women's Liberation presence within its ranks, thus signaling its wish to guarantee an ongoing instrument for Women's Liberation.

Indeed, it had done just that. The SNCC Black Women's Liberation Committee was to outlive its parent group, which would hold its last staff meeting the following year. The committee, under Beal's leadership, transformed itself into the Black Women's Alliance and went on to organize as an independent black Women's Liberation organization with, as Beal put it, "African American sisters raising our anti-racist banner within the women's liberation movement and our feminist one in the Black community."[72]

Black Power Influences the Feminism of Patricia Robinson and Poor Black Women

SNCC was not the only source of the rising influence of Black Power. The Black Power views of Malcolm X helped Patricia Robinson to sharpen her feminist theory. After his break with the NOI in March 1964 and subsequent exposure to anticolonial revolutionaries during trips to Africa and the Middle East that same year, Malcolm's politics shifted away from the NOI's cultural nationalist views to the revolutionary nationalism of the nations he had visited. The changes in Malcolm X's views on women were dramatic— a 180-degree turn. From the belief that women had no place in public life, and that they were by nature weak and duplicitous and needed the control of strong men, Malcolm had come to see women as equal partners in the movement for black self-determination.

In the months before Malcolm's assassination, he engaged in relentless self-criticism of his views on women. This process is reflected in his letter to his cousin-in-law: "I taught brothers . . . to spit acid at the sisters. They were kept in their places. . . . I taught the brothers that the sisters were standing in their way; in the way of the Messenger, in the way of progress, in the way of God Himself. I did these things brother. I must undo them."[73]

At a lecture at the Audubon Ballroom in Harlem on 20 December 1964 he was sharing lessons learned in Africa. Praising the Mau Mau in Kenya, who had fought and won a guerrilla war for national liberation from the British and were then running the country, Malcolm said the sisters in the Mau Mau were brave freedom fighters. "If they were over here," he observed, "they'd get this problem straightened up just like that."[74]

The change in Malcolm exemplifies Beal's view that revolutionary black nationalism provided a standard to which men could be held accountable. Malcolm held himself to this standard and began to hold other black men to it. He invited SNCC's Fannie Lou Hamer to share the podium with him at the Audubon Ballroom. He introduced her as "one of the best freedom fighters in America today." In her speech, Hamer described her struggle to vote: shots fired into her home, being thrown out of her home and fired from her job, and her terrible beating in the jail in Winona, Mississippi. When she finished, Malcolm took the stage and expressed his "hope that our brothers, especially our brothers here in Harlem, listened very well . . . to what I call one of this country's foremost freedom fighters. You don't have to be a man to fight for freedom. . . . all you have to do is . . . want freedom so badly that you'll do anything, by any means necessary, to get that freedom."[75]

Patricia Robinson attended the weekly talks at the Audubon that Malcolm gave in the final months of his life and consulted with him about her work in Poor Black Women. She searched tirelessly for opportunities for political education for members of her group. That she brought women from the group to his weekly lectures constitutes convincing evidence of Malcolm's rejection of male chauvinism.[76]

Another feminist who would not have attended had Malcolm's talks been riddled with sexism was Kathie Sarachild. Sarachild said she found the lectures "helping enormously in my adjustment to life back in the North after returning from Mississippi and the powerful positive experience of working with SNCC."[77] She was "very impressed by the fact that the master of ceremonies at these gatherings was a brilliant young female speaker Sharon Jackson," who she later discovered was also a SNCC worker.[78]

Robinson was in attendance when Malcolm X was assassinated on 21 February 1965. In "Malcolm X, Our Revolutionary Son and Brother," a eulogy she wrote in 1968, Robinson argued that Malcolm's revolutionary Black Power concepts freed black women for equal partnership with men in the black liberation movement.[79] In the eulogy, Robinson explained that "fathers have ruled the world" and "women and children are their subjects, their property. The sons, however, are to be bred and trained to continue the hierarchic male rule." With his departure from the NOI and Elijah Muhammad, Robinson said, Malcolm had broken with the father figure Muhammad who had "seduced" Malcolm to believe that he, Muhammad, was "in the images of sacred gods, existing high above women and children." But now, Robinson continued, "with the wisdom born from the betrayal of the black father . . . Malcolm turned to the poor masses, the women, and the young people."[80]

"How long had the poor black women of the world been . . . sunk in their slave acceptance of male and god rule?" Robinson asked. The black woman sought revolutionary sons with whom, according to Robinson, "she could help to overthrow the oppressor father and his aggressive, exploitive system." Malcolm had emerged as such a revolutionary son and brother. In his death, he passed on the "revolutionary responsibility" to those who, in Robinson's words, "gratefully and humbly accepted" it.[81] There was much truth in Robinson's argument. Malcolm said that he had believed Elijah Muhammad to be a divinity and Muhammad did teach women's inferiority and the necessity for male and God rule. Muhammad had betrayed Malcolm's trust and consequently, as Malcolm said on the day before he was assassinated, he felt "what I'm thinking and saying is now for myself."[82] Thus Malcolm welcomed women as equals in the struggle for black self-determination.

Black Power: Fight Your Own Oppressor

Black Power provided black women with theoretical training that they adapted to organizing for Women's Liberation. As Frances Beal put it, "people who are oppressed had the right, if not the duty, of organizing themselves along the lines of their own oppression." Beal made the analogy that just as "black people organizing as blacks was a legitimate form of political organization . . . women organizing themselves as women, taking on the questions of women's oppression was a legitimate form." Beal considered this "at a theoretical level . . . the most important thing we [black women] brought from the Black Power Movement."[83]

As Patricia Robinson organized Poor Black Women, she and the group broke this concept down further: "Poor black women in the U.S. have to fight back out of our own experience of oppression."[84] Poor Black Women was among the most class conscious of the black Women's Liberation groups and considered itself allied to "the have-nots in the wider world and their revolutionary struggles." Poor Black Women said its members understood themselves to be "at the bottom of a class hierarchy" as well as a sex hierarchy, and thus subjected to exploitation and oppression by black and white, middle- and upper-class men and women, and even poor men. They organized among themselves because they believed that only poor black women shared the same interests. Robinson backed up this position by quoting Lenin on male chauvinism "even among the proletariat."[85]

Black feminist Mary Ann Weathers, a member of both the Black Women's Alliance and the predominantly white Women's Liberation group Cell 16, wrote that the idea that "Nobody can fight your battles for you; you have to do it yourself" was "the premise for the time being for stating the case for black women's liberation."[86] Weathers differed from Robinson in her application of the concept. Weathers held that middle-class black women might be "prone to help in alleviating some of the conditions of our more oppressed sisters" because "though middle-class black women may not have suffered the brutal suppression of poor black people, they most certainly have felt the scourge of the male-superiority-oriented society as women." Weathers said that although women of color of various national origins in the United States were triply oppressed, because they had "female's oppression in common" they could "start building links" with "even white women."[87] For Weathers, a Women's Liberation group of their own gave women of color the leverage they needed in the predominantly white feminist movement as well as a power base within the Black Freedom Movement. Weathers saw black Women's Liberation, and Women's Liberation as a whole, as "a strategy for an eventual tie-up with the entire revolutionary movement."[88]

Another gift of theory that black feminists brought from Black Power, and from SNCC in particular, is what is currently referred to as "intersectionality theory." This is the notion that different systems of oppression—most notably those of class, race, and gender—not only add to the burden but interact to create experiences that reflect a mixture of influences.

Women in the SNCC Black Women's Liberation Committee and its subsequent incarnations drew this analytical approach, according to Frances Beal, from intense ongoing debates within SNCC on the relative weight of class oppression versus white supremacy as a basis for black oppression. Ella Baker brought into SNCC her rich background of immersion in this debate since the late 1920s on the Left in Harlem. Stokely Carmichael led those arguing that racism was the foremost if certainly not the only source of black oppression, while James Forman led those who placed a greater emphasis on class exploitation. Beal, Gwen Patton, and other SNCC Black Women's Liberation Committee founders were involved in this dialectic and now insisted that male supremacy be factored into the mix.

White Women Fight Their "Own Oppressors"

Black Power had unleashed a mighty theory. Did its male framers see it as a tool with which women or whites might fight sex or class oppression?[89] James Forman, a major theory leader in SNCC, described himself as conscious of the woman question and for Women's Liberation from his earliest days in SNCC.[90] Black and white feminists have supported his assessment.[91] Mary King said he had supported the women's strike in early 1964. Frances Beal said Forman had "thrown his weight behind" the formation of the Black Women's Liberation Committee. What about other Black Power framers? Did Stokely Carmichael think that white people had any oppressors to fight? That women did?

There is little written evidence of Carmichael's 1960s understanding of sexism. In his autobiography, written in the 1990s, he describes himself becoming conscious of the oppression of women in 1960 in the Nonviolent Action Group (NAG) at Howard University, a historically black college in Washington, D.C.[92] Describing the evolution of his views on gender, Carmichael said that half of NAG's core members were women—but that he "paid no real attention" to this at the time because "we didn't think in 'gender' terms." The women in NAG were "simply . . . fellow rebels . . . our comrades in struggle."[93]

It was only after a NAG woman got in trouble with the university administration for wearing her hair natural, said Carmichael, that "the men in NAG even began to think seriously about how these double standards affected our sisters." He became aware then of the "set of severely limiting 'women's roles' that were invidious and pervasive." To be "intellectually serious, politically engaged, self-defining young women, and to do so publicly," represented "for the sisters—a declaration of independence, a stubborn, public act of will and moral conviction that we men never had to take on in anything like the same way."[94]

Did Carmichael, well before he advocated Black Power in 1966, have the consciousness of sexism that he remembered himself to have gained in NAG? Certainly by the time he wrote his autobiography many years later, Carmichael consciously supported Women's Liberation. In the autobiography he reflected critically on his father's assumption "that the family's only son [himself] would become a physician" without considering whether his sisters might have "had a greater aptitude" for medicine. He called his father's view "male chauvinism" and a "patriarchal attitude."[95] Still, it is hard to assess what Carmichael's understanding of women's oppression may have been in the 1960s, based on his post–Women's Liberation memories.

What is clear, though, is that by 1966 Carmichael was advocating that white activists organize in the white community against class oppression as well as against racism. In a speech to a largely white audience at the University of California, Berkeley, in October 1966, after describing "institutions that . . . are clearly racist," Carmichael asked: "How can white people who say they are not part of those institutions begin to move?" He answered with three injunctions: (1) "move inside their own community and start tearing down racism"; (2) "organize poor whites so they can begin to move around the question of economic exploitation"; (3) "move out of that [the college campuses] into the white ghettos . . . and articulate a position for those white youth who do not want to go" to fight in Vietnam.[96] This was necessary, Carmichael said, "to form a coalition base for black people to hook up with. . . . If you want a coalition to address itself to real changes in this country, white people must start building those institutions inside the white community . . . tear down the institutions that have put us all in the trick bag."[97]

A month earlier in September 1966, in one of the earliest published discussions of the concept of Black Power, Carmichael said, "There is a vital job to be done among poor whites. We hope to see . . . a coalition between poor blacks and poor whites. . . . we see such a coalition as the major internal instrument of change in American society. SNCC has tried . . . to organize poor whites; we are trying again now, with an initial training program in Tennessee. . . . the job of creating a poor-white power bloc must be attempted. The main responsibility . . . falls upon whites." The "number of excluded whites [from upward mobility] in the U.S. is vast," Carmichael argued, because "exclusion is not based on race alone" and "criteria for upward mobility apply brutally to black and white everywhere."[98]

Carmichael had been familiar with theories of class struggle since going to the Bronx High School of Science in New York. Although he did not join, he was recruited to meetings of the Young Communist League by classmate Gene Dennis, who was the son of Eugene Dennis, the white leader of the Communist Party. Gene was a close friend, and they visited each other's homes. Carmichael said he read "Marx, Engels, Lenin, and Trotsky . . . for the study groups." He "was always at their rallies. . . . I participated publicly in all their activities." Carmichael named Paul Robeson, hero of the black and white Left, "one of my early heroes."[99]

Carmichael held that Marxism insufficiently addressed racism. Africans, as Carmichael called all black people, needed an analysis that more thoroughly addressed white supremacy. Marxism was necessary but insufficient. But he argued that white people ought to be fighting capitalism so that blacks, already conscious of their oppression, would have allies. Reflecting on Black Power's message to whites, he said that "the Black Power movement says to the white workers . . . you must . . . help wake up the white working class . . . and not leave it all on the shoulders of the African masses."[100]

This view was also argued by SNCC field secretary Julius Lester, a Black Power advocate who observed in 1968 that what was needed was a "coalition of those who know that they are dispossessed. . . . Whites in America are dispossessed . . . but the difference is that they will not recognize the fact as yet. Until they do, it will not be possible to have coalitions with them."[101]

Here, then, is evidence that male Black Power advocates in SNCC considered whites fighting class oppression at least as important as fighting racism in the white community. Carmichael, after all, had in 1966 called coalition with class-conscious whites "the major internal instrument of change in American society."[102]

The best evidence that feminist organizing was consistent with newly developing ideas of Black Power was SNCC's decision in spring 1965 to "loan" Casey Hayden to the Economic Research and Action Project (ERAP) of SDS to organize white welfare women. ERAP, as Hayden explained it, was "an emerging national effort to create the white side of a national interracial movement of the poor. . . . I was trying to follow the new line in SNCC," Hayden said. She told James Forman and Ruby Doris Robinson her plan. "They seemed to like it," she said. "I kept right on getting my paycheck, $9.64 a week." Organizing women in Chicago's white ghetto neighborhoods convinced Hayden that "a setting that lacked feminist consciousness" made organizing poor women very difficult. Feminism was needed to bring women into the planned interracial coalition of the poor.[103]

Black Women to White Women: Fight Your Own Oppressors

If male Black Power advocates did not discuss whether fighting one's own oppressor included Women's Liberation, black feminist Black Power advocates clearly held that white women too must fight sexism. Frances Beal held that "the exploitation of black people and women works to everyone's disadvantage and . . . the liberation of these two groups is a stepping-stone to the liberation of all oppressed people."[104] Gwen Patton said that "for white women to rise up against the sacred Victorian Philosophy is revolutionary. . . . Women, Black and white, have monopolies on typewriters and children while men [in the movement] have monopolies on . . . decision-making, and guns." Patton saw Victorian philosophy as "part, if not all . . . of the reason for capitalism."[105]

Black nationalist and feminist Myrna Hill agreed. "Blacks and women have the same enemy . . . a small group of white ruling-class men in whose hands is concentrated most of the wealth, and therefore the power," she said. "All women are potential allies, but . . . Black women who suffer the most from this system will lead the fight to liberate us all." Hill gave as an example the way that the Golden Drum Society, a black nationalist group at a New York community college, and the campus Women's Liberation group were "supporting each other's demands for Black control of the Black studies program and for . . . campus childcare facilities."[106]

Hill made a strong case that Women's Liberation demands were relevant to black women. These included free abortion—paired with no forced sterilization, twenty-four-hour community-controlled child care, and equal pay for equal work. "The issues of the women's liberation movement," Hill said, "far from being just a white thing, are even more relevant to the needs of Black women." She pointed out: "Four times as many Black women die from child-bearing related causes"; also "a larger proportion of Black women hold jobs than do their white sisters" and they "are most likely to have very young children with no child care facilities." In sum, "jobs and low wages [are] issues that most concern Black women."[107]

Borrowing from Black Power, black feminist Cellestine Ware named her book, the first history of the 1960s Women's Liberation Movement, *Woman Power*. The book's cover showed Black Power's signature clenched fist in the center of the female symbol, which was the symbol of Women's Liberation. One of Ware's central arguments was that having white women fighting their oppressors was to black women's advantage in their relations with their men. Ware argued:

> The strength of the resistance to women's independence is shown by the strong epithets directed against black women. The black male's reaction is the forerunner of what all feminists will face as they grow in strength. As women begin to assume positions of equality with men, they will meet virulent abuse, much like that endured by black women now. They will also discover that men will reject them for more "feminine" women. . . . "Uppity Women Unite" is a motto of the Women's Liberation Movement. As all women achieve self-determination, white women will cease to be preferred.[108]

When all women achieved independence, there would be no more submissive women for men to turn to.

Patricia Robinson and Poor Black Women called white women "our own oppressed white sisters."[109] In 1968 and early 1969 they met with a white women's welfare rights group and also with predominantly white Women's Liberation groups. Two members of the Poor Black Women branch in New

Rochelle, Maureen W. and Linda Landrine, said that they "appreciated hearing that the white women's 'ivory towers weren't so nice, you know, pedestals.'"[110] Their interest in white women talking about their own oppression is much like the views in "A Black Woman Speaks . . . of White Womanhood, of White Supremacy, of Peace," a poem by a black feminist poet and playwright of the 1950s, Beulah Richardson.[111]

In 1951 Richardson read the poem to some five hundred women, most of them white, at the Women's Workshop at the American People's Peace Congress in Chicago. It was published by American Women for Peace, a women's formation of the Old Left. The poem made its way into the Women's Liberation Movement, where the predominately white radical feminist groups Redstockings, Cell 16, and the Southern Female Rights Union distributed it. In the poem Richardson warned white women: "be careful when you talk with me. / Remind me not of my slavery, I know it well / but rather tell me of your own" for "White womanhood too is enslaved, / the difference is degree. . . . You bore him [your husband] sons. / I bore him sons. / No, not willingly. / He purchased you. / He raped me, / I fought! / But you fought neither for yourselves nor me."

Richardson compared the ways in which black women and white women were oppressed, repeatedly asking white women to fight their oppression. "I fought for freedom, / I'm fighting now for our unity. / We are women all, / and what wrongs you murders me / and eventually marks your grave / so we share a mutual death at the hand of tyranny."

Black feminists like Beulah Richardson and those in Poor Black Women knew that white women were oppressed better than many white women did. They expected white women to talk about their own oppression and fight for their own freedom. They expressed the hope to work together for the same goals, if not necessarily in the same group.

The Influence of Black Power on White Feminists

"'It's time to fight your own oppressors.' I remember he [Carmichael] used that phrase," recalled Kathie Sarachild. "And even then I was thinking, 'Fight your own oppressors,' what would that mean? I knew there was a class problem . . . I began thinking about it in connection with women's liberation . . . I almost thought it was my duty as a white organizer to start thinking about it."[112]

Casey Hayden too was reflecting on class and women when she decided to organize poor white women. "Working with whites . . . by now seemed the clear message. . . . It was unthinkable to me to go back to the white community of the segregated South." Because Hayden and her half sister had depended on their mother, who in a single-parent household had supported the family on a secretary's salary, Hayden "wanted to organize white welfare women."[113] In the summer of 1965, Hayden organized white welfare mothers in Chicago. She told her coworkers, "Women . . . should organize women . . . and that struck us all as . . . a very novel idea."

Realizing the need for feminist consciousness in this work, Hayden determined to raise it. Her first step was to begin writing "Sex and Caste." The "clear message" from the idea "fight your own oppressors" led Hayden to organize women and then, with King, to write the paper which located women's "oppressor" in a "sex-caste" system.[114]

Fighting one's own oppressor was also the theme of the Florida Paper, which in 1968 urged the emerging movement to "work for female liberation first, and now."[115] "People," Beverly Jones argued in the Florida Paper in what would become a classic feminist statement, "don't get radicalized (engaged with basic truths) fighting other people's battles." According to Jones, whites in the Civil Rights Movement thought they had no particular problems until they were "thoroughly shaken by Black Power."[116]

Jones analyzed the consciousness of whites in the Civil Rights Movement: "People who set about to help other people . . . maintain important illusions [about] the full measure of their own individual oppression."[117]

At a SNCC reunion twenty years after the Florida Paper helped to focus the logic of Black Power on the woman question, black scholar activist Bernice Johnson Reagon looked, as she put it, for the "strands of continuity," for "things that have continued to move from one group to the other as they try to grapple with restructuring their space in society." Reagon called the Civil Rights Movement the "borning struggle for this time," saying, "there's no progressive organizing that has come out . . . since that is not based on it, and that includes the women's movement." Reagon charged that "there was something racist working" to sever those "strands of continuity."[118] One way of severing the continuity is the view that Women's Liberation arose in reaction to the male chauvinism somehow inherent in the concept of Black Power. Jones drew lessons for Women's Liberation from her own fifteen-year experience in the Civil Rights Movement and its transition to Black Power, and she applied the fundamental truth in the concept of fighting one's own oppressor to women's oppression.

The Florida Paper jolted emerging women's groups toward independence from the New Left. Throughout the paper, Jones and coauthor Judith Brown gratefully acknowledged their debt to Black Power. Instead of feeling pushed aside, Brown, Jones, and Sarachild were attracted to Black Power's admonition "fight your own oppressors," and quickly applied it to women. But Hayden, the first to apply the lesson to women, did not share their excitement. As women began organizing women for feminism, she found it "unattractive," she said, because they were "emulating black nationalism."[119]

Women's Liberation did emulate black nationalism, and, like Hayden, some feminists and historians have found aspects of the relationship troubling. They have pointed to problems such as dedicated white women being pushed out of civil rights work and Black Power threatening the new influence of white women in the movement.[120] They also pointed to the new male chauvinist factions of black nationalism.

Again and again, however, like their African American counterparts, early white founders of Women's Liberation relied on Black Power theory. At the first national meeting of the emerging movement in 1968 in Sandy Springs, Maryland, Beverly Jones maintained: "If women want to gain equality or freedom, here's the analogy with the blacks . . . we have to organize against the people who are oppressing us. . . . Men are the enemy. . . . I am interested in organizing other women to organize other women to take their power away from them."[121] Representatives of New York Radical Women agreed: "we have to organize politically separately."[122] Later, NYRW cofounder Pam Allen observed: "Organizing separately mirrored the rise of black separatism . . . and is one way that movement influenced us."[123] Indeed, separatism distinguished the Women's Liberation or radical wing of the movement from the moderate branch led by NOW, which admitted men to membership and into leadership positions.

Black Power leaders in Florida were also supportive of separatist views on Women's Liberation. Recalling "real respect" from Black Power organizer Jack Dawkins, Judith Brown said, "He can be 'empathetic' the way white men can't be."[124] "He understands perfectly why I want to fight for my own self, my own sex," she wrote to contemporaries in 1968.[125] Black power leader Joe Waller (later Omali Yeshitela) also encouraged Brown. "He agrees right down the line. . . . he . . . welcomes any effort of a white person to organize other whites," Brown said. Brown reported that these men were interested in forming a Black Power–Women's Liberation coalition. "The most enlight-ened male response," Brown said, "comes from the very militant black power people."[126]

Another important early borrowing from Black Power by white Women's Liberation founders was the strategy taken by Shulamith Firestone and Jo Freeman at the National Conference for New Politics in Chicago in September 1967. The conference, attended by more than three thousand delegates from various organizations, included a black caucus. Although fewer than half of those in attendance were black, the caucus won a guarantee of 50 percent of the votes and 50 percent representation on committees.[127]

Shulamith Firestone and Jo Freeman followed the example of the black caucus. They wrote a resolution that called for, among other demands, 51 percent of the conference votes and 51 percent representation on committees because women were 51 percent of the population. Freeman threatened to "tie up the conference in procedural motions" to bring the resolution to the floor.[128] Although they lost the battle, as historian Alice Echols noted, "Black power enabled them to argue that it was valid for women to organize around their own oppression."[129]

"After that paper, there would be no turning back"

IN THE MOVEMENT'S founding years a struggle emerged, fueled by the radical logic of Black Power, over the need for a mass independent Women's Liberation Movement that classed men as well as racism and capitalism among women's oppressors. Debates raged both in black Women's Liberation groups and in predominantly white groups over whether men were among women's oppressors.

The "Dialectic": Opposing Arguments Produce Theory That Builds a Power Base for Women's Liberation

In 1967 Poor Black Women took on what they called "bourgie . . . educated Black women" for what they considered "simplistic nationalist" views.[1] The nationalist women did not agree with Poor Black Women's idea of men as women's oppressor and wrote to them saying, "Stop being so damned antagonistic to the Black man" and "work together with him."[2] Poor Black Women member Joyce H. responded that black women had been trying "for centuries . . . to work hand in hand with him" and he had just taken advantage. "Not this time," responded another. "No more masters, bluffers."[3]

Poor Black Women could be said to have held the radical feminist position that men, because of their vested interest in the systemic power imbalance that favored the male sex, should be, as "Toward a Female Liberation Movement" coauthor Brown put it, "for a time at least" a central target.[4] In 1969 black radical feminist Cellestine Ware cofounded New York Radical Feminists, a predominantly white group whose manifesto read, "We are engaged in a power struggle with men. . . . the agent of our oppression is man insofar as he . . . carries out the supremacy privileges of the male role. . . . men have set up institutions . . . to maintain this power."[5]

In contrast "politicos," as Marilyn Webb called herself and the women in her camp, held the opposing and at first majority position, at least among white radical women, that capitalism alone was to blame for women's oppression.[6] Said Webb, "we saw ourselves colonized in the same way as Fanon has described the Algerians, and our enemy was not men. . . . both men and women have their roles . . . shaped by advertisers for economic use in the consumer market."[7]

The culpability of men in the oppression of women was a key point of difference. But even as radical feminists and politicos debated it sharply, they shared some points of unity. The most important was that the status quo for women was intolerable and they were going to make it their business to change it. Sue Munaker of the West Side Group in Chicago put it this way: "We began to realize that the way in which we were radical women defined us as non-radical. . . . we were activists in . . . the black movement . . . or in SDS, but as women we accepted the status quo." They were beginning to see that "no group can be free . . . until each defines its liberation for itself." Thus Munaker counseled women playing a supportive role to men who refused the draft or who opposed the war in Vietnam by playing on female stereotypes to "see that work for what it is. It can be auxiliary."[8]

Another point of unity among radical women was opposition to capitalism. Black and white, politico and radical feminist, Women's Liberation founders opposed capitalism as the exploitive, oppressive system of labor within the United States and as the engine of imperialism, the source of war and exploitation around the world. They differed on the extent to which they understood capitalism to be the source and fuel of white supremacy and male supremacy, and, as Patricia Robinson pointed out repeatedly, on the class consciousness of their members and organizing strategies. Cellestine Ware said that radical feminists were "actively pressing for the inception of socialist institutions as the prerequisites to the emancipation of women," and that they wanted to "eliminate sexual class, economic and racial distinctions which are the bases for power and domination."[9] The politicos, for the most part, stuck to the view that capitalism oppressed women primarily in their role as brainwashed consumers.

The debates among the radical women helped give rise to the ideas upon which the coming movement was built. This "dialectic," as then-politico Peggy Dobbins later called it, was immensely productive, unlike its "nearly lethal" depiction in much of the later secondary literature.[10] The characterization of the debates as "corrosive," as Alice Echols called them, misses the immensely energizing and productive role they played in attracting participants and generating ideas that hastened the development of the mass power base of the Women's Liberation Movement.[11]

For example, consciousness-raising was developed as the radical feminist side of a debate over whether the basis of the new movement's theory and program should be women's daily experience or books about women.[12] The Florida Paper, the clarion call by Jones and Brown for an independent movement that targeted men as well as the economic system, was written in part in opposition to Webb's article exonerating men. Carol Hanisch's paper "The Personal Is Political" was written in an argument with Dottie Zellner and other women Hanisch worked with in the Southern Conference Education Fund (SCEF), who held that consciousness-raising was a form of therapy. Hanisch argued that consciousness-raising helped to flesh out the details of the unequal power relationship between men and women and thus was political exposure and analysis.[13] In this way, the debate between the politicos and the radical feminists unfolded in countless mimeographed position papers that by late 1967 had begun to spread about the nation, contending with each other's points.

The Formation of the First Women's Liberation Group

Jo Freeman and Shulamith Firestone, who were influenced by Black Power politics, went into action at the National Conference for a New Politics (NCNP) held in Chicago in September 1967.[14] Freeman had recently arrived in Chicago, fresh from the southern Civil Rights Movement. She had lived with black families in small towns in Alabama and South Carolina for more than a year doing voter registration work. There the contempt she had previously felt for women changed to respect—pride, almost. When Hosea Williams, her supervisor at the Southern Christian Leadership Conference, sent only male staff to the Meredith March in Mississippi in June 1966, Freeman organized a carload of women and took off for the march. There she heard the term "male chauvinism" for the first time.[15] She was beginning to understand that, like blacks, women faced oppression all their own. By the summer of 1967 she was actively looking for ways to organize women against female oppression.

While visiting the SDS office in Chicago, Freeman found out that Heather Booth and Naomi Weisstein were teaching a course on women. She also learned about NCNP, the big, wide-ranging conference to be held over Labor Day weekend, for which she wanted to propose a women's workshop. Jane Adams, a traveling SDS organizer who had also been on the SNCC staff, called a series of meetings to plan one. Although the plans failed, Freeman went to the NCNP and found a women's workshop already on the schedule.[16] In the workshop Freeman met Shulamith Firestone. This was Freeman's first experience with organizing around the issue of women's equality, and it had a remarkable result.

The workshop produced a resolution calling for equal pay for equal work and for abortion on demand. The resolutions chairperson pushed aside this feminist resolution in favor of a resolution for peace from the Women Strike for Peace (WSP), a veteran women's peace organization. The chair, ignoring that one resolution was for peace and the other for Women's Liberation, said that he would not accept two "women's" resolutions. Negotiations with the WSP brought a compromise that bore little resemblance to the original feminist resolution. So Freeman and Firestone drew up a radical new one that demanded a revamping of marriage, property, and divorce laws, free abortion and birth control, and an end to sexual stereotyping in the media.

Pressure on the conference leadership wrung a commitment to bring the Firestone-Freeman resolution to the floor. The two women rounded up a posse and passed out two thousand copies. At the last minute, instead of presenting the resolution, William Pepper, the conference chair, dismissed it in favor of "more important" issues. As the two women rushed up to the podium, Pepper gave Firestone a patronizing pat on the head and called her "little girl."[17] Firestone and Freeman were enraged.

When the conference was over, Firestone and Freeman called another meeting of the women with whom Freeman had originally tried to organize a workshop, including Heather Booth and Naomi Weisstein. They all began meeting in Freeman's apartment on Chicago's West Side. The group was furious over the treatment of Firestone and Freeman at the conference and the patronizing dismissal of their resolution. As one participant remarked, "rage at what had happened at the convention kept us going for at least three months."[18] They decided to exclude men from meetings and to develop a Statement of Principles based on the resolution Firestone and Freeman had written for the NCNP.

In the 13 November 1967 issue of *New Left Notes*, they went public with their plan "to take the initiative in organizing ourselves for our own liberation" by publishing the statement in an article titled "Chicago Women Form Liberation Group."[19] One of the most important things it did was use the phrase "Women's Liberation Movement."[20] Further, it demanded representation of women at all levels of society because women were 51 percent of the population. It condemned the mass media for sexist portrayals of women and called for equal opportunity in education and employment, communal child care centers, men and women equally sharing child-rearing and household work, and women's control over their own bodies. To meet these "minimal demands for equality," they said, required a total "social restructuring."

Although the women in the West Side Group were experienced organizers, they were in a quandary about how to proceed because they lacked a coherent theory about women's oppression.[21] Why were women oppressed, anyway? Who or what was responsible? "We asked ourselves what we should call the thing that was squelching us. Male supremacy? Female subordination? Male chauvinism? Capitalist debris?" recalled Weisstein.[22] Should they organize within the New Left or should they organize a movement for Women's Liberation independent of the New Left? Founding member Fran Rominski said the "main internal argument" was "Do we work with women already in the movement or with women who are totally unorganized?"[23]

The group was ready for action, yet these important issues were unresolved. Even the decision to exclude the men was difficult. Many of the women were under pressure from male coworkers in the New Left not to divide that movement by raising the woman question. But Firestone and Freeman saw the group as the start of a new independent movement, despite its continuing ambivalence. And so it was, holding together with enough glue to organize new groups and publish the first national Women's Liberation Movement newsletter.

New York Radical Women: A "Sister Chapter" Organizes

Barely a month after the group in Chicago was off the ground, Shulamith Firestone moved to New York City to organize a "sister chapter," as the

West Siders called it.[24] On her first day there, armed with names and phone numbers of contacts provided by the radical women in Chicago, Firestone wrote to Freeman that she was "very optimistic and excited."[25] Firestone took waitressing jobs to support herself, and started recruiting for what would become New York Radical Women (NYRW). She was not alone. Mississippi veteran Pam Allen, then in New York City, leapt at the chance to organize for Women's Liberation, and she and Firestone began to plan for a group in New York.

Allen had been growing more and more dissatisfied with her life since she left her civil rights work in Mississippi. There, she felt that she had been treated with respect as a woman. However, this did not seem to her the case in the larger society, in her new marriage or her new job as a social worker. From her positive Mississippi Freedom Summer experience, she concluded that her dissatisfaction had little to do with herself personally and everything to do with the arbitrary and unfair situation of women. She wanted to find like-minded women.

In November 1967, barely a month after Firestone's arrival in the city, she and Allen called their first meeting in Allen's apartment on the Lower East Side. Within a few weeks the group had regular participants—among them Kathie Sarachild (then Amatniek) who, since her introduction to SNCC work and ideas in Mississippi, had been closely following developments on the subject of Women's Liberation and had devoured the second Hayden and King paper when it appeared in *Liberation* magazine in 1966.[26] Anne Koedt, from SDS, was one of Allen's first recruits, and Mississippi veteran Carol Hanisch was also among the group's initial members.[27]

Sisterhood Is Powerful

Soon the "sister chapters" in New York and Chicago were planning their first action. They would perform street theatre and hold a "countercongress" in Washington, D.C., to take place at a large women's peace march called by the Jeannette Rankin Brigade. The Brigade, a coalition of women's peace groups composed mostly of Women Strike for Peace, held a march in January of 1968 on the opening day of Congress calling for an end to the war in Vietnam.[28]

In New York, Pam Allen wrote to Jo Freeman in Chicago: "Plans are underway for the N.Y. Radical women's Group to stage a funeral of 'weeping womanhood' . . . We are hoping that the Chicago group will want to participate in the funeral. . . . the idea is that we'll present the problem, you propose actions. How does that sound?"[29] For most of NYRW, the "problem" was to raise the feminist consciousness of their sisters in the Brigade.

The radical women saw the Brigade as mistakenly capitalizing on and re-inforcing the stereotype of "weeping womanhood" to bring their plea to the Congress. "Playing upon the traditional female role in the classic manner," as Shulamith Firestone characterized it, had already, as we have seen, been a point of contention with the peace women at the NCNP in Chicago.[30] Many in NYRW saw the tactic as impotent and ineffective. "This power is only a *substitute* for power," as Kathie Sarachild would argue in her speech to the Brigade women.[31] To gain real political power in affairs of state and over their own lives, she elaborated, women would need to organize a movement for their own liberation.

The West Side Group and NYRW agreed in deploring the Brigade's use of a male chauvinist stereotype of women to organize against the war. Heather Booth and other West Siders wrote in the aftermath of the action that un-til women "go beyond justifying themselves in terms of their wombs and breasts . . . they will never be able to exert any political power."[32] But the West Side Group tended to stress that the Brigade action was ineffective because it was not militant enough. The Brigade had resolved that there would be no civil disobedience and no arrests. Booth and the others held that the whole idea of petitioning Congress was off the mark, because effective antiwar work meant "talking to people about taking power."[33]

Despite this difference and heated negotiations over the content of the action, the West Side Group and NYRW forged ahead. The joint action impelled forward the new Women's Liberation Movement by practical ex-pansion on a number of fronts and by the presentation, by NYRW's chosen speaker, of a powerful new concept: "Sisterhood Is Powerful."

Sarachild came up with the slogan on a flyer she brought to the joint ac-tion along with the speech the group had been planning.[34] The flyer, with its focus on degrees of power and powerlessness, reflected the influence of Black Power, building up to a call for Sisterhood Is Powerful in contrast to the powerlessness of "uppity" women when they were struggling as individuals. Similarly, in the leaflet's affirmation that uppity women were beautiful, the influence of Black Is Beautiful, another Black Power concept, was evident.

Sarachild's speech was introduced by a funeral procession with a dummy representing Traditional Womanhood on a bier hung with curlers, garters, and other symbols of impotent, empty, trivialized femininity. "Why should we bury Traditional Womanhood while hundreds of thousands of human beings are being brutally slaughtered in our names?" Sarachild asked in her speech, referring to the war in Vietnam.[35] She then outlined the answer: that more women would mobilize to end the war if they were free of the oppressive traditional limitations on their lives. To wield political power, women, like black people and workers, Sarachild argued, explicitly making all these class, race, and gender connections, needed militant unity.

The national action in January of 1968 expanded the base of the budding movement by calling a meeting that brought together ninety women from fourteen states.[36] Most of the participants continued to emphasize organizing New Left women back in their local areas and getting the New Left to shape up on male chauvinism. Others wanted an independent mass movement.

But together the radical women's groups set up a newsletter to exchange information about their ideas and work. Jo Freeman agreed to edit what would soon adopt the name *Voice of the Women's Liberation Movement* (*VWLM*).[37] The meeting also generated a contact list used for the first mailing of the newsletter and to raise money for a theoretical journal that Dee Ann Pappas began planning.

The commitment to organize new groups almost doubled the size of the emerging movement. After the meeting Marilyn Webb, who had recently moved from Chicago to Washington, D.C., pulled together a Women's Liberation group there. Dee Ann Pappas organized a Women's Liberation group in Baltimore, and Anne Weills (then Scheer) organized Berkeley Women's Liberation. Weills had raised funds for the Jeannette Rankin action, but had to stay home because her husband wouldn't help with their new baby. When women returned to Berkeley all excited, her house became "a hotbed" of Women's Liberation meetings.[38]

Dee Ann Pappas got the idea for the theoretical journal, *Women: A Journal of Liberation*, at the Washington action and also decided then to start a Women's Liberation group. Since reading *The Second Sex* and *The Feminine Mystique*, she had been trying to analyze the situation of women. When she returned to Baltimore, she invited the women in her antiwar group to a Women's Liberation meeting. The women undertook a detailed examination of the concrete conditions of their lives. Pappas recalled herself as "applying Marxist ideas in the way I was analyzing the situation of women."[39]

Because of the joint action in D.C., new recruits flocked to the original "sister chapters." "We have gotten whole groups of new people lately, many of them from the Brigade contact, and some *very* promising," Firestone wrote to Freeman.[40] Freeman in Chicago wrote, "From a rather fitful and timid start we are growing far faster than any of us had ever imagined."[41] The collaboration of the two groups had borne fruit even as the activists disputed their political differences and sharpened their positions.

Still, Firestone and Allen stressed the shortcomings of the action with an eye on greater things in the future. The Brigade protest created opportunities that the West Side Group and NYRW had failed to make good on. In particular, there was a moment when five hundred women, frustrated by a sense of impotence, broke away from the Brigade to hold a countercongress. "We were not really prepared to rechannel this disgust, to provide the direction. . . . There was chaos," Firestone said. Allen wrote, "We had . . . no ready program for these women. . . . They wanted action, not rhetoric, and we had no action to offer."[42]

Moreover, there was very little press coverage. Considering that the five thousand women marching in the Brigade constituted the largest female protest since the days of the suffrage campaigns, here was more evidence of women's impotence.

Firestone and Allen were disappointed by the arguments between the New York and Chicago groups, albeit for different reasons. Allen saw the problem psychologically as "distrust and anger," but Firestone saw it politically as a difference in commitment to Women's Liberation.[43] The speech by the representative of the West Side Group "did not even mention women's oppression at all," Firestone said.[44] When NYRW fought for the time slot they had been promised for a speech, Firestone said the West Siders "insisted the feminist thing wasn't important enough to make a stink about."[45]

Firestone was right. Most of the West Side Group continued to be ambivalent about the new direction they were taking. They were out there on the edge, organizing a Women's Liberation Movement, all right, but was this really the way to go? In 1968 there was much more on the U.S. political scene to consider than Women's Liberation.

On January 30, the Viet Cong launched the Tet Offensive, and throughout most of February vivid images on TV and in the newspapers demonstrated that the United States had grossly overstated its success in Vietnam. In March, Lyndon Johnson, discredited by Tet and increasingly unpopular because of the war, declared he would not seek reelection as president in the fall. In April, Martin Luther King Jr. was assassinated; black communities all over America erupted in rebellions that were not put down for days. In May, a revolt of French students instigated a general strike of ten million workers that practically brought down the French government. In June, Robert F. Kennedy was assassinated.

Young radical women were active on many fronts, but to those who were also organizing for an independent Women's Liberation Movement, it was clear that women, as a second-class, divided, powerless oppressed group, had little chance of having much impact. Thus, for a time at least, Women's Liberation would have to come first. Otherwise, as Sarachild had pointed out in her speech and as the Brigade action clearly demonstrated, women would not be taken seriously.

Poor Black Women had already reached a similar feminist conclusion. They were not present at the Brigade action, but they had faced the predicament of opposing the war as women and not being able to make an impact on men as they did antiwar work in Harlem and in their Mount Vernon, New York, neighborhood during the summer of 1966.

"We got interested in the Vietnam War in 1966 when some of our young men began to come home in boxes," Poor Black Women wrote.[46] They read "material from the Vietnamese fighters themselves," like the *Vietnam Courier* from North Vietnam and writings from the National Liberation Front (Viet Cong) which Patricia Robinson brought them to read.[47] They compared what they learned in this material with "what we were being told by the Man," they said, and began arguing with young black men against enlisting, on the grounds that the war in Vietnam was "really a war against people like us."[48]

They also picketed an Army–Air Force recruiting office in Harlem with Black Women Enraged, a group organized by longtime black political activist and renowned actress Ruby Dee. "Black Men! . . . Stay Here and Fight for your Manhood" and "Protect us . . . women and children from the murder and rape of the white racist," read some of their flyers.[49] Some of the arguments, like those of the Brigade, were pitched on a traditional image of women.

"Our sons and brothers ignored us," said Poor Black Women. "We were just Black women." Poor Black Women also brought a class perspective to bear on the men's failure to heed them. "The schools had long ago convinced them not to listen to poor people (particularly women) who had never even finished high school," they said.[50] By the summer of 1968, Poor Black Women would develop an analysis that described capitalism as "a male supremacist society."[51] Their radical feminist analysis of the war was that the male oppressor appropriated "the surplus product of her [women's] body, the child, to use and exploit . . . as poorly paid mercenaries."[52]

On the other hand, if capitalism was the cause of women's oppression, as most radical women believed, why should not Women's Liberation groups take on capitalism wherever it was vulnerable? Why not oppose the war, the business order, and the Democratic Party as women? The women in the West Side Group questioned whether they should not be planning antiwar demonstrations for the Democratic Convention that fall. That the convention was in Chicago only increased the pressure on Women's Liberation founders there. In New York, Pam Allen and a number of others were also anxious that there be a women's presence at the protest of the convention. The new groups in D.C., Berkeley, and Baltimore shared their concern.

In contrast, Anne Koedt of NYRW further developed the argument against "storming the Pentagon as women, or protest[ing] the Democratic Convention as women" in a speech at a citywide meeting of radical women's groups at the Free University in New York City in February 1968.[53] Rather, she said, "We must begin to expose and eliminate the causes of our oppression as women. . . . we are confronted with the problem of assuring a female revolution within the general revolution."[54] Toward that end, Koedt argued, women must "confront the obvious male interest in keeping women 'in their place.'" Otherwise, women would end up with a "reformist revolution" that "simply transferred male supremacy, paternalism, male power onto the new economy."[55]

At the same citywide meeting Naomi Jaffe and Bernardine Dohrn presented the opposing position: "We are coming together . . . not to rage at our exploited status vis a vis men," they emphasized. Omitting women's role as reproducers, a cornerstone of Poor Black Women's theory, and even minimizing women's oppression as producing workers under capitalism, they presented what would soon be a widespread politico analysis of capitalism oppressing women as "consumers" because of a "culture of consumption" that was a necessary aspect of "domestic imperialism."[56] Their strategy for the liberation of women, Jaffe and Dohrn argued, would "focus on the unique quality of our exploitation as women, primarily in our vanguard economic role as consumers."[57] Radical feminist Ellen Willis would later characterize this position in her famous Redstockings paper "'Consumerism' and Women" as antiwoman and antiworker:

> Radical intellectuals have been attracted to this essentially reactionary position [anticonsumerism] . . . because it appeals to both their

dislike of capitalism and their feeling of superiority to the working class. . . . Consumerism as applied to women is blatantly sexist. The pervasive image of the empty-headed female consumer constantly trying her husband's patience with her extravagant purchases contributes to the myth of male superiority.[58]

"That started it if anything written started it"

Into this intensifying dialectic came the Florida Paper from Gainesville, with its trenchant critique of male chauvinism and its galvanizing call for a mass movement for Women's Liberation. For many reasons, the Florida Paper served to turn the tide. Naomi Weisstein of the Chicago group explained the impact of the document this way:

> After we got started, for months we were paralyzed. . . . was there any need for an independent women's movement? . . . the triumph of socialism would surely dismantle the patriarchy? Then the paper . . . transformed our thinking. . . . After that paper, there would be no turning back for us, or for the rest of the movement.[59]

What was the basis of the paper's influence among radical women? Most importantly, the paper effectively developed the general radical principle that the oppressed must fight their own oppressor, which had most recently been put forward by SNCC Black Power leaders explaining that whites should fight their own oppressors. When Jones stated in bold capital letters on the second page of the paper that "PEOPLE DON'T GET RADICALIZED FIGHTING OTHER PEOPLE'S BATTLES," she was applying this classic radical principle not first or only to women, but to the broad Black Freedom and New Left movements as a whole. "Any honest appraisal of their own condition," she reasoned, "would presumably lead people . . . first of all . . . to fight their own battles."[60] She then showed how the movement was radicalized by this: "One of the best things that ever happened to black militants happened . . . when they started fighting for blacks instead of the American dream." Whites, Jones continued, became radicalized when Black Power forced them "to face their own oppression in their own world . . . [and] they started fighting for control of the universities, against the draft, the war and the business order."[61]

Lastly, Jones applied the principle to women. She argued that men had too much to lose and would not give up their male privileges without the kind of battle that could only be made by a mass movement of women. What were the benefits a man received by oppressing women? Women, Jones said, were the "great maintenance force" who "wipe his ass and breast feed him when he is little, school him in his youthful years, do his clerical work and raise his . . . replacements later, and all through his life . . . in the restaurants, hospitals, and homes, . . . sew for him, stoop for him, cook for him, clean for him, sweep, run errands . . . and nurse him when his frail body falters."[62] The paper argued that, like blacks fighting white supremacy and men taking on the "business order," women aiming to eliminate male supremacy were also political and radical. The paper argued that women must "form their own group and work primarily for female liberation" both for "their own salvation" and "for the good of the movement."[63]

When Jones and Brown spoke of the "good of the movement," they spoke of the broad movement in whose service they had for years labored in life-risking, dues-paying ways that placed high hurdles before any retreat back into the establishment. When they said that Women's Liberation would advance both women and the Left, they spoke credibly and powerfully.

"As radical women, we must set the tone," Brown said, "organizing projects that . . . speak to American women about their condition. We have not conned ourselves into political paralysis as an excuse for inaction—we are a subjugated caste."[64] Urging women to work for "female liberation," Brown said: "We do not question the courage of radical men who now confront most of the manifestations of imperialism," but "radical men are not fighting for female liberation" and "regrettably" even "the best radical men . . . do not even have a political interest in female liberation."[65]

Jones and Brown came by their strategy of militancy in the southern Civil Rights Movement. Brown credited Patricia Stephens Due with teaching "a very high degree of militancy—and I had seen her make it work. Pat transformed the scary stuff into winning and converting more and more people. . . . this was my best model."[66] Brown's experience of Due's winning power with whites informed her strategy of calling men out militantly.

Also adding to the Florida Paper's influence was that it brought another radical feminist voice to fuel the momentum of the emerging Women's Liberation Movement. When Cell 16's *No More Fun and Games* came out that October and Poor Black Women's "The Sisters Reply" was published in *Lilith* in December 1968, the momentum grew exponentially.[67]

Fran Rominski of the West Side Group wanted to organize a mass movement of women. Yet her position on that issue, she wrote to Brown, "always fluctuated" until she read the Florida Paper. The reason the West Siders had not charged ahead for a mass power base and had chosen instead to focus on women within the New Left, Rominski said, was that they aimed to get the New Left "to adopt women's liberation as one of its major battles." But now she was ready to organize women in the larger society. "The thing that most excited me about the paper," she said, "it is something . . . I can give to anyone, unlike much of what has been written in the past . . . especially, what has come out of Chicago." But Rominski did "need a way to get in touch with more women . . . for myself and Chicago." She wanted to open a women's center to attract the curious but uncommitted. "Give me your opinion," she wrote.[68]

Brown's method for attracting uncommitted women had been the Florida Paper—this was the central reason she had coauthored it. Weisstein agreed, and put up her own money to mimeograph three hundred copies. She was joined by Marlene Dixon, a Marxist sociology professor who was not yet in a Women's Liberation group. Dixon, soon to be fired from the University of Chicago for her activism, had been the first woman appointed to her department in more than fifteen years. Dixon's firing and the massive protest over it gave her a national voice.

As Women's Liberation took off around the nation, Dixon praised the Florida Paper. "Then the publication of the central paper, 'Toward a Female Liberation Movement,'" she said. "That started it if anything written started it. That paper just laid it on the line."[69]

Outside of Chicago, too, the paper made a leap for the early movement. The editor of the *New South Student*, the journal of the Southern Student Organizing Committee, called the paper a "kind of 'what is to be done' for the movement."[70] SSOC distributed the paper, as did the New England Free Press, an alternative publishing house.

The paper was a "frontal assault" on the reluctance to clearly name men as beneficiaries of female oppression, and it outlined Women's Liberation demands and steps toward an independent movement.[71] Significantly, it spoke to several groups of women, including housewives with children and working husbands. Jones set forth in relentless detail the oppression of these women on a daily basis, at the breakfast table, in the bedroom, in routine conversations with men. Brown in turn gave a portrait of younger, childless, college-educated women in the New Left.

The Florida Paper spread rapidly across the United States. "I want to or-ganize a group. Can you help me?" inquired housewives with no connection to the New Left.[72] By December 1968 the paper had crossed the Atlantic. A Swedish radical journal published portions of it, along with translations of several of the articles in NYRW's *Notes from the First Year*. "An inquiry makes it clear that your views do have considerable impact on women," the Swedish editor wrote Brown.[73]

Once, the hope of reforming the peace and freedom movement to eliminate sexism, especially in their beloved SNCC, had given Hayden and King courage to write their critique of male chauvinism. But as the New Left resisted Women's Liberation, hope dwindled, producing a paralysis in those whose hopes had been the highest. The Florida Paper helped to dispel the paralysis. The very origin of the paper added to the optimism it generated. Gainesville was a small town in rural North Florida. It was the site of a conservative southern university. If women there could come out with a scathing indictment of male chauvinism and a call for a Women's Liberation Movement, then might not women of whom other movement founders were not yet aware, in other such towns, want one too?

"Serious disagreements . . . beautiful people": A Pivotal National Women's Liberation Meeting

One spring night in 1968, desperate to find such women, Brown began dialing telephone numbers in Baltimore on the "crazy chance" one of them might belong to a woman she had admired as a "toughie" while a teenager, years before at summer camp in Gainesville. Brown had read in *New Left Notes* that Dee Ann Pappas, a woman in Baltimore, was starting a theoretical journal about Women's Liberation. Even though the last name was different and Brown had no idea where her old friend Dee Ann was living, she called a string of numbers looking for her.

Brown could not believe her luck. Dee Ann Pappas *was* her friend from summer camp. She was working on *Women: A Journal of Liberation* and organizing a Women's Liberation group. Brown and Jones took off immediately for Baltimore. Pappas took them to D.C. to meet Marilyn Webb, whose position on working within the New Left they had attacked in the Florida Paper. Despite strong disagreements, the four began enthusiastically planning a three-day meeting of women who were organizing Women's Liberation groups or writing about Women's Liberation. Brown wrote Webb after their initial planning session: "We ought to emphasize that serious disagreements be settled through position papers . . . rather than try to insist that the group reach an immediate consensus on issues that could make for artificial divides." She signed off: "That Sunday evening was a milestone. You're some beautiful people."[74]

They originally intended to hold the meeting in Bev Jones's house, but the number of women expected soon grew too large. Pappas found a Quaker camp in Sandy Springs, Maryland, the Sandy Springs Friends School, that would rent for one dollar per woman per night.[75] On 2 August 1968 a score of women took their seats in the large meeting hall in the first gathering of the emerging movement since the Jeannette Rankin Brigade Protest.[76]

"All of them were true leaders," reflected Roxanne Dunbar, who had come from Boston, "militants with battle scars . . . from the front lines facing police dogs and jail in Mississippi and organizing antiwar demonstrations for the Students for a Democratic Society."[77] Webb and Pappas were veteran anti–Vietnam War organizers who had started out in local civil rights work. Jones and Brown had spent years in the southern Civil Rights Movement and also worked in SDS. From New York, Kathie Sarachild and Carol Hanisch were Mississippi civil rights veterans. From Chicago, Sue Munaker and Fran Rominski were longtime antiwar activists, and Jo Freeman had been a leader in the Berkeley Free Speech Movement and worked for projects of the Southern Christian Leadership Conference in Georgia, South Carolina, Alabama, and Mississippi. Sara Evans from Durham had been the North Carolina coordinator of Vietnam Summer, an antiwar project. The experience of the other participants was much the same. Their collective history and its accumulated wisdom charged the hall and filled their debates with passion and purpose.

Before they tackled questions of theory and ideology, local groups and representatives reported on their work. Reports from groups in New York, Chicago, D.C., Baltimore, and Boston broke the isolation of local organizing. New York Radical Women explained consciousness-raising, their new method for organizing women and analyzing women's oppression. Seemingly out of nowhere, a group was starting in Boston, organized by Roxanne Dunbar and Dana Densmore, two women who on arrival at Sandy Springs were unknown to the others there.

Roxanne Dunbar, like many Women's Liberation founders, had become feminist through reading *The Second Sex*. She later recounted that when a newspaper reported that "a superwoman power advocate" named Valerie Solanas had shot pop artist Andy Warhol, she believed it to be the start of the feminist revolution she had been waiting for.[78] In Mexico at the time, preparing to visit Cuba, Dunbar took off for Boston. She had decided Boston would be fertile ground for organizing because of its history as a nineteenth-century center of abolitionism and feminism. There she found Dana Densmore, who had been raised radical and feminist by her mother, Donna Allen, a founder of Women Strike for Peace. On July 4, Dunbar and Densmore called a Women's Liberation meeting, and now, only a month later, their group numbered eight. By October 1968 the first issue of their journal *No More Fun and Games* would be ready.[79]

Between the joint action of the West Side Group and New York Radical Women in January 1968 in Washington and the August meeting in Sandy Springs, the possibilities for a Women's Liberation Movement had greatly increased. Groups had formed in new cities, and in cities like New York and Chicago they had multiplied. They were also multiplying on the West Coast in Berkeley, San Francisco, and Seattle. Although more women had gone to the January meeting at the Brigade action, most came as individual activists. August, by contrast, saw most of the women at Sandy Springs representing groups.

The women at Sandy Springs argued vehemently over what one participant characterized as "disagreements . . . which are basic."[80] Some of the arguments included what to organize women around—"nitty gritty . . . problems with men," as one radical feminist held, or "where women are," such as around the upcoming Democratic National Convention—or about their hesitation to speak up in SDS meetings, as a politico woman argued.[81] This debate led to another: whether to first organize radical women or to "go for a mass movement" right away. They also argued fiercely about how, as white women, they should be organizing with black women. (This issue is discussed more fully in chapter 10 under "Black Power Women . . . Absolutely Essential.")

Then the question arose as to whether men or capitalism should be the "first concern" of Women's Liberation.[82] "Who is the enemy? There is no way to get out of this situation without fighting men," declared Beverly Jones. "Which is your final enemy?" said another participant. And another responded, "The capitalist system." Another said, "My final enemy is man. You can't have female liberation in a capitalist society, and a socialist society doesn't guarantee it." The argument grew more intense. One radical feminist said, "if women in this country get turned on by feminism, they are going to be so much more aware of capitalism than you are." At this point the transcriber recorded "bedlam."[83] These debates were not resolved at the conference and would continue to roil the movement.

A Collision Course of Collaboration

Meanwhile, New York and Gainesville women, as Brown put it, were on "a collision course of collaboration," because they were "fueled by some common movement and life experience and some common insights about what needed to be done."[84] Sarachild was ecstatic to discover the Florida Paper. Here were Beverly Jones and Judith Brown with their prestige as frontline southern activists in the Civil Rights Movement naming men as women's oppressor, calling for building an independent power base of women for Women's Liberation, and making the radical case that this was good for women and at the same time good for the Black Freedom and Left movements.

Jones and Brown were just as surprised as Sarachild to find new allies. Although they subscribed to the *Voice of the Women's Liberation Movement*, it had not reported the publication of *Notes from the First Year* or the existence of radical feminist views in New York Radical Women. The discovery of each other's work "changed my life," Brown said later.[85]

Brown listened carefully as Sarachild and Hanisch explained consciousness-raising. Here was just what she and Jones had been trying to do with the experiential detail of women in their paper. Brown, like Sarachild and Hanisch, found herself recalling mass meetings of the Civil Rights Movement where people "testified" about experiencing racism. And when she returned to Gainesville, armed with an organizing method, she immediately organized Gainesville Women's Liberation, the first Women's Liberation group in the South.

The Gainesville–New York alliance soon had important ramifications. Brown called it "an explosive intersection of thought, 'sparkling energy' and activism" from which "sparks have flown off and on ever since."[86] The women called their collaboration the Life Group, essentially a think tank of like-minded activists to develop the theory that would have a major impact on Women's Liberation.

Carol Hanisch was also excited that the evidence from Gainesville showed that the movement was rapidly developing nationally. She had already read the Florida Paper while working at the Louisville office of the Southern Conference Education Fund, the radical freedom movement organization. After Sandy Springs, she knew she had allies to develop a Women's Liberation organizing project in the South. Within a week, she presented a written proposal for it to SCEF. She wrote Brown that she "never would have written that proposal if it had not been for the Florida Paper."[87]

The excitement and optimism the conference engendered made itself felt in other ways. On the third day of the meeting, all the women at the conference laid another piece of the foundation for the new movement. Leaving unresolved their fierce debate on the nature of women's oppression, they moved ahead with plans for a much larger national conference for later that fall. Undaunted by their disagreements or the magnitude of the project before them, they committed themselves to a national conference in November 1968. This was a conscious decision to hold the meeting on the 120th anniversary of the meeting in 1848 that founded the nineteenth-century women's rights movement. The decision to hold the conference on the anniversary of this historic event spoke volumes about the increasing courage of the movement and its willingness to reclaim feminist history.

8 Support for Women's Liberation on the Left, New and Old

THE LEFT HELPED give rise to the Women's Liberation Movement—with both opposition and support. "Old Left" refers generally to the Marxist-inspired parties and individuals who held at their core "the emancipation of the working class" through its taking "ownership of the means of production and distribution." The Old Left, including the Communist Party, reached its pinnacle in the United States in the 1930s and 1940s. Political repression during the infamous McCarthy era drastically reduced the Old Left's ranks by the time the New Left came on the scene. The "New Left," especially in its early years, focused on black civil rights, university reform, and ending the Vietnam War, rather than on explicitly working-class issues.

The New Left roots of Women's Liberation are well established in the literature.[1] But the heat of women's fight against sexism in the New Left in the prefeminist gestation phase of Women's Liberation from 1965 to 1968 often overshadows the usefulness of the outcome. Women waged exhausting battles to win use of crucial resources and were angry over prices paid to obtain them. That they frequently came too little and late, however, must not obscure our understanding that the hard-won space for Women's Liberation classes and workshops, along with media access and experience of movement struggle, were building blocks for the new movement.

Before 1968, although a vast ferment of female rebellion against male domination rippled below the surface, only a handful of Women's Liberation groups had formed, and NOW, begun in 1966, had only one thousand members.[2] As pioneer feminist Cindy Cisler put it, locating the feminist movement then was "a little like trying to find the early Christians."[3] Contemporary Jo Freeman reflected, "I had my antennas tuned to any possible signs of female revolt. In 1966 I picked up a few tremors. . . . I first read of the National Organization for Women . . . in 1967. . . . The letters I wrote were never answered. . . . Clearly something was happening but I couldn't find it."[4]

By 1968 the movement began to develop its own newspapers and journals. Moreover, the protest of the Miss America Pageant in September of that year attracted the attention of the national media. Between 1965 and 1968, however, openings of space and support on the Left provided the most visible and often the only signs of the new movement's emergence.

Old Left Foremothers

Although few of the women who launched the Women's Liberation Movement were actually members of any of the Old Left parties or even well versed in Marxism, many were influenced and at times mentored by people who were. These influences included Simone de Beauvoir, who, when she wrote *The Second Sex* in 1949, was involved in the Old Left in France and, even while writing the book, held to the theory that "the class struggle" had to be fought before male supremacy could be tackled effectively. In a 1976 interview she observed:

> just as it is up to the poor to take away the power of the rich, so it is up to women to take away power from the men. And that doesn't mean dominate. . . . It means establish equality. . . . Put another way: once inside the class struggle, women understood that the class struggle did not eliminate the sex struggle. It's at that point that I myself became aware of what I have just said. Before that I was convinced that equality of the sexes can only be possible once capitalism is destroyed and therefore . . . it's this "therefore" which is the fallacy—we must first fight the class struggle. It is true that equality of the sexes is impossible under capitalism. . . . But it is not true that a socialist revolution neces-

sarily establishes sexual equality. . . . this consciousness among women that the class struggle does not embody the sex struggle—is what is new . . . most women in the struggle know that now. That's the greatest achievement of the feminist movement.[5]

Another influence was *The Golden Notebook*, by British feminist writer Doris Lessing, who had been an active member of the then banned Communist Party in the British apartheid colony of Southern Rhodesia before it became Zimbabwe. Casey Hayden reflected on reading *The Golden Notebook* in 1963, when she worked in the SNCC headquarters office in Atlanta. "It was enormously affirming," Hayden said, "to see a woman of the Left view her life in the same compartments as I viewed mine. . . . Andy Young remembered that I gave him the book to read during this time, turning him on to feminism."[6]

Award-winning African American feminist writer Alice Childress was active in the Civil Rights Congress, a post-WWII antiracist organization on the Left. Childress's plays and novels reflected her feminist, black, and anti-capitalist consciousness. Childress's work paved the way for African American women in theatre including Lorraine Hansberry, who reviewed *Florence*, Childress's first play, for Paul Robeson's magazine *Freedom*.

As the Women's Liberation Movement lifted off, Kathie Sarachild said Childress "cheered" her "involvement in feminism."[7] Redstockings members Sarachild and Myrna Hill attended the 1969 opening of Childress's play *Wine in the Wilderness*. The play's feminist heroine Tommy exposes the sexism and class bias of cultural nationalist middle-class black men who laud the image of an African queen but feel the "masses" of African American women should become more subservient.

In the 1970 roster of contributors to *Sisterhood Is Powerful*, Elizabeth "Betita" Sutherland Martinez described herself as "a tired old revolutionary writer-type."[8] Born in 1925, she was forty-three when she joined New York Radical Women. Her opposition to imperialism had begun in childhood. Her father had been involved in the Mexican Revolution and "every night I heard stories about our Revolution" and how the Yanquis had oppressed the Mexicans, Martinez said.[9] She dated her commitment to the broad struggle to 1959 when she worked with the legendary Robert Williams, the radical NAACP leader in Monroe, North Carolina, who was forced into exile in 1961 in Cuba and subsequently in China. From 1962 to 1968 Martinez worked on the SNCC staff.

In early 1968 she brought her accumulated years of movement work and radical thinking to NYRW. Her paper "Women of the World Unite—We Have Nothing to Lose But Our Men!" written with Carol Hanisch, warned women that

> we are . . . kept in "our place" by men and by a capitalist system that has institutionalized male supremacy. . . . If you're a black woman, it's also racism. . . . you have fight to change the whole thing. But we could change the economic system and women could still be victims of male supremacy, just as black people could still be victims of racism. To assure this doesn't happen, women have to organize themselves to fight male supremacy.[10]

Martinez opposed male supremacy in the Chicano movement, while at the same time making clear to white feminists that "the middle-class Anglo woman must beware of telling her black or brown sisters to throw off their chains."[11] Addressing herself to "women from colonized groups," she observed that "the struggle for 'Power to the People' is intimately linked to the women's liberation struggle."[12] Martinez produced a large body of writing on Chicana women's movement issues that reflected her lifelong activism trying to combine the anticapitalist, feminist, and antiracist struggles.

Tillie Olsen also helped to reignite the Women's Liberation Movement with her writing and encouragement to Women's Liberation founders. Redstockings called Olsen a "peerless exemplar of double militancy in art" who "eloquently fused the struggles of women and the working class for freedom."[13] Olsen, a longtime Communist Party activist, said, "The party certainly created feminists. . . . in the warehouse union, we really taught about . . . male chauvinism. One party woman, Lil Carlson, brought her guy, who was one of the heads of the Young Communist League in California, up on charges for male chauvinism. And she was not the only one. . . . We also read Lenin on housework."[14]

Olsen's 1961 story "Tell Me a Riddle," based on the life of her mother and father, both participants in the 1905 revolution in czarist Russia, was widely read by Women's Liberation founders. Its moving detail of the toll that male supremacy took on love between two people, across a lifetime of poverty and movement struggle, provided prowoman support for the power of consciousness-raising, then under attack as therapy. Olsen's early influence on the Feminist Press resulted in the reprinting of long erased and important prowoman, proworker books such as Rebecca Harding Davis's *Life in the Iron Mills* and Agnes Smedley's *Daughter of Earth*.

Although far from free of male supremacy, the Old Left opposed "male chauvinism." At its best, as African American Communist Party organizer Esther Cooper Jackson said, referring to several of the men—including her husband—in her branch in Alabama, "They actually thought [that] to be a good Communist you struggled on the woman question."[15]

Articles and lively letters to the editor on the "woman question" are found in the pages of Old Left publications of the period. Some of these foreshadowed the issues later raised by the Women's Liberation Movement: men sharing the housework, appearance issues, women doing the work while men take the glory,[16] and using "cheesecake" to sell the Party newspaper.[17] The U.S. Left of the 1920s through the 1940s had a rich tradition and literature on the "woman question." This no doubt evolved out of the radical tradition carried on in the classic works of Marx and Engels and further developed by Lenin, Mao, and others who wrote in opposition to the oppression of women and explained its origins in the private ownership of property.[18]

Until "Women's Liberation" protest surfaced in the mid-1960s, no such tradition and literature existed in the short life of the New Left, except occasionally where Old Left influences were felt.[19] In a 1967 article, "Sisters, Brothers, Lovers . . . Listen," the "four authoresses" observed of the Canadian New Left: "Old leftists . . . are astounded that we permit the degree of male chauvinism that abounds."[20]

Old Left Organizational Support

In a sign of the Old Left tradition, assistance came to New York Radical Women as the size of their weekly consciousness-raising meetings outgrew members' small apartments. Carol Hanisch, a founding member of NYRW, had gone to work for the Southern Conference Educational Fund as its New York office manager in 1966, fresh from Civil Rights Movement work in Mississippi. Hanisch was attracted to SCEF because—as SNCC had asked of whites—SCEF attempted to organize whites to join with black people to fight poverty and racism. At Hanisch's request, SCEF allowed NYRW to meet in its New York City office at Broadway and Eleventh Street.

SCEF was established in 1946 to organize against segregation and labor exploitation in the South. The organization had long been harassed by the House Un-American Activities Committee and was on the U.S. attorney general's list of "subversive" organizations. SCEF's directors, Carl and Anne Braden, were legends for bravery in standing up against segregation and political repression, and for the down-to-earth journalism of SCEF's newspaper, the *Southern Patriot*.[21]

In 1954 in Louisville the Bradens purchased a house in a white neighborhood for a black friend and political associate. The house was blown up by racist whites, Carl was fired from his job, and the Bradens were arrested for sedition on the grounds that they were Communists who were deliberately following a Party program to help black people get land in the South on which to establish a Black Nation. Carl was convicted and jailed. Anne's trial was delayed pending the outcome of Carl's appeal, which, eventually, he won.

SCEF support of NYRW meant the group had a free place to meet and office equipment, including a mimeograph machine. With dependable space, the group could more easily publicize weekly meetings, which grew to 50 or 60 participants.[22] After the Miss America Pageant protest in September 1968, the meetings swelled.

Hanisch had been on the SCEF staff for about two years in the summer of 1968 when, after discovering like-minded radical feminists in Gainesville, she submitted a proposal for a new Southern Women's Liberation project. She and Sarachild, close collaborators in New York City and with the Gainesville women, had reason to believe that SCEF would support Women's Liberation without attempting to dictate its policy. Sarachild wrote to Hanisch, "Carl played an important role in raising our consciousness . . . when he encouraged us in our thinking that maybe the woman question really could be the basis for a new mass movement in the country."[23]

Moreover, Carl and Anne Braden believed that women made outstanding radical organizers, and the majority of SCEF's paid staff were female. Additionally, in the mid-1960s SCEF's newspaper, the *Southern Patriot*, included opposition to the oppression of women on its masthead, a point Carl noted with pride (although a look at the 1968 masthead shows that this principle was no longer included).[24]

Hanisch's proposal, the "Freedom for Women" project, said SCEF should "establish its own women's liberation program" or be left "on the sidelines with its mouth hanging open" because "a real and important struggle is beginning."[25] Hanisch declared, "If SCEF does not see the need for this program, then I will have to leave SCEF."[26] The proposal was strong. "Radical women are tired of fighting in a male-dominated movement," Hanisch wrote, and "changing the economic/political system is not automatically going to free us from the domination of men. . . . SCEF . . . must include a program of women's liberation work."[27]

Hanisch saw as one aim and result of the project the building of a mass movement of women as a "leading force in the 'economic/political revolution' while its primary goal is liberation of women from the domination of men."[28] Hanisch proposed to travel the South "raising the consciousness of women" because "women's consciousness must be built like black consciousness has been."[29]

The proposal roiled the four-day SCEF meeting. Braden said he'd "been waiting . . . for a woman to want to organize Southern women" but denounced it as "reactionary" if it did not organize them on "class issues."[30] SCEF did not want feminist issues in the mix, except insofar as this might be necessary to attract women. Hanisch described arguments she'd had with Anne Braden in which Anne had "started in on how women's liberation would free women to work on 'more important' struggles."[31]

At the meeting Carl Braden asked angrily whether "everyone in the room" believed that "private ownership of the means of distribution and production" was at the root of the problem.[32] Hanisch said that when it was clear that her primary interest was to build an independent Women's Liberation Movement, "the lid blew off" and Carl "started . . . calling me and my proposal 'reactionary.'"[33] In the end, SCEF agreed to fund the project for six months on an "exploratory" basis. Anne Braden had voted for a modified form of the proposal, while Carl voted against even the modified exploratory project.[34]

Hanisch was shocked and indignant that Carl called into question her "dedication to the 'greater revolution.'" She saw the vote as disappointingly clarifying that SCEF mainly wanted "a women's liberation program . . . as something to be used to get women involved in other issues."[35] She was surprised to find during the debate that some SCEF staff had a similar view of Black Power. Hanisch told Sarachild, "Most people who profess to understand the black movement do not. . . . they are similarly going to see us as the enemy for disrupting the class struggle."[36]

Meanwhile in Gainesville, Judith Brown, relying on her credibility as a five-year front-line civil rights organizer well known to SCEF, wrote to Carl Braden in support of the project. Brown praised SCEF for insight and endurance and praised Hanisch: "There are pitifully few Carol Hanisch's in this country. . . . Now your Carol Hanisch informs you that a mass-based movement is about to get off the ground. She indicates her willingness to begin organizing. . . . Is SCEF jumping to seize this opportunity? I trust it is."[37]

Unfortunately, Brown's letter arrived after the vote on the project. Carl Braden tersely responded that "SCEF has had women's liberation as part of its program for 30 years."[38] Following the vote, Hanisch wrote to Brown:

> Thank you, thank you, for your encouraging letter! It really lifted my spirits . . . following the SCEF staff meeting. . . . I found the letter you wrote Carl beautiful, sad, and hilarious. I thrill now to your letter "And we are going to move . . . if every established movement group disowns us. . . . We are! . . . we are going to have to sustain *ourselves* . . . every established group *is* going to disown us . . ." Maybe I should make my headquarters Gainesville instead of Louisville.[39]

Brown strongly encouraged an unhappy Hanisch to accept SCEF's support. Brown's rationale for accepting what she clearly considered a compromise provides an insider's view of the state of the new movement in the summer of 1968. "Use SCEF for our movement," Brown wrote; "our movement is not legitimate enough yet to find and provide funds for independent organizers . . . keep this tie."[40] Sarachild wrote to Hanisch, "our complete liberation (as women) can only come from the development of an anti-male supremacist, anti-racist, anti-capitalist force and . . . we might as well try to work together from the beginning."[41]

Hanisch decided to go ahead. The project opened in Gainesville in January 1969, and Hanisch spread the consciousness-raising program to new groups forming around the South. During the project's short life, in an attempt to explain consciousness-raising to SCEF—which wrongly considered it a form of group therapy for specially victimized women—Hanisch wrote a memo to the women on the SCEF staff which later became the article "The Personal Is Political." This was the first written explanation of the concept and of the "Pro-Woman Line." (See chapter 9 for discussion of these concepts.)

SCEF had the Old Left's wisdom about the importance of making, as Anne Braden said, a "*specialized* effort" to gain women as a constituency.[42] But SCEF failed to grasp the extent to which an attack on male supremacy was needed for the mass mobilization of women. SCEF pulled out of the project after only three months, but its financial support allowed Hanisch to focus exclusively on Women's Liberation during its greatest period of theoretical and organizational growth.

Old Left influences were instrumental in organizing early Women's Liberation groups on the West Coast. Gloria Martin and Clara Fraser, two women associated with the Old Left, developed and taught the first Women's Liberation courses at the Free University of Seattle. Martin had been in the Young Communist League as a teenager and then in the Communist Party.[43] Fraser, a twenty-two-year veteran of the Socialist Workers Party and a member of its National Committee, had recently broken from the SWP to found and lead a new national party, the Freedom Socialist Party.[44]

Organizing women was a priority for Fraser, who hoped to bring them into the Freedom Socialists through the courses. Martin shared Fraser's priorities, and in October 1967 Fraser and Martin organized the women attending the Women's Liberation course into Seattle Radical Women.[45] The group challenged male chauvinism in the antiwar movement and organized women into leadership roles in various movement activities.

In the summer of 1968, groups of women broke away from Radical Women to form the Women's Majority Union and Women's Liberation Seattle. The Women's Majority Union established itself as an independent Women's Liberation group, and in December 1968 it published *Lilith*, the West Coast's pioneer Women's Liberation journal.[46] This journal, the first to publish the work of the black Women's Liberation group Poor Black Women, had a national circulation and spread to Europe. Janet Hews, a leader of the new group who had started out in Seattle Radical Women, said that their "free thinking" was being "somewhat stifled" by the "insistence on doctrinaire discipline and program formation" by a minority of the membership of Radical Women.[47] At the bottom, as in the split between SCEF and Hanisch, were political differences over whether abolishing capitalism was sufficient to liberate women or whether a fight against male supremacy was also necessary. This was being argued in Women's Liberation groups across the country.

Lilith argued for an independent movement for the liberation of women, rather than seeing itself as a way to interest women in a Left party. It championed the cause of Valerie Solanas, and it celebrated the birth of *The Bitch*, a political cartoon of a woman whose "mind is growing muscles."[48] *Lilith* raised consciousness about double standards and contradictions that women lived with every day, such as "Women are always playing hard to get" versus "No man likes an easy woman."[49] Fraser opposed the consideration of such "personal" matters as "subjective."[50]

Fraser, like the Bradens, saw women not as secretaries or cooks for the movement but as an important constituency, high on the Left's organizing agenda. In Seattle, the Freedom Socialist Party initiated the early challenges to male supremacy that laid the foundation for Women's Liberation. But as the movement took off, the party was opposed to fighting the oppression of women in its own right.

Women's Liberation Pioneers in the New Left

One of the benefits nascent Women's Liberation organizers gained from their participation in the New Left was the experience of arguing, organizing, marching, and going to jail to get out a perspective that contradicted the one put out by the powers that be. From this they gained the fortitude and skills to start a new movement—a major undertaking.

Before 1968 most Left organizations, New or Old, did not endorse early Women's Liberation (with the notable exception of SNCC). SDS documents at the national level show few women in leadership positions, certainly not as great a percentage as in SNCC, and we read little about women in the New Left who organized thousands of people or wrote columns in national newspapers. However, some of the women who would go on to found the Women's Liberation Movement were doing exactly this.

Jo Freeman's experience in the New Left was at the University of California at Berkeley, where in 1963 she was an officer of SLATE, the radical students' political party. She was the only woman on the negotiating team of the Free Speech Movement that met with Berkeley president Clark Kerr while the students held a police car hostage for thirty-six hours. At the largest of the 1964 sit-ins at Sproul Hall, when police rushed the students and arrested the main speaker, Freeman picked up the microphone and continued the speech until she too was arrested and jailed.

Freeman was arrested three times in the Berkeley protests before she went south with SCLC in 1965. When she helped to found the first Women's Liberation group in 1967, Freeman was a movement veteran. Her movement work earned her incarceration in six different jails in three states—and considerable boldness. "The men in the Free Speech Movement and the Civil Rights Movements had not been able to shut me up," Freeman said.[51]

Dee Ann Pappas's activism began with registering black voters in Baltimore in 1963. She moved on to antiwar civil disobedience on military bases and organized teachers against the war. In 1967 Pappas was working with the Baltimore Defense Committee when she started organizing for Women's Liberation. "We could put thousands of people in the street," said Pappas, recalling the antiwar demonstrations with pride; "my feminist consciousness grew in that context."[52]

Pappas was one of the handful of women who organized the first national meeting of the emerging Women's Liberation Movement in Sandy Springs, Maryland, in August 1968. Starting to work for Women's Liberation, she felt "moved by history. . . . It had to be done, I could do it, and I had to do it."[53] Pappas had learned, she said, "how to organize, go door-to-door, how to call meetings, how to start a group." When she started *Women: A Journal of Liberation*, "at that point I really believed that I was Lenin and the magazine was my *Iskra*, the spark, the tool to organize women in America."[54]

Judith Brown, also a local New Left leader, wrote to Freeman:

I am one of those exceptions . . . I have become, through tenacity and longevity the local "radical." . . . the movement guys are so up tight about female liberation and its espousal by one whom they know is the radical leader anyway (myself) . . . I am threatening because . . . I have organized or helped to organize every extant group here . . . I'm known as a militant person who has always taken a lead in changes in the movement and in getting racked up.[55]

Brown *was* an exception. But she was not a "token woman." She had been "from the beginning" with the Gainesville Band, as the local cadre called their circle of tested movement stalwarts.[56] With the exception of local Black Power leaders, Brown had incurred, by 1968, more jail time and counted more arrests in the previous five years of movement activity than any other Gainesville activist. She was one of the first two University of Florida students arrested for challenging segregation. In the next few years Brown led movement coworkers for academic freedom, in support of Black Power, and then for Women's Liberation. Brown did not feel exceptional among Women's Liberation founders, though. Referring to the women she met at Sandy Springs, Brown wrote Jo Freeman, "Let me tell you something, my sister, this is my reference group."[57]

Marilyn Webb (then Salzman) had risen to national leadership within the New Left by the time she began organizing for Women's Liberation. In the summer of 1967 she was director of Vietnam Teachers in the Schools on the national staff of the Vietnam Summer Project. The project organized more than twenty thousand door-to-door workers who spread opposition to the war on a community-by-community basis.[58] Webb coordinated the recruitment of high school teachers and developed antiwar curricula for them.

That same year Webb organized a Women's Liberation group in Washington, D.C., and later helped pull together the national Women's Liberation meeting in Sandy Springs. She went on to found the nationally distributed Women's Liberation newspaper *Off Our Backs*, the only early journal continuously publishing after four decades. A few years before she started *Off Our Backs*, she had been Washington bureau chief of the Left newspaper the *National Guardian*, where she honed skills that she brought to the feminist newspaper.

In the literature on Women's Liberation, one encounters Webb at a demonstration in Washington, D.C., where movement men greeted her speech for Women's Liberation by shouting, "Take her off the stage and fuck her."[59] Worse than the sexism of men in the audience was the failure of hitherto respected male movement leaders to try to stop the outrageous crowd behavior. Webb was alienated from the antiwar movement.

This experience was not, however, characteristic of Webb's previous five years in the movement. On the whole, Webb considered activists "the smartest people I ever met" and said the New Left gave her a "sense that there were things I could do to make a difference . . . a sense of hope and possibility."[60]

Historian Kirkpatrick Sale described early New Left activists as "extremely bright . . . intellectual . . . prodigious writers . . . they had a vision and they backed it up."[61] Sale had referred to men, but Ruth Rosen observed that female activists were "arguably more" capable.[62] Among the arguably more capable competition was Kathie Sarachild. Sarachild was, early on, a dedicated radical in TOCSIN, a movement group at Harvard, and an editor of the *Harvard Crimson*. From 1962 to 1964 her pathbreaking articles were the first in the Harvard community to expose and oppose increasing U.S. involvement in Vietnam. In 1967, when she went to the first meeting of NYRW, she was a veteran of Mississippi Freedom Summer and dedicating her skills in photography (from her work as a union assistant film editor) to work on the production of anti–Vietnam War films. Well versed in the "woman question," Sarachild's background is an example of the weaving together of Old and New Left.

Naomi Weisstein too was a red diaper baby. She had battled discrimination from faculty and fellow students in graduate school at Harvard to finish first in her class.[63] Weisstein described her life in the New Left then as "driven by a kind of moral force . . . and vision of what the world could be like."[64]

In the spring of 1966, universities across the nation were swept by massive protests against the Vietnam War. At the University of Chicago, students moved into the administration building for five days, beginning a series of confrontations that resulted in the university's ceasing to cooperate with draft boards. Inside the building students set up their own government based on participatory democracy. "We had such feelings of . . . being able to make the new world right there," Weisstein said. "We were setting up the institutions. . . . They were going to be . . . just and generous and democratic and all this was going on while the sexism was going on . . . schizophrenia . . . and yet feeling the ecstasy." By 1967, when she helped found the West Side Group, despite the sexism, Weisstein was a respected antiwar leader, chosen by the SDS chapter at Loyola as its official faculty advisor.[65]

These instances are not representative. The focus here is the formative experiences of particular Women's Liberation founders who, by virtue of being a bit ahead of others, were themselves exceptional. The discussion does not portray the full round of experience of the founders in the New Left where they confronted their share of sexism. Their positive experiences are important not because they were typical, nor because their experiences were exclusively positive, but because they were instrumental in the birth of the Women's Liberation Movement.

Rather than "leaving the Left," for most of its early proponents including the radical feminist militants, organizing the Women's Liberation Movement as a separate branch meant expanding and transforming the Left.[66] These Women's Liberation founders advanced a Left agenda and established credentials as radicals. But if they were taking their rightful place in the Left and achieving their goals, why did they start a movement for Women's Liberation?

According to Sara Evans, the reason was the ever-present male chauvinism that constituted a "threatened loss of new possibility."[67] But is the existence of a threat, however imminent, sufficient explanation for the start of a social movement? Are there not innumerable historical moments at which people threatened with losses simply lose without managing to organize to oppose the threat, much less advance their cause?

In the case of the Women's Liberation Movement, the impetus to start a new movement was not the threatened loss of new possibility. Rather, the impetus was a combination of experiencing new possibilities (the margin of freedom for women in the New Left) and at the same time developing newfound abilities to expand that margin in the movement and in the larger society as well. The margin at once supplied the vision, the thing to be defended and expanded, and the weapons with which to do so.

Vivian Rothstein, an early member of the West Side Group, compared the work of women in the larger society and the margin of opportunity for purposeful work experienced by Women's Liberation founders in the Left: "The movement gave me opportunities that barely existed for women in the larger society—to be a social critic, . . . to stand up to the power structure. . . . In contrast, the primary jobs for women outside the home in those days were in ghettoized female professions—as teachers, nurses, secretaries."[68]

The New Left was fluid enough to give the founders a vision to fight for and the means to do it. Understanding these forces enables us to reexamine the priority the literature has given to sexism as fuel for the movement.

He Kind of Became Active Through Me

The genesis of Women's Liberation is held to have depended, in great part, on "status deprivation" experienced by women in liaisons with men at the top levels of SDS.[69] Historian Ruth Rosen highlights, as a seminal and motivating grievance, women's complaints that their status in the movement depended upon their connection with a man in the SDS "inner circle." While this may well have been the case in the SDS "inner circle," it was not characteristic of women in the New Left who founded the Women's Liberation Movement, the majority of whom were not in the "inner circle."[70] Indeed, many Women's Liberation founders started off as the senior activist in the couple.

When Dee Ann Pappas and her future husband met, she said she "already had a certain level of political consciousness," while he "didn't want anything to do with activism." But, Pappas said, "I was just really adamant and he kind of became active through me . . . I pulled him along."[71]

Judith Brown also married a less experienced activist. She met "Brownie" on a picket line desegregating a restaurant in 1963. Married in 1966, they worked together in the movement. Brownie said he was "awe-struck" by Judith, who "had actually done my most noble and wished-for fantasy— she had been a subsistence worker doing voter registration. . . . She had worked . . . with Pat Due and CORE. . . . I was honored that she . . . married me."[72]

Brownie had deserted from a Marine reserve unit and done his share of antiwar organizing. He was a law clerk at the renowned radical law firm of

William Kunstler and Arthur Kinoy. Although he was catching up, neither Brownie, their activist band, or Judith considered her political standing dependent on his.

Sandra "Casey" Cason was a founding voice for Women's Liberation and the senior activist early in her marriage to future SDS leader Tom Hayden. When they met at a National Student Association conference in 1960, Casey had been in civil rights protests in Austin and committed herself to the newly formed SNCC. Casey was a speaker at the conference, while Tom saw himself as "a student writing about students taking action"—students such as Casey.[73] Tom interviewed Casey for his campus newspaper and quoted her eloquent remarks. Tom was not yet an SDS member when he and Casey married. The SDS gathering in Port Huron, Michigan, which signaled his leadership in the movement in 1962, was still a year away.

Tom joined SDS and the couple moved to Atlanta because of Casey's work in SNCC. So Tom set up an SDS office in Atlanta. His identity and moral authority as an activist who "put his body on the line," as the saying went, was developed on Casey's turf—the southern Civil Rights Movement. In the dangerous protests of 1961, Tom went to McComb, Mississippi, when local black NAACP leader Herbert Lee was murdered by white state legislator E. H. Hurst. A photograph of Tom on the ground being beaten by a white attacker went out over the wire services. He was, he said, "confronting commitment."[74] From this base, into which he was drawn by Casey, Tom emerged as an SDS leader.

That fall, they moved to Ann Arbor and Tom began graduate school. To pay the rent, Casey went to work as a secretary. Away from her beloved SNCC it was hard, she said, to maintain her "strong sense" of herself.[75] The couple split up that winter, and Casey returned to the South. "Tom and I held together as a couple well in the South. . . . We were close to SNCC," Casey observed.[76] She had begun as the senior activist in the couple, but away from her own movement base, despite the fact that she paid the bills, she lost power in the relationship.[77] Instead of taking her status from her husband, Casey enabled Tom's status to grow. But her status did not grow with the rise in his.

Women's Liberation founder Pam Allen experienced a similar reversal. Like Casey Hayden, Pam Parker was the senior activist when she and Robert Allen married. She "was so well known for her activism," wrote Evans, "her new husband joked about being 'Mr. Pam Parker.'"[78] In the next two years, Robert, an African American activist, took increasingly important responsibilities in the black draft resistance movement. Pam supported the family and felt that others considered her Robert's "appendage."[79]

Ann Weills (then Scheer), cofounder of an early Women's Liberation group on the West Coast, also began marriage as the senior activist.[80] Weills was the protégée of the Hallinan family, next-door neighbors in Marin County, California. She was a tomboy playmate of the six Hallinan boys whose mother, Vivian, was a leader in Women Strike for Peace and whose father, Vincent, was the attorney for Harry Bridges, head of the Left-led International Longshoremen's and Warehousemen's Union. After graduating from high school, Weills joined the W.E.B. DuBois Club, a youth group of the Communist Party. DuBois Club members formed a core in the Bay Area Coalition to End Discrimination where Weills began civil rights work. When she met Robert Scheer, "I was the 'heavy.' I had already been arrested and jailed," Weills said, while "he was a beatnik." Scheer courted Weills by going to her trial. "He definitely deferred to me," she said.[81] That changed as Scheer developed as a movement journalist and Ann ended up with ever-increasing unshared responsibilities for child care.

Thus several Women's Liberation founders were or had been in relationships in which they were the senior activist. They did not rise in the New Left because of these relationships. On the contrary, some, like Hayden, Allen, and Weills, started out as the senior activist in the couple but saw their own status diminish as their husbands became more influential. Unlike many of their sisters in the larger society, the liaisons of these women included respect for political commitment from men who followed their leadership. For Hayden, Weills, and Brown, such deference was a part of the courtship.

Most Women's Liberation founders did not make it into SDS's "inner circle." But far from being the most oppressed women in the New Left, they appear, as leading organizers in their own right, to have been among the least oppressed.[82]

Institutional Support by the New Left

The New Left provided support that helped get the emerging Women's Liberation Movement off the ground. In the fall of 1968 Marilyn Webb used her influence to get support for a "woman's project" from the Institute for Policy Studies, including stipends for three organizers and related expenses for the first conference of the emerging movement in Lake Villa, Illinois.[83]

Support also came from "free universities" modeled after SNCC's Freedom Schools. In 1965 and 1966 free schools were organized across the country as part of a New Left mission to make relevant and "redefine the vocation of the intellectual."[84] The free schools were the site of Women's Liberation classes that were building blocks for the earliest groups in Chicago, New Orleans, Seattle, and Gainesville.

Women's Liberation workshops and meetings at New Left conferences also built the constituency for the emerging movement. A workshop on Hayden and King's "Sex and Caste" at a national SDS conference in December 1965 generated feminist momentum. In the fall of 1965 Heather Booth (then Tobis) was a freshman at the University of Chicago in an introductory social science course taught by Richard Flacks. Flacks, Booth said, told her about "Sex and Caste" and "encouraged me to go" to the conference.[85] Marilyn Webb also attended the SDS workshop before going on to teach Women's Liberation classes in Washington, D.C., and to start D.C.'s first Women's Liberation group. The workshop played the same role in Cathy Barrett's initiation of a course on women at the Free School in New Orleans. Her course was a forerunner of the group that formed there, which was among the earliest in the South.

Before the 1965 SDS workshop provided the first public discussion of "Sex and Caste," the document had reached a much smaller circle. Now "Sex and Caste" was distributed with other conference papers to approximately 360 attendees from sixty-six SDS chapters around the nation.

In 1966, for the first time, plans for the national SDS conference included child care. Child care provisions were announced in hopes that "This will . . . resolve the age-old debate about who should stay home. Equal amounts of time will be spent [in child care] by both parents."[86]

By 1967, New Left conferences saw two pivotal Women's Liberation workshops, one at the national SDS conference in Ann Arbor in June, the other at the National Conference for a New Politics in Chicago that September. At the June SDS conference, the women's workshop brought to the convention floor an analysis of women's oppression and an agenda for action that included free public child care, repeal of abortion laws, and shared housework.[87] And the workshop at the NCNP, as we have seen, prompted the founding of the West Side Group in Chicago. Coverage of the NCNP in the *Guardian* also brought new strong feminists into NYRW.

Women's meetings at New Left conferences were vital to the formation of the new movement because its pioneer organizers recruited there for the earliest Women's Liberation groups. A women's caucus at a regional SDS conference supplied the first recruits for the first meeting of NYRW. NYRW cofounder Pam Allen said, "Shulie . . . found out about the meeting and we'd planned our first women's meeting so I could announce it there."[88] According to Allen, when she proposed independence the women argued against it. Still, when the meeting ended, six women came up to explain that they too were hoping to find others interested in organizing an independent movement. Allen recruited them to the meeting, thus adding Anne Koedt to NYRW. Koedt's work would prove essential to the formation of the new movement.

Women forming Gainesville Women's Liberation, the South's first Women's Liberation group, used conferences of the Southern Student Organizing Committee.[89] Judith Brown led consciousness-raising sessions at SSOC conferences which inspired Women's Liberation groups in Sarasota and St. Petersburg, Florida. Brown wrote, "Hearteningly . . . from our little presentation at SSOC . . . *two* new groups have formed. They want us to come immediately. . . . After we gave our presentation, a young woman cornered us and said, 'OK how do I start a group?'"[90]

The Pivotal Support of Men

Perhaps least touched upon in the literature were men on the Left who "helped spread word of women's liberation," as historian Ruth Rosen put it. But Rosen stipulated that such help came "only through repeated derision and ridicule."[91] The examples of ridicule Rosen supplied were repeated many times as Women's Liberation founders raised the woman question. There were, however, instances in which men spread word of Women's Liberation with notable effect and did not frame it derisively.

SNCC leader James Forman supported Women's Liberation directly and also helped to promote the leadership of women in SNCC like Ruby Doris Robinson and Zoharah Simmons. He trained Ruby Doris Robinson when she was his assistant in the Atlanta SNCC office and supported her election to his position as executive secretary when he stepped down. He was also instrumental in Simmons's assuming directorship of what became the Amazon Project in Laurel, Mississippi.

At the least, Forman encouraged and supported what was probably the earliest influential action in the founding of Women's Liberation—the women's sit-in strike for equality that Robinson led in the Atlanta office in the spring of 1964. Forman also said that he encouraged discussion of the feminist paper at SNCC's Waveland conference that same year.[92]

His support of Women's Liberation, consistent throughout its founding years, can be seen in the second half of the decade when, as Frances Beal said, he "threw his weight behind" the establishment of the SNCC Black Women's Liberation Committee.[93] "This made others" support it as well, Beal said, noting that "mostly men attended that staff meeting in New York City."[94] He aided the TWWA by developing revolutionary theory workshops to use in political education work. Also, Beal said she found Forman's "belief in women's equality as a legitimate concern" personally sustaining.[95]

More often than not, supportive men had roots in the Old Left where they learned about the "woman question." This was the case with longtime feminist W. E. B. DuBois, who grew increasingly radical in the post-WWII period and, in the last few years of his life, joined the Communist Party. Probably the best-known black feminist influenced by DuBois was award-winning writer and activist Lorraine Hansberry. Hansberry was also influenced by black leaders Paul Robeson and Louis Burnham, for whom she worked as associate editor of Robeson's newspaper *Freedom*. DuBois also influenced Patricia Robinson, who had been his neighbor.

Jesse Lemisch, who consistently and publicly denounced sexism in the New Left, was a "red diaper baby." Lemisch's understanding of male chauvinism came in part from his mother, a woman he "totally respected and admired."[96] His wife, Naomi Weisstein, called Lemisch's mother "an oil-burning communist, tough as a brick, and pretty good on 'male chauvinism.'"[97] The couple conferred with her about sexism as the woman question began to heat up the New Left.

Richard Flacks, Heather Booth's professor at the University of Chicago, recognized in Booth a budding feminist. Hayden and King's paper had been circulating less than a month, but Flacks had read it and thought it was important. "Oh yes, I knew there was a woman question," Flacks reflected. "I was raised as a red diaper baby."[98] Equality for women was part of life at Camp Wo-chi-ca, the experimental Communist summer camp Flacks attended. One summer the twelve-year-old Flacks saw antisexist lessons brought to life in a play produced at the camp's theatre, as a counselor taught campers how to create theatre out of everyday camp doings. A group of boys had protested the camp's policy of sexually integrated ball teams, and this was developed into a theatrical production in which the balls, bats, and gloves went on strike until the boys let the girls play. Years later, Flacks brought these antisexist values into SDS.

Bill Price, a reporter for the *Guardian*, understood that the phenomenon he described at the National Conference for a New Politics was male chauvinism. Price, then in his fifties, had learned about sexism in the Old Left. Price knew his insight was unusual. As he put it, "Another pattern appeared, too, visible most easily to older veterans of campaigns against male chauvinism. This was the minimal role played by young women."[99] Price denounced the "pattern" and gave as an example women activists doing the clerical work at the conference yet having "no visible role on the convention floor."[100]

Unlike most young people coming of age in the 1950s, these men needed no introduction to the concept of male chauvinism. When women did most of the housework and cooking, or male organizers tried to seduce a new female recruit, they knew that was male chauvinist. Compared with most of the New Left who were not red diaper babies, had never heard of a "woman question" and did not think twice about stereotypical sexual behavior all around them, these men were able to support the Women's Liberation Movement.

Price met Shulamith Firestone at the NCNP. When she moved to New York from Chicago shortly afterwards, they stayed in touch. Meanwhile, Kathie Sarachild read Price's article and began looking for him. When she found him, he put her in touch with Firestone and Pam Allen, who were recruiting for the newly forming NYRW, the nation's second Women's Liberation group and the first in New York City. Carol Hanisch too found NYRW through Price. He introduced her to Firestone and she became a key member. Hanisch said she had "good discussions with Bill, [who] had a consciousness of the woman question."[101] Thus Bill Price spread word of the nascent movement to some of the very women whose work would be fundamental in its creation.

A handful of men in the New Left defended the emerging movement in public letters, talks, and courses, although other men viewed a male supporter as a traitor to his sex. Price, for example, said that the *Guardian* editor disapproved of his profeminist coverage of the NCNP and began excluding him from the paper's staff meetings.[102] Naomi Weisstein recalled that her husband Jesse was beaten up by "some SDS asshole" for advocating Women's Liberation.[103] This did not deter Lemisch, who went on to develop courses on Women Liberation and to fire off angry letters to editors protesting male chauvinism in the Left press. In July 1968 he wrote to the *Guardian* protesting a cartoon that approvingly depicted "The Movement" as a macho male about to rape a fawning female labeled "Establishment." If the movement favorably portrayed itself as a rapist, Lemisch wrote, it had "nothing to contribute to human progress" and "deserves to be . . . brought to a dead stop."[104] His public advocacy for Women's Liberation appears to have begun when he and Weisstein married and they gave talks around Chicago about equality in marriage.

Perhaps the most striking instance of men in the Left spreading word of Women's Liberation in these critical years was the workshop on *The Second Sex* organized by Ed Richer, a serious Beauvoir advocate who sought to foment a feminist revolt. Richer got his wish when his workshop turned out to be the birthplace of the Florida Paper.

Support for Women's Liberation and virulent male chauvinism coexisted within the Left. So it was that in 1967 male radicals respected Naomi Weisstein as SDS faculty advisor even while an SDS member beat up her husband Jesse for his feminism. Sexism and feminism coexisted within the same man. Ed Richer advocated Beauvoir. At the same time, however, he used male privilege to take advantage of women in traditional roles.

Thus in the prefeminist mid-1960s, key organizers of the incipient movement were encouraged to pursue the woman question by feminist men. These events were not typical, they were generative. Little known compared to the wide currency of the hoots at Webb or Carmichael's quip, they were pivotal because of the critical moment at which these men acted, and because the women they influenced went on to found the new movement.

Women's Liberation in the Left Media

Attention to the oppression of women and to Women's Liberation in the Left media was minimal and often sexist. Rather than a broad review, the focus here is on the few venues that employed feminist pioneers or published work that influenced the rise of Women's Liberation in its start-up years. The press of the black Left appears to have been a bit better on the woman question than that of the predominantly white Left, perhaps because in the 1950s and much of the 1960s it was more firmly rooted in the Old Left.

For example, Paul Robeson's journal *Freedom*, which came out from 1951 through 1955, did not espouse an explicitly feminist view. But *Freedom* routinely highlighted women's leadership in the broad peace and justice struggle and did so without the cheesecake or double entendre that was ubiquitous in the period. In *Freedom* women were treated as serious activists with important work to do beyond that of wives and mothers—in labor unions, in world affairs, and as "great fighters for . . . people's rights."[105]

Black feminist Alice Childress's regular column "Conversation from Life" brilliantly put forth radical political positions on the issues of the day in the words of a fictional black domestic worker named Mildred talking to her friend Marge.[106] Mildred shared politics with Marge rather than recipes or gossip. Lorraine Hansberry was an ardent feminist by at least age twenty-three, when she was associate editor of *Freedom*.[107] She covered everything from foreign affairs to subscriptions, and wrote reviews of the plays of Childress, who was an influence on her.[108]

In 1961 a collective including black feminists Esther Cooper Jackson and Dorothy Burnham came out with *Freedomways*. According to longtime member of the Freedomways collective Jean Carey Bond, they purposefully took the word "freedom" to show a connection with Robeson's journal.[109] Described as a "veritable Who's Who of arts and letters—as well as workers and students,"[110] *Freedomways* went a step further than *Freedom* to publish talks, poetry, fiction, and political commentary by African American women characterized by Jackson as "pioneers in criticizing degrading and stereotypical portrayals of women."[111]

Before 1968 contributors of feminist work to the journal included poet Beulah Richardson, founding *Freedomways* member Augusta Strong, Alice Childress, poet and novelist Sarah E. Wright, and Lorraine Hansberry. In 1965 Wright, for example, offered a scathing critique of the portrayal of women in literature as "mere sexual animals" and "strangling mother[s]" by African American and white male writers.[112] Wright called such portrayals "attacks on women" fueled by the desire for "popular recognition of what is fictitiously called 'manhood.'"[113] Childress refuted accusations that black women emasculated black men, and she defended black women's strength. "Facing the world alone makes a woman strong," Childress said.[114]

Freedomways also published international calls for the "emancipation of women." A report on the first Afro-Asian Women's Conference in Cairo in 1961 said that women in anticolonial struggles had developed "new consciousness" and would not endure "shameful discrimination because of color or sex."[115]

A black radical journal, the *Liberator*, describing itself as "the voice of the Afro American protest movement in the United States and the Liberation

Movement of Africa" began publishing in 1961.[116] The journal sold the works of Alice Childress, Lorraine Hansberry, and Simone de Beauvoir through its Book Service and published letters to the editor from female readers critical of male chauvinism on its pages.

In May 1966 the *Liberator* took up the allegations of a black matriarchy and its emasculation of black males. The issue ignited a firestorm of debate which by 1970 saw the *Liberator* denouncing Women's Liberation. An article by Louise Moore, vice president of the Domestic Personal Service Workers, initiated the debate.[117] Moore told black men to fight their own oppressor— the white man—rather than taking out frustrations with racism on black women. She had been helped with the article by Patricia Robinson and had discussed her ideas with members of Poor Black Women.

In "Afro-American Woman: Growth Deferred" Betty Frank Lomax agreed with Moore, saying, "the black man, frustrated by white america, turns inward to a perverted form of male supremacy in his relationship with the Black woman . . . [which] is just as immoral as white supremacy, in that it prevents the female from . . . realizing her full potential."[118]

In "Sisters—Stop Castrating the Black Man!" Evelyn Rodgers called upon black people to "apply our own definitions and meaning to such reports as the Moynihan Report rather than accept their evaluation."[119] But Rodgers herself criticized black women for castrating black men. Later Jean Carey Bond and Patricia Peery in "Has the Black Male Been Castrated?" argued that the "myth of Black male emasculation" was "so successfully popularized" "through the *The Negro Family: The Case for National Action*, by Daniel Patrick Moynihan—that even blacks have swallowed his assumptions . . . hook line and sinker."[120]

In an article titled "Black Men vs. Black Women," Moore wrote, "just recently I was forced to realize who my immediate oppressor really was; it was men—Black men. I can truly say I was shocked and sickened for I have loved my Black man, my race, my people."[121] Moore had realized, she said, that although she considered herself a revolutionary, she had not been applying a radical standard to relations with men because she had "overlook[ed] too much and accept[ed] too little for what is our human right as women, wives, and mothers."[122]

Subsequent issues published vehement letters for and against Moore's position. In October the *Liberator* carried a supportive letter from "Two Black Sisters" in Mount Vernon.[123] They did not give names but wrote very much in the style of Poor Black Women. Since Poor Black Women in Mount Vernon had exchanged ideas with Moore on the first article, it is likely that they followed the debate. After that, the series of articles by Moore stopped.

Interestingly, the August 1970 issue of the *Black Panther* carried the new Panther position in support of Women's Liberation.[124] The next month, the September *Liberator* appeared to respond to the Panthers with a rhetorically headlined article asking if Women's Liberation was "A New Cop-Out on the Black Struggle."[125]

The *Liberator* stopped publishing in 1971. *Freedomways* continued through 1985 with support for Women's Liberation. Important black Women's Liberation material by Shirley Chisholm, Angela Davis, Linda LaRue, Johnnetta Cole, and Kathleen Cleaver, among others, also came out in the *Black Scholar*, which began publishing in 1969. *Palante*, the newspaper of the radical Puerto Rican party the Young Lords, was better on Women's Liberation than most of the Left press. This was, perhaps, because the Women's Liberation Movement was strong by 1969 when *Palante* began publishing.

The predominantly white Left press provided needed publicity for Women's Liberation on the one hand and derision on the other. In city after city, signals of feminist protest in the New Left press brought together the new movement's founding organizers. In 1967 and 1968 Brown and Jones worked on the Florida Paper in Gainesville in secret until the snippet in *New Left Notes* about Dee Ann Pappas's planned journal led Brown out of isolation. In Boston, Roxanne Dunbar and Dana Densmore placed an ad in the *Avatar*, a local counterculture newspaper: "ANNOUNCING: Formation of the FEMALE LIBERATION FRONT FOR HUMAN LIBERATION."[126] The ad brought eight women to the first meeting of Cell 16, the first Women's Liberation group in Boston and one of a half dozen in the nation.

The alternative media also publicized early Women's Liberation literature. In July 1968 the *Guardian* reviewed NYRW's groundbreaking journal *Notes from the First Year* and the *Voice of the Women's Liberation Movement*. Pandora, the pseudonymous (male) *Guardian* reviewer, noted, "A women's liberation movement is developing. . . . unlike previous efforts . . . this movement will not be denied."[127]

This publicity gave early Women's Liberation organizers the advantage of circulation to numbers far greater than they could yet reach themselves. "Sex and Caste" was published in the radical pacifist monthly magazine *Liberation* in 1966, bringing it to ten thousand readers.[128] Mary King observed that this "increased by a quantum leap the number of people circulating it."[129] In

July 1968 when the *Guardian* reviewed the *Voice of the Women's Liberation Movement* and *Notes from the First Year*, thirty thousand *Guardian* readers learned how to subscribe to the first Women's Liberation newsletter, which at the time reached a mailing list of fewer than six hundred.[130] In October 1968 the *Guardian* published Pam Allen's critique of the new movement, and those readers learned that a manifesto from Florida had caused a national debate by calling for a Women's Liberation Movement independent of the New Left.[131] *Voice* editor Jo Freeman wrote Allen, "The *Guardian* readership is a source we should reach."[132]

Alternative radio also helped spread word of the growing movement. On 5 May 1968 black activist Julius Lester, an advocate of Women's Liberation, interviewed Allen on his program *Conversation* on WBAI, the New York City affiliate of the progressive Pacifica Foundation.[133] WBAI shared programs with Pacifica stations KPFA in the San Francisco Bay area and KPFK in Los Angeles, reaching hundreds of thousands of listeners. In the interview, Allen explained that the new movement was organizing all-female groups to confront male chauvinism on the Left and in the larger society. Lester responded with understanding: "Everything that you are going to say is going to spark a response from men that is very similar to the response that whites had at first to black power."[134] The newly forming groups circulated the interview as a pamphlet.

The Left was the first among a very few institutions to publicize accusations of sexism against itself. In April 1967 *New Left Notes*—which was, after all, the SDS newspaper—circulated to a membership estimated betweeen fifty and one hundred thousand[135] and published charges against SDS by one of its high-ranking female staff members, SDS regional traveler Jane Adams. Adams's article pointed out, "As long as almost all the organizers and staff are male," SDS was treating women "like second class citizens."[136]

In November 1967 *New Left Notes* published, as an article, a letter headlined "To the Women of the Left" from the newly formed West Side Group in Chicago. The letter urged the many thousands of female readers to organize for Women's Liberation independently of the Left. This was needed, the Chicago group argued, because as women who worked in SDS "sought to apply the principles of justice, equality . . . and dignity which we learned from the movement to the lives we lived as part of the movement, [we came] up against a solid wall of male chauvinism."[137] Thus SDS not only criticized itself in its own newspaper; it also invited female readers to work outside the organization.

Perhaps the most remarkable case of the Left spreading word of Women's Liberation at its own expense was the distribution of the Florida Paper by SSOC and the New England Free Press.

The Florida Paper criticized New Left hero Fidel Castro and the whole New Left, including the exciting leaders of the recent weeklong "siege" of Columbia University. It attacked male leaders at Columbia for asking the women to cook for the demonstrators and Castro for what amounted to the same thing. Brown called a radical male lover or coworker the "most immediate oppressor . . . the foreman on the big plantation of maleville."[138] The attack was unparalleled, and the Left credentials of its authors were impeccable. Moreover, Jones and Brown were married to men with outstanding activist credentials who publicly supported Women's Liberation. This made the paper's critique all the more difficult to dismiss.

Brown had not intended to distribute the paper through New Left channels.[139] But she was enthusiastic about SSOC bringing out the paper. "SSOC [has] committed itself to the considerable expense of reproducing our paper, adding it to their mailing list, and sending it out on request to anybody," she wrote to Carol Hanisch.[140] The New England Free Press sold the Florida Paper at a far lower price than earlier editions and advertised it widely, making it more readily available than ever.

NYRW's Notes from the First Year was no less critical of male chauvinism than the Florida Paper. Moreover, Notes, while clearly anticapitalist, identified male supremacy as women's primary target of struggle. Notes editors refused New Left offers of publication. In October 1968 NYRW declined an Institute for Policy Studies offer to produce Notes in bulk for the first national Women's Liberation conference.[141] NYRW had no more money than the other early groups. What NYRW did have, however, was the free use of SCEF's mimeograph machine. So it was that the most scathing critiques of male chauvinism in the Left were in one case distributed by the Left press and, in the other, printed on its equipment.

After the protest of the Miss America Pageant in September 1968, the mainstream press could not get enough of Women's Liberation.[142] Also, exponentially proliferating Women's Liberation groups started their own publications to spread the word of theoretical debates, meetings, and more.

This turn represented a political shift from fighting male chauvinism within the New Left. Women's Liberation groups put out their own newspapers and used mainstream publishing houses and newspapers, not only because it had become possible to do so, but because they now sought a mass constituency.

Perspectives on Support for Women's Liberation on the Left

Women's Liberation pioneers used openings on the Left between 1965 and 1968 to lay the foundation for the new movement. The openings were pivotal because of the power of the ideas that were spread; because the women who first pushed through the openings were among Women's Liberation's prime movers; and because the Left was almost the sole provider of meeting and publishing space.

But the significance of the openings and sometimes support is distorted by its successes. On the one hand, improvements in equality for women and public consciousness of sexism today magnify the severity of male chauvinism on the Left in the 1960s. Thus the treatment of women by male movement colleagues appears disproportionately sexist by today's standards, whereas in those prefeminist years, bad as it was, it was often slightly better than the norm in the wider society. On the other hand, openings and support on the Left in the 1960s appear insignificant compared with what we have come to expect today from the larger society.

How unimportant an opportunity to present a paper on some gender-related issue seems today when thousands of such papers have been presented at hundreds of conferences for as long as young women can remember. How important can a single recruit to a feminist organization appear, or a debate over discrimination against women, when there are dozens of such organizations, and debates over sex discrimination routinely occur in legislatures and courtrooms? As ubiquitous as women's broad public participation in society is now, just so normal was women's absence from such activity in the mid-1960s. "Sex class" was, to paraphrase Shulamith Firestone in 1970, "so deep as to be invisible."[143]

Understanding the importance of the Left to feminism's rebirth requires understanding its context from several perspectives. First, as has been said, aside from a conference on the Left, in 1965 there were few venues in which sexism was debated.[144] Even rarer were those that allowed critiques of sexism within the very institution putting on the conference. Moreover, in 1965, students in most college courses were not informed of new feminist work, much less encouraged to pursue it, as Richard Flacks encouraged Heather Booth.

These seemingly small incidents—the student referred to the workshop, the new recruit from an SDS meeting—were important because each case positioned a prime mover of Women's Liberation to move. When Kathie Sarachild found Price's article in the *Guardian*, for example, and when Judith

Brown saw Pappas's announcement, they were ripe for Women's Liberation leadership. For these women, prepared by family traditions of feminism and radicalism and infused with the power and brilliance of grassroots organizing in the Civil Rights Movement, the article and the announcement provided the stimulus to take the next bold step.

When recruiting at the SDS meeting brought Anne Koedt into NYRW, a nascent leader was positioned to come into her own. Within a year Koedt would write "The Myth of the Vaginal Orgasm," a brief essay that made public and exposed by simple logic the unnamed experiences of millions of women. She argued that vaginal orgasm was a physiological impossibility and that "frigidity has generally been defined by men as the failure of women to have vaginal orgasms."[145] "Women," Koedt said, "have . . . been defined sexually in terms of what pleases men." The article alerted thousands of sexually active young women, recently freed from fear of pregnancy by the pill, that what they secretly worried was a personal "hang-up" was a form of sexual exploitation. Koedt called for "new guidelines which take into account mutual sexual enjoyment . . . new techniques."[146] These ideas so radically changed the nation's sexual landscape that in today's milieu of vibrator toys, pop songs about women masturbating, and tips in popular magazines on how to come to clitoral orgasm, it is difficult to grasp the power of Koedt's argument then. Indeed, we are so surrounded by Women's Liberation successes that its giant steps before 1968 do not appear impressive.

9

Making the Women's Liberation Movement

IN 1967 AND 1968, as the Women's Liberation Movement formed, the idea that a mass-based movement of women was both possible and needed was, as has been indicated, neither obvious nor well accepted. A number of views contended for influence in several important debates: Should there be a mass movement rather than a lobby, a vanguard, a legalistic approach, caucuses within the Black Freedom Movement and the Left? Should men be in the Women's Liberation Movement, or were men among women's oppressors? Was capitalism, racism, male supremacy, or some combination of all three the main target of the Women's Liberation Movement? Were women complicit in their subordination? Should antihierarchical structures be established in a women's movement? These questions were hotly debated without movement-wide agreement.

In 1967 women seeking to eliminate male chauvinism in the movements in which they participated were beginning to win some of their demands, such as the provision of child care at conferences. They were also demanding that child care, abortion, an end to forced sterilization, an analysis of women's oppression, and other specifically women's liberation issues be added to the social change agenda of the Black Freedom Movement and the Left. Their position was based, in part, on theories that the capitalist economic system and/or the colonial status of African Americans were the basis of women's oppression, and therefore sexism was a proper target of movements against white supremacy and capitalism. By 1968 these demands evolved into the position that, along with racism and the Vietnam War, sexism deserved not just inclusion but high priority on the agenda of the radical movement.

After caucusing, disrupting, and issuing demands, in 1967 some women active in the New Left had begun forming independent anticapitalist women's groups such as the West Side Group and Berkeley Women's Liberation. These groups argued that the war and Wall Street were women's liberation issues because, like male chauvinism, they helped to maintain the capitalist system, which in the end was the cause of male domination.

Women opposing this view argued that in order to end male supremacy in the whole society, as well as in the radical movement, a mass movement of women as an independent power base was needed to fight sexism directly and immediately. As radicals they opposed capitalism, but they pointed out that women in socialist countries had not achieved freedom from male domination.

While white radical feminists often pointed to male chauvinism in the Soviet Union or Cuba, Patricia Robinson found material by African feminists "going at male supremacy" of the anticolonialist African men trying to build socialism in the newly independent nations. Poor Black Women studied a letter from Effa Okupa in Nigeria who complained that "Africa is still a man's paradise. . . . African men talk socialism but practice oligarchy and dictatorship."[1]

Poor Black Women began taking a feminist turn in 1966. This can be seen in the letter its members (they did not give names but signed simply as "black sisters") sent to the *Liberator* in support of columnist Louise Moore's article that named black men as black women's "immediate" oppressor. By mid-1967 Poor Black Women was exchanging letters arguing with "middle class nationalist" women who failed to confront men on male supremacy.[2]

By mid-1968, the debate within the New Left was shifting toward an independent movement. In September 1968 Pam Allen wrote to Judith Brown in Gainesville, "I have . . . seen a significant change in the attitude of many SDS women regarding the idea of an independent movement. They are no longer hostile."[3] Still, the question of where to aim the movement remained.

Poor Black Women held that black women must first fight white supremacy and male supremacy and then join together with poor and working-class whites to take on capitalism. They explained this sequence in "Letter to a North Vietnamese Sister from an Afro-American Woman": "smashing the myths supporting white and male supremacy," then "working together . . . to-ward smashing imperialism and capitalism."[4]

Brown argued that, for a time at least, men were the enemy, whereas Pam Allen saw capitalism as the most immediate source of women's domination by men. In New York, although Allen and Shulamith Firestone worked to-gether to organize the nation's second group, they differed on this question, with Firestone and Anne Koedt leading those who named male supremacy as the new movement's primary target.

The first and second national Women's Liberation meetings exemplify forward motion despite unsettled debates over the movement's target. The women's desire for freedom was more important than their differences over whom or what was in the way of it. Of the twenty women who came together in August in Sandy Springs, Maryland, at the first national meeting, most held that capitalism should be the target of the Women's Liberation Move-ment. The question was fiercely debated and there was no agreement. None-theless, their differences starkly before them, they plunged into planning the first national conference for November 1968.

In Gainesville, organizers of Women's Liberation were divided on the is-sue of men as a target of the movement, and once even came to blows over it. Yet a few months after they had thrown punches at each other in a politi-cal argument, the women in the two groups met to develop and deliver a "Declaration of Continued Independence" to Gainesville's New Left.[5] The declaration stated:

> Women's liberation has been used in recent Left meetings . . . as a polit-ical football. . . . We demand that SDS, YSA, and similar groups recog-nize that women's liberation is a totally separate movement of women whose goal is to aid [in ending] our own oppression. . . . We are not a part of any existing male group or movement.[6]

Because they were in agreement on the need for an independent movement, they worked together to organize one.

"Sisterhood Is Powerful" and "Consciousness-Raising": Ideas That Built the Movement

Advocates for a mass Women's Liberation Movement stressed political soli-darity, a union of women many millions strong, to put power behind femi-nist demands embodied in the slogan Sisterhood Is Powerful. To organize women and to develop new theory based on their experience, its advocates came up with "consciousness-raising." This program would develop their own and other women's awareness that they were members of an oppressed group—"female class consciousness," as its originators referred to it.[7]

Sisterhood Is Powerful and consciousness-raising have been revised many times since their original articulation and movement-building use in the late 1960s. Perhaps it will clarify these ideas to say what, at that time, they did not mean. Sisterhood Is Powerful did not mean, as later versions have suggested, a sense of female community or female culture based on universal and essential "female" values. Neither did it mean spiritual bonding among women, or nonhierarchical organizational or intellectual processes based on traditional "female" values.[8] Sarachild, who came up with the phrase Sisterhood Is Powerful, explained, "People don't seem to realize that solidarity means militant unity not this lovey dovey, Emily Post sisterhood."[9] The idea was not to deny or gloss over race and class-based divisions and priorities with appeals to behave in a sisterly manner. Rather, the point was that women unified against their mutual oppressor would gain power to control their lives.

Similarly, consciousness-raising was not defined by its developers as an apolitical therapeutic process that, as later proponents held, would "give individual women tools with which to go forward in their own lives."[10] Indeed, it meant precisely the opposite, because it was conceived specifically to foster the understanding that problems were collective—not individual.

Studying the original sources of Sisterhood Is Powerful and consciousness-raising reveals how revised versions of the concepts differed significantly from the original meanings. In the original form, both of these concepts embody and expand upon influences from the Black Freedom Movement, Simone de Beauvoir, and the Left. There are clear trails of transmission of these concepts from such sources.

Sisterhood Is Powerful and consciousness-raising were carefully crafted by their developers. The right ideas at the right historical moment, these concepts prevailed over others because they excavated from women themselves the actual conditions women faced. Participants learned from consciousness-raising that problems they had been trying to overcome as individuals were shared with many other women. Thus they were "sex-class" problems, as Shulamith Firestone later called them.[11] Once women saw this, they saw the point of working collectively to change social conditions, instead of relying primarily on individual strategies.

"I think we have a lot more to do just in the area of raising our own consciousness"

Consciousness-raising was a method of creating the female equivalent of the Marxist concept of working-class consciousness. Poor Black Women called their feminist consciousness-raising sessions "systematic self-criticism," a process of self-examination done with other women.[12] They did not say why they chose the term "self-criticism," but Rosario Morales, who described herself as a "feminist communist and Puerto Rican independentist," called "criticism and self-criticism" a "more congenial name" for consciousness-raising whose "universalization" was a "great achievement of the Chinese cultural revolution."[13] Given the worldwide scope of Patricia Robinson's revolutionary study and contacts, it is likely that the Cultural Revolution in China was the source of Poor Black Women's decision to call their consciousness-raising learning process "systematic self-criticism."

Joyce (last name not given), a member of the Mount Vernon branch of Poor Black Women, described how it worked: "you have to examine yourself inside and out. . . . a lot of times you . . . don't like what you see. . . . But, you know, after you get started, you're not going to be alone. That's the wonderful thing about it."[14] Joyce said that Louise Moore, the head of the Domestic Workers Union who had written the inflammatory radical feminist article in the *Liberator*, had been participating in systematic self-criticism sessions with Poor Black Women.

As it was developed in late 1967 and early 1968 in NYRW, consciousness-raising owed the Old Left for the concept of class consciousness and the Black Freedom Movement for the concept of black consciousness. Anne Forer proposed the idea of women telling their experiences in an NYRW meeting soon after she joined.[15] Forer said that she understood that workers were oppressed as a group, but that she had only just begun thinking about women that way. After asking women in the group to give their experiences, she began to do this herself. She spoke about feeling that she never measured up to all the ways women were supposed to be attractive. She gave examples of how she had played dumb, faked niceness, gone on diets, and used the latest makeup. The women in the group recognized their own struggles. Forer had raised everyone's feminist consciousness.

The group was surprised and elated by all that they had learned from asking and answering questions. If they could learn so much this way, other women surely would too. Forer suggested, and the group agreed, that at each meeting they would ask who benefited from, who had an interest in women's continued investment in individual solutions.

Sarachild was in the meeting where Forer testified from her experience. "Kathie was sitting behind me," Forer said. "From then on she sort of made it an institution and called it consciousness-raising."[16] Shulamith Firestone and Anne Koedt, also in the meeting, saw Sarachild as "the originator of the concept of 'consciousness-raising.'"[17]

From then on Sarachild led in developing the method into a program. At the first national Women's Liberation conference, in November 1968, she presented it as "Radical Feminist 'Consciousness Organizing' Workshop."[18] Sarachild said that the program was "planned on the assumption that a mass liberation movement will develop as more and more women begin to perceive their situation correctly. . . . Therefore our primary task right now is to awaken 'class' consciousness . . . on a mass scale."[19]

Carol Hanisch and Betita Martinez (then Elizabeth Sutherland), who were also in NYRW when consciousness-raising was being developed, quoted Malcolm X on the idea for a program of consciousness-raising: "the primary job is consciousness-raising. Malcolm X said it about black people in 1964 and it's equally true for us: 'You can't give people a program until they realize they need one.'"[20]

Arguments in NYRW to try examining women's experience as the raw data for a theory of women's oppression and as a program for the emerging movement prevailed over opposing arguments advanced by Peggy Dobbins. According to Sarachild, "Dobbins said that what she wanted to do was to make a very intensive study of all the literature on the question of whether there really were any biological differences between men and women." Sarachild argued to reject "what some authorities in the name of science are arguing over what we are" in favor of learning it from "the realities of our own lives."[21] Sarachild likened the struggle over what to study—books or experience—to the "study nature, not books" challenge to scholasticism during the seventeenth-century scientific revolution.[22] Carol Hanisch referred to Mao Tse-tung's *Oppose Bookworship* (1930) to validate their argument.[23]

The Program for Feminist Consciousness-Raising

The Program for Feminist Consciousness-Raising developed out of debate about the appropriate sources for a political program for the movement. It outlined aspects of consciousness-raising that included giving testimony ("recalling and sharing our bitter experiences" by going around the room answering questions on particular topics), questioning the testimony ("cross examination"), and looking for a common root for different feelings and experiences. The program explained forms of false reasoning, such as believing one had "power behind the throne" or failing to reveal problems with a man because of loyalty. It proposed training consciousness-raising organizers who would dare to speak out about their "bitter experiences," exposing apparently personal experiences so as to organize new groups. The plan was for each woman in the "bitch session cell group" to train as a consciousness-raising organizer.[24]

Finally, the program called for developing radical feminist theory with consciousness-raising:

> understanding oppression wherever it exists in our lives—our oppression as black people, workers, tenants, consumers, children . . . as well as our oppression as women . . . analyzing . . . privileges we may have— the white skin privilege, the education and citizenship of a big power (imperialist) nation privilege, and seeing how these help to perpetuate our oppression as women, workers.[25]

Thus the Program for Feminist Consciousness-Raising called for getting to the roots of divisions among women and resolving what the developers, borrowing from Mao Tse-tung, called "contradictions among the people."[26] This was in opposition to reflexive assumptions that divisions did not exist. Here the assumption was that they existed and that consciousness-raising would uncover and confront them.

Moreover, the program challenged women to "take off the rose colored glasses" and "face the awful truth."[27] It emphasized the view that women themselves were the experts on their own behavior, motives, and feelings. It recognized the "survival reasons" that women sometimes resisted consciousness-raising.[28] Sarachild and the team that proposed the program argued for holding all existing theory to the test of women's experience. Raising consciousness in the manner explained in the program almost always produced intense, deep, and lasting emotions of relief and anger, accompanied by the excitement of learning. As a member of the Women's Majority Union in Seattle put it, in consciousness-raising one feels her "mind is growing muscles."[29]

Consciousness-Raising and Black Women's Liberation

Black feminist scholars Johnnetta Cole and Beverly Guy-Sheftall observed that "women's movement scholars have tended to assume that these [consciousness-raising] sessions took place primarily among middle class white women." Cole and Guy-Sheftall said this "needs to be challenged," because "consciousness-raising was an important strategy of Black feminist organizations."[30] Evidence for this is abundant, not only with Poor Black Women with its "systematic self criticism," but in black communities around the nation.

The SNCC Black Women's Liberation Committee held consciousness-raising sessions regularly and continued to do so as it developed into the Black Women's Alliance and finally into the Third World Women's Alliance.[31] There were intermittent periods during which the TWWA invited men to the consciousness-raising sessions with the idea of teaching them feminist thought from a position of strength—as a group rather than as individual women with their own men. For Beal, as for Sarachild, the Civil Rights Movement was the source of the term and the practice of consciousness-raising. Beal said that the phrase was "very common" in SNCC and had to do with "what it meant to be black and to fight for freedom."[32]

Consciousness-raising groups spread through the black community between 1968 and 1970. Guy-Sheftall remembered attending weekly consciousness-raising sessions in Atlanta as a graduate student in 1968. From the late 1960s through the early 1970s, Cole attended consciousness-raising meetings in Pullman, Washington.[33] The Woman's Workshop, a black women's group formed at a Malcolm X conference in 1969 in New York, called consciousness-raising "the rap." They audiotaped their consciousness-raising sessions, one of which was transcribed and published in the 1970 anthology *The Black Woman*.[34]

Vanquishing the Female Version of the Horatio Alger Myth

Feminist consciousness felt astounding because in the mid-1960s, although women experienced sexism on a daily basis, the idea that sexism was a social force was simply unknown to most women. Women struggled for happiness, security, better-paying and more rewarding work, and satisfying love relationships, never factoring in the power imbalance between the sexes as a reason that these goals were difficult to attain. Thus women sought individual remedies that never seemed to solve the problems and, worse, often left them feeling more inadequate than before.

To listen to ten or fifteen women telling the ways in which each worked toward a goal, and to see that even the seemingly successful and beautiful, the seemingly happily married, felt they had failed, brought home a message. The faults an individual woman saw in herself were not the problem. Instead something bigger, something systemic, was stacked against her. Suddenly a participant in a consciousness-raising group felt years of self-blame fall away. Women stopped thinking they were not intelligent enough, not attractive enough, not trying hard enough, or had not yet found the right strategy. They stopped thinking that just "trying a little harder" was the answer.

The female version of the Horatio Alger myth was being vanquished. In the same moment of female class-conscious insight, women felt freedom from self-blame and realized a vast, sometimes overwhelming, fury at whatever or whoever was discovered to be the beneficiary of their previously low consciousness. Anselma Dell'Olio, an early member of NYRW and NOW, described her discovery of feminist consciousness this way: "the ecstasy of relief . . . from a tension . . . between who I was, and who and what I was supposed to be. . . . Feminism allowed me to make the leap from rumbling volcano . . . to rebel with a cause. It was like teaching an illiterate to read."[35]

Louise Moore's flash of rage in her article in the *Liberator* showed the fury of newly raised consciousness when she wrote, "As a Black woman I am being forced to realize that I must kill a Black man . . . if I and my Black sisters all over the world are ever to be free."[36]

Judith Brown described the anger this way: "I am recognizing the machinery of our oppression in such detail that I really feel as if I am having to begin all over in my relationships with men. I am so furious at all men for what I am only beginning to see as the depth of our oppression."[37]

Finally, along with insight, relief, and anger, new group consciousness often brought with it a generalized love for women that the Life Group called the Pro-Woman Line. Black feminist Myrna Hill described her experience of consciousness-raising in Redstockings:

> To see how exciting women are for the first time, to see bravery in a female, to see their beauty, their value—is overwhelming. To see that other blacks and women could really see each other, too, not just whites and men, and to have the internal fortitude to stick to that vision in loyalty to their OWN group, not just the oppressor, I found electrifying.[38]

Women participating in consciousness-raising groups grew proud to be women: women were strong, not weak; smart, not dumb; angry, not cheerfully accepting of their lot; "messed over, not messed up" as Carol Hanisch put it.[39]

Men were more surprised by all of this than women were. A male newspaper reporter wrote, "How could we guess that Lady Clairol gloss covered up the mind of a revolutionary?"[40] Feminist consciousness produced a kind of solidarity that shocked many women too. Forer described the change: "Up to that point my big problem with women was that I saw them as competition. I walked into that meeting and saw something different. Women were seeing their interests as one. It was the most wonderful thing that ever, ever happened."[41]

From Testifying to "Bitch, Sisters, Bitch"

For many Women's Liberation pioneers, the idea of raising female class-consciousness had been jump-started in the Civil Rights Movement, where they experienced the power of testifying. Pam Allen reflected, "I was a freedom school teacher in '64 and . . . steeped in the idea of using people's own experiences . . . concrete examples of racism like streets in the white neighborhood being paved and streets in the black not being paved, although everybody paid taxes. This being an example of unfair, discriminatory treatment, not inferiority."[42] Sarachild said, "We were applying to women and to ourselves as women's liberation organizers the practice a number of us had learned as organizers in the Civil Rights Movement in the South in the early 1960's."[43]

Testifying, as the practice was called in the Civil Rights Movement, had helped to produce unity. SNCC field organizer Charles Sherrod, in a tough campaign in Albany, Georgia, described the process this way: "Our only hope was unity. This had been the real reason for the mass meeting—to weld the community into one bond of reason and emotion. The force to do this was generated by accounts of the released students who individually described the physical situation and mental state of each, in jail."[44]

Brown said her immediate, favorable reaction to feminist consciousness-raising came from mass meetings in which Patricia Stephens Due, the young black CORE field secretary who was Brown's supervisor, insisted that Brown, like the black participants, speak from personal experience about why she was there. This was difficult at first because, as Brown said, "This exercise that Pat put me through was entirely unfamiliar to me. . . . I took to consciousness-raising as legitimate because of what I slowly learned in this manner."[45] Brown also remembered her surprise at the forthrightness of Due's family, who shared problems that at first seemed personal and private. The lack of embarrassment with which they recounted these experiences suggested to Brown that the family attributed responsibility for the problems to racism rather than to personal failure. This was just what Brown wanted consciousness-raising to do for women.

The Women's Liberation group in New Orleans held that, unlike raising class consciousness, raising women's consciousness was just "therapy." But they allowed "therapy type sessions" because, as one member said, "many women have very serious personal problems that they feel they have to straighten out first before they can engage in anything outside of themselves."[46] From Gainesville, where the consciousness-raising method was being spread across the South, Judith Brown wrote to the New Orleans group, "We do not believe there are such things as 'personal problems' for oppressed people." Using the example of a male worker, Brown argued: "When he feels subjectively his objective oppression by capitalism, [he] is feeling a political problem. To call his problem 'personal' is to ignore the power relationship in which he suffers daily."[47]

Brown believed that the New Orleans group feared disapproval from the Left—much of which saw consciousness-raising as therapy. To show that consciousness-raising was espoused by revolutionaries in other nations, she included in her letter SDS leader Greg Calvert's description of Guatemalan guerrillas organizing a new village:

> They do not talk about the "anti-imperialist struggle" . . . they gather together the people one by one. Then the guerrillas rise and talk . . . about their own lives . . . how the things they've striven for . . . were frustrated by the society in which they lived. . . . The guerrillas encourage the villagers to talk about their lives. . . . people who thought that their deepest problems were their individual problems discover that their longings are all the same. . . . out of the discovery of their common humanity comes the decision that men must unite . . . to destroy their common oppression.[48]

The method used by the Guatemalan cadre appeared to transform the consciousness of the villagers much as consciousness-raising did with women in the United States. The method had been used in the same way in the Chinese revolution, where it was described as "Speak Pains to Recall Pains." There, cadre had posed questions about landlords and tenants such as "who needs who." The peasants came together in village meetings to answer the questions based on their experiences and to talk over their conclusions.[49]

Kathie Sarachild, Carol Hanisch, and Irene Peslikis created a poster combining the Chinese slogan "Speak Pains to Recall Pains" with the Black Freedom Movement slogan "Tell it like it is" and a new slogan, "Bitch, sisters, bitch."[50] They brought it to NYRW meetings and hung it on the wall.[51]

Colette Price, a member of NYRW who read *Fanshen*, said of the method of learning about the economic relationship between landlords and peasants, "We were asking many of the same questions about the relations between men and women. *Fanshen* encouraged me with its startling indication that what we were on to with consciousness-raising was truly a universal, radical, mass revolutionary process."[52] The Chinese and Guatemalan radicals were clearly not conducting therapy sessions. But when women in the United States applied the same process to discussions of housework or sex, portions of the Left still called this therapy.

Carol Hanisch's classic radical feminist essay "The Personal Is Political" was, as we have seen, originally written as a letter to the women of SCEF to dispel the notion that consciousness-raising was therapy. "These analytical sessions," Hanisch wrote, "are a form of political action." She explained:

> I do not go . . . to talk about . . . "personal problems." In fact I would rather not. As a movement woman, I've been pressured to be strong, selfless . . . not admit I have any real problems that I can't find a personal solution to. One of the first things we discover . . . is that personal problems are political problems. There are no personal solutions at this time. There is only collective action for a collective solution.[53]

The Purposeful Transmission of Consciousness-Raising before 1970

Patricia Robinson took notes on Poor Black Women's systematic self-criticism sessions and to "further awareness" mailed the notes to women in groups including Moore's Domestic Workers Union, "women who went to groups like the NAACP, the Urban League and Black sororities," "simplistic nationalists," and predominantly white Women's Liberation groups in New York City, New Rochelle, and Canada.[54] In "A Historical and Critical Essay for Black Women in the Cities, June 1969," Patricia Robinson and Group agreed that the most important thing for black women to do at this point was to "break out of these deathly myths" perpetrated by white and male supremacy. Systematic self-criticism was the best weapon against those myths, and Poor Black Women spread this view by visiting other groups as well as sending out their "study papers."[55]

When she learned consciousness-raising at the Sandy Springs meeting, Brown had seen immediately the potential of this approach to unify women. In September of 1968 she wrote to Sarachild for help: "Kathie, would you please send me a list of topics you people have discussed? Also I would like a model phrasing of questions."[56] Sarachild responded by sending NYRW's questions and the questions she had written for the group she'd visited in Berkeley, with a caveat that she found Berkeley's style "too formal."[57] Brown wrote to Hanisch, "It would be well to get to a few women quickly with the 'New York' approach. One of our members—previously on the staff of Vietnam Summer—and a hard line feminist, just moved to Miami and she's starting a group there."[58] Brown meant consciousness-raising when she referred to the "New York approach." Later Brown wrote to Sarachild about the effectiveness of the material Sarachild sent her and of plans to use it: "Those minutes you sent are priceless; the N.C. stronghold and the Sarasota group want them immediately."[59]

After Hanisch opened the Freedom for Women project in Gainesville, she visited the group that was developing in Miami and reported to SCEF:

> Someone suggested we go around the room with the question "Do you think your mother messed you up?" We began to see that our mothers were just giving us one side of the contradiction . . . [the testifiers'] mothers . . . encouraged them not to have sex before marriage . . . they had chosen the other side of the alternative—having sex without marriage. The common root of both alternatives is that men leave you if you sleep with them and leave you if you don't.[60]

Hanisch and others visited groups in Sarasota and St. Petersburg, and Brown shared questions and demonstrated consciousness-raising at SSOC conferences in Atlanta and Tallahassee.

The spread of consciousness-raising from Gainesville exemplifies its dissemination to a number of other cities. From New York, for example, it was taken to Boston by Sarachild on a visit to movement activist Nancy Hawley, and to Berkeley by NYRW's Jenny Gardner.

Consciousness-raising then spread nationally via Women's Liberation's first national conference at Lake Villa, Illinois. In the months preceding the national conference, Gainesville Women's Liberation and New York Radical Women had been working together on consciousness-raising strategies. An early draft of Sarachild's "Radical Feminist 'Consciousness-Organizing' Workshop" was sent to Judith Brown and me in Gainesville.[61] At the conference, consciousness-raising was demonstrated in a workshop, debated in plenary sessions, and disseminated in written form to more than two hundred women from thirty-seven states and Canada. These women formed the nucleus of the organizers of the movement in 1968. From the conference, the program was carried back to groups across the nation.

Thus consciousness-raising was put together by specific women out of particular traditions, and purposefully disseminated before 1969, along routes that are traceable. Like the need for a Women's Liberation Movement that the concept Sisterhood Is Powerful stood for, consciousness-raising, the movement's central organizing strategy, was first advocated by only a minority of founders. But then, like Sisterhood Is Powerful, the method took root even among many of those who had first opposed it.

By 1969, consciousness-raising groups were multiplying faster than the originators and early advocates of the program could keep track of. Founders organized with the method, and women in the groups they had organized then organized more consciousness-raising groups. More than any other strategy, feminist consciousness-raising created a mass national Women's Liberation Movement that, for a time, was a political movement and not an individual support network.

Not Leaving the Left

Although the movement they built was organizationally independent of the Left, Women's Liberation was, in its rebirth years, a movement on the Left.[62] Tens of thousands of women coming into Women's Liberation before 1970 "accepted," as Brown put it, "a radical placement of their oppression."[63] "In my own group," Brown wrote later in 1968 to Roxanne Dunbar in Boston, "I see middle class women beginning to call themselves revolutionaries."[64] "Let me report to you," she wrote that same year to Pam Allen in San Francisco, "that the first group (first white group) in Gainesville which is openly socialist, [and which] openly calls itself revolutionary is the Women's Liberation Group."[65] Hanisch also held the radical feminist position that men were women's immediate oppressor and found that Women's Liberation organizing turned women against capitalism. So did Hanisch's coworker on the staff of SCEF, Margaret McSurely, then organizing against strip mining in Appalachia. Quoting a recent letter, Hanisch shared McSurely's perception with Brown: "I see you guys working things out with new women all the time," McSurely had written; "they get turned on as anti-capitalists."[66] McSurely's observation was also true of the few early Women's Liberation founders who had not started out as radicals. Ti-Grace Atkinson was a registered Republican until 1967, when she began feminist organizing. Atkinson said later, "My *feminism* radicalized me on other issues, not vice versa."[67]

Moreover, for feminist radical women, independence in organization meant independence in thinking also, rather than just going along with received Left theories. The Old Left, for the most part, relied on Engels's *Origins of the Family, Private Property, and the State*, where Engels tried to show that male domination originated with the advent of private property.[68] The New Left struggled awkwardly to show the ways in which this would work by drawing causal connections between private property and female oppression—for example, the consumer theory of women's oppression. But, as discussed in chapter 7, the connections were unconvincing.

Proponents of consciousness-raising cited as their source the mass meetings in the Black Freedom Movement rather than Left perspectives on women's oppression. But they considered consciousness-raising consistent with, and indeed a positive application of, Marxism. Consciousness-raising embodied the Marxist principle of critically examining the "objective conditions." "Materialism insists that all ideas have at their base an observable objective cause. A materialist approach . . . would search for those objective relationships between men and women, worker and capitalism, or blacks and racism which would cause an individual to behave in a particular way," wrote Judith Brown.[69] Consciousness-raising, as its proponents argued with those on the Left who called it therapy, was an application of what Lenin called "the most essential thing in Marxism, the living soul of Marxism, a concrete analysis of concrete conditions."[70]

New theory based on conscious-raising provided a better analysis of women's oppression—one that was not dogmatic, could break abstractions down, and was tested against people's experiences. The everyday issues testified about in meetings produced a spate of vastly popular and widely anthologized consciousness-raising theory papers, such as Pat Mainardi's "The Politics of Housework" and Anne Koedt's "The Myth of the Vaginal Orgasm."[71] These papers were as accessible in style and language as the testimony that generated them. Patricia Robinson saw women's experience as the "base for breaking out of narrow nationalism," since a woman was "forced to be more realistic because of her biology."[72]

Rather than challenging dialectical materialism as a method, radical feminist analysis tried to expand the content to which it was being applied so that it could be used to explain all production and reproduction. These feminists argued that the central form of exploitation of women was their unpaid childbearing and child-raising work, and it was this work that Marxist theorists had been unable to derive from capitalism. As Firestone put it, "we have not thrown out the insights of the socialists; on the contrary, radical feminism enlarges their analysis, granting it an even deeper basis in objective conditions."[73]

In addition to trying to improve the theory of the broad radical movement, Women's Liberation also provided radical political education to the female public. For example, *Triple Jeopardy*, the newspaper of the TWWA, reviewed *Enter Fighting: Today's Woman*, a book by Clara Colon, who wrote on the woman question in the Communist Party newspaper the *Daily World*.[74] The review explained and critiqued Colon's application of dialectical materialism to understand women's oppression. Patricia Robinson brought "revolutionary history: the Paris Commune, the Soviet and Chinese revolutions," as well as the *Guardian* newspaper, Mao's *Little Red Book*, and *The Spark*, a radical newspaper from Ghana, to poor women in the black community of Mount Vernon, New York.[75] The women said that their men warned them to "be careful of radical people," but they ignored the men's advice.[76]

Clara Colon expressed "gratitude to the WLM in jogging us [the Left] into a greater awareness on the question of women's freedom" in a series in the *Daily World* in the spring of 1969.[77] The focus of the series was Colon's critique of "Toward a Female Liberation Movement" (the Florida Paper), which she said had "elicited wide-ranging and sometimes heated discussion in the left press."[78] Although Colon disagreed sharply with the separatist strategy, she praised those advancing it for "going right ahead and sparking the apathy of the entire movement on the question of women's freedom. They have elicted a positive response."[79]

On the West Coast, Women's Liberation pioneer Laura X (Murra) also began a campaign of political education. She wanted to put International Working Women's Day, the socialist holiday based on an event in the United States, back into U.S. history. On 8 March 1908, immigrant women in New York City demonstrated for the vote and to end sweatshops and child labor. This inspired the Second International in 1910 to declare a day of celebration.

International Women's Day had been dropped out of U.S. culture, but it was celebrated in many parts of the world.

To revive this celebration, in 1969 the Berkeley women led a march dressed in the turn-of-the century garb of the immigrant women. Their campaign raised awareness of International Women's Day until by 1970 its history had spread through the movement, and the day was celebrated in cities and towns around the nation. Laura X began the project hoping that women in the New Left might gain the respect of male comrades if the men knew of women's radical accomplishments. It turned into an education for U.S. women about the history of the Left.

As the Women's Liberation Movement took off between 1968 and 1970, new participants who had not been in the Black Freedom Movement or the Left were introduced to the history and current activities of the Left in the United States and internationally. Hundreds of thousands of women were introduced by a local Women's Liberation group to blacklisted Left films with feminist themes such as *Salt of the Earth*, to reports of visits to Cuba with the Venceremos Brigade, and to the progress, and lack of progress, that socialist nations made on the woman question. They learned about revolutions in the Third World—especially those in Cuba, Vietnam, Algeria, and China—and they were exposed to Marxist analysis and to the classic Marxist texts whose usefulness for Women's Liberation was then under debate. The cause(s) of women's oppression may not have been settled, but by the fall of 1968 women weren't waiting for the origins to be found. They were coming into the movement at a great rate. The troops were already in motion, and there was no slowing them down.

The Pro-Woman Line

If a social movement could concentrate enough power to democratize the situation between men and women, then many hundreds of thousands of new women were going to have to join. Sarachild came to believe that, like the everyday black people with whom she lived and worked in Mississippi and who came together to fight white supremacy, everyday women would be up to the challenge of standing together against male supremacy. For Judith Brown, the lesson came this way: "I compared the subservient behavior of black people with that of women."[80] Living for years in the South before the Civil Rights Movement, Brown, without knowing what to make of it, had seen black people dissemble around whites. In the movement, she said, "seeing black people from the inside, strong, open, debating me, telling me I was wrong, teaching me, it was easy to think that women too were really this way."[81] Brown began to think of how much she hated wearing makeup and pretending to be dumb around men—began, as she said, to "immediately transfer" to women what she had learned about blacks' supposedly cheerful acceptance of their lot. "It was a tactic for survival," Brown said, "a strong thing, not a meek, weak thing."[82]

This understanding provided evidence to Women's Liberation founders that women would unify and fight. Not just the women in the New Left or college-educated women—there were not enough of these—but the very women who, because of their numbers, were needed to make people-power effective. Knowing that women were not satisfied, although they might appear to be, provided a basis for mass organizing and became known as the Pro-Woman Line. Brown, Sarachild, Hanisch, and others interpreted female behaviors like "playing dumb" as survival techniques—dissembling that was necessary under the conditions of male domination. Brown said the Pro-woman Line was the "basic radical idea of feminist groups"—fuel for making sisterhood powerful.[83]

The Debate Is Settled

The proponents of the strategy of Sisterhood Is Powerful held that the movement's power would draw on the cross-class and multiracial nature of women's oppression. In early 1968 Firestone and Koedt wrote: "What is . . . exciting . . . is that if you could appeal to women in general you would be appealing to 51% of the population . . . spread evenly through all classes. . . . you could crack the system right down the middle."[84]

The Redstockings Manifesto argued that repudiation of privilege to "crack the system" was not just a moral matter but a strategic one: a battle plan meant to maximize the power of the movement by uncovering and then dealing with divisions among women. "We repudiate all economic, racial, educational, or status privileges that divide us from other women," the Manifesto said in 1969.[85] In a debate with SCEF's Anne Braden over whether the new Women's Liberation Movement would be anticapitalist and antiracist, Hanisch wrote, "We can show in personal terms how women's liberation not only means destruction of the capitalist system, but a strong attack on racism. . . . The movement . . . will make a majority of the population *want* . . . to give up their privileges to get their liberation."[86]

But how would this play out on a daily basis? Brown and Sarachild began to discuss a movement code with a common interest at its core. A woman who had the money to avoid a struggle with her husband over the housework by hiring a housekeeper should see that it was more in her interest to insist that her husband share the housework than take the bait of exploiting a less privileged woman. If a sister was in jail, no other woman should go out with her boyfriend. "If we are going to work in a mass movement," Sarachild wrote to Brown, "we're going to have to give up such personal outs, our racial and economic privileges."[87] Consciousness-raising could uncover divisions upon which such a code might be based and also build, as Firestone said, "group consciousness [and] . . . the power that comes through its development."[88]

The infinite portability of consciousness-raising, along with its exponential way of expanding, brought ever-increasing numbers of women into the movement. Consciousness-raising spread, too, because any woman could take part in it—and even lead it. The method itself contained the message of its underlying concept: that women themselves were the experts on women. No teacher or "facilitator" was required. Unlike a book or a course, consciousness-raising was free, and there was no outside reading. There was no paperwork. It required no license or permit, no public space. Most consciousness-raising was done in participants' homes in groups no larger than ten or fifteen. A woman need only come up with a question and invite a few friends and neighbors over for a meeting. Invariably, existing groups gave rise to more groups as enthusiastic participants moved and started new groups, or as groups grew too large for participants' living rooms. And often the result was a desire for action. Consciousness-raising literally made sisterhood powerful.

From 1963 to 1970, women made history speed up for their sex; change came at a pace that made just about everyone's head spin. What made women mobilize so readily? Actually, the question more typically asked is, why did women wait so long? Women's reentry into the paid labor force had returned their presence to its previous wartime level by 1950. In the late 1950s, *The Second Sex* had already gone through several U.S. editions. By 1957, Lorraine Hansberry was growing impatient. She had read *The Second Sex* in 1953, the year it came out in the United States, and was thrilled by it. "Four years have passed . . . since . . . *The Second Sex.* . . . It is four years since . . . [that] revolutionary treatment of the 'woman question' exploded upon the consciousness of . . . American book readers," Hansberry said. "Four years and one waits."[89] During the long wait, underlying changes were occurring that helped to erode women's economic dependency on men. So the ideas of consciousness-raising and Sisterhood Is Powerful found favorable social conditions and a receptive constituency in which to stir feminist consciousness and organize a Women's Liberation Movement.

The Movement Goes Nationwide

1968–1970

IN 1970 FOUR OUT OF FIVE Americans knew there was a Women's Liberation Movement.[1] Between 1968 and 1970, as Anne Forer observed, from "just a few women meeting in a room" the movement would go "nation-wide and international."[2] Women's Liberation took off, a mass grassroots movement that was powerful, popular, radical.

Lawmakers rushed to catch up with Women's Liberation. At the least, sexist laggards could expect to be disrupted by direct action, sued in class action lawsuits, or find their male chauvinist ways detailed in the morning papers or a new popular book. Corporate offices across the country were picketed and occupied by throngs of women, as was the stock market, and much else from the U.S. Senate to the Whitney Museum opening in New York City. Angry Women's Liberation "truth squads" confronted men on sexist behavior, and photographs of grimacing women breaking boards in all-female karate classes appeared in the news. Litigation and formal complaints of sex discrimination proliferated. Women filed charges against the entire state system of universities in Florida, California, and New York. Female employees at just about every major newsmagazine charged sex discrimination. Stewardesses sued the airlines, and female officers sued the armed forces. Among the several lawsuits against states were class actions by hundreds of female plaintiffs who had been denied abortions. Legal action was almost always combined with picketing, sit-ins, and press conferences.

Union women, too, wanted Women's Liberation. Several unions, including the Hotel, Restaurant Employees, and Bartenders Union and the International Chemical Workers Union, were sued by female members who sought higher-paying jobs traditionally reserved for men. These unions had sided with management when women sought relief through the Equal Employment Opportunity Commission.[3] The unions, along with states and employers, justified keeping women out of "male" jobs on the basis of protective labor laws mandated by the Supreme Court in *Mueller v. Oregon* in 1908. For decades, the AFL-CIO and liberal labor supporters such as Eleanor Roosevelt had opposed the ERA, fearing that it would be used to overrule hard-won protective legislation and to subject women to heavy work and long hours. Nonetheless, the rush of complaints from blue-collar union women right after the EEOC was established showed their desire for the better-paying jobs that they were being denied.

In the professions and in academia, women formed caucuses to challenge male domination. In May 1969 Judith Brown, then employed in psychiatric research, formed the first women's caucus at an annual meeting of the American Psychiatric Association in Miami, Florida. The caucus included female psychiatrists and the wives of male psychiatrists. Its resolution was not endorsed by the APA board, but a sympathetic male psychiatrist read it into the board minutes. In September 1969 women organized caucuses in the American Sociological Association, the American Political Science Association, and the American Psychological Association. That December the Modern Language Association set up a commission on the status of women in the field. The Coordinating Committee for Women in the Historical Professions grew out of letters and petitions that Bernice Carroll submitted to the American Historical Association in October of 1969.[4]

The new movement pushed ahead on college campuses as well. On many campuses activists won day care centers, birth control at university infirmaries, lifting of curfews and dress codes, and the beginnings of a revamped curriculum that included women in general courses and offered specialized courses on women, opening a new field of "women's studies." In 1969 universities such as Cornell and New York University offered credit courses on women. San Diego State University in California established its renowned multicourse program in 1970. The year's end saw women's studies courses at more than a hundred colleges and universities.

The churches were under attack, from within, for male supremacy. In July 1969 the National Coalition of American Nuns sought equality for women in the Catholic Church. In December 1969 the women's caucus in the National Council of Churches sought reform of America's churches, calling them "male dominated and male-oriented."[5] Female Baptists demanded reform by the American Baptist Convention in 1970, saying that the church used women as "tokens."[6] Demands for ordination of women spread across religious communities. All of these challenges occurred between 1968 and 1970.[7]

How did the Women's Liberation Movement grow from a handful of groups in 1968 to something that included masses of women in every walk of life by 1970? Perhaps the most influential force was a series of consciousness-raising sessions in NYRW sparking the protest of the Miss America Beauty Pageant in September 1968. The protest propelled Women's Liberation into the national spotlight, setting off a media blitz that over the next two years brought Women's Liberation into every home in the United States with access to public broadcasting.[8] Consciousness-raising organizers developed an effective form of action called the "zap." A zap was conducted with the singular goal of raising public consciousness, as opposed to winning demands. Like the method that produced it, the zap action was portable, requiring only courage and a local consciousness-raising group.

Zapping the Miss America Beauty Pageant

Sure of women's potential for revolt, Shulamith Firestone argued with Naomi Weisstein, "If you are worried about their [women's] complacency . . . they have very strong beefs which will come out very soon with actions designed to stir an already dormant consciousness."[9] The zap of the pageant proved Firestone right. The Miss America protest brought women into the movement in droves. The protest was replicated across the nation and spread to Europe. Countless women, fed up with expensive, uncomfortable, and unachievable beauty standards, and undaunted—even delighted—by the label "bra burner," made hometown and campus beauty pageants popular targets.

For years the Miss America Pageant set the standard for all U.S. women, including women of color, even though they had never been among the contestants since the first pageant in 1921. In the 1930s, Rule 7 was added, stipulating that "Contestants must be in good health and of the white race."[10]

Versions of Rule 7 specified the number of generations used to determine "whiteness."

The Miss America Pageant protest of 7 September 1968 cut deep into women's everyday routines, hopes, and fears. First of all, regulation of women's appearance was widespread and restrictive. In most of the country, from kindergarten through graduate school, in historically black colleges and predominantly white ones, dress codes forbade pants, no matter what the weather. Domestic workers wore skirts, as did women in the pink-collar ghetto, where a skirt and hose and heels, not to mention bras, girdles, and makeup, were required. Putting on lipstick was like brushing one's teeth— you just did it. These were the requirements, some explicit, some implicit, but backed up by the threat of punishments that ranged from getting restricted to the dormitory for the weekend to losing one's job, getting cheated on by one's mate, or not getting dates and being shunned by other women, themselves afraid of the fate of "losers."

As bad as the regulation was the no-win, intensely competitive, and almost impossible-to-drop-out-of beauty rat race—expensive, time consuming, and mysterious, with ever changing rules. Women who refused to participate were still judged by these rules. Most women participated twenty-four hours, seven days a week. Whatever the woman's individual weight and shape, she was manipulated and squeezed toward a standard model in boned, wired, and rubberized girdles and bras. Walking on high heels not only deformed, weakened, and hurt feet and legs, but it made balance, speed, and grace something one had to work at. Most women never felt they were getting it all right.

Although Black Power had begun to provide some relief from white beauty standards, black women's burden was still heavier than white women's. For example, the establishment black media, whose advertising accounts included companies that sold products to straighten hair and bleach the skin, continued to promote these products even as they carried messages of race pride.

In the early 1960s black women continued to face the onerous burden of straightening their hair or enduring, at best, "quiet disapproval." Zoharah Simmons, who like many of the SNCC women wore an Afro, recalled being summoned to the dean's office at Spelman College and told her hair was a "disgrace."[11]

Tananarive Due, daughter of civil rights leaders Patricia Stephens and John Due, who came of age in the 1970s, still experienced the imposition of white beauty standards. She remembered that she "couldn't stand having kinky hair, and I couldn't stand having it straightened. I couldn't stand my hair hardly at all."[12] As black feminist Patricia Hill Collins put it,

Judging white women by their physical appearance objectifies them. . . . Black men's blackness penalizes them. But because they are men, their self-definitions are not as heavily dependent on their physical attractiveness as those of all women. But African-American women experience the pain of never being able to live up to external defined standards of beauty—standards applied to us by white men, white women, Black men, and, most painfully, one another.[13]

Miss America communicated the rules—showing millions of women the uniform of their inequality. The pageant's message was, if you want to get along, get ahead, or get love, here is what you should look like.

The idea for the pageant protest had come to Carol Hanisch as she watched the feminist movie *Schmeerguntz* with other members of NYRW. After the Sandy Springs meeting, even with all its divisions, she was ready to show the world that a Women's Liberation Movement was "afoot in the land."[14] NYRW did consciousness-raising on how members were affected by the pageant. This evoked a gaggle of ideas for how to protest the 1968 pageant and even more enthusiasm for going ahead.

On September 7, more than one hundred women marched up the boardwalk in Atlantic City, chanting and waving picket signs. Their marching feet on the wooden boardwalk, which was some distance off the ground, made a loud, rhythmic, insistent sound.[15] Led by Florynce Kennedy, the intrepid black feminist attorney, the women ranged from young mothers with baby strollers to grandmothers. They came from Florida, New York, New Jersey, Massachusetts, Michigan, and D.C. Some were chained to a giant red, white, and blue Miss America puppet. Others paraded a live sheep which was crowned Miss America. On the sidelines men jeered "Go back to Russia" and "Mothers of Mao," and commented lewdly.[16] Nevertheless, female bystanders came up seeking protest literature.

Singing and exclaiming, the demonstrators threw "instruments of female torture" such as high heels and girdles into a Freedom Trashcan. No fires were set, but the protesters had intended to burn all the instruments of torture, bras included, in the spirit of the antiwar movement's burning of draft cards. Reluctantly, in order to be able to continue protesting on the boardwalk where regulations outlawed fires, they did not set one.[17]

Protesters posing as convention-goers had obtained seats in the balcony. As Miss America approached the microphone, four women involved in the preplanned inside action, including Hanisch and Sarachild, unfurled a large banner with the words "Women's Liberation" over the balcony. They tied the banner to the balcony and shouted "Freedom for Women" and "No More Miss America" until the police "hustled us out of the hall," as Hanisch put it.[18] Several protesters released "stink bombs" on the convention floor, and one of them, Peggy Dobbins, was arrested and taken to jail. The "stink bombs" were actually part of the Toni Home Permanent package, and Toni was one of the sponsors of the pageant. Hanisch later said, "we were targeting and challenging . . . the *uniform* of women's inferior class status. . . . Beneath this 'appearance thing' is male prerogative and control. . . . it's about power."[19]

Incredibly, 1968 saw *two* protests of the Miss America Pageant, one asserting the beauty of black women, the other opposing the racism of the pageant but mainly targeting its sexism. "Miss America does not represent us because there has never been a black girl in the pageant," said Saundra Williams, who was crowned Miss Black America in a counterpageant held the same day four blocks from the official pageant.[20] Sponsors of Miss Black America called it a "positive protest."[21]

In fact, black women were involved in both of the protests. Florynce Kennedy and Bonnie Allen were among the Women's Liberation protesters, and racism was a high-priority target, the second point on the flyer for the demonstration:

> Since its inception in 1921, the Pageant has not had one Black finalist. . . . this has not been for a lack of test-case contestants. There has never been a Puerto Rican, Alaskan, Hawaiian, or Mexican-American winner. Nor has there ever been a *true* Miss America—an American Indian."[22]

Black feminists in consciousness-raising sessions in the SNCC Black Women's Liberation Committee and then the Third World Women's Alliance discussed the politics of beauty. Frances Beal said that their analysis of beauty standards had begun "in relationship to white women." After they drew conclusions to "honor our own physical characteristics," they began to see that "there was something deeper here. There was something wrong with still accepting the male/female ideas . . . Why should women be defined by physical characteristics at all?"[23] In 1968 Miss Black America Saundra Williams conformed to standards of slimness and makeup. But her hair was natural in a short Afro and she was not light skinned.

Remarkably, much of the media sympathized with the feminist protest-ers. This no doubt resulted, at least in part, from the policy publicized before the demonstration: the protesters would speak only with female reporters. Shana Alexander, writing for *Life* magazine, said the protest had not gone far enough. The *New York Times*, whose female reporter had ridden to At-lantic City on the bus rented by the protesters, headlined the protest, say-ing that a "Women's Liberation Movement" was at work.[24] New York's *Daily News*, with more than 3 million readers, noted: "Some women who think the whole idea of such contests is degrading to femininity took their case to the people. . . . gals say they're not anti-beauty, just anti-beauty contests."[25] News of the protest went out over the wire services and was picked up from coast to coast and around the globe. As the movement surfaced in England in 1969 and 1970, what one observer called a "rerun" of the pageant protest occurred in London when one hundred women disrupted the Miss World beauty contest.[26]

In the weeks that followed the Miss America protest in Atlantic City, femi-nists were interviewed on news and talk shows. Jacqui Ceballos and Kate Millett of NOW, who had joined the protest, and Rosalyn Baxandall, repre-senting NYRW, appeared on the nationally syndicated *David Susskind Show*, a popular television talk show. "Every day in a woman's life is a walking Miss America contest," Baxandall told Susskind, and gave NYRW's address.[27]

As Firestone predicted, the Miss America protest elicited "strong beefs." NYRW was overwhelmed with letters from women who weren't stopped by the word "radical" in the group's name. A frequent theme in the letters was "I've been waiting all my life for something like this to come along."[28] The women wanted to join Women's Liberation. Weekly meetings of NYRW jumped in size.

The First National Conference

The growth of the new movement was also evident at the first national conference, which had been in the works since the Sandy Springs meeting and was held Thanksgiving weekend of 1968. Marilyn Webb had obtained funding to bring together representatives of Chicago's West Side Group and NYRW to prepare for the conference, which was held at a YWCA camp in Lake Villa, Illinois, near Chicago. For their part, radical feminists came up with a large donation that covered the cost of renting the conference facili-ties. Anxious to include the position that male domination should be a target of the new movement, Brown wrote to newfound ally Carol Hanisch noting that Marilyn Webb had made it clear that if radical feminists wanted a hand in the conference, "it will rest with us to propose topics."[29]

Approximately two hundred women attended, most representing groups in thirty-seven states and Canada.[30] The New York–Gainesville Life Group contingent including Sarachild, Brown, and Hanisch had met in Gainesville shortly before the conference to talk broadly about theory and strategy and how to advance the organizing implications and importance of consciousness-raising and the "pro-woman line" at the conference. Kathie Sarachild brought with her copies of a proposal for a Radical Feminist "Consciousness Organizing" Workshop.[31] The women from New York and Gainesville argued in the plenary sessions for using consciousness-raising for mass organizing and theory building. Hanisch later called the arguments over consciousness-raising a "heavy, hard debate."[32]

Indeed, like the earlier meeting at Sandy Springs, the conference debated the causes of women's oppression, the main target of Women's Liberation, and the need for a mass movement of women for Women's Liberation. Radical sociology professor and movement activist Marlene Dixon, who attended the conference, said "much of what passed for 'ideological struggle' . . . the real split . . . hinged upon the significant audience that women addressed: other women or Movement men."[33] Dixon decried the "needless polarization" which resulted in "no national organization . . . nothing of the structural framework" for a "national radical women's movement" being put in place. Still, she said, "the long range effect" of the debate was crucial "to furthering the intellectual maturity of the women's movement."[34]

The conference showed that new Women's Liberation groups were forming throughout the country and that the movement was indeed national. Dana Densmore, representing Cell 16 in Boston, found the conference "exhilarating" despite her sharp disagreement with the predominant views there. Densmore said that too many women held on to the belief that male chauvinism could be educated away. Densmore held that men "chose their behavior because it was to their advantage" and they "wouldn't voluntarily change." But, she said, "The general impression was one of tremendous richness. Women came from all around the country."[35] For Freeman, the gathering was most significant because it prompted further growth. "Disagreements [were] sharp," Freeman said, "but the women returned to their cities turned on by the *idea* of women's liberation, to organize more and more groups."[36]

Despite the unresolved arguments, Webb continued to hope that the growing movement would emphasize capitalism rather than male supremacy as the target, and would somehow be affiliated with the New Left. She believed that "the potential of a mass movement was so great" that the debate among the founders would be resolved and the New Left won over as well.[37] Webb was partially right. The New Left, mostly, was won over; the debate was not resolved, but the mass movement was established anyhow. Dixon was right, too. One of the most serious vulnerabilities of the new movement was that, while it was led by the truth of its theory in the rebirth years, its lack of organizational structure later resulted in the ousting and erasure of many of the very women who had come up with the ideas that attracted women to the movement and gave it its power.

In the short run the conference provided organizing momentum for women of different ideological persuasions. A number of women in the Gainesville contingent who held the politico view were inspired to form a new group to advance their position. At the same time, the conference promoted the continuing shift among women in Chicago's West Side Group toward an independent movement. Amy Kesselman, a founding West Sider, said the conference was "enormously stimulating. It pushed my thinking deeper about issues of personal life, and it convinced me of the importance and the viability of an autonomous women's movement."[38]

Black Power Women: "Absolutely Essential"

The conference did not reflect the extent of African American women's leadership in Women's Liberation, because few African American feminists were there. Feminist scholar Alice Echols argued that, given the political climate of the late 1960s that was created by Black Power, "it is extremely unlikely that black women, had they been approached, would have chosen to participate."[39] But Rivka Polatnick said black women did attend the conference at Lake Villa.[40]

At the earlier meeting in Sandy Springs in August 1968, white feminists had argued heatedly about whether to invite black women to the Lake Villa conference.[41] The debate ended inconclusively—at least in the transcript of a tape of the session—with the tentative proposal to hold a special conference to meet with black women and to ask black feminist Kathleen Cleaver to help with it.

Later Roxanne Dunbar, who had participated in the discussion, remembered the proposal for conference planning with Kathleen Cleaver as the final plan for the national conference in Chicago. Rather than trying to distance themselves from black women, Dunbar wrote that the white feminists

at Sandy Springs "felt that they shouldn't even go public until they had obtained the 'approval' of leading black women."[42] Dunbar also said that she
did not agree that black women would reject Women's Liberation. Scholar
of Women's Liberation Benita Roth argued that Sandy Springs was not representative of most predominantly white Women's Liberation groups, which
"desperately wanted women of color to join *them*."[43]

Carol Hanisch, who had also participated in the discussion, recalled later
that the men-are-oppressors faction, including herself, argued to invite African American women.[44] This is supported by a letter from Kathie Sarachild
to Judith Brown about two months after the argument at Sandy Springs,
but before Lake Villa. Sarachild wrote, "I don't think we will be able to get
very far in either our understanding of the woman problem, racism, and the
inter-relationship thereof until there are black women in the groups. . . . I
think black women who are feminists and poor women who are feminists
will make *absolutely essential* contributions to our theory."[45] Those words appear in the Sandy Springs transcript as one participant, probably Sarachild,
argued: "If we are going to find out what is common in our oppression vs
what's different . . . It's absolutely essential for our ideology that we have
militant black power women in on the formation of our ideology."[46]

The counterarguments in the transcript ranged from an assertion that
Black Power women thought Women's Liberation was "a pile of shit" to "I
don't want to . . . hear a black militant woman tell me she is more oppressed
and what am I going to do about it."[47] Benita Roth interpreted the argument
as having been about "keeping the politics of women's liberation focused on
gender oppression."[48]

Yet a number of black feminists who were known to women at Sandy
Springs gave fighting gender oppression a high political priority. Florynce
Kennedy had a major role at the Miss America demonstration and called it
"the best fun I can imagine anyone wanting to have on any single day of her
life."[49] She offered her legal services pro bono for the arrested "stink bomb"
thrower and marched all day buoying morale with her withering and hilari-
ous feminist backtalk to male harassers. She had defended *SCUM Manifesto*
author Valerie Solanas after Solanas shot Andy Warhol. Who could doubt
Kennedy's commitment to Women's Liberation or her willingness to work
with white women?

Moreover, Kennedy, an early NOW member, was involved in several
NOW campaigns, including the boycott of Colgate Palmolive for sex discrimination. A month before the Lake Villa conference, Kennedy made a

high-profile exit from NOW with Ti-Grace Atkinson to form what would later become the Feminists. But remarkably, the transcript showed that Kennedy was mentioned at Sandy Springs as someone who could help bring black women to the conference but would "probably would not want to be included."[50]

In addition to Kennedy, Poor Black Women were "militant black power women" known to at least some white feminists for strong feminist views and for working with white women. Since 1967 Poor Black Women had been circulating its "working papers" to audiences including middle-class black women and poor black and white women, to "further awareness of other sisters" and "stir and stimulate."[51]

Pam Allen met with Patricia Robinson in December 1967, soon after she and Firestone began organizing NYRW. She said of the meeting, "It was clear to me that Pat came to see me as a gesture of solidarity that she was acting as a link. . . . Pat was saying Black women are in fact aware of and concerned about these same questions of women and women's oppression."[52] However, Allen left New York for California in August 1968 and did not attend the Sandy Springs meeting.

White feminists argued on August 2–4 about inviting black women to the Lake Villa conference. In September, Patricia Robinson mailed out a set of Poor Black Women's papers that "question aggressive male domination and the class society which enforces it, capitalism."[53] However, the papers weren't published and read widely until December 1968 in the inaugural issue of *Lilith*, a new Women's Liberation journal from the Women's Majority Union in Seattle. This was, of course, after both conferences had taken place.

Lilith's editor called the papers "remarkable," and they were indeed.[54] They discussed woman's childbearing work in capitalism as "giving him [the male] the surplus product of her body, the child to use and exploit," and quoted Lenin that "even" proletarian men were male chauvinist.[55] This was better feminist analysis of capitalism and male supremacy intertwining to oppress women than the predominantly white groups had come up with, or the Marxist Left, for that matter. The papers make clear that Black Power feminists could also be radical feminists. With the publication of their work in *Lilith* that December, Poor Black Women "suddenly had become a national political presence . . . receiving letters from white women's liberation groups . . . radical intellectuals and professors," Polatnick said.[56] They responded to the white groups in writing and met with some of them.

Also in September 1968, a month and a half before the Lake Villa conference, Mary Ann Weathers, "a young, militant Black power-turned feminist" (as Sarachild called her), joined Cell 16, the predominantly white Women's Liberation group founded in Boston by Roxanne Dunbar and Dana Densmore.[57] Sarachild visited Cell 16 that September and met Weathers. In mid-October Weathers visited NYRW in turn and met with the predominantly white group for "sixteen hours straight."[58] Weathers held that although black women's oppression was "tripled," they had "female's oppression in common" with "even white women."[59]

The work of black feminists before and during the fall of 1968 shows that the women at Sandy Springs who argued that Black Power women were not interested in Women's Liberation were wrong, as was Echols's later assessment. Given their ongoing work with white feminists, why wouldn't Kennedy, Robinson, and Weathers, among other women with Black Power politics, have been willing to continue to meet with them at the Lake Villa conference?[60] The work of Kennedy, Robinson, and Weathers also calls into question the argument of feminist scholar Wini Breines, who said that white socialist feminists "reached out to them [black women] and were met with indifference or anger."[61] Indeed, it appears that it was the black women who did most of the "reaching out."

The Struggle for Reproductive Freedom

Within three months of the Lake Villa conference, on 13 February 1969, the campaign to repeal all abortion laws gained national attention when a new group, soon to be called Redstockings, disrupted a hearing of a New York State legislative committee. The abortion campaign attracted women from different sides of the movement's unresolved debates. Lucinda Cisler, who led the campaign in New York—and, for a time, in the nation—called abortion "a great point of unity."[62] Moreover, countless women who were not in any movement came into the Women's Liberation Movement through this campaign.

In consciousness-raising sessions, women listened to each other's experiences of unwanted pregnancies. Some had had to quit school, some had been deserted by men who wanted no responsibility, some had given up babies for adoption or put them into foster care. Others spoke of marrying men they did not want to marry. Still others had struggled to scrape up money for an abortion, only to suffer through nightmarish, painful experiences with blindfolds, dirty instruments, and untrained abortionists.

Hearing many different experiences reinforced women's conviction that mere reform, covering only a particular subset of conditions, could never solve their problems. Most, after all, had not been impregnated as incest victims. Nor did they already have four children or mental instability. Nor were they likely to die in pregnancy. Thus, for the radical feminists, only repeal—no law at all—was the answer. Repeal was not only the practical solution, it was, as Cisler said, based on the principle of "*justice*: woman's right to abortion."[63]

Into the fight for legal abortion, Women's Liberation brought what Lucinda Cisler called the "grass-roots force" of women facing the problem.[64] Before then, a small group of abortion reformers, mostly liberal male doctors, lawyers, and clergy, sought relief for various highly specific subgroups by appealing to lawmakers or medical boards for altruistic concern.[65]

The Women's Liberation strategy regarding abortion laws was just the opposite. First of all, rather than educating the lawmakers, Women's Liberation sought to raise the consciousness of women that unwanted pregnancy was a political rather than a personal problem. Second, rather than proposing a law encompassing a particular set of conditions, they sought total repeal, meaning that no laws beyond those regulating routine outpatient procedures would govern abortion. Abortion would be treated as just another medical procedure—no longer the only one with legislative regulations attached to it. No time or age limits would be imposed, and no permissions required. Repeal activists illustrated this by holding up a blank sheet of paper.

For black women, repeal was not enough. Controlling one's own fertility also meant freedom from forced sterilization. Sterilization, sometimes without consent or even knowledge, was known by African American women to be a danger, particularly in the South. The issue of forced sterilization was raised in June 1967 in a meeting in Indianola, Mississippi, organized by the National Council of Negro Women. The meeting was part of a tour of the South for influential northern women including Florynce Kennedy, among other outspoken black feminists. Dorothy Height, president of the NCNW, and Fannie Lou Hamer were both present. Although Hamer did not say that she herself had been forcibly sterilized, some people there knew it and raised the issue because of her experience.[66]

Sterilization was widespread in the 1930s, and the black community spoke out against it. In the 1950s welfare recipients in many states were subjected to agreements to be sterilized in order to continue to receive assistance. Later, when Fannie Lou Hamer spoke out against the threat of sterilization faced by poor women in the South, she spoke from experience. Hamer had been sterilized when she entered the hospital to have a uterine tumor removed in 1961. She did not give permission and was not told that she would be, or had been, sterilized. She learned about it after the fact through friends who worked for the doctor and heard him talking about it. Hamer confronted the doctor and wished she could have sued him but, as she later told a newspaper reporter, had she done so, "I would have been . . . screwing tacks in my own casket."[67]

SNCC's Black Women's Liberation Committee and its later incarnations, the Black Women's Alliance and the TWWA, held that sterilization of women in the black community and the Third World was part of the white power structure's genocidal campaign against African Americans. At the same time, noting that in New York City 79 percent of deaths from illegal abortions were among black and Hispanic women, they advocated the right of women to decide for themselves whether to have children or not—full birth control rights including the right to abortion.[68]

Black feminist congresswoman Shirley Chisholm grew into an advocate for abortion repeal. "When I was in the [New York] Assembly," Chisholm said, explaining her learning process, "I had not been in favor of repealing all abortion laws." Since then, however, the experiences of her young friends had "compelled . . . some heavy thinking on the subject." "Experience shows," Chisholm said, "that pregnant women who feel they have compelling reasons for not having a baby . . . will break the law and . . . risk injury and death if they must, to get one." Chisholm said that the question then became whether women should be forced to continue having dangerous ones or, by repealing laws criminalizing abortion, could have "clean, competent ones."[69]

Abortion was more than simply another issue. Legalizing abortion meant a qualitative leap toward women's freedom. It was, as Firestone said at an abortion rally in New York in March 1968, "as important as their own self determination." An illegal abortion literally meant risking one's life. The alternative was lifelong physical, economic, and other responsibilities, disruptions, and sacrifices undesirable enough to force countless thousands of women into taking that risk. "Let's not kid ourselves," Firestone said to the women at the 1968 rally, "it is not a distant aunt who faced this problem. We ourselves do. Think of your female friends . . . those of them who have had the problem outnumber those who haven't."[70]

The disruption of the 13 February 1969 hearing on abortion reform by the New York State legislature was the first public action of the new group soon to be called Redstockings. "Now let's hear from some *real* experts—the women," Kathie Sarachild shouted out, rising from her seat.[71] Ellen Willis soon joined in.

The problem, as Redstockings saw it, was that the experts the legislators had called to testify at the hearing were fourteen men and a nun. Indeed, Sarachild had leapt to her feet and interrupted just as a male expert made the point that a woman should be permitted an abortion after her fourth child. As Willis put it, Redstockings was "interested in exposing the concept of expertise, as opposed to letting people make decisions about their lives."[72]

The legislators, unsuccessful at quieting the Redstockings, adjourned the hearing to a private room. But the locked-out women staged a sit-in in the hall. Irene Peslikis testified about the illegal abortion she had at age seventeen. Another woman testified that at seventeen she gave up a baby for adoption because she could not get an abortion. The testimonies were broadcast in the evening news.[73] The next day the New York papers ran stories headlined "Gals Squeal for Repeal" and "Abortion Law Protestors Disrupt Panel."[74] The *New York Times* quoted Sarachild as "Mrs. Amatniek" arguing for repeal of abortion laws.[75] Later Willis wrote about the action in the *New Yorker's* "Talk of the Town" column.

Redstockings then came up with a new form of consciousness-raising action—the speak-out. They would hold their own public hearing at which women, the "real experts," would be the ones giving the testimony. Redstockings called their speak-out "Abortion: Tell It Like It Is," after the popular civil rights slogan. On 21 March 1969 at Washington Square Methodist Church in Greenwich Village, before an audience of three hundred, twelve women dared to speak out. They told about their illegal abortions. There was a woman who had sought certification as mentally unstable and was offered an abortion in exchange for sterilization. One woman spoke of continuing a pregnancy against her will and then giving the baby up for adoption.

Sometimes the audience chimed in sympathetically. Other times men called out angrily, "Lesbians." A black man in the audience told Ellen Willis that the "supercharged" tension was like a black confrontation with whites. "We're hoping the idea will catch on," Willis said, "and become the equivalent, for the women's movement, of the Vietnam teach-ins."[76] Irene Peslikis, who had done most of the work of recruiting the other speakers and was the first woman to testify, said the speak-out "showed the power of consciousness-raising, how theory comes from deep inside a person's life, and how it leads directly to action."[77] After the speak-out, the abortion campaign was consciousness-raising in action. As one commentator put it, speak-outs made the "'unspeakable' speakable, clearing the way for campaigns for women's right to abortion."[78]

News of the speak-out spread far and wide and, the idea did catch on. Susan Brownmiller, who had previously testified about her illegal abortion in NYRW, wrote "Everywoman's Abortions: The Oppressor Is Man," a front-page story for the *Village Voice*.[79] Gloria Steinem, not yet active in the movement, was in the speak-out audience as a journalist. She listened, recalled her own secret abortion, and wrote her first major piece on Women's Liberation, including a line about the Redstockings speak-out.[80]

In Chicago the *Voice of the Women's Liberation Movement* carried Brownmiller's article to activists throughout Women's Liberation and speak-outs spread around the country.[81] On the West Coast, Women's Liberation groups in Washington State, operating within the New and Old Left, led a statewide referendum on abortion to victory.[82]

In the fall of 1969 Shirley Chisholm became the founding president of the National Association for the Repeal of Abortion Laws (NARAL). Not able to function as an active officer because of her busy schedule as a congresswoman, she asked NARAL to allow her to be its "honorary president." To take such a high-profile stand, Chisholm said, was for her as a black politician "an even more serious step than for a white politician . . . because there is a deep and angry suspicion among many blacks that even birth control clinics are a plot by the white power structure to keep down the numbers of blacks." But, Chisholm said, "I do not know any black or Puerto Rican *women* who feel that way. . . . to label family planning and legal abortion programs 'genocide' is male rhetoric. . . . Poor women of every race feel as I do, I believe."[83]

Chisholm was not correct about all poor women, however, for although Poor Black Women's statement on birth control had preceded all others, the group believed that the white power structure did commit genocide against people of color. Still, they argued in favor of abortion rights because women could not fight genocide overburdened with child care responsibilities.[84]

The right to abortion was also supported by Dara Abubakari, the female vice president of the nationalist Republic of New Africa, even though the group she led officially opposed abortion. In 1970 Abubakari argued that black women must make their own decisions about bearing children. "Men shouldn't tell us. Nobody should tell us," Abubakari said.[85]

Shortly after the spread of news of the Redstockings speak-out, a consciousness-raising group in Austin, Texas, was getting started. The group was making referrals for illegal abortions and decided they too would hold a speak-out. Among the early members of Austin Women's Liberation was a young attorney named Sarah Weddington. Several years earlier, Weddington had crossed the border to Mexico for an illegal abortion. She was not among the women to testify at the speak-out.[86] She was not ready for that, but she was ready to make abortion legal. Weddington found a cocounsel, Linda Coffee, and a pregnant plaintiff seeking an abortion, Norma McCorvey, who became "Jane Roe." In March 1970 the women filed *Roe v. Wade*. In May a federal court ruled in favor of the plaintiff, the State of Texas appealed, and the suit was on its way to the Supreme Court.[87]

In the weeks after *Roe* was filed, the New York State legislature passed a law permitting abortions through the second trimester. The new law was not repeal, but it was the most liberal abortion law in the nation and, until the final decision in *Roe*, made New York the nation's abortion capital. The Cook Bill, signed into law on 11 April 1970 by Governor Nelson Rockefeller, had no residency requirements, abortions did not have to be performed in hospitals, and there were no consent provisions. Three years later, the Supreme Court would use the New York law as its model in the *Roe* ruling.

Thus *Roe v. Wade*, the ruling that legalized most abortions in the United States, owed a tremendous amount to consciousness-raising and the repeal strategy. On the one hand, consciousness-raising in Austin Women's Liberation was the impetus for Weddington to bring the suit. On the other, the Supreme Court modeled its ruling on a liberal New York law that had passed under pressure to stave off repeal, and after an onslaught of protest by women for whom consciousness-raising had made the "unspeakable speakable."

The next five years saw Women's Liberation in France, England, Italy, and a host of other nations use consciousness-raising in winning campaigns in which women, including Simone de Beauvoir, went public with their experience of illegal abortion.

The immense popular response to the abortion campaign, like the mobilization against beauty standards, rested on the importance of these issues to women. If the beauty issue meant casting off the "uniform" of second-class citizenship, the right to abortion meant self-determination for women. These struggles arose directly from the retelling of women's day-to-day experience of sexism. Consciousness-raising spread the understanding that these experiences were political rather than personal problems. Once raised and understood politically, these issues swelled the ranks of the movement with women who were new to any kind of political activism.

Moreover, Women's Liberation pioneers of differing views understood the centrality of control over one's fertility. Those who would fight for Women's Liberation through the Left and the Black Freedom Movement and those who sought an independent movement had little choice but to continue to lead the burgeoning movement they had created. Otherwise, there were others now coming around who would lead it on behalf of the establishment.

The power of sisterhood got the attention of the corporate world, mainstream politicians, and government agencies. These included the Central Intelligence Agency and the Federal Bureau of Investigation, as Women's Liberation founders began to suspect, and as the Senate's Church Committee investigations would soon confirm.[88]

Women of Color and White Women Organize Separately and Together

Throughout 1969 and 1970, women of all ages, races, and social classes formed feminist groups in high schools and colleges, in their churches, unions, professions, and in their neighborhoods. Support for Women's Liberation spread through the black community in the same late-sixties years that saw feminist ideas take hold among whites. By 1972 polls showed that black women supported Women's Liberation in considerably higher proportions than white women.[89]

Black women in the Civil Rights Movement had helped to start the Women's Liberation Movement, in part by rallying white founders to a standard of militancy with men that white women at last dared to risk. Black women's early feminist leadership, such as the 1964 strike for equality in the SNCC headquarters office and Dona Moses going back to her maiden name, exemplified that standard.

Although black women such as Florynce Kennedy, Cellestine Ware, Mary Ann Weathers, and Aileen Hernandez (NOW) were among the leaders of predominately white Women's Liberation groups and NOW, more frequently African American women preferred to fight male chauvinism together with other black women than in predominantly white groups. In 1970 black feminist Toni Cade said of the increasing numbers of black women espousing feminism, "It is obvious that we are turning to each other."[90]

There were a number of reasons for this, among them white women's racism and differences in the ways in which racism combined with male domination to complicate black women's oppression. Another less frequently discussed reason is that black feminists meeting apart from white women could avoid the danger of their honest testimony being turned into ammunition against African American men, especially in view of whites' already exaggerated views of black male chauvinism. Black feminist playwright Ntozake Shange refers to this phenomenon as a "conspiracy of silence."[91]

Because of the historically racist stereotype of the black man as rapist or macho stud, many white women already wrongly considered black men particularly sexist. It was not in black women's interest to give white women firsthand information that could validate their racist assumptions. Had not Emmett Till had been tortured and murdered only fifteen years earlier for possibly whistling at a white woman? Were not white women complicit in the Red Record brought to light by Ida B. Wells?[92] Was not Stokely Carmichael's sexist humor getting far more attention than the Moynihan Report in white feminist circles and on its way to being considered a cause of the rebirth of feminism? Black women were, of course, far more conscious of black male sexism than white women could ever be. But testifying about it in a consciousness-raising group with white women could increase the negative outlook for black males' chances in a white supremacist society.[93]

By June 1969, Gainesville, Florida, had a black Women's Liberation group. Judith Brown wrote to Kathie Sarachild and Carol Hanisch that "the black women are scared to make the existence of their group known. . . . the reason . . . : the double standard on tomming. They meet once a week. They don't want to be accused of doing a 'white thing.'"[94]

Brown became aware of what she called the "double standard on tomming" when Gainesville Women's Liberation (GWL) visited the Black Power group Junta of Militant Organizations (JOMO)—which would later become the African People's Socialist Party, sometimes referred to as the Uhuru Movement—in St. Petersburg, a city on Florida's west coast commonly thought of as a haven for retirees. GWL had been invited by JOMO chair Omali Yeshitela to consult with JOMO's women's caucus about a feminist plank in their platform for an upcoming mayoral election.

While the white women waited to meet with the caucus, male JOMO members chatted casually with them—and then loudly harassed the black women about meeting with white women. They themselves, however, could meet with white political leaders, and talk with white feminists, without questions being raised about loyalty to the race.

The black and white women did some consciousness-raising, and instead of working on an election platform, came up with feminist arguments the black women needed in their fight to serve on the armed community defense patrols. Women's exclusion from these patrols was a feminist complaint throughout the Black Power Movement and a battle the JOMO women soon won. The issue of the "double standard on tomming" raises the question of how many other black Women's Liberation groups may have been meeting like the one in Gainesville—keeping its existence to itself.

Women in the Puerto Rican Independence Movement and the Puerto Rican Socialist Party also worked for Women's Liberation within their own groups. But some sought out the Black Women's Alliance and asked to join. This prompted the BWA to expand into the Third World Women's Alliance in the summer of 1970. From there, the TWWA established connections with Chicana feminist groups and grew into a broad-based organization including women of Puerto Rican, Mexican, African, Lebanese, Chinese, Korean, and Japanese backgrounds. By November its New York City membership had reached two hundred, and there were members organizing chapters in other parts of the country.[95] In order to accommodate expansion while guaranteeing the continuity of its radical politics, the TWWA developed a democratic centralist decision-making structure.[96]

TWWA published *Triple Jeopardy*, an antisexist, antiracist, anti-imperialist newspaper for women of color. The newspaper reflected TWWA's analysis that economic exploitation was the basis of racism and sexism and that women of color in the United States were united with women of color in Third World nations in the struggle against imperialism. *Triple Jeopardy* published feminist articles demanding free twenty-four-hour day care centers, and a critical analysis of the Miss Black America contest headlined "Black Women on Auction Block Again," along with news and analysis of the Black Freedom Movement and articles on women in Third World nations such as Guinea-Bissau and Mozambique. Readers could expect explanations and diagrams of female anatomy and physiology in the same pages with explanations of dialectical materialism published in Spanish and English.[97]

The TWWA distributed the "Black Women's Manifesto," which declared that "the black woman is demanding a new set of female definitions."[98] Eleanor Holmes Norton proposed that black women "pioneer in establishing new male-female relationships around two careers."[99]

By 1970 feminism was widely apparent in the black community. Groups like Poor Black Women, the National Welfare Rights Organization, and the Black Panthers organized the poorest women. Toni Cade described the spread of black Women's Liberation:

Throughout the country . . . Black women have been forming work-
study groups, . . . cooperative nurseries, cooperative businesses,
consumer education groups, women's workshops on the campuses,
women's caucuses within existing organizations, . . . women's magazines . . . working papers, . . . correspondence with sisters in Vietnam,
Guatemala, Algeria, Ghana . . . alliances on a Third World Women
plank. They . . . have not . . . been duped by prevailing notions of
"woman" . . . they . . . use the Black Liberation struggle rather than the
American Dream as their yardstick.[100]

Margaret Wright, a member of a black Women's Liberation group in Los
Angeles called Women Against Repression, observed, "Now the black man
is saying he wants a family structure like the white man's . . . he's got to be
head and women have to be submissive. . . . Hell, the white woman is already
oppressed in that set up."[101] As black feminists opposed "that set up," some
began to see themselves as charting a new course for all women.

Black Women's Liberation spread into small towns, among artists and writers, and more. Painter Faith Ringgold, a leading figure in the New York art
world, had gone from "making a statement in my art about the Civil Rights
Movement" in the mid-1960s to forming the Ad Hoc Women's Group and
the Women Students and Artists for Black Art Liberation with her feminist
daughter Michelle Wallace in 1970.[102] The Ad Hoc Women's Group picketed
the Whitney and won increased showing of work by female artists. Black
composer and performing artist Abbey Lincoln called on black women to
"get evil enough and angry enough . . . [to] be moved to some action that will
bring our men to their senses."[103]

Women's Liberation Influences Black Power and Other Freedom Struggles

Throughout 1969 and 1970 Women's Liberation politics and positions were
increasingly recognized in sexually integrated, male-led organizations of the
black Left, most notably the Black Panther Party (BPP). By 1969 there were
at least forty Panther chapters in cities from coast to coast, and countless
unaffiliated Panther-type formations. The Panthers served free hot breakfasts to more than 50,000 children and ran free health clinics, free legal aid
clinics, free clothing distribution programs, and other "survival services."[104]
Political education, including equal rights for women, went hand in hand
with the services. Panther leader Kathleen Cleaver spoke out publicly against
male chauvinism in the BPP and the larger society. Cleaver's feminist analy-

sis of male supremacy was published in the black press, in Women's Liberation Movement newspapers, in the Left press, and in the mainstream white
press.[105]

Although Cleaver remained within the Black Panther Party, she was in
favor of the independent Women's Liberation Movement and commented
that the "organization of any movement for the liberation of women . . . [is]
the most revolutionary element in changing the social order of the world."
Her analysis of the roots of women's oppression held that women's childbearing and rearing role was "the most crucial factor in the reproduction of the
species and the maintenance of society. But . . . this most crucial work . . . is
the basis for women's position of inferiority."[106]

The Panthers engaged in public self-criticism on sexism. Far from indicat-
ing the severity of male chauvinism in the party, this should be understood
as precisely the opposite—an expression of the growing strength of feminist
forces within the BPP. That this self-criticism took place while the party was
subjected to attack by the FBI and local police is a remarkable indication not
only of feminism within the party but also of the party's courage.

The popular image of the Panthers was of macho males. But unlike its media image, by 1969 the party's membership was two-thirds female. Many of
these women held leadership positions in their chapters.[107] Cleaver defended
the BPP against its image as a "bastion of sexism," explaining, "What . . . is
distinctive about gender relations within the Black Panther Party is . . . that
it put[s] a woman in a position, when such treatment occur[s], to contest
it."[108]

In 1969 the BPP developed a press packet of Panther women discussing
goals of "women's emancipation" and fighting male chauvinism in the party:
"we're tired of sitting home and being misused," said one; "unless we stand
up, male chauvinism will still show itself. . . . unless we . . . teach the brothers
what's correct . . . then it'll still be here." Another chimed in: "black men have
to understand that their manhood is not dependent on keeping their black
women subordinate."[109]

These Panther women discussed a previous sex-segregated division of labor within the party—which now, they said, thanks to women's protest, was
being corrected. The Panther women saw the party as a vanguard in providing an antisexist example to the rest of the movement and the community,
but they did not describe the BPP as having eliminated male chauvinism
in its ranks. "We believe male chauvinism must be stomped out," said one,
but "we're very new at it . . . so whether or not we'll be able to provide the

example to lead other organizations towards women's liberation will come through our practice."[110]

In 1970 the party took an official position against male supremacy. It recognized that both women and gays were oppressed, and called for an alliance with the Women's Liberation and Gay Liberation Movements.[111] Also in 1970, the Panthers held a Revolutionary People's Constitutional Convention in Philadelphia attended by somewhere between 6,000 and 15,000 representatives from the Black Freedom Movement, the Women's Liberation Movement, the Gay Liberation Front, the American Indian Movement, Chicano and Latino groups such as the Brown Berets and the Young Lords, a radical Asian American group called I Wor Kuen, the student movement, and the Yippies. Planks in the resulting convention platform were proportional representation for minorities and women, shared housework by men and women, day care, and replacing the word "man" with "people" to "express solidarity with the self determination of women, and to do away with all remnants of male supremacy, once and for all."[112]

The Panthers' work on Women's Liberation advanced the spread of feminism into low-income urban neighborhoods, reaching young people who neither could nor would have learned about it elsewhere. As scholar activist George Katsiaficas wrote, "It is difficult to overestimate how much the Panthers transformed young African Americans: hardened criminals rose before 6:00 am to serve free breakfasts to thousands of school children; drug addicts kicked their habits and worked to expel dealers from the neighborhoods; and men used to having their way with women learned to listen to and respect their female counterparts."[113]

Radical black women were not alone in their opposition to male domination. In 1970 the National Association for the Advancement of Colored People adopted a women's rights platform at its annual convention and the National Council of Negro Women established a Woman Power Project. Latina and Chicana feminists began organizing out of the Puerto Rican Independence Movement and the Young Lords on the East Coast and the movements of Mexican American Chicano radicals on the West Coast and in the Southwest. Both these communities had traditions of feminism dating to revolutionary periods in Puerto Rico and Mexico.

The Young Lords, a revolutionary Puerto Rican nationalist group, evolved from a street gang that adopted radical politics. By 1969 it had a Women's Caucus that met regularly to formulate feminist positions, study Latina history, and develop feminist political education. An early achievement was bringing about a change in the Young Lords' Thirteen Point Program and Platform, which originally included equality for women while calling for "revolutionary machismo." Denise Oliver, a leader of the Women's Caucus, said that "machismo was never gonna be revolutionary. Saying 'revolutionary machismo' is like saying 'revolutionary fascism' or 'revolutionary racism'— it's a contradiction. And so, through our political growth . . . that point in the program was changed." Point 5 now read: "We want equality for women. Down with machismo and male chauvinism."[114]

Some of the positions of the Women's Caucus were for "revolutionary day care centers," rearing children being "the responsibility of the man as well as the woman," and "End all genocide. Abortions under community control." Oliver said there was "still male chauvinism in the Party" but "a new man . . . [was] evolving. It's not just the women who are pointing out male chauvinism, the men are even disciplining other men because of it."[115]

By 1970 there were at least two Chicana feminist organizations, Las Hijas de Cuauhtemoc at Long Beach State University in California, which was independent, and the Chicana Caucus of El Partido de la Raza Unida in Texas.[116] Las Hijas adopted the name from a Mexican feminist group that fought for women's equality during the Mexican Revolution. They studied Chicana history, did political education, helped women get abortions, put out a newspaper, and developed an analysis through consciousness-raising.

The Chicana Caucus of La Raza developed their positions into a party document that called for equal pay for equal work, "legalized medical abortions to . . . protect the human right of self-determination," child care centers, and representation "in all levels of La Raza Unida party."[117]

By the year 1970 there were women's uprisings in virtually every ethnic group and economic class. From the trade unions to the upper echelons, in cities, suburbs, and beyond, feminist consciousness soared. Women could see the social nature of their predicament and were eager to work together for change. Older women started OWL, Older Women's Liberation. Young women started groups in their high schools. Women of color organized groups. Women's caucuses flourished in professional organizations. Within and without the movements of the 1960s, from the Black Panther Party to the counterculture, from cosmopolitan elites to country radio fans, women across the nation rose up and began to fight male chauvinism passionately and collectively.

The Movement Is Established

1970

THE PIONEERING black Women's Liberation groups led the way for black women and often for the predominantly white movement as well. Poor Black Women had developed a movement-wide influence, sending their working papers out to black and white women's groups of all sorts. The group also published their working papers in the black press, Women's Liberation journals, and predominantly white movement newspapers such as the *Guardian*. They met in Canada with revolutionary Vietnamese women in order, as one put it, "to find out how did they get from underneath the man to actually get out here in the battlefield."[1]

Poor Black Women developed critical consulting relationships with founding white Women's Liberation groups, most notably the groups organized by Roxanne Dunbar and Pam Allen.[2] Poor Black Women repeatedly advised white Women's Liberation groups to pay attention to class.

Perhaps the capstone event of 1970 for the spread of black feminist influence was the weeklong hearing called that September by Eleanor Holmes Norton, then New York City human rights commissioner. Norton said "the chief organizing factor" for the hearing was to counter the "public conception" of the Women's Liberation Movement "as a white, affluent, educated women's movement."[3]

The hearing brought together officially recognized experts and women whose expertise came from their activism, such as black feminist Beulah

Sanders, vice chair of the National Welfare Rights Organization (NWRO). Representatives from feminist groups ranged from Frances Beal to Betty Friedan. Also included were famous scholars such as Margaret Mead, elected officials such as Shirley Chisholm, and representatives of domestic workers and largely female labor unions. Dorothy Height, president of the National Council of Negro Women, representing its four million members, spoke to "the inescapable task of working to eliminate racism and sexism" faced by black women, who were "found largely in the lowest paid jobs."[4] Patricia Jones, representing domestic workers, gave detailed testimony on the "slave labor" conditions she faced working five and a half days a week, fourteen hours a day, caring for a ten-room house and two young children. "Is this human dignity for women, black, white, or domestic?" Jones asked.[5]

Within six months of the hearing, the New York State legislature passed into law a bill extending minimum wage protection to household workers, two-thirds of whom were black women. Norton said "testimony received at the hearing led us to organize a campaign to get the minimum wage for household workers." The victory "illustrate[d] what has been missing from the movement for women's rights" and what was happening to "move it ahead," Norton said. She held up the campaign as an example for the feminist movement because it "illuminated three essential components of a success-ful strategy for women's rights in this country: . . . [that it] must be a 'politi-cal' movement"; that to "embrace all women" it must include "labor or class" issues; and it must be "willing to make alliances" with "legislators, women's groups, minority community groups, labor unions, and others."[6]

Another example of the type of coalition work promoted by Norton oc-curred when NOW president Betty Friedan, NRWO's Beulah Sanders, and a representative of Redstockings, among other organizations, conducted a press conference calling on women across the nation to defeat the confir-mation of G. Harrold Carswell, then President Nixon's appointee to the Su-preme Court.[7] Carswell had a record of ruling against civil rights activists, and in his personal life was a leader of a segregated country club. The labor movement considered him an enemy of workers' rights. And feminists were incensed when, as we shall see, Carswell ruled in 1969 that mothers of pre-schoolers could be denied employment.

Women's Liberation, NOW, and the NWRO were on the cutting edge of the alliance with the labor movement and the Black Freedom Movement that was successful in defeating Carswell's confirmation. Here was a broad-based campaign with national impact in which Women's Liberation struggled simultaneously against male supremacy, white supremacy, and capitalism. Black feminism did much to point the movement in that direction.

Although among lower-income women there were numerically more whites than blacks, a greater percentage of black women were low income. Thus black feminist demands were likely to be stronger than white feminist demands on class and/or labor issues, and so to be universal or, as Norton put it, to "embrace all women." This made black feminist leadership indispensible to ensure a movement that was not only inclusive of black women but also broad-based enough to emcompass the needs of most white women and to rally the enormous potential female power base of half the population.

Another campaign that demonstrated the mass appeal of feminism began when Betty Friedan called for a twenty-four-hour general strike "on the unfinished business of women's equality" on 26 August 1970, the fiftieth anniversary of winning the vote.[8] A coalition of NOW and Women's Liberation organized the Women's Strike for Equality. The demands were twenty-four-hour public child care, abortion on demand, and equal opportunity in employment and education.

NOW sought to involve the radical feminists. Friedan said NOW "needed the emotional verve and style of the young radicals. I admired that verve and style in the Miss America protest."[9] To the *New York Times* Friedan said that "women's lib people . . . they're the way the troops we need come up."[10]

Friedan got more troops on August 26 in New York City than she had anticipated. "There were more women than anyone had ever seen. . . . we . . . couldn't believe it," she said as fifty thousand supporters, ranging from the Third World Women's Alliance to suffragists from the First Wave, marched down Fifth Avenue.[11] Stretched across the avenue was huge banner reading "Women of the World Unite," echoing the title of the 1968 article in New York Radical Women's *Notes from the First Year* by Carol Hanisch and Elizabeth Sutherland with its automatic play on "Workers of the World, Unite!"

The radical feminists conducted an integral part of the organizing. Far beyond the reach of the thirty then-extant NOW chapters, tens of thousands of women demonstrated in more than ninety cities and small towns in forty-two states.[12] Jo Freeman, visiting Women's Liberation groups abroad, organized a press conference on the strike in Norway. Norwegian women turned out in solidarity. Women in Quebec demonstrated for the strike demands. In the Netherlands, Dutch Women's Liberation, called the Dolle Minas, marched on the U.S. embassy in support, and French feminists in Paris joined a march on the Arc de Triomphe.[13] In a speech to the New York marchers Friedan said, "We learned . . . the power of our solidarity . . . Sisterhood is Powerful . . . August 26th made that power visible to the world."[14]

The strike was heralded as the "largest protest for women's equality in U.S. history."[15] National publicity in the weeks before the strike was intense. Friedan believed the threat of the approaching strike and the powerful coalition that put it on caused the House to pass the Equal Rights Amendment (ERA). The ERA had not received the attention of the full House since its introduction in 1923. On August 10, sixteen days before strike day, it passed by a vote of 352–15.[16]

That same year, trade union feminists called statewide conferences on sex discrimination in the AFL-CIO. In March, in Wisconsin, the first of these conferences endorsed the ERA and came out against protective legislation. In April the United Auto Workers, under unrelenting pressure from its Women's Department, was the first major union to endorse the ERA. One after another followed, until in 1973 the AFL-CIO reversed its position and supported the ERA.

Women who were not in unions also fought for their rights. In 1966 Ida Phillips earned six dollars a day plus tips as a waitress. In response to an advertisement, she applied for an assembly-line job at Martin Marietta Corporation that started at $2.25 an hour. Phillips was denied the job because she had a preschool-age child. Since fathers of such children were hired, Phillips sued on the grounds of sex discrimination. When the case came before his court on appeal, Judge G. Harrold Carswell upheld the company's position.

In the end, however, Carswell's decision prompted feminist participation in the coalition that influenced the Senate's rejection of his nomination to the Supreme Court. And Phillips won her case, including back wages. "It wasn't just for myself," Phillips said, "but for other women in the same shoes. . . . This is my way of letting people know I'm more than just a dumb little waitress."[17] There were more than four million women in the United States in Phillips's "shoes"; mothers with children under six constituted about 40 percent of employed mothers.

By 1970, black feminists rose to leadership in the National Welfare Rights Organization, and the organization advocated reproductive freedom, free universal child care, and a universal guaranteed annual wage that included women's reproductive work. Eleanor Holmes Norton introduced the NWRO as the "vanguard of the women's movement" at the hearing on women's rights.[18] The organization described itself as "frontline troops of women's freedom."[19] NWRO first vice chair Beulah Sanders said they were working for these goals together with "women's liberation which we have a great admiration for."[20] Indeed, NOW and Women's Liberation, including the Southern Female Rights Union and Redstockings, made these same demands. The Florida Paper had declared the guaranteed annual income "of direct relevance to women."[21]

In May 1970 lesbians "came out" (as the then-preeminent gay organizing strategy was called) at the second Congress to Unite Women in New York City. On the opening day of the conference a new group, Radicalesbians, took the stage by surprise, announced themselves as lesbians, and protested discrimination against lesbians in the movement.

They distributed their position paper, "The Woman-Identified Woman," which cast lesbians as a feminist vanguard and opened a national debate in the movement on the relationship between lesbianism and feminism. "A lesbian is the rage of all women condensed to the point of explosion," declared the paper. "Until women see in each other the possibility of a primal commitment which includes sexual love, they will be denying themselves the love and value they readily accord to men, thus affirming their second-class status."[22]

Lesbians had been active in the feminist movement from the beginning, and the politics of their presence had been stirring beneath the surface. Until 1970, however, lesbians worked on the feminist issues of the day and did not focus on sexual orientation. After 1970, like the Radicalesbians, a number of lesbian and heterosexual feminists argued that lesbianism was—or at least should become—a central concern to the heterosexual majority of women. They saw lesbianism as "one road to freedom—freedom from oppression by men," as radical lesbian feminist Martha Shelley put it.[23]

Feminist and lesbian activists Sidney Abbott and Barbara Love helped to raise lesbian feminist consciousness within Women's Liberation during the rebirth years. They analyzed and detailed its rise chronologically in their pathbreaking 1972 book *Sappho Was a Right-On Woman* and concluded:

> In the beginning, the highest aspiration of most Lesbians in the women's movement was just that—to be included. For the first two years of the second wave of Feminism, this desire to be included was the perspective from which Lesbians viewed the women's movement. In the midst of fighting for Women's Liberation, they continued to submit to oppression by hiding so that they could be included, or worse, defensively trying to prove the obvious—that they were also "real" women.[24]

In 1969, observed Abbott and Love, the birth of the Gay Liberation Movement raised their expectations as lesbians.

Although no Women's Liberation pioneer wrote of lesbianism as a founding influence on the development of her feminist consciousness or the need for a new movement, several addressed the lesbian question early on. Beauvoir devoted a section of *The Second Sex* to it and argued that "homosexuality can be for woman a mode of flight from her situation or a way of accepting it. The great mistake . . . is . . . to regard it as never other than an inauthentic attitude. . . . if nature is to be invoked, one can say that all women are naturally homosexual."[25]

Beauvoir vigorously defended lesbians from accusations that they imitated sterotypical male-female roles, saying, "The woman who turns lesbian because she haughtily declines male domination is often pleased to find the same proud amazon in another." Indeed, declared Beauvoir, there was "Nothing less natural than to dress in feminine fashion."[26]

In July 1968, well before the lesbian question emerged as a high-profile issue in the new movement, Judith Brown urged women to "begin an open discussion of homosexuality in the hope that future conferences and private thinking will consider the issue."[27] After making a case for all-female communes as a needed bastion of strength in the coming struggle, Brown wrote eloquently and presciently of what was to come:

> Women who turn from men for a time, to look to each other for political relationships . . . are bound to see here and there someone they love. The slightest measure of female liberation will bring with it the ability to perceive again the precise qualities and degree of responsivity which inhere in other women. . . . political content will not suffice to fill the need every human has for that place where one "slackens the pace at the crossroads." . . . Exploring the possibilities of non-elitist, non-colonial love may teach us forms of political strength.[28]

Brown compared charges of homosexuality with red-baiting and said that "a fear of homosexuality may be the one last strand by which the male order can pull us back into tow."[29]

In 1970, in *The Dialectic of Sex*, Shulamith Firestone argued that bans on homosexuality had originally arisen because "full sexuality threatened the continuous reproduction necessary for human survival . . . and sexuality had to be restricted to reproductive purposes." Firestone contended: "A feminist revolution based on advanced technology" would eliminate the "need for sexual repression . . . allowing for the first time a 'natural sexual freedom'"

which would include "the freedom of all women and children to do whatever they wish to do sexually. . . . all forms of sexuality would be allowed and
indulged."[30]

But neither Brown nor Firestone argued that lesbian relationships were
the road to Women's Liberation. In 1970, Ti-Grace Atkinson was perhaps the
only founder to support, for a time, the Radicalesbian position. "Lesbianism
is to feminism what the Communist Party was to the trade-union movement," Atkinson argued.[31]

Atkinson, although not a lesbian except "in the political sense," joined
the New York chapter of the Daughters of Bilitis (DOB), a lesbian civil rights
group begun in 1955.[32] By "the political sense," Atkinson meant "a total commitment to this [feminist] Movement." Still, "Some lesbians have challenged
my right to hold any opinion on this question, since by their definition I am
not 'lesbian,'" Atkinson said, meaning that she was not sexually involved
with women.[33]

The lesbian question surfaced in the mainstream media in connection
with Women's Liberation in December 1970 when feminist theorist Kate
Millett was disapprovingly referred to as bisexual in *Time* magazine.[34] In
response, a coalition of feminist groups and Daughters of Bilitis defended
Millett at a press conference. DOB had, from the start, debated what priority
to give the cause of feminism, and many DOB members were activists for
lesbian civil rights and feminism.[35]

Articles about lesbian feminism were published in at least three of the
spate of anthologies of Women's Liberation material that came out in 1970.[36]
After the founding years that are the subject of this study, and throughout
the decade of the 1970s, varieties of lesbian feminist groups, some within
the movement and others as lesbian separatists, organized across the nation.
Debate over the relationship between lesbianism and feminism roiled the
Women's Liberation Movement. This is widely discussed in the secondary
literature and has been referred to as the "gay-straight split."[37]

Women's Liberation: A Mass Radical Movement

The establishment of Women's Liberation nationally was documented in
1970 in *The Mushroom Effect*, a directory of Women's Liberation groups in
thirty-four states including hundreds in rural areas in Iowa, West Virginia,
North Dakota, Nebraska, New Mexico, and Kansas.[38] It also gave addresses
for Women's Liberation groups in Argentina, Australia, England, France, the
Netherlands, and Canada.[39]

The informal organization of Women's Liberation made precise numbers difficult to determine. Unlike NOW, which had chartered chapters, membership applications, cards, dues, and formal structure, Women's Liberation had none of these. In 1970 there were three thousand NOW members in about thirty chapters around the nation.[40] That same year, radical feminist Robin Morgan counted more than two hundred consciousness-raising groups in New York City.[41] Most groups averaged ten to fifteen, which suggests that three thousand women were in the movement's Women's Liberation branch in New York City alone.

Feminist author Caroline Bird commented delightedly on the movement's surprising growth.[42] After the "uphill work" of writing *Born Female* between 1967 and 1968 when people "kept telling me that most women wouldn't like the book . . . In 1970, I find like-minded women wherever I go."[43]

Bird attributed the dramatic change to the rise of young radical feminists who through the "technique of consciousness-raising" solved the "gut problem of any social action—how to recruit new members."[44] These women, Bird said, unlike "the middle of the road New Feminism of the National Organization for Women . . . want to remake the world . . . from top to bottom." Bird called their approach a "startling innovation," the movement's "secret strength" that "propagates itself by contagion."[45] "Virtually non-existent in 1966," Bird said, the radical feminists were "in every sizable city in 1970."[46]

That same year, Women's Liberation activist Robin Morgan reported groups in Sweden, Germany, Mexico, Tanzania, Japan, and a half dozen other countries.[47] In the summer of 1970, Jo Freeman visited groups in Norway and Denmark and reported that the whole movement in Denmark named itself Redstockings, after the New York group.[48] In France, the first feminist anthology carried Carol Hanisch's "The Personal Is Political."[49] England saw a mass Women's Liberation meeting in March 1970. Women's Liberation took on relevant issues in countries around the world. The Tanzanian Women's Association, for example, protested that if men could have more than one wife, they would take additional husbands. Indonesian women also protested polygamy.[50]

And what were the Women's Liberation founders we've been following doing in 1970? The SNCC Black Women's Liberation Committee, with Frances Beal in the lead, developed into the Third World Women's Alliance and soon began bringing out their newspaper *Triple Jeopardy*, with the subtitle "Smash! Capitalism, Racism, & Sexism."[51] Kathie Sarachild was busy with Redstockings organizing and actions, including planning a multigroup sit-in at the *Ladies' Home Journal*, out of which came a special section of the magazine written by Women's Liberation, which reached millions of women.[52] Judith Brown and Marilyn Webb were part of collectives working on Women's Liberation newspapers. Carol Hanisch had moved to Gainesville at the start of her SCEF Freedom for Women project and was organizing with Gainesville Women's Liberation. Poor Black Women explored alliances with the revolutionary women of Vietnam. Heather Booth had established Jane, an underground feminist service that gave thousands of illegal abortions to women. Naomi Weisstein operated a national speakers bureau and trained women to agitate for the cause. Shulamith Firestone was writing *The Dialectic of Sex* and continuing to organize in New York City, founding New York Radical Feminists with Anne Koedt and African American feminist Cellestine Ware. Firestone and Ware left Redstockings and Koedt left the Feminists to start this new group. With Anne Koedt, Firestone edited *Notes from the Second Year.* Jo Freeman traveled abroad meeting with Women's Liberation groups. Roxanne Dunbar set up the Southern Female Rights Union in New Orleans to organize an interracial group of poor women.

Women's Liberation in 1970 was geographically widespread, mobilized massive numbers of women, and moved deeply into the culture, organizing across race and class lines. Its impact was felt in enclaves known for internal loyalty and lack of public protest from within, such as the church, sports, and the military.

By 1970, as polls indicated, most Americans knew that the Women's Liberation Movement was in their midst. They knew about the movement because a neighbor, a family member, or a coworker was in a consciousness-raising group. They knew because an acquaintance had used a movement abortion referral network or joined a demonstration for legalized abortion or protested a beauty pageant. They knew because female coworkers were whispering about sex discrimination or were using the label "male chauvinist pig" for an office sexist. In 1970 Women's Liberation was, as *Life* magazine said, the "liveliest conversational topic in the land."[53]

It was strikingly clear that the argument for Sisterhood Is Powerful had prevailed. The mass base of Women's Liberation expanded rapidly, and participants coming into the movement from outside of the Left exceeded those coming from within. One journalist observed, "The WLM is growing so rapidly . . . even its most cheerful proselytizers are surprised, spreading . . . into a political territory where anti-Vietnam petitions have rarely been seen."[54] Women's Liberation pioneers continued to write and organize for the movement, but now, with a mass movement, their work reached mass audiences.

Women's Liberation—the Liveliest Conversational Topic in the Land

The popularity of the new movement in 1970 was apparent in the aggressive coverage of the mass media. The extent of the coverage showed that editors believed the public wanted to know what Women's Liberation was doing.

Three forces collided in an explosion of news about the movement. First, there was a surfeit of newsworthy activity. As *Glamour* magazine editorialized, "women's liberation has surfaced and . . . the media . . . seized upon the colorful goings on with delight."[55] Second, the public wanted to know about these "goings on." The rapid growth of the movement was itself a source of astonishment and interest. *Life* observed, "Awareness of the movement for women's liberation has burst upon most Americans with jarring suddenness."[56] Ida Lewis, the editor-in-chief at *Essence*, a mainstream fashion magazine for black women, said in the July 1970 issue, "Everybody's talking about the women's liberation movement. Overnight it seems to have grown into a national issue."[57] In December of that year the *Chicago Defender*, a leader of the black press, editorialized that due to "thinking women" a "woman power revolution" was "dawning."[58]

The *Chicago Defender*

Coverage of Women's Liberation by the *Chicago Defender*, a nationally circulated daily serving a general black readership, is an indicator of the interest of the black public. With such editorial pronouncements as "Women, like blacks, have too long been second class citizens,"[59] the newspaper was both following and leading. The *Defender*'s serious, positive coverage challenges the predominant image of the media disparaging the Women's Liberation Movement in the years of its resurgence, and it pierces the myth that black women were distanced from Women's Liberation and saw it as a white movement.[60] Indeed, the *Defender* not only covered black feminist activities positively but highlighted predominantly white feminist events and groups and gave contact information for them. By 1970 the *Defender* believed that the reading public was interested in attending feminist events. This is attested by its ongoing provision of advance publicity and calendar listings for events, including phone numbers.[61]

The *Defender* was mainstream black press, yet the secondary literature contains sweeping allegations that both black and white mainstream reportage maligned feminism. Remarkably, the *Defender* has been cited to show that "the black press was generally uninterested in the woman's movement."[62]

True, the *Defender* supplied plenty of standard male-chauvinist women's page fare. It also published columns by critics of the movement. Noteworthy about the *Defender*'s coverage, however, was the extent to which it broke from the traditional male-chauvinist milieu to satisfy the interest of its readers, not the ways in which it was consistent with the everyday male chauvinism of the time.

The *Defender*'s view on reader interest may have been based, in part, on polls and surveys. The newspaper's own Inquiring Photographer polled passersby about feminism on several occasions. The published results showed a profeminist majority.[63] In the fall of 1970, the *Defender* also published the results of two surveys on teenage girls' interest in Women's Liberation. The articles were sympathetically headlined "Teen Girls Want Liberation, Too" and "Teen-Age Feminists in Agreement With Adult Counterparts." Bylined positive headlines about Women's Liberation such as "Women's Lib Helps Men" and "First Black YWCA Executive Director Feels Organization Is Women's Movement" defied journalism's standard of objectivity and assumed readers' favorable attitudes.[64]

The *Defender*'s 1969 and 1970 presentation of feminist news made it clear that the paper considered Women's Liberation newsworthy. In 1969 the *Defender* wrote about the newly organized Congress to Unite Women, and in 1970 it gave advance publicity to the August 26 Women's Strike for Equality. The newspaper called constitutional equality for women a "sound goal" and defended NOW's campaign for the Equal Rights Amendment (ERA) against Happiness of Womanhood (HOW), a group that organized against it.[65]

The *Defender* agreed with black feminist opposition to the Moynihan Report. When female Black Panthers opposed as myth Moynihan's view of the "emasculated black man in a matriarchal society," the *Defender* praised them as "strong feminists" and quoted them as saying that "the liberation of women is a part of the same struggle that all victims of the capitalistic system are fighting."[66]

Linda Lumsden, a scholar of journalism history, found the *Defender* the most profeminist of the black press between 1968 and 1973.[67] The *Defender* may have been the best, but it was not the first. It stood in a long tradition of black newspapers and journalists that supported equality for women. Frederick Douglass's *North Star*, which bore on its masthead "Right is of no Sex—Truth is of no Color," exemplified the tradition, as did black feminist and race leader Ida B. Wells's *Free Speech and Headlight*, W. E. B. DuBois's *Crisis*, and the *Defender*'s own internationally respected Ethel Payne, who was a Shirley Chisholm supporter.

By 1970, front-running mass circulation black magazines *Ebony* and *Jet* also offered profeminist coverage. In April *Ebony*, in an early, positive use of the phrase "black feminism," observed that the "black feminist movement must obliterate" the "message" of black women as "sex kittens."[68]

Jet newsmagazine, with more than half a million working-class readers, devoted its December 4 cover story to the election of black feminist Aileen Hernandez as president of the predominantly white NOW.[69] On the cover was a riveting photograph of Hernandez on a political visit to Chicago. "Black Woman Heads Drive to Liberate All Women" read the headline. Hernandez looked like the right woman for the job, confident, dignified but not chic, standing tall in a well-cut suit on a city sidewalk. *Jet*'s inside coverage, a five-page article with five photographs, was long for the magazine, which specialized in "peppy" "news nuggets," as one journalism historian put it.[70] Under the large-print all-caps headline "Feminist Likens Sexism to Racism Against Blacks" were photographs of Hernandez meeting with the Chicago Urban League head, a black man, and meeting with a white female representative of the Chicago NOW chapter. By the second paragraph, *Jet* proudly let readers know that Hernandez had been voted in as NOW's president by a "mostly white middle-class, well educated" membership.[71] *Jet*'s forthright tone suggested that it did not believe that this information would alienate readers.

The article's black feminist reporter, Valerie Jo Bradley, presented statistics that showed black women were the "biggest victims of sexism." She quoted Hernandez's assertion that black women could tell white women "how it goes" on the "fundamental kinds of things." Hernandez also held that "white women need to be as intimately involved in dealing with racism . . . as they are with doing away with sexism," and that too many of them considered racism "a side issue."[72]

Hernandez said she was seeking to "coordinate the black, student and woman's revolutions . . . for the most profound social revolution there ever has been."[73] Implicit in the article was the significance of white, middle-class women choosing to be led to liberation by a black woman who criticized them for racism. Its clearest message was that feminist demands such as equal pay and public child care centers were in black women's interest.

Women's Liberation Turns the Mighty Establishment Media to Its Advantage

The sheer number of newsworthy feminist activities and the strength of public interest in Women's Liberation combined with a third force to create an explosion of feminist news. That force was the conversion to feminism of female employees of the corporate media, whose engaged reportage helped to bring the message of Women's Liberation to millions of women. As Women's Liberation mushroomed, women working in major media outlets challenged their employers. Inspired by the movement and fed up with consignment to the research department while men wrote the breaking stories, the media women took action. They filed charges of sex discrimination against their employers, including the National Broadcasting Company (NBC), *Newsweek*, and the Time Inc. publications *Time, Life, Fortune*, and *Sports Illustrated*. At NBC, women also disrupted a corporate board meeting and won two million dollars in back pay.

The top-story status of Women's Liberation, combined with the movement strategy of refusing to talk with male reporters initiated by NYRW at the Miss America protest, fueled the media women's fight. If the press wanted the scoop on Women's Liberation, they would have to send female reporters. They did just that. Said *Newsweek*: "the feminists won't even talk to male journalists. . . . For this week's coverage, *Newsweek* sought out Helen Dudar, a topflight journalist who is also a woman."[74] In a six-article series on Women's Liberation, the *Florida Times Union* explained why it had added a female reporter: "The reason is several militant ladies would grant interviews only if their views were reported under a woman's byline."[75]

The female journalists were converted to Women's Liberation as they gathered material for their stories. They explained their learning process to their readers, replacing the journalistic convention of "objectivity" with a fresh and convincing personal approach.

Helen Dudar, who researched and wrote *Newsweek's* cover story on the movement, was one of the journalists converted by her assignment. Speaking of a "gravely infectious" anger toward men that came with consciousness-raising, Dudar wrote, "I came to this story with a smug certainty of my ability to keep a respectable distance between me and any subject I reported on. The complacency . . . died. . . . I found myself offering . . . obscenities to a . . . male colleague who 'only' made a casual remark along the lines of 'just-like-a-woman.'"[76]

In her article, Dudar revealed that she had realized in the course of interviewing feminist pioneers that she had been rejecting Women's Liberation because she secretly prized her exclusive status as a token successful woman. "Superiority is precisely what I had felt and enjoyed," Dudar said. "One of the rare and real rewards of reporting is learning about yourself." Now, Dudar said, she felt a "sense of . . . kinship with all those women who have been asking all the hard questions. I thank them and so . . . will a lot of other women."[77]

Dudar's conversion was repeated across the nation. In the *Florida Times Union*, for example, Pamela Howard reported: "Despite my own attempts to remain objective . . . I was . . . hooked. . . . So why not a woman in the White House? Why not a man in the home at the sink—at least half the time."[78]

The February 1970 issue of *Mademoiselle*, the popular magazine for young women, featured a cover story on Women's Liberation. In a lead article, "Women's Liberation Loves You," associate editor Amy Gross began with her first impression of the movement as "sick" and "paranoid." Gross, too, changed her mind while talking with founders. Interviewing Naomi Weisstein, she found herself agreeing that, as Weisstein said, "Only with equal power can people act with dignity and humaneness." "That's why," Gross said, "I like women's lib more all the time . . . it says out loud what we've all learned not to say even silently." *Mademoiselle* also offered a quiz called "Are you ready for liberation?" Rating the scores, *Mademoiselle* said of those in one range, "You need further consciousness-raising. Get four or five other girls together. Start a group."[79]

Essence featured in its July 1970 issue an interview by editor-in-chief Ida Lewis with Eleanor Holmes Norton, who was then the legal advisor to SNCC's Black Women's Liberation Committee, head of the Women's Project at the ACLU, and attorney for the women who had just filed charges of sex discrimination at *Newsweek*. Norton came directly to the point: "Unless black women find that they have been treated with total equality, they had better find the women's liberation movement relevant." Lewis agreed immediately: "The fact is that black women have not been treated equally."[80]

Newsweek's Helen Dudar interviewed Roxanne Dunbar and Ti-Grace Atkinson, whom she called "leading feminist theoreticians," and reported extensively their views on men and marriage. Quoting from a Women's Liberation journal that recommended karate, Dudar explained as if it were her own view the radical feminist position "that women are a class, probably the original oppressed class of human history"—and if women are a class, then rape is a political act, and karate an appropriate political solution.[81]

To be sure, there was antifeminist coverage and distortion. But when the founders refused to speak with male reporters, demanded female reporters, and then raised the reporters' feminist consciousness, they effectively used the media to advocate for Women's Liberation.

The Market Is Ripe for Feminist Literature

Mainstream publishing houses joined the press in seeking to capitalize on the movement's growing popularity. The year 1970 saw at least thirteen mass market books on Women's Liberation and women's history, with more under contract. Publishers had gotten the message that, as Jones presciently observed two years earlier in the Florida Paper, the "market is ripe for feminist literature." Women's Liberation activists were the first editors and writers of these books.

In 1969 Leslie Tanner, soon-to-be editor of *Voices from Women's Liberation*, one of five anthologies of movement documents published in 1970, was starting a consciousness-raising group on New York's Lower East Side. Tanner said, "We avidly read and circulated everything we could get our hands on. There was never enough to go around within our own growing group, and nowhere near enough to pass along to other women who expressed an interest in Women's Liberation."[82] So Tanner began gathering the movement's mimeographed papers for a mass market anthology.

The publishers were eager to meet the women's demand, because they wanted to sell books. Unlike Betty Friedan, Women's Liberation founders were not women that publishers would seek out for their professional writing experience. But their position papers, circulated hand to hand, had helped to start a new movement that was spreading widely. The founders' track record of readership was the movement itself. Tanner said that for her anthology she gathered the "papers that . . . had opened up our heads to new ideas, to a totally new way of thinking. Why not make a book of the 'voices from Women's Liberation?'"[83]

At least nine of the thirteen books published in 1970 were written or edited by activists.[84] The anthologies were collections of founding movement papers. Another two were by pro–Women's Liberation journalists who extensively interviewed and quoted the founders, even publishing pages of interview transcripts.

Five of the books by black feminists were Toni Cade's *The Black Woman*; Maya Angelou's *I Know Why the Caged Bird Sings*; Shirley Chisholm's *Unbought and Unbossed*; *Crusade for Justice: The Autobiography of Ida B. Wells*, edited by Wells's daughter, Alfreda M. Barnett Duster; and *Woman*

Power: The Movement for Women's Liberation, by Cellestine Ware. *Woman Power* was the first history of the new movement.

The Black Woman grew out of editor Toni Cade's "impatience," as she put it, that writing about Women's Liberation did not meet the growing demand of black women dealing with three liberation struggles: "white people, whiteness, or racism; men, maleness, or chauvinism; America or imperialism."[85] Black women, said Cade, were not "duped by the prevailing notions of 'woman' but . . . have maintained a critical stance."[86] *The Black Woman* was for them.

In *Unbought and Unbossed*, Congresswoman Shirley Chisholm daringly spoke out about making referrals for illegal abortions. She provided income statistics from the Labor Department that showed the average wages for white men, black men, white women, and black women. "Measured in uncontested dollars and cents," Chisholm asked, "which is worse—race prejudice or anti-feminism? White women are at an economic disadvantage even when compared with black men, and black women are nowhere on the earnings scale."[87] Like Ware and Cade, Chisholm noted the rising popularity of Women's Liberation: "most men will jeer at the women's liberation groups springing up. But . . . countless women, including their own wives and especially their daughters . . . applaud the liberation groups."[88]

Award-winning writer, actress, and activist Maya Angelou was as bold as Chisholm. In her bestselling autobiography, *I Know Why the Caged Bird Sings*, Angelou broke the code of silence about exposing to whites' judgment the crimes of black men against black women and children. She revealed that her mother's boyfriend had raped her when she was eight.[89] She was hospitalized, and the boyfriend was killed in retaliation after his deed was revealed. Angelou blamed herself and became mute for five years. In 1970 Angelou was among the earliest incest survivors to speak out publicly. As the first black woman to do so in a way that brought incest to the attention of the nation, Angelou told a "race secret," as black feminist scholars Johnnetta Cole and Beverly Guy-Sheftall put it.[90] Incest occurs in all races and classes and is difficult for survivors of both sexes to disclose. But pressure on women of otherwise oppressed groups to protect the group by concealing abuse is especially onerous. Angelou made a feminist analysis of the situation: "The Black female . . . in her tender years . . . is caught up in the tripartite crossfire of masculine prejudice, white illogical hate, and Black lack of power. . . . That the adult American Negro female emerges a formidable character . . . is seldom accepted as an inevitable outcome of the struggle."[91]

Four of the five anthologies by white editors carried the founding articles of the first black Women's Liberation group, Poor Black Women.[92] Two also included Mary Ann Weathers's "An Argument for Black Women's Liberation as a Revolutionary Force."[93] Most of the work in the anthologies had appeared first in the dozens of Women's Liberation newspapers and several theoretical journals that now circulated around the country.

Three of the anthologies included part or all of the Florida Paper, and two carried the "Program for Feminist Consciousness-Raising." Most represented an array of Women's Liberation activist writings by names familiar from the debates described in previous chapters. Many included the Redstockings Manifesto. Virtually all of the material, as Tanner said, had been passed from hand to hand when it first ran off the mimeograph machines as the pamphlet literature of the movement.

The appearance of Kate Millett's opus *Sexual Politics*, from Doubleday, was a news item in itself. The book was twice reviewed in the *New York Times*, and the 31 August 1970 cover of *Time* was a portrait captioned "Kate Millett of Women's Lib." Millett the activist and theorist toured the country and Europe as a feminist celebrity. Shulamith Firestone's *The Dialectic of Sex: The Case for Feminist Revolution* and the first of the anthologies, Robin Morgan's *Sisterhood Is Powerful*, came out that October. *The Dialectic* argued that women were the first oppressed class, and it made, as the subtitle proclaimed, "the case for feminist revolution." Here was the theory whose debate fueled the rise of the movement and spread through *Newsweek* magazine the radical feminist claim that "women are . . . probably the original oppressed class of human history." Like *Sexual Politics*, *The Dialectic of Sex* and *Sisterhood Is Powerful* were widely reviewed and became Women's Liberation classics.

Sisterhood Is Powerful, named for the concept that helped give birth to the movement, set the tone for those to come. In her introduction, editor Robin Morgan said that working on the book had taken her from "Lady Bountiful actions about other people's oppression" to realizing that "it isn't until you begin to fight in your own cause that you *a*) become really committed to winning, and *b*) become a genuine ally of other people struggling for their freedom."[94]

This Book Is an Action

Morgan called her book "an action" because it was an organizing strategy to recruit women to the movement.[95] Toward that end, Morgan provided a

comprehensive list of Women's Liberation Movement contacts, including national organizations. She also listed by state and city the names and addresses
of Women's Liberation groups and included abortion referral services with
names, telephone numbers, and information on how to use the services. Later
that year, Tanner's anthology, Joan Robins's *Handbook of Women's Liberation*,
and Julie Ellis's *Revolt of the Second Sex* would also provide addresses and
contacts. Ellis offered abortion contacts as well. Joan Robins and Cellestine
Ware gave addresses for ordering protest literature.

The 1970 publications recruited for Women's Liberation by teaching
consciousness-raising. The editors of *Sisterhood Is Powerful* and *Voices from
Women's Liberation* excerpted Sarachild's "Program for Feminist Consciousness-Raising" and endorsed it from firsthand experience. Sookie Stambler
recommended that women join consciousness-raising groups to participate
in the "very process from which feminist ideologies are born" and "begin to
see that . . . personal problems are actually political problems."[96] Stambler included an article explaining how to organize a consciousness-raising group
with questions and actual responses.

Cellestine Ware's *Woman Power* defined consciousness-raising as a "close
examination of the individual lives of group members to determine how
society must be changed to eliminate the oppression to which all women
can testify."[97] Ware highlighted her own group, New York Radical Feminists,
which she said used the method to "create an understanding of the nature of
politics."[98]

To women who liked what they read, the mass distribution of contact information for groups and the explanations of consciousness-raising brought
the capability of joining and organizing the movement. Moreover, the publications were sparky and engaging. They were full of movement songs, symbols, poetry, chants from demonstrations, and photographs of women in
action from karate classes to marches and guerrilla theater.

Amazingly Relevant for Today

In the prefeminist 1960s, the First Wave had almost disappeared from the
historical record.[99] In 1968 Shulamith Firestone in *Notes from the First Year*
and Jones and Brown in the Florida Paper sought to reclaim the women's
rights movement from erasure. In "The Women's Rights Movement in the
U.S.: A New View," Firestone said, "What does the word 'feminism' bring
to mind? A granite faced spinster obsessed with the vote? . . . Chances are

whatever image you have . . . is a negative one. . . . a young woman intellectual . . . will be ashamed to identify with the early women's movement."[100] Noting that even the few historians interested in the nineteenth-century movement complained of inadequate access to documents, Firestone argued that the First Wave had been erased because of its "dynamite revolutionary potential."[101]

Women's history was one of the demands of the Florida Paper. "Women must learn their own history," Jones insisted,

> because they have a history to be proud of. . . . What defense is there for a people so ignorant they will believe anything said about their past? To keep us from our history is to keep us from each other. . . . To keep us from our history is to deny to us the group pride from which individual pride is born. To deny to us the possibility of revolt . . . That's why there is no black or female history in high school texts. . . . Courageous women brought us out of total bondage to our present improved position. We must . . . learn from them. . . . The market is ripe for feminist literature, historic and otherwise.[102]

The publications of 1970 sought to develop the movement-inspired passion for learning about the First Wave. Leslie Tanner introduced her anthology with the phrase "amazingly relevant for today," a quote from First Wave founders' introduction to their six-volume *History of Woman Suffrage*. She agreed with Firestone and Jones that "deliberately women had been left out of our history books. Strong, courageous, brilliant women! . . . I became angry," she said, "I felt cheated."[103] Tanner included early papers, among them Abigail Adams's now well-known letter to Mercy Otis Warren, excerpts from essays of Frances Wright and Mary Wollstonecraft, two speeches by Sojourner Truth, and work by the Grimke sisters, Ernestine Rose, and, of course, Stanton and Anthony.

While the 1970 anthologies did include Sojourner Truth, it was the publication that year by Alfreda Duster of the autobiography of Ida B. Wells that broke through the whitewash of the First Wave. Duster's introductory description of her mother as a "fiery reformer, feminist, race leader" put "feminist" before "race leader."[104] Gerda Lerner's *Black Women in White America* (1972) also corrected the record by publishing pioneers Maria Stewart, Anna Julia Cooper, Fannie Barrier Williams, Mary McLeod Bethune, Amy Jacques Garvey, Josephine St. Pierre Ruffin, and Mary Church Terrell.[105]

In *The Dialectic of Sex*, Firestone called the erasure of the First Wave and its substitution by the stereotype of the grim suffragist "The Fifty-Year Ridicule."[106] She explained the substitution as a backlash against the First Wave and a bulwark against its reappearing. Only the "prodding of today's Women's Liberation Movement," as Tanner said, restored the First Wave "to its rightful place."[107] In particular, Tanner was referring to the long-out-of-print six-volume *History of Woman Suffrage* which, at the "prodding" of the movement, had just been reissued by Arno Press.

Public demand sustained the publishing explosion through 1971. Shana Alexander, whose *Life* magazine editorial on the protest of the Miss America Pageant said the protesters had not gone far enough, contracted for a state-by-state guide to women's legal rights. Alexander said that "feminism looked like a good bet to base a book on, even a book of statistical research."[108] The year saw three more anthologies of founding documents, another history, Florynce Kennedy and Diane Schulder's *Abortion Rap*, and U.S. publication of Australian feminist Germaine Greer's best seller *The Female Eunuch*. These books also published contacts for Women's Liberation groups and addresses to order literature.

The Female Eunuch got rave reviews, and Greer took a widely publicized American tour including a week of television appearances and her photograph on the cover of *Life*. When *The Female Eunuch* came out in England in 1970, it had brought the founding debates, along with excerpts of founding Women's Liberation documents in the United States, to a wider British public than ever before. Greer highlighted Jones and Brown's debate with Marilyn Webb over the need for an independent movement. Siding with Jones and Brown, Greer reprinted the Florida Paper's nine-point program and observed that it had "become more or less basic in the young women's liberation groups."[109]

The Female Eunuch had seven printings in the United States in 1971, plus a Book-of-the-Month Club edition, and was serialized in several magazines. Even in the hinterlands, Greer said of her U.S. tour, "the most radical ideas are gladly entertained."[110] Greer referred to her injunction that women— "the true proletariat"—withhold labor from capitalism to reach the goals of "liberty and communism."[111] Indeed, the view that women were a class, and that regardless of the ways in which capitalism, racism, and male supremacy intertwined or which came first, all must be opposed, was widely held in the mass radical Women's Liberation Movement.

Epilogue

THE PREDICTION THAT had so impressed Anne Forer was coming true: from "just a few women meeting in a room," a movement that was radical and feminist had "gone nationwide and international." Soon its victories would include the legalization of divorce in Italy and the legalization of abortion in Italy and France. In the United States the derailing of the Carswell appointment to the Supreme Court by the coalition of NOW, Women's Liberation, the Black Freedom Movement, and the AFL-CIO demonstrated the promise of the political strength of these constituencies when they mobilized their combined forces.

In 1971 black Women's Liberation continued to expand. The TWWA had established itself on the West Coast, and Poor Black Women was writing its prescient, revolutionary analysis *Lessons from the Damned: Class Struggle in the Black Community.*[1] The *Black Scholar* published "Reflections on the Black Woman's Role in the Community of Slaves," Angela Davis's classic attack on the Moynihan Report, while Davis was still in jail. Her supporters had organized a high-profile worldwide mobilization of antiracist, Left, and Women's Liberation forces in her defense.

Also reflective of the movement's momentum was the passage of the ERA in the Senate in 1972, Congresswoman Shirley Chisholm's pathbreaking presidential campaign, and of course, in 1973, the Supreme Court's *Roe v. Wade* ruling that legalized most abortions. The Chisholm campaign represented the zenith of Women's Liberation and at the same time contained within it the clearest sign, on the national level, of the rise of centrist forces within the movement and the beginning of radical mass Women's Liberation decline.

In 1972 Shirley Chisholm may have been the best-known feminist in the nation, rivaled only by Betty Friedan and Angela Davis. Davis had just begun to publicly criticize male chauvinism, whereas Chisholm's record as a feminist had been building for more than four years. One journalism scholar said that by 1972 Chisholm's name was a "household word," and called her presidential campaign the "feminist story of the year."[2]

When Chisholm won a landslide election to Congress in 1968, she became a national figure because she was the first black woman in Congress—and she was outspoken on controversial progressive issues, especially those advancing the cause of women and of African Americans. She was on national television in public service announcements for the National Association for the Repeal of Abortion Laws, and she publicized that she referred women for then-illegal abortions. She pushed for government-funded child care centers, equal opportunity for women in employment and education, and other feminist goals.

Chisholm broke ranks with black and white liberal legislators to seek freedom for Angela Davis, who had been the FBI's most wanted criminal and the subject of a national manhunt (womanhunt?) as an allegedly armed and dangerous person charged with kidnapping and first-degree murder. Davis had been captured as a high-profile fugitive from justice, who publicly declared herself a Communist and a revolutionary opposed to the "male chauvinism which prevails in our society."[3]

Chisholm characterized herself as a "real radical" if not an "all-out" one.[4] She championed Davis and took strong positions on many fronts. She supported Black Power, calling it "a real American political truth." At the same time she declared that "of my two 'handicaps,' being female put many more obstacles in my path than being black." She had been speaking out against the war in Vietnam since early 1968, although this was not the official position of her party. She told the nation that money spent on the war was needed for early childhood education programs—that the United States must "use its strength . . . [for] people . . . not for profits and war."[5]

Her opponent in the congressional race was the well-known black male civil rights leader James Farmer, who had headed CORE, and who campaigned against her by invoking the stereotype of the black matriarch. Chisholm was elected and reelected from her district in Brooklyn, which was overwhelmingly working-class black and Puerto Rican. Among registered voters in the district, women outnumbered men more than two to one. Chisholm attributed her victory over Farmer to the female voters.

Both Chisholm and Davis were branded out-of-control black matriarchs, and such was the feminist consciousness in the nation that both were able to turn the insult to their advantage. The prosecuting attorney at Davis's trial had described her crime to the jury as motivated by sexual lust and lust for power. Davis attributed the jury's verdict of innocent to its female jurors, who had voted for her acquittal after listening to her rebuttal of the prosecutor for building his case on male chauvinism. Davis said she could see "the receptive expressions" of the female jurors "as I spoke about the male supremacist character of Harris' case."[6]

In 1971, the year before her bid for the presidential nomination, Chisholm with Betty Friedan, Gloria Steinem, and Bella Abzug had founded the National Women's Political Caucus for the purpose of electing feminist women to national office. Chisholm was precisely the sort of candidate the caucus had been created to support. But Steinem and Abzug sought to maneuver the caucus to support Democratic contender George McGovern for the presidential nomination, a move black feminist Paula Giddings characterized as an attempt to "consolidate their own position as power-brokers between women and the Democratic Party."[7] They proceeded to damn Chisholm with faint praise, insisting on introducing her and then making a poor introduction. Chisholm finally told them she didn't "need that kind of help."[8] Ultimately she resigned from the caucus in disgust.

Some white feminists were able to follow black feminist leadership. NOW, which was predominantly white, endorsed Chisholm and campaigned for her. When Florynce Kennedy organized the Feminist Party to support Chisholm's campaign, the radical feminist *Woman's World* newspaper supported her campaign.[9] Ti-Grace Atkinson, founder of the Feminists, Florence Rush, organizer of Older Women's Liberation (OWL), prostitutes' rights leader Margo St. James, and a host of others joined the Feminist Party and organized for Chisholm. The Feminist Party was a predominantly white feminist group led by Kennedy, a black feminist, in support of Shirley Chisholm, a black feminist.

The *Chicago Defender* covered Chisholm's campaign positively in articles such as "NOW Campaigns for Shirley" and "Mrs. Chisholm Educating America."[10] *Defender* columnist Louis Martin castigated men who criticized her as a matriarch, writing, "You really have to be a male chauvinist pig not to admire Rep. Shirley Chisholm."[11]

Chisholm was clearly the candidate that best represented the interests of women, African Americans, and poor and working class people. Her campaign sought to mobilize these constituencies into the same powerful coalition that had defeated Carswell's appointment to the Supreme Court two years earlier. To counter what Chisholm called "the United States moving to the right," the "movement toward justice" needed "a new national coalition."[12] Continuing to build this coalition could capitalize on and maximize the influence of the vast grassroots movement for Women's Liberation.

Yet most of those in positions of influence close to the Democratic Party who could have helped Chisholm gain delegates to the nominating convention opposed her campaign, although some gave it lip service. Black male political power brokers condemned her as a matriarch and "captive of the women's movement," although Giddings speculated that that "may have been a cover for some Black politicians who were uncomfortable with Chisholm's controversial political stands," notably her support for Angela Davis.[13]

While Chisholm was popular with Women's Liberation at the grassroots level, she was too much "unbought and unbossed," as she called herself, to be useful to the women who were moving into leadership of the movement by the early to mid-1970s. Giddings characterized the turn from radical to moderate leadership of the movement in the seventies as "crush[ing] the momentum of the mainstream women's movement."[14] Soon, black feminist Linda La Rue projected in 1970, "those few women participating in the 'struggle' will be outnumbered by the more traditional middle-class women. This means that the traditional women will be in a position to take advantage of new opportunities, which radical women's liberation has struggled to win."[15] Giddings said that La Rue's prediction was accurate and called it "distressing."[16]

La Rue and Giddings were right. Radical Women's Liberation organizers lost the leadership of the movement in a nationwide wave of antileadership politics that convulsed the movement. As Naomi Weisstein said, "the question of leadership . . . was to rend the women's movement from coast to coast. . . . the movement ate its leaders: in city after city, they went down."[17] Judith Brown, Shulamith Firestone, Marilyn Webb, Naomi Weisstein, Ti-Grace Atkinson, and other radical Women's Liberation founders were displaced by women less oriented to fundamental change, to "going all the way," as the Redstockings Manifesto put it.[18] Instead, the newer feminists led the movement into projects such as feminist businesses, women's communities, cultural festivals, matriarchal religious rituals, and self-help projects.

The newer feminists, for the most part, had not come into the movement through the Black Freedom Movement and the New Left, which were by then in decline. They began to redefine some of the founding concepts. In 1972 a new women's magazine, Ms., funded with one million dollars from Warner Communications, began publication.[19] Radical feminist Patricia Mainardi, speaking as a sometime contributor to the magazine who had been subjected to its editing, said Ms. was "watering down" her ideas.[20] Ellen Willis, a cofounder of Redstockings and then on staff at the New Yorker, had worked as a contributing editor at Ms. for two years. Willis resigned from Ms. in 1975, in part because, as she put it, Ms. had a "self improvement, individual liberation philosophy" in contrast to her own view of "the need for militant resistance" to male domination in which women were "uniting to combat that power."[21]

As opposed to a slogan for taking a collective approach to changing oppressive conditions, "Sisterhood Is Powerful" became individual "empowerment." Thus whatever made a woman feel powerful—"power nails," "power suits," "power lunches"—could be and often was called feminist. Instead of a consciousness-raising analysis that revealed the political basis of problems considered personal, "The Personal Is Political" was inverted to a prescriptive injunction that defined feminism in terms of decisions an individual might make, such as wearing natural clothing or not eating meat. Instead of a way of analyzing the experiential data of oppression so as to get to the root and make radical change, consciousness-raising groups became support groups.

Radical feminists Kathie Sarachild and Barbara Leon described the ejection of the movement's radical leaders:

The feminism that has drawn us to the movement, all the brilliant but stark truths . . . the honesty, had mostly disappeared in a flurry of wishful thinking, of boring illusions, of lies. . . . the very women who we found ourselves learning the most from . . . All of a sudden we looked around us and almost all of these women had "dropped out" of their organizations, stopped speaking, writing or just plain disappeared. One by one all these women had been picked off.[22]

It was an enduring victory of the movement that some of its work was taken up by the establishment: all sorts of institutions had affirmative action officers, local police departments had rape victim advocates, schools and universities took on the teaching of women's history and women's studies, and local governments funded battered women's shelters. But founding activists were not hired for this work, because they were seen as agitators rather than professionals. Thus, as important as this victory was, these gains became "services" rather than ways of organizing for change to root out the problems at their source. Consequently, as Giddings observed, the momentum of the movement did slow until it eventually lost the thrust of offense and became defensive. Whereas radical feminists of the 1960s spoke of "going all the way," by the 1980s NOW was responding to right-wing attack with the slogan "We Won't Go Back."

By the mid-1970s the movement, as Kathie Sarachild put it, was "spread very wide, but it has also spread thin." She presciently noted in 1974, "The liberals have taken over, claiming credit for the radicals' achievements. If this goes on much longer, feminism will go under once again and we will lose almost all of what we have gained in the last years—both the radical consciousness and many of the practical reforms. It won't be long now until the liberals will be gone too."[23]

Even as the radical cutting edge of Women's Liberation dulled, NOW too took a centrist turn as it devoted itself to passing the ERA by using the failing strategy of appealing, as Giddings observed, to "those women who, in the end, became the amendment's most effective opponents."[24] As organized feminism encountered the backlash from the right in the form of Phyllis Schlafly's Stop ERA campaign, NOW tried to compete in reaching white, antifeminist upper-middle-class housewives instead of, as Giddings said, "consolidating those constituencies most responsive to the ERA . . . labor women . . . and Black women.[25]

In 1979, the year the ERA faced its first ratification deadline, NOW ignored the suggestions of its minority task force led by Aileen Hernandez and failed, for the second election in a row, to elect any black officers. Hernandez and other black NOW leaders resigned and publicly urged black members of the rank and file to resign as well. Giddings has convincingly argued that withdrawal of black female support led to the defeat of the ERA in Illinois, where black political strength was vital.

Radical black Women's Liberation also diminished as the decade wore on, although black Women's Liberation did not appear to reject its radical founders. Poor Black Women went out of existence by 1975, and the TWWA ended in 1978. Members of Poor Black Women offered various explanations: "We went backwards . . . because we was movin' too fast" or "There were things we left undone so we could dedicate ourselves to the struggle. And they had to be dealt with."[26] There is no evidence, though, that they turned on Patricia Robinson.

The National Black Feminist Organization, founded in 1973, ended in 1977; the Combahee River Collective, its 1974 successful offshoot which was instrumental in the publication of important black feminist work including *This Bridge Called My Back* and *Home Girls*, was also gone by 1980.[27] Contrary to much secondary commentary, neither black nor predominantly white Women's Liberation is best characterized as a 1970s movement.

While Women's Liberation continued the decline that began in the 1970s, many of its gains were maintained by majorities of the female public. Foremost among these has been feminist consciousness, which has slowly and consistently risen. In 1970, for example, polls showed that slightly more than half of women held that marriage and motherhood was "one of the best parts of being a woman." But by the 1980s that figure had halved. Polls in the 1980s also showed that more women were aware of and opposed to "male chauvinism" and sex discrimination than in the 1970s. By 1989, a poll showed that 64 percent of white women, 70 percent of Latina and Chicana women, and 85 percent of African American women agreed with the statement "The United States continues to need a strong women's movement to push for changes that benefit women."[28]

The momentum generated by the movement has been maintained by women themselves in other areas as well. The percentage of women attending college, entering the professions, and breaking into all-male jobs such as law, medicine, and a number of blue-collar trades has risen continuously. More and more local, state, and national elections are "gender gapped"—that is, women voting in a bloc prove decisive—and percentages of female elected officials at all levels of government are rising. Despite the terrible erosion of reproductive freedom, majorities of women continue to support *Roe v. Wade* and low-cost, easily accessible birth control.

The life of the radical Women's Liberation Movement was short, perhaps no longer than four or five years. But the fires lit by the movement blazed so intensely that even the powerful backlash of conservatism and religious fundamentalism that gained power in the United States since the 1970s could not extinguish the impact of Women's Liberation or dull the desire for freedom in the hearts and minds of women.

Notes

Introduction

1. Freeman, *Politics*, 44. Freeman is also a founder of the Women's Liberation movement.

2. Beauvoir, *The Second Sex*. In 1975, at a time when political shifts in the movement were burying *The Second Sex* and its importance to feminism's resurgence, the Redstockings anthology *Feminist Revolution*, in its first (and later 1978) edition, traced and highlighted *The Second Sex*'s crucial influence. In the anthology see, for instance, Kathie Sarachild, "The Power of History," passim.

3. The research that establishes the movement by 1970 contradicts a considerable body of work that, a priori, calls women's liberation a 1970s movement. For example, Gloria Steinem calls the 1970s feminism's "beginning," saying that by that decade "almost all the early reformers had become feminists" and "The '70's bring an awareness of our need to reclaim control over our own bodies" (*Ms.*, December 1979, 59, 68, 63); see also Klein, *Gender Politics*, 1; Shreve, *Women Together, Women Alone*; Faludi, *Backlash*.

4. The names of even the most important Women's Liberation pioneers are unknown today outside a small circle of historians of the movement and Second Wave veterans. The well-known names are those of Betty Friedan, founder of NOW and author of *The Feminine Mystique*, and Gloria Steinem, editor of *Ms.* magazine (1972).

5. Betty Friedan refers to NOW as an NAACP for women in "'The First Year': President's Report to NOW, Washington, D.C., 1967," in *It Changed My Life*, 138.

6. This includes Guy-Sheftall, *Words of Fire*; Springer, *Still Lifting, Still Climbing* and *Living for the Revolution*; Cole and Guy-Sheftall, *Gender Talk*; Roth, *Separate Roads*.

7. Evans, *Personal Politics*, 133. The other key ingredient common to black civil rights organizing in the South and Women's Liberation organizing was that in both

cases the oppressed themselves were organizing, in contrast to white college students organizing the inner-city white poor in the North.

8. Hansberry, "Simone de Beauvoir," 129.

9. Women's Liberationists for a long time thought the term "woman question" came from circles around the Communist Party (CP), where it was used in publications and conversation. Kathie Sarachild has reminded me that the term was part of a far older radical heritage in the United States that the CP contributed to keeping alive. She gives an example of an 1838 article in the *Liberator* by its editor, abolitionist William Lloyd Garrison, in which he declared: "We contend that the 'woman question' . . . is not an irrelevant question" (in Papachristou, *Women Together*, 17). Garrison used the term repeatedly.

10. Bernice Johnson Reagon, "SNCC Women and the Stirrings of Feminism," in Greenberg, *A Circle of Trust*, 150.

11. Sara Evans, in *Personal Politics*, first pointed out that a number of Women's Liberation founders were raised in Old Left families. Kate Weigand explores legacies of the CP for Women's Liberation in *Red Feminism*. Ruth Rosen calls the link "an important story that still needs to be recovered" (*The World Split Open*, 34). Gerda Lerner's *Fireweed: A Political Autobiography*, Betty Friedan's *The Feminine Mystique*, and Daniel Horowitz's *Betty Friedan* also draw these connections. Friedan is clear in *The Feminine Mystique* that she worked in the Left in the 1940s, but she does not say that is how she learned about the woman question.

12. By feminism I mean understanding that there is an all-encompassing imbalance of power between the sexes that favors men at the expense of women, and conscious advocacy for equitable rearrangement of that power.

13. Many of the organizers of successful anticolonial revolutions had been educated beyond those they were organizing. Black radical C. L. R. James observed, for example, that "the leaders of a revolution are usually those who have been able to profit by the cultural advantages of the system they are attacking." Toussaint L'Ouverture, enslaved in Haiti, led the world's only successful slave revolt. He was inspired to action by reading the French revolutionary Abbé Raynal. L'Ouverture had been taught to read some French and Latin by his godfather. See James, *The Black Jacobins*, 19, 20.

14. In 1975 Jo Freeman wrote about "cooptable networks" in the New Left and black women's leadership in the Civil Rights Movement (*Politics*, 61). Sara Evans described the status of women in the New Left as "marginally freer" than in the society as a whole (*Personal Politics*, 116).

15. Recent work making this point about the New Left includes Baxandall and Gordon, *Dear Sisters*.

16. Jo Freeman also noted the leadership of many early Women's Liberation organizers in the New Left (*Politics*, 61, 62).

17. See for example BPP cofounder Bobby Seale's statement "The Party says no to this . . . they [women] just want to be treated as human beings on an equal basis, just as blacks want the liberation of their people," in Foner, *The Black Panthers Speak*, 86, 87. The Young Lords Party, a radical Puerto Rican group, had as the fifth point on its thir-

teen-point program "We want equality for women. Down with machismo and male chauvinism" (Abramson and Young Lords Party, *Palante*, 150). In fall 1968, SDS passed a resolution stating: "oppression of women through male supremacy [was] . . . greater than the oppression of working people" (Sale, *SDS*, 508). Brotha Dalou and the Attica Brothers, inmates of Attica prison who had been indicted after the uprising there, wrote, "what good is a revolution if the men will not change their attitudes toward the women in the struggle??? . . . I or any other man, can easily do house-work, cooking, childrearing. . . . This article is . . . an attempt to show that Attica has conscientious Brothas who understand our Sista's struggle" (Attica Brothers, *Fighting Back*, 64).

18. Simmons, "Mama Told Me Not to Go," 118.

19. Simmons, interview by author, Gainesville, 8 July 2007.

20. Norman, "Brightly Shining Lights," 2.

21. Ibid.

22. Ibid.

23. Ibid., 3.

24. Evans, *Personal Politics*, 212–13.

25. Echols, *Daring to Be Bad*, 26.

26. Evans, *Personal Politics*, 221.

27. This is the case with virtually all the early literature. See for example the first anthologies of that literature such as Morgan, *Sisterhood Is Powerful*, or facsimiles of the mimeographed papers as they were first published by the movement itself from 1967 to 1970, in RWLAA.

28. See, for example, Jaggar's *Feminist Politics and Human Nature* and Shreve's *Women Together, Women Alone*.

29. While singling out Rosen, Moses also mentioned DuPlessis and Snitow, *The Feminist Memoir Project*, and Baxandall and Gordon, *Dear Sisters* (Claire Moses, College Park, Md., to author, New York City, 14 May 2001).

30. Barbara Winslow, "Primary and Secondary Contradictions in Seattle: 1967–1969," in DuPlessis and Snitow, *The Feminist Memoir Project*, 235–36.

31. DuPlessis and Snitow, *The Feminist Memoir Project*, 6.

32. Baxandall and Gordon, *Dear Sisters*, 7.

33. Ibid., 10.

34. Evans, *Personal Politics*, 41, 116.

35. Ibid., 100.

36. Rosen, *The World Split Open*, 121.

37. If I had read Rosen before I reread Evans and Echols, I too would have thought that Rosen was onto something new.

38. Janny Scott, "The Feminist Mystique," review of *The World Split Open*, by Ruth Rosen, *New York Times Book Review*, 2 April 2000, 3, 26.

39. Susan E. Reed, review of *The World Split Open*, by Ruth Rosen, *American Prospect*, 17 July 2000, 41.

40. Baxandall and Gordon, "Second-Wave Soundings," 28.

41. Evans, *Tidal Wave*, 240.

42. Ibid., 240. Evans singles out Marge Piercy's "Grand Coolie Damn" and Robin Morgan's "Goodbye to All That."

43. Kathie Sarachild in "The Power of History," 14–16, began capturing the process of the elimination of women's agency from the history of the new feminist revival, focusing on the invisibility of the specific grassroots pioneers and the failure of scholars to work with the primary source documents of these pioneers. She observes (21) that concepts like "changing times" sometimes eliminated women's role completely.

44. Evans, *Tidal Wave*, 16.

45. This is the case with Sara Evans, Rosalyn Baxandall, Linda Gordon, Ruth Rosen, Ann Snitow, Jo Freeman, Barbara Winslow, and probably others whose participation I am not aware of.

46. Sarachild, "Civil Rights Movement: Lessons."

47. Judith Brown, Gainesville, to Kathie Amatniek (later Sarachild), New York, 15 August 1985, RWLAA.

48. Cleaver and Katsiaficas, *Liberation, Imagination*, 124.

49. Ibid.

50. Frances M. Beal, interview by author, 8 August 2007.

51. I refer to the work of Belinda Robnett, Cynthia Griggs Fleming, Benita Roth, Paula Giddings, and others whose views in this regard are discussed in the chapters to come.

52. Cleaver and Katsiaficas, *Liberation, Imagination*, 124, 126.

53. My earliest encounter with sexism in the student movement came in Gainesville in 1967 when, filled with excitement over new radical insights, I eagerly sought to volunteer for more movement work. The response I got from an admired male leader was an invitation to "go fuck on the steps of Tigert Hall" (the University of Florida administration building) in order to confront the establishment. When I declined, he could think of no political work for me to do. Female leaders in our SDS chapter helped me grow as an activist. Among widely read firsthand accounts of male chauvinism in the New Left are Beverly Jones and Judith Brown's "Toward a Female Liberation Movement" and Marge Piercy's "Grand Coolie Damn." All the monographs on the movement are filled with similar anecdotes.

54. Selma James, "The American Family: Decay and Rebirth," *Radical America*, February 1970.

55. Lucinda Cisler, Ellen Willis, Dana Densmore, Laura X, Peggy Dobbins, and Anne Koedt are among those whose leadership far exceeds my discussion of it. My decision about which early organizers to focus on was based, for the most part, on who "went first," as Kathie Sarachild put it in "The Power of History," 26.

56. The founding texts and manifestos of the movement assert leaderlessness as both the style and the goal. See for example Shulamith Firestone on the movement's structure: "One of its major stated goals is internal democracy. . . . if any revolutionary movement can succeed at establishing an egalitarian structure, radical feminism will" (*The Dialectic of Sex*, 44, 45).

Chapter 1. Toward a Female Liberation Movement

1. Beauvoir, *The Second Sex*, xxvii.

2. U.S. Department of Labor, *Educational Attainment*, 5.

3. Hymowitz and Weissman, *Women in America*, 326.

4. Friedan, *Life So Far*, 134.

5. U.S. Department of Labor, *Handbook on Women Workers*, 15.

6. Friedan, *The Feminine Mystique*, 368. This book has generally been considered the first important sign of the impending feminist revival.

7. Murray, "Liberation of Black Women," 196. The statistics here depend on those in Murray's article, first published in 1970.

8. Beal, "Double Jeopardy," 97. African American women were subjected to involuntary sterilization as well, an outrage not inflicted on white women.

9. Freeman, "Origins," 172.

10. Chafe, *The American Woman*, 218.

11. Chafe, *The Paradox of Change*, 200.

12. Bouchier, *The Feminist Challenge*, 27.

13. Ibid., 31.

14. A number of African American women voted against the mystique and led high-profile, public political lives, among them Rosa Parks; Autherine Lucy, who attempted to integrate the University of Alabama; Daisy Bates, who led the integration of schools in Little Rock, Arkansas; and Constance Baker Motley, who worked on briefs for *Brown v. Board of Education* and tried cases for James Meredith to enter the University of Mississippi.

15. The details of the political maneuvering, positive and negative, in the passage of the Civil Rights Act hold lessons for the relations between the movements of African Americans, labor, and women. For instance, the National Woman's Party, one of the few organizations that remained intact since the First Wave of feminism, although less influential than at its height, was a significant actor, mainly behind the scenes. Caroline Bird discusses the inclusion of Title VII in *Born Female*, chap. 1. See also firsthand accounts in Friedan, *It Changed My Life*, 112–15; Murray, *Autobiography*, 354–56.

16. Equal Employment Opportunity Commission, *Second Annual Report*, 6.

17. Friedan, *It Changed My Life*, 89.

18. Fleming, *Soon We Will Not Cry*, 36.

19. Simmons, interview by author, Gainesville, 8 July 2007.

20. Simmons, "Mama Told Me Not to Go," 116, 117.

21. King, *Freedom Song*, 54, 55.

22. In 1896 Terrell, then eighty-six, founded the National Association of Colored Women. Also in the 1890s, she pressured the National American Woman Suffrage Association (NAWSA) to recognize that the black woman faced two "handicaps to overcome—her sex and her race" (quoted in Hine et al., *Black Women in America*, 1157).

23. Lester with Norton, *Fire in My Soul*, 43.

24. Ransby, *Ella Baker*, 367.

25. Ransby said that Baker's "construction of a gender identity was less than conventional" (ibid., 33).

26. Ibid., 32.

27. Ibid., 33.

28. Ibid.

29. Ibid., 34.

30. Judith Brown, Gainesville, to Kathie Sarachild, New York, n.d., RWLAA.

31. Carol Hanisch, personal communication, 14 July 2007. This quote comes from a memoir Hanisch is writing.

32. Firestone, *Airless Spaces* 151, 153.

33. Marilyn Webb, interview by author, New York, 22 May 2002.

34. SDS was the largest and most prominent organization of the New Left student movement in the 1960s.

35. Kennedy, *Color Me Flo*, 2.

36. Freeman, "Origins," 171.

37. Benita Roth argues that the Second Wave is best described as made up of "feminisms," and feminist "movements." She finds this a way to discuss the feminist work of African American and Chicana women, which has been erased by the "fiction of feminist unity." Scholars looking for these women in predominantly white feminist groups did not find many, so they sought to explain why African American and Chicana women were not interested in feminism. This, of course, was not the case and exacerbated what Roth rightly calls the "whitewashing" of the feminist movement by obscuring groups that were African American and Chicana only; see Roth, *Separate Roads*, 6. Commenting on the whitewashing of Women's Liberation, black scholar and former SNCC leader Bernice Johnson Reagon warned that "people really try to make stuff White, even if it ain't," in Greenberg, *A Circle of Trust*, 151.

38. Beal, interview by author, 31 July 2007.

39. Height, "We Wanted the Voice of a Woman," 90.

40. Roth argues that "black feminism arose as an organizationally distinct movement in response to the changes that had occurred in the Civil Rights/Black Liberation movement. . . . a resurgent masculinism within the Black movement sought to contain women in the domestic sphere after having had positions of responsibility . . . in the Civil Rights Movement" (*Separate Roads*, 127).

41. Ransby, *Ella Baker*, 310.

42. Wynn, quoted in Robnett, *How Long, How Long?* 42.

43. Baker, "Developing Community Leadership," 351. Baker was one of SCLC's three founders and its first paid staff—she pulled it up off the ground from nothing and led it, although this was not acknowledged by the male SCLC leaders she trained and developed.

44. Robnett, *How Long, How Long?* 43.

45. Bates, *Long Shadow*, 26.

46. Bates, quoted in Olson, *Freedom's Daughters*, 138.

47. Cole and Guy-Sheftall, *Gender Talk*, 90.

48. Neither black nor white feminists called themselves "feminist" until the twentieth century.

49. Maria Stewart, quoted in Hanisch, *Promise and Betrayal*, 7.

50. Stewart, "Lecture Delivered at the Franklin Hall," in Guy-Sheftall, *Words of Fire*, 30; Beal, "Double Jeopardy," 92.

51. Conrad, "I Bring You General Tubman."

52. Terborg-Penn, *African American Women in the Struggle for the Vote.*

53. Cooper, "Status of Woman," 43–45. This review of African American women's feminist traditions is indebted to Guy-Sheftall. Some scholars call the triple oppression of black women "intersectionality" to encompass the mixing of class, race, and gender as well as the tripled burden; see Roth, *Separate Roads*, 11.

54. Cooper, "Status of Woman," 43.

55. Beal, "Double Jeopardy," 92.

56. James Forman, who was in the office at the time, said the protest was about "the conditions of women in SNCC" (*Black Revolutionaries*, xvii). Fleming said the women were protesting "unequal treatment" (*Soon We Will Not Cry*, 153).

57. Evans refers to early legends about Robinson in *Personal Politics*, 74. Her sources on the strike are interviews with Ella Baker, Fay Bellamy, Mary King, Cathy Cade, Nan Grogan, and Jean Wiley (248n17).

58. Reagon, in Sicherman and Green, *Notable American Women*, 585. The SNCC Freedom Singers spread freedom songs throughout the southern movement, the nation, and beyond.

59. Wise, quoted in Fleming, *Soon We Will Not Cry*, 151, 152.

60. Yancy, quoted in Fleming, *Soon We Will Not Cry*, 152. Black SNCC staffer Martha Prescod Norman says that Judy Richardson organized the strike ("Brightly Shining Lights," 21n11); Mary King said she, Judy Richardson, and Betty Garman "rounded people up for it" (*Freedom Song*, 453); black SNCC executive secretary James Forman said it was his idea (*Black Revolutionaries*, xvii). Robinson's biographer, African American scholar Cynthia Griggs Fleming, offers convincing evidence from Wise, Robinson's coworker, that Robinson led the strike. Fleming does not provide a date but says the strike was in spring 1964. King places the date in January 1964.

61. Wise, quoted in Fleming, *Soon We Will Not Cry*, 151.

62. Simmons, "Mama Told Me Not to Go," 116. Simmons began working with SNCC as a volunteer in the spring of 1963 while a student at Spelman College in Atlanta. She came on the SNCC staff shortly before the first orientation for Freedom Summer 1964.

63. Ibid., 117.

64. Simmons has not said who her assailant was but has said (interview by author, 8 July 2007) that he was not a volunteer.

65. Simmons, "Mama Told Me Not to Go," 118.

66. Simmons, personal communication, 8 February 2008.

67. Evans, *Personal Politics*, 162.

Chapter 2. The "Borning" Movement

1. Historian Clayborne Carson calls the rise of the woman question in SNCC "new tensions" (*In Struggle*, 147). See also McAdam, *Freedom Summer*, 105–11; Pouissant, "Stresses." Some newer work has highlighted the democratic opening for women in SNCC. See Dittmer, *Local People*; Payne, *Light of Freedom*, 266–78; Ransby, *Ella Baker*.

2. Joking about the position of women refers to the many accounts of Stokely Carmichael's fabled quip that women in SNCC were "prone." For just a few, see Carson, *In Struggle*, 148; Chafe and Sitkoff, *History of Our Time*, 230.

3. Sarachild, "Civil Rights Movement: Lessons," 8.

4. Norton, "Great Movements of My Time."

5. Lester with Norton, *Fire in My Soul*, 147.

6. Norton, "Great Movements of My Time."

7. Chana Kai Lee, Hamer's most recent biographer, makes this clear in *For Freedom's Sake*.

8. Beal, interview by author, 8 August 2007.

9. Norman, "Brightly Shining Lights," 6.

10. Ransby, *Ella Baker*, 296, 297.

11. Ibid., 34.

12. Myrna Hill, interview by author, 5 July 2007.

13. Donaldson, quoted in Ransby, *Ella Baker*, 296.

14. Fleming, *Soon We Will Not Cry*, 124.

15. Ibid., 51.

16. McAdam, *Freedom Summer*, 183; also Olson, *Freedom's Daughters*, 354.

17. May, *Homeward Bound*, 15.

18. Robnett, *How Long, How Long?* 38.

19. In *I've Got the Light of Freedom*, 268, Charles Payne attributes SNCC's distinctive ability to develop female leadership to its having been "founded by a woman."

20. Barbara Ransby in *Ella Baker* has described Baker's influence on black and white women in SNCC.

21. The workshop, under the auspices of the NAACP, was held in Atlanta and was the first time Parks had traveled outside the Montgomery area. According to Parks, Baker was a profound influence on her life; see Ransby, *Ella Baker*, 142.

22. Grant, *Ella Baker*, 108.

23. Baker, "Developing Community Leadership," 352.

24. J. Williams, *Eyes on the Prize*, 131.

25. The Freedom Rides began in the spring of 1961 and renewed a campaign CORE had begun in the 1940s.

26. J. Williams, *Eyes on the Prize*, 149.

27. Fleming, *Soon We Will Not Cry*, 94.

28. Greenberg, *A Circle of Trust*, 143.

29. Hine et al., *Black Women in America*, 1085.

30. Greenberg, *A Circle of Trust*, 36.

31. Carmichael, *Ready for Revolution*, 217.

32. Ibid., 217.

33. Olson, *Freedom's Daughters*, 150.

34. Ransby, *Ella Baker*, 272.

35. Ibid., 144.

36. Grant, *Ella Baker*, 141, 142.

37. Ransby, *Ella Baker*, 367.

38. Lester with Norton, *Fire in My Soul*, 121. When Norton asked a friend to fix her up with a date, her friend said, "You're too smart. Why would you need a man."

39. King, *Freedom Song*, 456.

40. Hayden, "Fields of Blue," 346.

41. Ibid., 352.

42. Ibid., 340.

43. Ibid., 342.

44. Olson, *Freedom's Daughters*, 372.

45. Norton, "Great Movements of My Time."

46. Fannie Lou Hamer, "Testimony," 22 July 1964. Voices of Freedom, www.calvin. edu/academic/cas/programs/pauleyg/voices/fhamer.htm.

47. Norton, "A Memory of Fannie Lou Hamer," 51.

48. Lee, *For Freedom's Sake*, 99.

49. Ibid., 172.

50. King, *Freedom Song*, 470.

51. Judith Brown, Gainesville, to Kathie Sarachild, New York, 22 November 1985, RWLAA.

52. Brown to Sarachild, 15 August 1985, RWLAA.

53. Ibid.

54. See Evans, *Personal Politics*, 51.

55. Rabby, *The Pain and the Promise*, 120.

56. Since slavery, the recurring rape of black women by white men was unacknowledged and unpunished by white society. Black women fought back, and putting a stop to it was one of the reasons the National Association of Colored Women was founded in 1895. W. E. B. DuBois condemned the rape of black women. The mother of Arkansas NAACP president and leader of Little Rock school integration Daisy Bates was raped and murdered by local whites. Bates cites her father's lesson to her about her mother's death—"if you hate, make it count for something. . . . any Negro speaking out alone will suffer . . . but more and more will join together . . . one day"—as "a priceless heritage . . . that was to sustain me throughout the years to come" (*Long Shadow*, 29, 31, and 14–31 passim).

57. Rabby, *The Pain and the Promise*, 77–79 passim.

58. Due and Due, *Freedom in the Family*, 40, 41.

59. According to Clayborne Carson, sit-ins in Hampton, Virginia, on February 10 were the first outside of North Carolina (*In Struggle*, 11). Students sat in on February 12 in Rock Hill, South Carolina, and on February 13 in Tallahassee (Meier and Rudwick,

CORE, 104). The Nashville sit-ins also took place on February 13 (Morris, *Origins*, 206).

60. Meier and Rudwick, *CORE*, 106.

61. Peck, *Freedom Ride*, 79.

62. Rabby, *The Pain and the Promise*, 106.

63. Ibid.

64. The students who were jailed at Rock Hill in January 1961, among them Diane Nash, are usually credited with the tactic of the jail-in or "jail, no bail," but the tactic was used by Due and Tallahassee CORE in February and March 1960. See Due and Due, *Freedom in the Family*, 70, and Meier and Rudwick, *CORE*, 106.

65. Dan Harmeling, Gainesville, to author, 29 June 1991, JBE.

66. Brown to Sarachild, 15 August 1985, RWLAA.

67. Brown to Sarachild, 21 November 1988, RWLAA.

68. Rabby, *The Pain and the Promise*, 165.

69. Ibid., 174.

70. Brown, "CORE Voter Registration Drive," 42–45.

71. Rabby, *The Pain and the Promise*, 173.

72. Ibid., 178.

73. Brown to Sarachild, 15 August 1985, RWLAA.

74. Bettie Wright, interview by author, Salisbury, Md., 10 September 2000.

75. Dan Harmeling, interview by author, Gainesville, 4 September 2000.

76. Beal, "Sisterhood Is Still Powerful," 4–5.

77. Norton, "Great Movements of My Time."

78. Lester with Norton, *Fire in My Soul*, 114.

79. Norton, "Great Movements of My Time."

80. Lester with Norton, *Fire in My Soul*, 112.

81. Norton, "Great Movements of My Time."

82. J. Williams, *Eyes on the Prize*, 225.

83. Norton, "A Memory of Fannie Lou Hamer," 51.

84. Hayden, "Fields of Blue," 340, 342; McAdam, *Freedom Summer*, 71.

85. Booth, in Martinez, *Letters from Mississippi*, 127.

86. Ibid., 151.

87. Pam Allen, interview by author, 2 January 2001.

88. Olson, *Freedom's Daughters*, 309.

89. Allen, interview by author, 2 January 2001.

90. Allen, letter to author, 21 December 2000.

91. McAdam, *Freedom Summer*, 127.

92. Olson, *Freedom's Daughters*, 352.

93. Curry et al., *Deep in Our Hearts*, 19.

94. Among those whose lives were taken by white authorities in the early years of SNCC was black farmer Herbert Lee, who participated in a voter registration drive. He was shot to death in Liberty, Mississippi, in September 1961 by E. H. Hurst, a Mississippi state legislator, who was never brought to trial. See Dittmer, *Local People*, 109.

Lee's name became legend in "We'll Never Turn Back," the anthem of the Mississippi Freedom Summer Project.

95. Sarachild, "Civil Rights Movement: Lessons," 7.

96. Ibid.

97. Ibid., 8.

98. Sarachild, in Firestone, *First Year*, 21.

99. The two papers are in King, *Freedom Song*, 567–74.

100. Hayden, "Fields of Blue," 365.

101. King, *Freedom Song*, 569.

102. Ibid.

103. Ibid., 571.

104. Ibid., 573.

105. Ibid., 574.

106. Sarachild, statement read at the Simone de Beauvoir Memorial Speak Out (hereafter Beauvoir Speak Out), New York, 1 May 1986, RWLAA.

107. Sarachild, "Civil Rights Movement: Lessons," 7.

108. Ibid.

109. Sarachild, in Greenberg, *A Circle of Trust*, 149.

110. Sarachild, "Civil Rights Movement: Lessons," 7.

111. Ibid., 8.

112. Heather Booth, interview by author, Washington, D.C., 15 April 2001.

113. Olson, *Freedom's Daughters*, 352.

Chapter 3. "Something had to be there already"

1. Brown, "Origins of Consciousness-Raising in the South," 3.

2. Bettie Wright, interview by author, Salisbury, Md., 10 September 2000.

3. Julian Brown, Pierre, S.D., to author, Gainesville, 29 June 1991, JBE.

4. Ibid.

5. Julian Brown, interview by author, Gainesville, 29 January 2001.

6. Judith Brown, Gainesville, to Kathie Sarachild, New York, 13 July 1985, RW-LAA.

7. The University of Alabama expelled Lucy because NAACP attorneys filed a contempt of court suit against the university on Lucy's behalf.

8. Judith Brown, interview by author, Gainesville, 9 April 1990, videotape 1, JBE.

9. Eberlein, diary entry, 316.

10. Free Acres Association, *Constitution*, 4.

11. Bierbaum, "Free Acres."

12. Christopher Benninger, interview by author, New York, 8 December 1999.

13. Pam Allen, interview by author, 2 January 2001.

14. Murray, "Liberation of Black Women," 197.

15. Murray, *Autobiography*, 75.

16. Ibid.

17. Ibid., 107.

18. Ibid., 183.

19. Ibid., 217.

20. Ibid., 214.

21. Ibid., 217.

22. Ibid., 224.

23. This included several rounds of public appeals and letter-writing campaigns—including a letter from President Franklin Roosevelt at the behest of Eleanor Roosevelt, with whom Murray developed a strong friendship; see Murray, *Autobiography*, 244.

24. Kwame Nkrumah was then president of Ghana. Nkrumah was an influential Pan-Africanist and pursued a socialist agenda.

25. Murray, *Autobiography*, 347–48.

26. Lester with Norton, *Fire in My Soul*, 106.

27. Ibid., 45.

28. Ibid., 107.

29. Ibid., 146.

30. Black feminist scholar Barbara Ransby gives an extensive analysis of Baker's association with Schuyler in *Ella Baker*, 78–91 passim.

31. Baker, "The Black Woman in the Civil Rights Struggle," in Grant, *Ella Baker*, 229.

32. Ibid.

33. Grant, *Ella Baker*, 147.

34. Baker, quoted in Grant, *Ella Baker*, 229.

35. Ibid., 65.

36. Ibid., 227.

37. Patricia Robinson, letter for Beauvoir Speak Out, RWLAA.

38. Polatnick, "Strategies," 46.

39. Weigand, "Vanguards of Women's Liberation," 276.

40. E. M. Moss, "Pat Murphy—Big Brother," undated clipping, archives of the Afro-American Newspapers, Baltimore.

41. Robinson explains her dedication to Planned Parenthood and birth control in Polatnick, "Strategies," 46.

42. Rodrique, "Birth Control Movement," 338.

43. Ibid.

44. Ibid., 342, 343.

45. Beal, interview by author, 31 July 2007.

46. Beal, interview by author, 8 August 2007.

47. Weisstein, in DuPlessis and Snitow, *The Feminist Memoir Project*, 32.

48. Naomi Weisstein, eulogy for Mary Menk Weisstein (1905–1999), read by Jesse Lemisch, Riverside Memorial Chapel, New York, 7 February 1999, author's files.

49. Naomi Weisstein, letter to author, 22 October 2000.

50. Sarachild, statement at Beauvoir Speak Out, RWLAA.

51. Evans, *Personal Politics*, 63.

52. Sarachild, lecture for a course, "Feminist Activism: Learning from History" (University of Florida, Gainesville, 31 January 1994), author's lecture notes.

53. Jackson, quoted in Kelley, *Hammer and Hoe*, 207.

54. Sarachild, "Civil Rights Movement: Lessons," 2, 3.

55. Schwarz, *Radical Feminists of Heterodoxy*.

56. Ibid., 1.

57. Cott, *Grounding of Modern Feminism*, 38.

58. A. Davis, *Angela Davis*, 108.

59. Dorothy Burnham, "Biology and Gender: False Theories About Women and Blacks," in Jackson, *Freedomways Reader*, 252.

60. A. Davis, "Black Woman's Role," passim.

61. Davis went underground when she was falsely charged with first-degree murder, kidnapping, and conspiracy in connection with her political advocacy on behalf of the Soledad Brothers: George Jackson, John Clutchette, and Fleeta Drumgo, prisoners at Soledad Prison who did political education of other prisoners and had been accused of killing a guard.

62. Davis, in Guy-Sheftall, *Words of Fire*, 215.

63. Aptheker, *Woman's Legacy*, 130.

64. A. Davis, *Angela Davis*, 363.

65. Aptheker, *Woman's Legacy*, 130.

66. Kennedy, *Color Me Flo*, 40.

67. Kennedy, in Guy-Sheftall, *Words of Fire*, 102.

68. Kennedy, *Color Me Flo*, 53.

69. Hanisch, correspondence with author, 14 July 2007.

70. Chisholm, *Unbought and Unbossed*, 27.

71. Ibid.

72. Ibid., 38

73. Ibid.

74. Evans, *Personal Politics*, 120n.

75. Ibid.

76. Ibid., 119–20.

77. Evans, *Personal Politics*, 124. See also Weigand, *Red Feminism*, and Rosen, *The World Split Open*, for their observations about the leadership of "red diaper babies" in the Women's Liberation Movement.

78. Weigand, "Vanguards of Women's Liberation," 279. In 2000 Weigand published findings from her 1995 dissertation in *Red Feminism*.

79. Weisstein to author, 1 March 2001.

80. Brown to Sarachild, 15 December 1985.

Chapter 4. The Influence of Simone de Beauvoir

1. Beauvoir, *The Second Sex*, xxiv, xxviii, 698, 755, 800.

2. Robinson, letter for Beauvoir Speak Out, RWLAA.

3. Ibid.

4. Hansberry, "Simone de Beauvoir," 129, 133.

5. By 1968, 900,000 copies of the Bantam paperback edition (1961) had been sold.

6. Hansberry, "Simone de Beauvoir," 130.

7. Margaret B. Wilkerson, "Lorraine Vivian Hansberry," in Hine et al., *Black Women in America*, 535.

8. Hansberry, "Simone de Beauvoir," 139.

9. Sarachild, statement at Beauvoir Speak Out, RWLLA.

10. Ibid.

11. Ibid.

12. Ibid.

13. Redstockings, *Feminist Revolution*, dedication page.

14. Firestone, *First Year*, 7.

15. Firestone and Koedt, *Second Year*, 76–78, 79–80.

16. Yaffe, "The Second Sex: A Work in Progress," 59.

17. Firestone, *The Dialectic of Sex*, dedication.

18. Ibid., 7.

19. Ibid.

20. Firestone, statement at Beauvoir Speak Out, RWLLA.

21. Firestone, "Anticredentials."

22. Firestone, statement at Beauvoir Speak Out.

23. Stephen Elliott, "5 Gals Call It a Bridle Veil, Ask Salaries in Marriage Contracts," *New York Daily News*, 24 September 1969.

24. Beauvoir, *A Transatlantic Love Affair*, 65–67.

25. Millett, "Simone de Beauvoir . . . Autobiographer," 3.

26. Ti-Grace Atkinson, statement at Beauvoir Speak Out, RWLLA.

27. Roxanne Dunbar, "Outlaw Woman: Chapters from a Feminist Memoir-in-Progress," in DuPlessis and Snitow, *The Feminist Memoir Project*, 91.

28. Ibid., 93.

29. Dunbar-Ortiz, *Outlaw Woman*, 128.

30. *No More Fun and Games* (Somerville, Mass.), no. 2 (February 1969), RWLAA.

31. Allen, interview by author, 1 January 2001. Evans, *Personal Politics*, 196n, also mentions Robinson advising white Women's Liberation organizers.

32. Sarachild, New York, to Patricia Robinson, San Franscisco, [ca. 1986], RWLAA.

33. Millett, *Sexual Politics*. On crediting Millett, see for example Brownmiller, *In Our Time*, 43: "Millett was inventing a whole new field called feminist literary criticism."

34. Frank J. Prial, "Feminist Philosopher Katharine Murray Millett," *New York Times*, 27 August 1970.

35. Irving Howe, "The Middle-Class Mind of Kate Millett," *Harper's*, December 1970, 110.

36. Bair, *Simone de Beauvoir*, 654.

37. Ibid.

38. Millett, "Simone de Beauvoir . . . Autobiographer," 3.

39. National Organization for Women, "An Invitation to Join," in Papachristou, *Women Together*, 220.

40. Beauvoir, *All Said and Done*, 455.

41. Friedan, "No Gods, No Goddesses."

42. King, *Freedom Song*, 77.

43. Ibid.

44. Ibid., 76.

45. Ibid.

46. Ibid., 444.

47. Ibid.

48. Okely, *Simone de Beauvoir*, 18.

49. Ibid., 17, 18.

50. Rosalyn Baxandall, statement at Beauvoir Speak Out, RWLAA.

51. Ibid., 455.

Chapter 5. Next Steps to Women's Liberation

1. "SNCC Position Paper (Women in the Movement)," in Evans, *Personal Politics*, appendix, 233–35.

2. Sarachild, in Greenberg, *A Circle of Trust*, 148. Only four months after the conference, Sarachild's SNCC coworker Cris Williams told her that Robinson presented a feminist paper at the Waveland conference that had been written by Hayden and King. But in an article written in 1969, Linda Seese, also a white Freedom Summer volunteer who was there at the time, attributed the authorship of the paper to Robinson; see "You've Come a Long Way, Baby: Women in the Movement," in Cooke, Bunch-Weeks Morgan, *The New Women*, 175–84, esp. 180.

3. Mention of Robinson leading the discussion group appears in Hole and Levine, *Rebirth of Feminism*, 110, and in correspondence in 1975 from Mary King to Sara Evans, in Evans, *Personal Politics*, 84, 249n2. Yet King does not mention attending the discussion group in her memoir, *Freedom Song*. Scholar of the movement Rosetta E. Ross says in *Witnessing and Testifying*, 211, that in summer 1964 Robinson "led a women's group in discussing the movement's failure to achieve gender equality." Ross also maintains that Robinson presented the paper.

4. King, *Freedom Song*, 568.

5. Ibid., 569.

6. Bernice Johnson Reagon described this distortion well: "The implication is . . . [the paper] was not generated by SNCC. . . . That document moved through society as an aberration without any acknowledgment that this . . . is a SNCC document. . . . We really have to watch racism, because if the group is integrated . . . when it [the paper] is transmitted to the larger culture, and other people start to read into it, they will separate it out as if it was not created by the structure that made it possible"

(quoted in "SNCC Women and the Stirrings of Feminism" in Greenberg, *A Circle of Trust*, 150–51).

7. Hayden, "Fields of Blue," 365. The minutes of the meeting show that black SNCC staff member Prathia Hall requested discussion of the paper (T. James, "*Sisters in Struggle*," 34).

8. Hayden, "Fields of Blue," 365. The accounts of Hayden and King differ. For example, King said (*Freedom Song*, 444) that she typed it alone and "secretly" after she "consulted" with Hayden. Also, in contrast with Hayden, King said (*Freedom Song*, 452) that Robinson "repudiated" the paper.

9. Simmons, interview by author, Gainesville, 8 July 2007. Simmons's account differs dramatically from King's.

10. This account relies on King, *Freedom Song*, 452.

11. Washington, in Evans, *Personal Politics*, 239.

12. Rosen, *The World Split Open*, 109.

13. Ibid., 153.

14. Norman, "Brightly Shining Lights," 18.

15. Ladner, in Greenberg, *A Circle of Trust*, 144, 145.

16. Moynihan, *The Negro Family*.

17. Giddings, *When and Where I Enter*, 329.

18. Aptheker, *Woman's Legacy*, 129–51 passim.

19. Ibid., 134.

20. More than three thousand civil rights demonstrators were arrested in Birmingham alone in April and May 1963 (Carson, *In Struggle*, 90).

21. Baldwin, in Jackson, *Freedomways Reader*, 81.

22. Ibid.

23. Olson, *Freedom's Daughters*, 281.

24. Ibid.

25. UPI photo in Olson, *Freedom's Daughters*, 281.

26. Bird, *Born Female*, 5.

27. Lee, *For Freedom's Sake*, 87.

28. Olson, *Freedom's Daughters*, 320.

29. Lee, *For Freedom's Sake*, 87, 95.

30. According to Carson, *In Struggle*, 123, "The MFDP 'was open to all Mississippi residents' and 'had followed Mississippi rules regarding party operations.'"

31. *Newsweek*, quoted in Lee, *For Freedom's Sake*, 118.

32. Giddings, *When and Where I Enter*, 329. Cole and Guy-Sheftall also support Giddings's view that the report influenced black attitudes (*Gender Talk*, 81).

33. C. Eric Lincoln, "A Look Behind the 'Matriarchy,'" *Ebony* 21, no. 10 (August 1966), 112–13.

34. Davis, in Guy-Sheftall, *Words of Fire*, 201.

35. Ibid., 216.

36. Ibid., 201. Jackson was shot and killed by guards at San Quentin Prison in 1971.

37. Patton, "Victorian Ethos," 145–46.

38. Bond and Peery, "Has the Black Male Been Castrated?" 114.

39. In the decades that followed, black feminists continued to criticize black men for following the Moynihan Report. In an article attacking the report, the radical black women of *Bottomfish Blues: A Voice for the Amazon Nation*, a feminist black nationalist newspaper of the 1980s, wrote, "'Yes, boss, you're right' say the . . . puppet Black middle-class men. Criminalizing Black women has become a career for more than just Daniel Patrick Moynihan in this Land of Equal Opportunity" ("Moynihan-Ism: The Attack on Black Women," *Bottomfish Blues*, no. 3 [Winter 1987], 30). Black scholars Johnnetta Cole and Beverly Guy-Sheftall agreed, saying that the views of "psychologist, cultural nationalist, and one time coeditor of *The Black Scholar* Nathan Hare revealed the extent to which Moynihan's problematic assumptions about gender and Black families had been embraced by Black activists" (*Gender Talk*, 84).

40. Lester with Norton, *Fire in My Soul*, 187, 188. Norton could not have agreed with all of Moynihan's conclusions, because she did not say that black women should step back. She laid the "major responsibility" on the government for the "increasing number of black women" who ended up raising "the children of the black nation alone" even as she argued "we cannot avoid personal responsibility."

41. Hayden and King, in King, *Freedom Song*, 571–74.

42. King, *Freedom Song*, 457. This supports Zoharah Simmons's recollection that Dona Richards may have called the meeting that produced the 1964 position paper.

43. King, *Freedom Song*, 574.

44. Ibid., 458.

45. Ibid.

46. Ibid., 573.

47. King, *Freedom Song*, 462–63. Martha Prescod Norman, SNCC field secretary for Mississippi and later Alabama, reflected that she had taken Hayden's discussions of "women's place in the society at large with great seriousness" ("Brightly Shining Lights," 22).

48. Jones and Brown, "Female Liberation Movement."

49. Beverly Jones, interview by author, New York, 2 November 1999.

50. Jones, in Jones and Brown, "Female Liberation Movement," 386–87.

51. Brown, in Jones and Brown, "Female Liberation Movement," 392.

52. Ibid.

53. Brown, Gainesville, to Carol Hanisch, New York, 8 September 1968, RWLAA.

54. Brown to Sarachild, 15 July 1986, RWLAA.

55. Evans, *Personal Politics*, 157.

56. Hole and Levine, *Rebirth of Feminism*, 112.

57. Varying views on Garrett's role can be found in King, *Freedom Song*, 467, and Evans, *Personal Politics*, 162–63.

58. Olson, *Freedom's Daughters*, 353.

59. Echols, *Daring to Be Bad*, 35.

60. "December Conference Impressions," *New Left Notes*, 28 January 1966, 4.

61. "Liberation of Women," *New Left Notes*, 10 July 1967, 4.

Chapter 6. The Influence of Black Power on the Rise of Women's Liberation

1. Carmichael, *Stokely Speaks*, 19. Black feminist Myrna Hill said Carmichael's explanation of Black Power was what she defined as "revolutionary black nationalism." "By the time . . . Carmichael's original intended meaning of the term . . . got to me, in 1967, the Black Power Movement came to mean . . . reactionary male supremacist stuff . . . brothers and sisters who dressed in dashikis . . . but didn't want to actually do anything drastic to overthrow capitalism" (correspondence with author, 29 November 2007).

2. Carmichael, *Stokely Speaks*, 18.

3. Ibid., 32.

4. Ibid., 132.

5. The March against Fear was a joint effort of SCLC, SNCC, and CORE, and led by Martin Luther King Jr., leaders of SNCC including Stokely Carmichael, and Floyd McKissick of CORE.

6. Beal, interview by author, 8 August 2007.

7. Beal, "Double Jeopardy," 91.

8. Grant, *Ella Baker*, 209. Baker read the "Black Proclamation" at a public meeting of the Coalition of Concerned Black Americans, which had formed to fight for Angela Davis's release from prison.

9. Ibid., 220.

10. There were diverse interpretations of Black Power within SNCC. Baker believed that black movements and communities should be led by black people, indeed, by their own indigenous representatives, but she did not endorse separatism and opposed the coming exclusion of whites from SNCC. For Baker, Carmichael, and Forman, Black Power included socialism, but they differed in the emphasis they placed on class.

11. Beal, interview by author, 8 August 2007.

12. Beal, "Double Jeopardy," 92.

13. Patton, "Victorian Ethos," 145.

14. There is a political/historical dispute over whether the group's name is US or Us. The author and many activists from the 1960s continue to use the name US, whereas Karenga's current Web site and some scholars of today use the name Us, or the Us Organization.

15. Later Eldridge Cleaver and Karenga also changed positions.

16. "Black Cultural Nationalism's . . . US is a cultural organization": Karenga, "From *The Quotable Karenga*," 162. For a black feminist view of cultural nationalism, see Cole and Guy-Sheftall, *Gender Talk*, 79.

17. Karenga, "From *The Quotable Karenga*," 162.

18. Giddings, *When and Where I Enter*, 320.

19. Baraka, "Black Woman" (1970), in *Raise Race Rays Raze*, 148.

20. Hill, personal communication, 28 May 2008.

21. Hill, "Feminism and Black Nationalism."

22. Hill, "Zulu Woman: A Book Review," 6.

23. Robinson, "Malcolm X," 61.

24. Kwame Nkrumah, "African Socialism Revisited" (1967), quoted in Robinson, "Malcolm X," 59. SNCC leaders James Forman and Stokely Carmichael both considered Nkrumah a mentor. Neither of them held that Africa had been a place where women were free, or subordinate and happy with it.

25. Cade, "On the Issue of Roles," in *The Black Woman*, 104.

26. Black Unity Party, "Birth Control Pills and Black Children," quoted in Polatnick, "Strategies," 75.

27. Robinson et al., "The Sisters Reply."

28. Beal, "Double Jeopardy," 96–98.

29. Abubakari, "Liberated in Her Own Mind," 587.

30. Hill, "Feminism and Black Nationalism."

31. Black nationalism, like Black Power, has been blamed for an intensification of male chauvinism in the Black Freedom Movement. Yet as black feminist Myrna Hill showed in her article "Feminism and Black Nationalism," there was nothing inherently male chauvinist in the view that African Americans constituted a colony or "nation within a nation."

32. Fleming, *Soon We Will Not Cry*, 167.

33. Ibid.

34. Grant, *Ella Baker*, 229.

35. Beal, interview by author, 8 August 2007.

36. Lester with Norton, *Fire in My Soul*, 148.

37. Beal, "Double Jeopardy," 93.

38. Beal, "Sisterhood Is Still Powerful," 4.

39. Malcolm X, quoted from interviews in Paris, 28–29 November 1964, by Cole and Guy-Sheftall in *Gender Talk*, 97–98.

40. For example, NAACP chapter president Robert Williams fled Monroe, North Carolina, in 1961 to exile in Cuba, where he broadcast black news analysis to the United States on Radio Free Dixie (R. Williams, *Negroes With Guns*). In 1964, SNCC staff traveled to newly socialist Guinea as guests of the government and met with Guinean president Sékou Touré; that same year Malcolm X traveled in Africa and the Middle East; Stokely Carmichael visited newly independent nations in Africa in 1966; Diane Nash visited North Vietnam in 1966; Poor Black Women met in Canada with female Viet Cong guerrillas; the Venceremos Brigade brought U.S. volunteers to work in Cuba, including Patricia Robinson; SNCC and the BPP had international affairs coordinators. These people shared what they had learned in press conferences, interviews, articles, and speaking tours.

41. On 9 October 1967, for example, the front page of the *New York Times* featured a large photograph of a petite young Vietnamese woman, her hair in braids, carrying a rifle aimed at a downed U.S. Air Force pilot. A year later the *Times* opined, "Despite the traditional subordination of the woman's role in Asia, the Vietcong have always recog-

nized the political potential of woman power" ("Vietcong Spokesman: Mrs. Nguyen Thi Binh," *New York Times*, 4 November 1968).

42. Weathers, "Black Women's Liberation as a Revolutionary Force," 159.

43. Rowbotham, *Women, Resistance, and Revolution*, 215.

44. Carrietta G., quoted in Polatnick, "Strategies," 109.

45. Ibid., 114.

46. Fanon, *Wretched of the Earth*; Pontecorvo, *The Battle of Algiers*. Pontecorvo's 1966 film was discussed, among other places, in an article in Toni Cade's 1970 anthology *The Black Woman*. In 1969, Black Panther leaders Eldridge Cleaver (widely known for his controversial bestseller *Soul on Ice*) and Kathleen Cleaver, in political exile in Algiers, set up an international Panther headquarters there which also raised Algeria's profile in the United States.

47. Fanon, *A Dying Colonialism*, 109.

48. Cade, "On the Issue of Roles," in *The Black Woman*, 103, 106.

49. Ibid., 108.

50. Beal, "Double Jeopardy," 99, 100.

51. Ibid., 92.

52. Beal, interview by author, 14 August 2007.

53. Bond and Peery, "Has the Black Male Been Castrated?" 118.

54. Ibid., 115, 118.

55. Forman, *Black Revolutionaries*, 513.

56. Ibid., xvii.

57. Ibid., 475.

58. Stokely Carmichael, "Free Huey," in *Stokely Speaks*, 114. Originally given as a speech on 17 February 1968.

59. Forman, *Black Revolutionaries*, 519.

60. Carmichael, quoted in Fleming, *Soon We Will Not Cry*, 121.

61. Robnett, *How Long, How Long?* 180.

62. Ibid.

63. Ransby, *Ella Baker*, 310.

64. Fleming, *Soon We Will Not Cry*, 162.

65. Ibid., 157, 163.

66. Robnett, *How Long, How Long*, 182.

67. Ransby said that cultural nationalist rhetoric about women stepping back to support men "was not a commonly held view in SNCC" (*Ella Baker*, 310).

68. Ransby, *Ella Baker*, 310.

69. Carson, *In Struggle*, 272.

70. Beal, interview by author, 31 July 2007.

71. Ibid. H. Rap Brown later changed his name to Jamil Abdullah Al-Amin.

72. Beal, "Sisterhood Is Still Powerful," 3.

73. Malcolm X, quoted in Barbara Ransby and Tracye Matthews, "Black Popular Culture and the Transcendence of Patriarchal Illusions," in Guy-Sheftall, *Words of Fire*, 530. The quote comes from a letter Malcolm had written to his cousin-in-law Hakim

Jamal. For more on the evolution of Malcolm X from misogynistic sexist to pro–Women's Liberation, Ransby and Matthews refer to Paul Lee, "Malcolm X's Evolved Views on the Role of Women in Society" (unpublished manuscript, 1991).

74. Malcolm X, "At the Audubon," 133–34.

75. Ibid., 135.

76. Polatnick, "Strategies," 59–61.

77. Sarachild, personal communication, 8 September 2006.

78. Jackson later changed her name to Amina Abdur-Rahman.

79. Robinson, "Malcolm X," 56.

80. Ibid., 57, 61.

81. Ibid., 62, 63.

82. Malcolm X, in Theodore Jones, "Malcolm Knew He Was a 'Marked Man,'" *New York Times*, 22 February 1965, quoted in Robinson, "Malcolm X," 57.

83. Beal, interview by author, 8 August 2007.

84. Robinson et al., "The Sisters Reply."

85. Robinson and Group, "Position of Poor Black Women," 194, 196, 197.

86. Weathers, "Black Women's Liberation as a Revolutionary Force," 158.

87. Ibid., 159, 161, 160.

88. Ibid., 158.

89. Men were not the only framers of Black Power. Ruby Doris Robinson and Ella Baker also influenced its development.

90. Forman, *Black Revolutionaries*, xvii.

91. Beal, interview by author, 8 August 2007.

92. NAG existed before SNCC and would supply many of its leaders.

93. Carmichael, *Ready for Revolution*, 160, 161.

94. Ibid., 161.

95. Ibid., 110.

96. Carmichael, *Stokely Speaks*, 51, 53. Black feminist scholar Barbara Ransby mentions only Carmichael's charge to whites to fight racism in the white community (*Ella Baker*, 348). White feminist scholar Alice Echols said Julius Lester was the only Black Power advocate she had found who believed that whites were oppressed (*Daring to Be Bad*, 311n69). However, black scholar and 1960s feminist activist Cellestine Ware held that "Stokely Carmichael's message to white radicals was to look to their own oppression. This admonition was one of the inspirations of the new feminist movement. . . . Black is Beautiful is the direct antecedent to Women Are People" (*Woman Power*, 11).

97. Carmichael, *Stokely Speaks*, 51, 52.

98. Ibid., 28, 12.

99. Carmichael, *Ready for Revolution*, 92, 93.

100. Greenberg, *A Circle of Trust*, 170.

101. Lester, *Look Out Whitey!* 139.

102. Carmichael, *Stokely Speaks*, 28.

103. Hayden, "Fields of Blue," 369.

104. Beal, "Double Jeopardy," 95.

105. Patton, "Victorian Ethos," 147, 144.

106. Hill, "Feminism and Black Nationalism," 3.

107. Ibid.

108. Ware, *Woman Power*, 81, 89.

109. Patricia Robinson and Group, "A Historical and Critical Essay for Black Women in the Cities, June 1969," in Cade, *The Black Woman*, 199.

110. Polatnick, "Strategies," 101.

111. Richardson, "A Black Woman Speaks."

112. Sarachild, in Greenberg, *A Circle of Trust*, 148.

113. Hayden, "Fields of Blue," 368, 369.

114. Ibid., 368.

115. Brown, in Jones and Brown, "Female Liberation Movement," 398.

116. Jones, in Jones and Brown, "Female Liberation Movement," 364.

117. Ibid., 365.

118. Reagon, in Greenberg, *A Circle of Trust*, 150.

119. Hayden, "Fields of Blue," 371.

120. See for example the discussions of Casey Hayden's reaction to black nationalism in Rosen, *The World Split Open*, 112–13, and in Evans, *Personal Politics*, 99, 100.

121. Sandy Springs meeting transcript, 10, RWLAA.

122. Sarachild, in Sandy Springs meeting transcript, 15.

123. Allen, New York, to author, March 2001.

124. Brown, Gainesville, to Sarachild, New York, 22 November 1985, RWLAA.

125. Brown to Sarachild, 8 September 1968, RWLAA.

126. Ibid.

127. Price, "Behind the NCNP Meeting," 9.

128. Freeman, *Politics*, 60.

129. Echols, *Daring to Be Bad*, 49.

Chapter 7. "After that paper, there would be no turning back"

1. Transcript of audio recording, in Polatnick, "Strategies," 69. Poor Black Women taped some of the meetings in which they formulated their positions.

2. Ibid.

3. Ibid., 70, 329. With the exception of Linda Landrine, members of Poor Black Women allowed themselves to be cited only by first name and last initial.

4. Jones and Brown, "Female Liberation Movement," 397.

5. Ware, *Woman Power*, 58. Ware also attended meetings of the black Women's Liberation group the Black Women's Alliance.

6. Marilyn Webb called advocates of this tendency, of which she was a leader, "intellectual politicos" ("Common Enemy," 15). Sara Evans mistakenly notes that "radical feminists . . . labeled their opponents 'politicos' . . . an unfair designation" (*Tidal Wave*, 29). But the sting was in the other direction—intended as an indication of the intellectual, political nature of "politico" arguments as opposed to the personal, nonpolitical

nature of those who saw men among women's oppressors. Indeed, Webb labels such a view "personal" in the "Common Enemy" article. Alice Echols gives some history of the designation "politico" in *Daring to Be Bad*, 314n2. Black Women's Liberation founders did not use the term "politico."

7. Webb, "Common Enemy," 15.

8. Sue Munaker, "A Call for Women's Liberation," *Resistance*, January 1968.

9. Ware, *Woman Power*, 166–67.

10. Peggy Dobbins, e-mail to Kathie Sarachild, 28 June 2007.

11. Historian Alice Echols calls the debates "corrosive" and refers to the "near lethal politico-feminist schism" (*Daring to Be Bad*, 51, 52).

13. This debate is developed more fully in the section on consciousness-raising in chapter 9.

13. Shulamith Firestone and Anne Koedt named the paper "The Personal Is Political" when they published it in *Notes from the Second Year* in 1970. Hanisch's original title in February 1969 was "Some Thoughts in Response to Dottie's Thoughts on a Women's Liberation Movement" (Hanisch, "New Intro").

14. This account of the convention is taken from Freeman, "Origins," 179–80.

15. Ibid., 175.

16. Ibid., 178, 179. The workshop had been organized by Barbara Likan, whom Freeman described as believing that woman "deserved more respect for her role as first educator." Freeman said she believed that Likan had been able to persuade NCNP conference organizers to include a women's workshop by recruiting Madalyn Murray O'Hair, widely known as the plaintiff in the Supreme Court's decision to forbid prayer in public schools, to lead the workshop.

17. Ibid., 180.

18. Anonymous by request, quoted in Hole and Levine, *Rebirth of Feminism*, 114.

19. "Chicago Women Form Liberation Group," *New Left Notes*, 13 November 1967, 2. The article, not bylined, was provided by the women who would soon be known as the West Side Group.

20. Poor Black Women was organized in 1960 and in summer 1967 had begun to develop and circulate its political analysis of male supremacy; see Polatnick, "Strategies," 73, 76. Although it did not call itself a Women's Liberation group until fall 1968, it could and perhaps should be considered to have been as early as the Chicago group.

21. The group did not name itself the West Side Group until sometime later that year. At that point it was virtually alone on a cutting edge. NOW consisted of only about 1,200 members, who saw themselves mainly as a lobbying group at the national level (Freeman, *Politics*, 80). See also Susan Brownmiller's discussion (*In Our Time*, 3) of her rejection from early NOW by Betty Friedan, who had informed her that NOW was "not soliciting general members" and "was to be a select committee of professional women who would lobby Congress."

22. Weisstein, in DuPlessis and Snitow, *The Feminist Memoir Project*, 39.

23. Fran Rominski, Chicago, to Judith Brown, Gainesville, 19 September 1968, JBE.

24. See note 19.

25. Shulamith Firestone, New York, to Jo Freeman, Chicago, 17 October 1967, JFPF.

26. Casey Hayden and Mary King, "Sex and Caste: A Kind of Memo," *Liberation*, 10 April 1966, 35–36. Sarachild was also in a group interview in SNCC's New York office on the subject of women in the movement for the article " . . . because he was black and I was white," by Elizabeth Martinez, a northern SNCC support staffer, which appeared in *Mademoiselle*, April 1967. Three black and three white women anonymously participated in the interview.

27. Chude Pam Allen, "The Women's Liberation Movement," unpublished article in author's files.

28. Jeannette Rankin was the first congresswoman, and the sole member of Congress to vote against both WWI and WWII.

29. Allen to Freeman, 31 December 1967, JFPF.

30. Shulamith Firestone, "The Jeanette Rankin Brigade: Woman Power?" in *First Year*, 18; also at scriptorium.lib.duke.edu/wlm/notes/#rankin.

31. Sarachild, "Funeral Oration," 21.

32. Booth, Munaker, and Goldfield, "Women in the Radical Movement."

33. Ibid.

34. "Traditional Womanhood Is Dead," leaflet written by Kathie Amatniek (Sarachild) for New York Radical Women, 15 January 1968, in Redstockings, *Feminist Revolution*, 154. This was the first known use of the slogan "Sisterhood Is Powerful," and the leaflet clearly defines it as a militant union of women organizing to gain and wield political power for women's freedom as "full human beings."

35. Sarachild, "Funeral Oration," 21.

36. "Contact List from Radical Women's Caucus at Jeannette Rankin Grigade [sic]" n.d., RWLAA.

37. *VWLM* (Chicago, March 1968–June 1969, 7 issues, RWLAA) published material from various cities, and radical women activists of all stripes subscribed to it, but until 1969 it did not include radical feminist material. It was the first and last Women's Liberation newsletter of national scope.

38. Anne Weills, interview by author, New York, 14 June 2001.

39. Dee Ann Pappas, interview by author, New York, 11 June 2001.

40. Firestone to Freeman, March 1968, JFPF.

41. Freeman, "Genesis of the Women's Liberation Movement," JFPF. This unpublished paper was probably written in February 1968 shortly after the action at the Brigade.

42. *VWLM*, March 1968, 3.

43. Allen to Freeman, 6 February 1968, JFPF.

44. Firestone to Freeman, March 1968, JFPF.

45. Ibid.

46. Damned, *Lessons from the Damned*, 93. "The damned" was Poor Black Women, who put together this book containing several of their early papers.

47. Ibid. Some of this discussion also draws from Polatnick, "Strategies," 62–63.

48. Polatnick, "Strategies," 62.

49. Ibid., 64.

50. Ibid., 62, 63.

51. Robinson and Group, "Position of Poor Black Women," 196.

52. Ibid.

53. Koedt, in Firestone, *First Year*, 26.

54. Ibid.

55. Ibid., 27.

56. Naomi Jaffe and Bernardine Dohrn, "The Look Is You . . . Two Tits and No Head," *New Left Notes*, 18 March 1968, 5.

57. Ibid.

58. Ellen Willis, "'Consumerism' and Women," ca. 1969, mimeograph, in *Redstockings First Literature List*, 19–23, RWLAA.

59. Weisstein to author, 23 June 1991, JBE.

60. Jones and Brown, "Female Liberation Movement," 365.

61. Ibid., 365, 366.

62. Ibid, 367.

63. Ibid, 366, 364.

64. Ibid., 413.

65. Ibid., 392.

66. Judith Brown, Gainesville, to Kathie Sarachild, New York, 15 July 1985, RWLAA.

67. Letters in the Redstockings Archives and the personal files of Jo Freeman from Janet Hews of the Women's Majority Union in Seattle put the publication at 2 December 1968. "The Sisters Reply" was sent to the Black Unity Party by Poor Black Women (Robinson et al.) in September 1968.

68. Rominski to Brown, 19 September 1968, JBE.

69. Robins, *Handbook of Women's Liberation*, 105.

70. Dave Nolan to Brown, 21 September 1968, JBE. For SSOC history, see Michel, *Struggle for a Better South*, and Greene, "We'll Take Our Stand." SSOC formed to organize white college students in the South against white supremacy and poverty.

71. "Indeed, the 'Florida Paper' was nothing less than a frontal assault on the politico position" (Echols, *Daring to Be Bad*, 63).

72. Brown to Hanisch, 27 August 1968, RWLAA.

73. Lars Backstrom, Stockholm, to Brown, 25 December 1968, JBE.

74. Brown to Marilyn Webb, Washington, D.C., July 1968, RWLAA.

75. Webb to invitees to the Sandy Springs meeting, 27 July 1968, JBE.

76. The precise number in attendance is unclear. Handwritten notes on the transcripts of tape-recorded portions of the meeting, made at the time, show 19 (Sandy Springs transcript, RWLAA). Alice Echols (*Daring to Be Bad*, 104) says 20 women attended, as does Brownmiller (*In Our Time*, 31). Jo Freeman, who was there, says 22 were present (*Politics*, 106).

77. Dunbar-Ortiz, *Outlaw Woman*, 139.

78. Ibid., 119.

79. Cell 16, flier for journal issue no. 1, RWLAA.

80. Sandy Springs meeting transcript, 15. The transcript is incomplete and does not name the speakers.

81. Ibid., 13.

82. Ibid., 16.

83. Ibid., 25, 26.

84. Brown, "Origins of Consciousness-Raising in the South," 3.

85. Ibid.

86. Ibid.

87. Hanisch to Brown, 31 August 1968, RWLAA.

Chapter 8. Support for Women's Liberation on the Left, New and Old

1. See for example the discussion in Freeman, *Politics*, 56–68; see also Evans, *Personal Politics*, 218–20.

2. Freeman, *Politics*, 87.

3. Echols, *Daring to Be Bad*, 74.

4. Freeman, *Politics*, xi.

5. Gerassi, "Interview."

6. Hayden, "Fields of Blue," 351–52.

7. Kathie Sarachild, personal communication, 21 June 2007.

8. Morgan, *Sisterhood Is Powerful*, 601.

9. Betita Martinez, interview by author, 8 November 2008.

10. Carol Hanisch and Elizabeth Sutherland, "Women of the World Unite—We Have Nothing to Lose But Our Men!" in Firestone, *First Year*, 12; available from www. redstockings.org and at scriptorium.lib.duke.edu/wlm/notes/#ourmen.

11. Sutherland, "Colonized Women: The Chicana," in Morgan, *Sisterhood Is Powerful*, 378.

12. Ibid., 378–79.

13. Redstockings, "For the Tillie Olsen Memorial Celebration," 17 February 2007, RWLAA.

14. Cusac, "Tillie Olsen Interview."

15. Esther Cooper Jackson, quoted in Kelley, *Hammer and Hoe*, 207.

16. Weigand, *Red Feminism*.

17. Edwards, "Male Supremacy on the Left," 26.

18. Engels's *Origin of the Family* was among the books most frequently debated by the radical women.

19. Sara Evans in *Personal Politics*, 116–19 passim, compared the New Left unfavorably on male chauvinism with the Old Left and noted that "those around the new left with a background of experience in old left organizations were sometimes shocked by the crassness of anti-female sentiments" (118).

20. Bernstein et al., *Sisters, Brothers, Lovers*, 6.

21. Anne Braden discusses the housing battle and sedition conviction in *The Wall Between*. See also Fosl, *Subversive Southerner*.

22. Redstockings Membership List, 1968, RWLAA.

23. Sarachild, New York, to Hanisch, Louisville, 15 August 1968, RWLAA.

24. Enclosing a scrap of the *Patriot*'s masthead, Carl Braden wrote, "SCEF has had women's liberation as part of its program for 30 years. Guess nobody bothered to read the masthead" (Braden, Louisville, to Brown, Gainesville, 29 August 1968, RWLAA).

25. Hanisch, New York, to SCEF Women, Louisville, "Proposal for a Women's Liberation Program," 10 August 1968, RWLAA.

26. Ibid.

27. Ibid.

28. Ibid., 2.

29. Ibid.

30. Ibid.

31. Hanisch, Louisville, to Sarachild, New York, 12 August 1968, RWLAA.

32. Hanisch to Sarachild, 31 August 1968, RWLAA.

33. Hanisch to Sarachild, 23 August 1968, RWLAA.

34. Ibid.

35. Hanisch to Sarachild, 12 and 23 August 1968.

36. Hanisch to Sarachild, 23 August 1968, RWLAA.

37. Brown to Carl Braden, 27 August 1968, RWLAA.

38. Braden to Brown, 29 August 1968, RWLAA.

39. Hanisch, Bancroft, Iowa, to Brown, Gainesville, 31 August 1968, RWLAA.

40. Brown, Gainesville, to Hanisch, New York, 8 September 1968, RWLAA.

41. Sarachild, New York, to Hanisch, Louisville, 15 August 1968, RWLAA.

42. Anne Braden, Louisville, to Brown, Gainesville, 17 September 1968, RWLAA.

43. For more on the rich tradition of argument on the woman question, see Weigand, *Red Feminism*.

44. To the Communist-led Left, the "Old Left" does not include people with a background in organizations such as the Socialist Workers Party that are guided by the ideas of Leon Trotsky, a theorist and military leader in the Bolshevik Revolution. I have included such organizations based on when they originated, not political interpretation.

45. Barbara Winslow, interview by author, New York, 1 June 2001. A year later Women's Liberation Seattle became independent.

46. The journal *Lilith* was named for the legendary first wife of Adam, who preceded Eve and was his equal. There is a current Jewish feminist magazine, *Lilith Magazine*, which also takes its name from this legend.

47. Janet Hews, Seattle, to "Sisters," 2 December 1968, RWLAA.

48. Women's Majority Union, *Lilith* (Seattle), 2 December 1968, 15.

49. Ibid.

50. Barbara Winslow, unpublished manuscript, 19 July 1999, 10.

51. Freeman, *Politics*, 187.

272 Notes to Pages 155–160

52. Ibid.

53. Ibid.

54. Pappas, interview by author, New York, 23 September 1995. Russian for "spark," *Iskra* was the name of an underground newspaper founded by Lenin in 1900.

55. Brown, Gainesville, to Freeman, Chicago, 26 July 1968, JFPF.

56. M. Jones, *Berkeley of the South*, 138.

57. Brown to Freeman, 3 October 1968, JFPF.

58. Sale, *SDS*, 354.

59. See for example Rosen, *The World Split Open*, 134; Evans, *Personal Politics*, 224; Echols, *Daring to Be Bad*, 117; Brownmiller, *In Our Time*, 57.

60. Webb, interview by author, New York, 13 June 2001.

61. Sale, *SDS*, 89.

62. Rosen, *The World Split Open*, 116.

63. Jesse Lemisch, "Remarks on Naomi Weisstein," read at the Thirtieth Anniversary of the Women's Liberation Movement, Honoring Founders and Activists, 13 December 1997.

64. Weisstein, quoted in Evans, *Personal Politics*, 172.

65. Weisstein to author, 11 June 2001.

66. "Leaving the Left" is the title of chapter 4 in Rosen, *The World Split Open*, 94–140. I discuss this further in chapter 9.

67. Evans, *Personal Politics*, 221. This point is conclusive for Evans. She states, "Feminism was born in that contradiction—the threatened loss of new possibility."

68. Rothstein, in DuPlessis and Snitow, *The Feminist Memoir Project*, 31.

69. Rosen, *The World Split Open*, 117–20.

70. Only four of the women Rosen mentioned as suffering status deprivation took part in formative Women's Liberation work. They were Casey Hayden, Ann Weills, Marilyn Webb, and Vivian Rothstein. The others did not go to early conferences, nor write feminist papers in 1967 and 1968.

71. Pappas, interview by author, New York, 14 June 2001.

72. Julian Brown, Pierre, S.D., to author, 29 June 1991, JBE.

73. Tom Hayden, quoted in Miller, *Democracy Is in the Streets*, 48.

74. Ibid., 59.

75. Hayden, "Fields of Blue," 349.

76. Ibid., 347.

77. Ibid., 349.

78. Evans, *Personal Politics*, 202.

79. Pam Allen to author, 21 December 2000.

80. Weills, interview by author, New York, 15 June 2001.

81. Ibid.

82. Not all Women's Liberation founders were married. A few later identified as lesbians. All complained about sexism inside and outside the movement.

83. Echols, *Daring to Be Bad*, 107; Laya Firestone, Helen Kritzler, Charlotte B. Weeks, Marilyn S. Webb, Washington, D.C., "[Letter] to Women . . ." 8 November

1968, RWLAA: "we are making $25/week each . . . We do not see our work . . . as the center of a new bureaucracy," the women working at IPS wrote. .

84. Miller, *Democracy Is in the Streets*, 158.

85. Booth, interview by author, New York, 15 April 2001.

86. Evans, *Personal Politics*, 186.

87. Sale, *SDS*, 248.

88. Allen to author, 21 December 2000.

89. SSOC was organized in 1964 to attract white southern students to activism against racism and poverty. See Michel, *Struggle for a Better South*.

90. Brown to Sarachild, 10 February 1969, RWLAA.

91. Rosen, *The World Split Open*, 131.

92. Forman, *Black Revolutionaries*, xvii.

93. Beal, interview by author, 31 July 2007.

94. Beal, personal communication, 21 January 2009.

95. Ibid.

96. Weisstein to author, 20 May 2001.

97. Ibid.

98. Richard Flacks, interview by author, New York, 28 May 2001.

99. Price, "Behind the NCNP Meeting," 9.

100. Ibid.

101. Hanisch, interview by author, New York, 15 October 2000.

102. William A. "Bill" Price, interview by author, New York, 11 February 2001.

103. Weisstein to author, 20 June 2001.

104. Jesse Lemisch, New York, to *Guardian*, 23 July 1968.

105. Gregory, "Poet Demands Equality for Negro Womanhood."

106. Mildred was the domestic worker and protagonist in Childress's acclaimed 1956 book *Like One of the Family*.

107. Hansberry describes spending "months of study" on *The Second Sex* at age twenty-three ("Simone de Beauvoir," 130).

108. Elizabeth Brown-Guillory, "Alice Childress," in Hine et al., *Black Women in America*, 235.

109. Jean Carey Bond, "Freedomways and the Civil Rights Movement," presentation at the symposium "The American Left and the Origins of the Modern Civil Rights Movement," Tamiment Library, New York University, 28 October 2006.

110. Julian Bond, in Jackson, *Freedomways Reader*, xvii.

111. Jackson, *Freedomways Reader*, 291.

112. Sarah E. Wright, in Jackson, *Freedomways Reader*, 291, 292.

113. Ibid.

114. Alice Childress, in Jackson, *Freedomways Reader*, 296.

115. Jackson, *Freedomways Reader*, 105.

116. Liberation Committee for Africa, *Liberator* 3, no. 8 (August 1963): 2.

117. Moore, "When Will the Real Black Man Stand Up?" 4.

118. Lomax, "Afro-American Woman: Growth Deferred," 18.

119. Rodgers, "Sisters—Stop Castrating the Black Man!" 21.

120. Bond and Peery, "Has the Black Male Been Castrated?" 114.

121. Moore, "Black Men vs. Black Women," 16.

122. Ibid.

123. Two Black Sisters, letter to the editor, *Liberator* 6, no. 10 (October 1966): 22.

124. Newton, "Women's Liberation and Gay Liberation Movements."

125. Banks, "Women's Liberation," 5–9.

126. Dunbar-Ortiz, *Outlaw Woman*, 126.

127. *Guardian* (New York), 20 July 1968, 17. Pandora was known to be Irwin Silber, longtime editor of the Left journal *Sing Out*.

128. Circulation figure from Buhle, Buhle, and Georgakas, *Encyclopedia*, 443.

129. King, *Freedom Song*, 468.

130. *VWLM* circulation from Jo Freeman, Chicago, to Pam Allen, San Francisco, 5 October 1968, JFPF; *Guardian* circulation from Buhle, Buhle, and Georgakas, *Encyclopedia*, 531.

131. *Guardian*, 5 October 1968, 11.

132. Freeman to Allen, 5 October 1968, JFPF.

133. The station had been owned by a liberal millionaire who gave it to the Pacifica Foundation.

134. Julius Lester, interview with Pam Allen, 5 May 1968, box XA-2, 3, RWLAA.

135. Miller, *Democracy Is in the Streets*, 259.

136. Jane Adams, *New Left Notes*, 17 April 1967, 4.

137. [West Side Group], "Chicago Women Form Liberation Group," *New Left Notes*, 13 November 1967, 2.

138. Brown, in Jones and Brown, "Female Liberation Movement, 397.

139. Brown to Freeman, April 1968, JFPF.

140. Brown to Hanisch, 8 September 1968, RWLAA.

141. Freeman, Chicago, to Laya Firestone, Washington, D.C., 18 October 1968, JFPF.

142. There were exceptions in the mainstream media before the pageant protest, e.g., on 10 March 1968 the *New York Times Magazine* published an article on the new movement by Martha Weinman Lear, "What Do These Women *Want*? The Second Feminist Wave," coining the term "second wave" (24). Also, the appearance on TV of WLM leaders on the nationally popular *David Susskind Show* followed the pageant protest but was scheduled before the protest; see Rosalyn Baxandall, New York, to Kathie Sarachild, New York, 7 August 1968, RWLAA.

143. Firestone, *The Dialectic of Sex*, 11.

144. Commissions on the Status of Women, the Woman's Party, the National Council of Negro Women, the League of Women Voters, the Berkshire Conference of female historians, women's departments of unions, and Daughters of Bilitis, a national lesbian rights group, are among the exceptions.

145. Anne Koedt, "The Myth of the Vaginal Orgasm" (1968) in Firestone, *First*

Year, 11; available from www.redstockings.org and at scriptorium.lib.duke.edu/wlm/notes/#myth.

146. Ibid.

Chapter 9. Making the Women's Liberation Movement

1. Polatnick, "Strategies," 67.

2. Ibid., 68, 69.

3. Allen, San Francisco, to Brown, Gainesville, 5 September 1968, RWLAA.

4. Poor Black Women, quoted in Polatnick, "Strategies," 114. The letter was published in 1970 in Cade, *The Black Woman*, 189–94.

5. Gainesville would soon become the site of eight Women's Liberation groups, including a high school group and a black group.

6. Gainesville Women's Liberation, "Declaration of Continued Independence."

7. Kathie Sarachild, for example, called women a class and used the term "class consciousness" to refer to feminist consciousness in "A Program for Radical Feminist Consciousness-Raising," November 27, 1968; see Redstockings, *Feminist Revolution*, 202.

8. Jaggar in *Feminist Politics*, 84, explained sisterhood as a route to self-affirmation. Fox-Genovese in *Feminism Without Illusions*, 16, said that feminist sisterhood meant "bonding among female peers." For a critical discussion, see Brooke Williams in Redstockings, *Feminist Revolution*, 79, and Willis, *No More Nice Girls*, 152. A distortion of the concept in current use as a decision-making style called "feminist process" is found in various documents of NOW.

9. Sarachild, New York, to Hanisch, Gainesville, 8 February 1969, RWLAA. Sarachild first came up with the slogan and put it on the flyer she made for NYRW's Burial of Traditional Womanhood demonstration in D.C. on 15 January 1968.

10. Shreve, *Women Together, Women Alone*, 14.

11. Firestone, *The Dialectic of Sex*, 1.

12. Poor Black Women, quoted in Polatnick, "Strategies," 72.

13. Morales, in Redstockings, *Feminist Revolution*, 199.

14. Joyce, Poor Black Women, quoted in Polatnick, "Strategies," 69.

15. Sarachild said Forer proposed the elements of what became consciousness-raising "shortly after the group formed" in September 1967 as they were "planning our first public action," the Burial of Traditional Womanhood, in January 1968. Sarachild quoted Forer as saying, "I think we have a lot more to do just in the area of raising our own consciousness" (Redstockings, *Feminist Revolution*, 144). Carol Hanisch was also at the meeting at which Forer made the proposal. Hanisch said they didn't consciously adopt consciousness-raising until after the Burial action (Hanisch, in Ezekiel et al., Comments, 27 May 2006).

16. Brownmiller, *In Our Time*, 21. When Forer spoke of the phrase "consciousness-raising" ringing in Sarachild's mind, Forer was referring to Sarachild's firsthand account of the origins of consciousness-raising, the first to relate Forer's contribution; see Redstockings, *Feminist Revolution*, 144.

17. Firestone and Koedt, *Second Year*, 78.

18. Kathie Sarachild, "Radical Feminist 'Consciousness Organizing' Workshop," originally published with no author listed, workshop description and notes on Lake Villa Conference, 27 November 1968, folder 1968.27, RWLAA. See also Redstockings, *Feminist Revolution*, 202–3. Sarachild removed "Radical" from the title and changed "organizing" to "raising" when the program was published in Firestone and Koedt, *Notes from the Second Year*, and in subsequent reprints such as the 1970 anthologies Morgan, *Sisterhood Is Powerful*, xxiii–xxiv, and Tanner, *Voices from Women's Liberation*.

19. Redstockings, *Feminist Revolution*, 202.

20. Firestone, *First Year*, 15.

21. Redstockings, *Feminist Revolution*, 145.

22. Ibid.

23. Ibid., 185.

24. Sarachild, in Redstockings, *Feminist Revolution*, 203.

25. Ibid.

26. Mao, *On New Democracy*.

27. Sarachild, in Redstockings, *Feminist Revolution*, 203.

28. Ibid.

29. [Janet Hews], "The Bitch," *Lilith* (Seattle), December 1968, 7.

30. Cole and Guy-Sheftall, *Gender Talk*, 5.

31. Springer, *Living for the Revolution*, 118–22 passim, provides a discussion on the TWWA's use of consciousness-raising.

32. Springer, *Living for the Revolution*, 118.

33. Cole and Guy-Sheftall, *Gender Talk*, 6.

34. Adele Jones and Group, "Ebony Minds, Black Voices," in Cade, *The Black Woman*, 180–88.

35. Anselma Dell'Olio, "Home Before Sundown," in DuPlessis and Snitow, *The Feminist Memoir Project*, 150.

36. Moore, "Black Men vs. Black Women," 16.

37. Brown to Sarachild, 16 October 1968, RWLAA.

38. Hill, e-mail, 6 July 2008.

39. Redstockings, *Feminist Revolution*, 204. Some women did not take to consciousness-raising. Women passed in and out of groups easily, as there were no formal memberships in Women's Liberation.

40. Bill Hager, "How Could We Guess That Lady Clairol Gloss Covered Up the Mind of a Revolutionary?" *Gainesville Sun*, 5 January 1969.

41. Brownmiller, *In Our Time*, 21.

42. Allen to author, 27 June 2002.

43. Redstockings, *Feminist Revolution*, 145.

44. Forman, *Black Revolutionaries*, 247.

45. Brown to Sarachild, n.d., RWLAA.

46. Dottie Zellner, quoted in Brown, Gainesville, to "Women's Liberation Group,

New Orleans," c/o SCEF, Louisville, 9 June 1969, RWLAA. SCEF's Anne Braden also understood consciousness-raising this way—strong women didn't need it, but more oppressed women did; see Fosl, *Subversive Southerner*, 318.

47. Brown to Women's Liberation Group, New Orleans, 9 June 1969.

48. Redstockings, *Feminist Revolution*, 184.

49. Described in detail in Hinton, *Fanshen*, a book about the Chinese Revolution that provided reinforcement to consciousness-raising organizers when attacked by the Left for holding therapy sessions.

50. Sarachild, in Redstockings, *Feminist Revolution*, 30.

51. This poster later found a home in the New York City Redstockings office, there catching the attention of the mass media when it was quoted in its entirety in a *Life* magazine article on the Women's Liberation Movement in December 1969; see Redstockings, *Feminist Revolution*, 30.

52. Colette Price, "The Cultural Revolution, the Women's Liberation Movement and the Spirit of the '60s," speech given at the symposium "China's Great Proletarian Cultural Revolution: Its Goals, Achievements, and Significance," Hunter College, 23 April 1987, 3, RWLAA.

53. Hanisch, "The Personal Is Political," 76.

54. Polatnick, "Strategies," 74, 75, 80.

55. Ibid., 104.

56. Brown to Sarachild, 1 September 1968, RWLAA.

57. Sarachild to Brown, 3 September 1968, RWLAA.

58. Brown to Hanisch, 18 September 1968, RWLAA.

59. Brown to Sarachild, 10 February 1969, RWLAA.

60. Carol Hanisch, "Freedom for Women, Report #7 Miami," to SCEF, Louisville, 13 March 1969, RWLAA.

61. Sarachild, New York, to Judith Brown and Carol Giardina, Gainesville, 24 Nov 1968, RWLAA.

62. The reference "Leaving the Left" is to the title of chapter 4 in Rosen, *The World Split Open*, 94–140.

63. Brown to Hanisch, 27 August 1968.

64. Brown to Roxanne Dunbar, Boston, 11 December 1968, RWLAA.

65. Brown to Allen, 18 October 1968, RWLAA.

66. Hanisch to Brown, 17 December 1968, RWLAA.

67. Quoted in Echols, *Daring to Be Bad*, 168.

68. Engels, *Origin of the Family*.

69. Brown, editorial, 2.

70. Lenin, "Communism," 143.

71. Mainardi, "The Politics of Housework," in Morgan, *Sisterhood Is Powerful*, 447–54; Koedt, "The Myth of the Vaginal Orgasm" (1968) in Tanner, *Voices from Women's Liberation*, 157–65.

72. Polatnick, "Strategies," 74.

73. Firestone, *The Dialectic of Sex*, 13.

74. Third World Women's Alliance, "Book Review," Triple *Jeopardy*, October 1971, 12, 13.

75. Polatnick, "Strategies," 54.

76. Ibid.

77. Clara Colon and Irena Knight, "Marxists in the Women's Freedom Struggle," *Daily World*, 24 April 1969.

78. Clara Colon and Lenore Weiss, "Marxists in the Women's Freedom Struggle," *Daily World*, 22 April 1969.

79. See note 77.

80. Judith Brown, interview by author, Gainesville, 9 April 1990, videotape 3, JBE.

81. Ibid.

82. Ibid.

83. Brown, editorial, 2.

84. Firestone and Koedt, New York, to Naomi Weisstein, Chicago, 1 March 1968, JFPF.

85. Redstockings, "Redstockings Manifesto," 8.

86. Hanisch, New York, to Anne Braden, Louisville, 17 October 1968, RWLAA.

87. Sarachild to Brown, 18 September 1968, RWLAA.

88. Firestone and Koedt to Weisstein, 1 March 1968, JFPF.

89. Hansberry, "Simone de Beauvoir," 128–29.

Chapter 10. The Movement Goes Nationwide

1. Hole and Levine, *Rebirth of Feminism*, 397.

2. Polatnick, "Strategies," 128.

3. Equal Employment Opportunity Commission, *Second Annual Report*, 45; Babcock et al., *Sex Discrimination and the Law*, 361.

4. Nupur Chaudhuri and Mary Elizabeth Perry, "Achievements and Battles: Twenty-five Years of CCWHP," *Journal of Women's History* 6, no. 2 (1994): 97–105.

5. Hole and Levine, *Rebirth of Feminism*, 413.

6. Ibid., 422.

7. Judith Hole and Ellen Levine provide a detailed chronological record of feminist "events, issues, and activities" from 1961 to 1971 in *Rebirth of Feminism*, 401–27. More examples of many of the activities referred to can be found there.

8. Jo Freeman used the term "blitz" to describe the flood of attention the media gave the movement in is rebirth years (*Politics*, 148). Reporters even sneaked into neighborhood consciousness-raising groups, only to be discovered and sometimes physically ejected.

9. Firestone, New York, to Weisstein, Chicago, March 1968, JFPF.

10. "Primary Sources: 1948 Pageant Contract," *American Experience*, http://www.pbs.org/wgbh/amex/missamerica/filmmore/ps.html.

11. Simmons, quoted in Fleming, *Soon We Will Not Cry*, 174. For more on black women discussing white beauty standards, see Fleming, 172–76 passim.

12. Due and Due, *Freedom in the Family*, 22.

13. Collins, *Black Feminist Thought*, 80.

14. Carol Hanisch, "What Can Be Learned: A Critique of the Miss America Protest," 27 November 1968, in *Redstockings First Literature List and a Sampling of Its Materials*, RWLAA.

15. The author joined the protest, representing Gainesville Women's Liberation. My picket sign read "Can Make-Up Cover the Wounds of Our Oppression?" Photograph in Papachristou, *Women Together*, 233.

16. Hanisch analyses the action in "Two Letters," 198.

17. Ibid.

18. Ibid., 200.

19. Ibid., 200, 201.

20. Saundra Williams, quoted in Judy Klemesrud, "There's Now Miss Black America," *New York Times*, 9 September 1968.

21. Charlotte Curtis, "Miss America Pageant Is Picketed by 100 Women," *New York Times*, 8 September 1968.

22. NYRW, "The Ten Points We Protest."

23. Beal, quoted in Springer, *Living for the Revolution*, 120.

24. See note 21.

25. *Daily News*, 8 September 1968.

26. Bouchier, *The Feminist Challenge*, 105.

27. Baxandall, quoted in Hanisch, "Two Letters," 198.

28. Hanisch, "Two Letters," 200.

29. Brown to Hanisch, 27 August 1968, RWLAA.

30. Hole and Levine, *Rebirth of Feminism*, 131. There were two national gatherings in 1968. I sometimes refer to the first, in Sandy Springs in August, as a national "meeting" because it was much smaller and many of the women there did not represent groups.

31. "Radical Feminist 'Consciousness Organizing' Workshop," 27 November 1968, folder 1968.27, RWLAA.

32. Hanisch, quoted in Brownmiller, *In Our Time*, 53.

33. Dixon, "Where Are We Going?" 34, 35.

34. Ibid., 37, 34, 35.

35. Dana Densmore, "A Year of Living Dangerously: 1968," in DuPlessis and Snitow, *The Feminist Memoir Project*, 83, 82.

36. Freeman, *Politics*, 107.

37. Webb, quoted in Brownmiller, *In Our Time*, 53.

38. Kesselman, "Our Gang of Four: Friendship and Women's Liberation," in DuPlessis and Snitow, *The Feminist Memoir Project*, 41.

39. Echols, *Daring to Be Bad*, 107.

40. Polatnick, "Strategies," 174. More investigation of the question of African American women's conference attendance is needed. Polatnick writes that "only a few Black women attended" but she does not provide their names or the groups they may have represented.

41. There were no black women at the Sandy Springs meeting. The discussion about inviting African American women is in Echols, *Daring to Be Bad*, 369–77.

42. Dunbar-Ortiz, *Outlaw Woman*, 142.

43. Roth, *Separate Roads*, 195.

44. Polatnick said that Sarachild and Hanisch argued that black women must be invited ("Strategies," 171).

45. Sarachild to Brown, 9 October 1968, RWLAA.

46. Echols, *Daring to Be Bad*, 373.

47. Ibid., 375.

48. Roth, *Separate Roads*, 195.

49. Kennedy, *Color Me Flo*, 62.

50. Echols, *Daring to Be Bad*, 372.

51. For "militant black power women," Sarachild, quoted in Echols, *Daring to Be Bad*, 373; for the "further awareness" comment, Cade, *The Black Woman*, 189; for "stir and stimulate," Patricia Robinson, quoted in Polatnick, "Strategies," 75.

52. Pam Allen, quoted in Polatnick, "Strategies," 121.

53. Robinson and Group, "Position of Poor Black Women," 197.

54. [Janet Hews], *Lilith*, 1968, 9, RWLAA.

55. Robinson and Group, "Position of Poor Black Women," 196, 197.

56. Polatnick, "Strategies," 79, 81.

57. Sarachild to Brown, 29 September 1968, RWLAA.

58. Sarachild to Brown and Giardina, n.d., RWLAA.

59. Weathers, "Black Women's Liberation," 161–62.

60. The author attempted to ask Robinson and Weathers about this but was unable to reach them. Kennedy died in December 2000.

61. Breines, *The Trouble Between Us*, 81. Breines has written in rebuttal of accusations of racism in socialist feminist women.

62. Cisler, "On Abortion and Abortion Law," 89.

63. Ibid. The women of SisterSong (www.SisterSong.net) have developed a new, more advanced and useful theory of reproductive freedom—Reproductive Justice. See Loretta J. Ross's articles, electronic and print, titled "Understanding Reproductive Justice."

64. Cisler, "On Abortion and Abortion Law," 90.

65. The best short discussion of the earlier movement is feminist abortion pioneer Cisler's "On Abortion and Abortion Law." Lawrence Lader, also an activist, discusses this in *Abortion* (1966) and *Abortion II* (1973).

66. Mills, *This Little Light of Mine*, 200, 202.

67. Hamer, quoted in Mills, *This Little Light of Mine*, 22. Small wonder that African Americans charged genocide.

68. Beal, "Double Jeopardy," 97.

69. Chisholm, "Facing the Abortion Question," in *Unbought and Unbossed*, 127, 128.

70. Firestone, "Abortion Rally Speech," in *First Year*, 24.

71. Sarachild, quoted in Edith Evans Asbury, "Women Break Up Abortion Hearing," *New York Times*, 14 February 1969.

72. Ellen Willis, quoted in Margie Stamberg, "The New Feminism," *Guardian*, 19 April 1969, 11.

73. Irene Peslikis, communication with author, n.d.

74. "Gals Squeal for Repeal," *Daily News*, 14 February 1969; "Abortion Law Protesters Disrupt Panel," *New York Post*, 14 February 1969.

75. See note 71.

76. Willis, "Up from Radicalism," 118–19.

77. Peslikis, quoted in Brownmiller, *In Our Time*, 108.

78. Luker, *Abortion and the Politics of Motherhood*, 97.

79. Brownmiller, "Everywoman's Abortions," 1.

80. Steinem, "After Black Power, Women's Liberation," 10.

81. Brownmiller, "Everywoman's Abortions," reprinted in *WLM*, April 1969.

82. Activist-scholar Barbara Winslow's forthcoming book about feminism in Washington State deals with this campaign.

83. Chisholm, *Unbought and Unbossed*, 128.

84. Polatnick, "Strategies," 52, referring to Robinson et al., "The Sisters Reply."

85. Abubakari, "Liberated in Her Own Mind," 587.

86. Brownmiller, *In Our Time*, 119.

87. Weddington, *A Question of Choice*.

88. In 1975 the U.S. Senate committee chaired by Frank Church (D-Idaho) exposed the CIA and FBI for overstepping their authority. The committee hearings revealed that the spy agencies gathered information on the Women's Liberation Movement and NOW. See *Hearings before the Select Committee to Study Governmental Operations with Respect to Intelligence Activities* (Washington, D.C.: U.S. Government Printing Office, 1975), 6:98–103, 360–66, 540–85. CIA activity in the Women's Liberation Movement is discussed in the report of a governmental commission headed by Nelson Rockefeller, *Report to the President by the Commission on CIA Activities Within the U.S.* (Washington, D.C.: U.S. Government Printing Office, 1975, 144. The CIA called its mission targeting the movements of the 1960s "Operation Chaos." Government surveillance, infiltration, and disruption in the Women's Liberation Movement deserves more than one book of its own.

89. A 1972 poll showed 67 percent of black women and 35 percent of white women approved of the work of Women's Liberation groups; see F. Davis, *Moving the Mountain*, 363.

90. Cade, *The Black Woman*, 9.

91. Ntozake Shange, quoted in Tate, *Black Women Writers at Work*, 158–59.

92. Wells, *A Red Record*. Wells, turn-of-the-century antilynching crusader and women's suffrage organizer, exposed rape charges as specious grounds for whites lynching black men by showing that the real motive was eliminating black economic and political competition.

93. Cole and Guy-Sheftall, *Gender Talk*, 128–53 passim. See also Chrisman and Allen, *Court of Appeal*.

94. Brown to Sarachild and Hanisch, 9 June 1969, RWLAA.

95. Roth, *Separate Roads*, 93.

96. Kristin Anderson-Bricker, "'Triple Jeopardy': Black Women and the Growth of Feminist Consciousness in SNCC, 1964–1975," in Springer, *Still Lifting, Still Climbing*, 61. Kimberly Springer characterized TWWA as "decentralized" and rejecting hierarchical decision making (*Living for the Revolution*, 67). But democratic centralism, the traditional structure of political parties on the Left, is not decentralized.

97. Review of issues of *Triple Jeopardy*, 1971–75, RWLAA. Kristin Anderson-Bricker discusses *Triple Jeopardy* in Springer, *Still Lifting, Still Climbing*, 62, 63. See also Springer, *Living for the Revolution*, 91, 92; Roth, *Separate Roads*, 89–93.

98. Lynch, "Black Women's Manifesto."

99. Lester with Norton, *Fire in My Soul*, 148.

100. Cade, *The Black Woman*, 9, 10.

101. Margaret Wright, "I Want the Right to Be Black and Me," in Lerner, *Black Women in White America*, 608.

102. Faith Ringgold, quoted by Ann Lee Morgan in Scanlon, *Significant Contemporary American Feminists*, 246.

103. Abbey Lincoln, "Who Will Revere the Black Woman?" in Cade, *The Black Woman*, 83.

104. Lader, *Power on the Left*, 268.

105. See for example Karen Lewis, "My Place Is in the Revolution," *St. Petersburg (Fla.) Times*, 9 January 1970; also Kathleen Cleaver, "Interview."

106. Cleaver, " Interview," 20, 21.

107. Ericka Huggins, Patricia Hilliard, and Elaine Brown were among female Panthers holding national leadership positions.

108. Cleaver, "Women, Power, and Revolution," in Cleaver and Katsiaficas, *Liberation, Imagination*, 124, 126.

109. Heath, *Off the Pigs!* 339, 341, 343.

110. Ibid., 347.

111. Newton, " Women's Liberation and Gay Liberation Movements."

112. George Katsiaficas, "Organization and Movement," in Cleaver and Katsiaficas, *Liberation, Imagination*, 149.

113. Ibid., 144, 145.

114. Denise Oliver, "Revolution Within the Revolution," in Abramson and Young Lords Party, *Palante*, 52, 150.

115. Ibid., 50, 51, 52.

116. According to Roth, Chicana feminist groups "were popping up all over the Southwest." My account of Las Hijas relies on Roth, *Separate Roads*, 140.

117. "Some Demands of Chicana Women," in Papachristou, *Women Together*, 243.

Chapter 11. The Movement Is Established

1. Carrietta G., quoted in Polatnick, "Strategies," 109.

2. Pam Allen went on to organize in Union Women's Alliance to Gain Equality (Union WAGE), which sought to link Women's Liberation and the labor movement; see Balser, *Sisterhood and Solidarity*, 89.

3. Norton, in New York Commission on Human Rights, *Women's Role*, 23.

4. New York Commission on Human Rights, *Women's Role*, 83, 84.

5. Ibid., 349.

6. Ibid, 22, 23, 24.

7. Friedan, *It Changed My Life*, 178. There was plenty of friction between black and white feminists. Black feminist Bernice Johnson Reagon later described coalition politics as "feel[ing] as if I'm gonna keel over any minute and die. That is often what it feels like if you're *really* doing coalition work . . . you feel threatened to the core and if you don't, you're not really doing no coalescing" (in Smith, *Home Girls*, 356).

8. Friedan, *It Changed My Life*, 178.

9. Ibid., 187.

10. Susan Brownmiller, "Sisterhood Is Powerful," *New York Times Magazine*, 15 March 1970, 129.

11. Friedan, *It Changed My Life*, 201. The numbers vary; see also Lader, *Power on the Left*, 299.

12. Carabillo, Meuli, and Csida, *Feminist Chronicles*, 57.

13. F. Davis, *Moving the Mountain*, 116.

14. Friedan, *It Changed My Life*, 203, 207.

15. Hole and Levine, *Rebirth of Feminism*, 420.

16. Friedan, *It Changed My Life*, 210.

17. *New York Post*, 30 January 1971.

18. New York Commission on Human Rights, *Women's Role*, 475.

19. Johnnie Tillmon, quoted in Nadasen, *Welfare Warriors*, 214.

20. New York Commission on Human Rights, *Women's Role*, 479.

21. Jones and Brown, "Female Liberation Movement," 18.

22. Radicalesbians, "The Woman-Identified Woman."

23. Martha Shelley, "Notes of a Radical Lesbian," in Morgan, *Sisterhood Is Powerful*, 306.

24. Abbott and Love, *Sappho Was a Right-On Woman*, 135.

25. Beauvoir, *The Second Sex*, 381, 382.

26. Ibid., 393, 397.

27. Brown, in Jones and Brown, "Female Liberation Movement," 27.

28. Ibid., 27, 28.

29. Ibid., 28.

30. Firestone, *The Dialectic of Sex*, 236, 237.

31. Atkinson, *Amazon Odyssey*, 134. Atkinson wrote the article in December 1970 for the op-ed page of the *New York Times*, but they did not publish it.

32. Ibid., 132, 189.

33. Ibid., 132, 137.

34. "Women's Lib: A Second Look," *Time*, 14 December 1970, 50.

35. Gallo, *Different Daughters*, chaps. 7–9 passim.

36. These include Morgan, *Sisterhood Is Powerful*; Stambler, *Women's Liberation*; Cooke, Bunch-Weeks, and Morgan, *The New Women*.

37. See, for example, Echols, *Daring to Be Bad*. The so-called "gay-straight split," Echols held, "crippled the movement" (204).

38. Martelli, *The Mushroom Effect*.

39. In 1967 Canada had a Women's Liberation group (possibly preceding the West Side Group) that called itself "a rising militant Feminine Caucus . . . secretly organizing a hard-core Liberation Front . . . linked with cadres . . . across North America." Doris Lessing and Beauvoir were on its reading list. See Bernstein et al., *Sisters, Brothers, Lovers*. One of the authors, Linda Seese, was in Mississippi Freedom Summer in 1964.

40. Schneir, *Feminism in Our Time*, 130.

41. Morgan, *Sisterhood Is Powerful*, xxv.

42. Bird, *Born Female*. First published in 1968, the book also had printings in 1970.

43. Ibid., ix, x.

44. Ibid., 215. Bird compared radical feminists to "politically conscious girls" in her class of 1935 who joined the Communist Party (210).

45. Ibid., 215, 216, 206, 207.

46. Ibid., 204.

47. Morgan, *Sisterhood Is Powerful*, xxv.

48. Freeman, " Origins," 194.

49. Judith Ezekiel, in Ezekiel et al., Comments, 31 May 2006.

50. For London, Tanzania, and Indonesia, see Komisar, *The New Feminism*, 130, 133.

51. Third World Women's Alliance, *Triple Jeopardy*, front cover, 1970, RWLAA. For subsequent issues, the newspaper bore the name *Triple Jeopardy: Racism, Imperialism, Sexism*.

52. The supplement, "The New Feminism," came out in the August issue, introduced by *Journal* publisher John Mack Carter in "Why You Find the New Eight Pages in the *Ladies' Home Journal*," August 1970, 63.

53. "Women Arise," *Life*, 4 September 1970, 16b.

54. Steinem, "After Black Power, Women's Liberation," 10. In 1969 Steinem was a celebrity journalist with a column, "The City Politic," in *New York Magazine*. She covered Women's Liberation and by summer of 1970 had become an open supporter, raising money for the upcoming Women's Strike. *Ms.* was launched in 1972.

55. "Are You a Mere Sex Object? If Not, Do You Know Anybody Who Is?" *Glamour*, September 1969, 44.

56. "Women Arise," *Life*, 4 September 1970, 18.

57. Ida Lewis, interview with Eleanor Holmes Norton, *Essence*, July 1970, 47.

58. "Woman Power Age Dawns in 1970," *Chicago Defender*, 28 February 1970, 2, quoted by Linda Lumsden in "The *Chicago Defender* Rides the Second Wave," 1. The material from the *Defender* depends on Lumsden's research, and I am grateful to her for permission to use it. A revised version of her paper is to appear in the Fall 2009 issue of *Journalism History*.

59. "The Ladies Organize," *Chicago Defender*, 24 September 1970, 19, quoted in Lumsden, "*Defender* Rides," 6.

60. There were, of course, women of color who were critical of Women's Liberation. The movement had its share of white female critics as well.

61. Examples include a meeting at the University of Chicago, "Women at U of C. Schedule Confab," 4 October 1969; "What Is New Direction for Feminist Movement?" 21 March 1970, 22; "New NOW Head to Speak Here," 4 May 1970, 2; "Ebony's Helen King to Speak on WTTW's Liberation Panel," 24 August 1970, 17; "Seminar on Women Scheduled," 10 November 1970, 18; "Media Women Will Air 'Lib' Views Here," 16 November 1970, 17; "Women's Lib Top Bill at College," 10 October 1970, 2 (Lumsden, "*Defender* Rides," 25).

62. Bradley, *Mass Media*, 118.

63. Lumsden, "*Defender* Rides," 11, 27.

64. Ibid., 28.

65. Ibid, 6.

66. "Meet Women of the Black Panthers," *Chicago Defender*, 24 January 1970, 19, quoted in Lumsden, "*Defender* Rides," 7.

67. Lumsden, "*Defender* Rides," 22.

68. "A New Crop of Eligible Girls," *Ebony*, 25 April 1970, 123, quoted in Lumsden, "*Defender* Rides," 20.

69. Hernandez had been vice president under Betty Friedan, NOW's first president, and had come up through the ranks of California NOW. Before that, Hernandez was a leader in the International Ladies' Garment Workers Union (ILGWU).

70. Wolseley, *The Black Press, U.S.A.*, 144.

71. Valerie Jo Bradley, "Feminist Likens Sexism to Racism Against Blacks," *Jet*, 4 December 1970, 46, 47.

72. Ibid., 49, 50.

73. Ibid., 50.

74. Dudar, "Women's Lib," 71.

75. Howard, "We Want to Be Free."

76. Dudar, "Women's Lib," 73.

77. Ibid., 78.

78. Howard, "We Want to Be Free."

79. Amy Gross, "Women's Liberation Loves You," *Mademoiselle*, February 1970, 232, 288, 106.

81. Dudar, "Women's Lib," 73, 74.

82. Tanner, *Voices from Women's Liberation*, 13.

83. Ibid.

84. The books were Angelou, *I Know Why the Caged Bird Sings*; Chisholm, *Unbought and Unbossed*; Ware, *Woman Power*; Duster, *Crusade for Justice*; Tanner, *Voices from Women's Liberation*; Cade, *The Black Woman*; Stambler, *Women's Liberation*; Morgan, *Sisterhood Is Powerful*; Firestone, *The Dialectic of Sex*; Millett, *Sexual Politics*; Robins, *Handbook of Women's Liberation*; Hennessey, *I, B.I.T.C.H.* Several founding papers came out in Roszak and Roszak, *Masculine/Feminine*.

85. Cade, *The Black Woman*, 7.

86. Ibid., 10.

87. Chisholm, *Unbought and Unbossed*, 179.

88. Ibid., 183.

89. In 1970 alone, Angelou's book went through six printings and was a Book-of-the-Month Club and *Ebony* Book Club selection. It was reprinted five more times in 1971.

90. Cole and Guy-Sheftall, *Gender Talk*, 142.

91. Angelou, *I Know Why the Caged Bird Sings*, 231.

92. The papers by Poor Black Women were published in whole or in part in Tanner, *Voices from Women's Liberation*; Morgan, *Sisterhood Is Powerful*; Stambler, *Women's Liberation*; Roszak and Roszak, *Masculine/Feminine*. They had first appeared in *Lilith*, the publication of the Women's Majority Union in Seattle.

93. Weathers's 1969 article for Cell 16's *No More Fun and Games* appeared in 1970 in Stambler, *Women's Liberation*, and Tanner, *Voices from Women's Liberation*, as well as in Guy-Sheftall, *Words of Fire*.

94. Morgan, *Sisterhood Is Powerful*, xiv.

95. Ibid., xiii.

96. Stambler, *Women's Liberation*, 11.

97. Ware, *Woman Power*, 109.

98. Ibid., 112.

99. Exceptions include the work of Eileen Kraditor, Gerda Lerner, Elinor Rice Hays, Eleanor Flexner, and Yuri Suhl.

100. Firestone, *First Year*, 1; also at scriptorium.lib.duke.edu/wlm/notes/#new view.

101. Ibid.

102. Jones, in Jones and Brown, "Toward a Female Liberation Movement," 390, 391.

103. Tanner, *Voices from Women's Liberation*, 13.

104. Duster, *Crusade for Justice*, xiii.

105. Lerner, *Black Women in White America*, 573.

106. Firestone, *The Dialectic of Sex*, 27.

107. Tanner, *Voices from Women's Liberation*, 14.

108. S. Alexander, *Talking Woman*, 116.

109. Greer, *The Female Eunuch*, 323.

110. Ibid., 2.

111. Ibid., 13.

Epilogue

1. Damned, *Lessons from the Damned*.

2. Bradley, *Mass Media*, 252, 251.

3. Davis quoted from her May 1972 courtroom speech to her jury in *Angela Davis: An Autobiography*, 363. Davis publicly declared herself a Communist in 1969 when the California Board of Regents accused her of being one.

4. Chisholm, *The Good Fight*, 155.

5. Chisholm, *Unbought and Unbossed*, 150, 12, 111.

6. *Angela Davis: An Autobiography*, 363.

7. Giddings, *When and Where I Enter*, 338.

8. Chisholm, *The Good Fight*, 77.

9. "We Support Shirley Chisholm's Candidacy for President of the United States," editorial, *Woman's World*, March–May 1972, RWLAA. See also Colette Price, "The Feminist Party," in the same issue.

10. *Chicago Defender*, 10 June 1972, 3, quoted in Lumsden, "*Defender* Rides," 28.

11. Ibid.

12. Chisholm, *The Good Fight*, 149, 151.

13. Giddings, *When and Where I Enter*, 339.

14. Ibid., 340.

15. Linda La Rue, "The Black Movement and Women's Liberation," in Guy-Sheftall, *Words of Fire*, 170. La Rue's paper was written in 1970.

16. Giddings, *When and Where I Enter*, 307. Besides Giddings, other analyses of the national antileadership wave include Sarachild, "The Power of History"; Echols, *Daring to Be Bad*; F. Davis, *Moving the Mountain*; Bouchier, "The Deradicalization of Feminism."

17. Naomi Weisstein, "Days of Celebration and Resistance," in DuPlessis and Snitow, *The Feminist Memoir Project*, 358.

18. Redstockings, "Redstockings Manifesto." RWLAA.

19. Klagsbrun, *The First Ms. Reader*, 266. According to *Ms.*, although Warner was the major investor, it promised not to take financial or editorial control.

20. Patricia Mainardi, "*Ms.* Politics and Editing: An Interview," in Redstockings, *Feminist Revolution*, 168. The interview was conducted in 1973 by *Village Voice* writer Robin Reisig.

21. Ellen Willis, "The Conservatism of *Ms.*," in Redstockings, *Feminist Revolution*, 170.

22. Editorial, *Woman's World*, July–August 1971. RWLAA.

23. Sarachild, "The Power of History," 14, 13. The Second Wave did not, of course, go completely under, nor did the liberals and the radicals. New organizations and campaigns too numerous to mention have continued to spring up to carry the baton in what can still be considered the Second Wave. Among the feminist organizations formed in the 1960s, NOW, Redstockings, and Gainesville Women's Liberation are fighting effectively for Women's Liberation into the new millenium. For information

about their current work, see www.NOW.org, www.redstockings.org, and www.wo-mensliberation.org. Commentator Stephen Colbert referred to the movements of the sixties as the "gift that keeps on giving" (quoted by Bill Ayers on Democracy Now news show, www.democracynow.org, 14 November 2008).

24. Giddings, *When and Where I Enter*, 341.

25. Ibid., 343, 344. Black feminist historian Mary Frances Berry also makes this analysis in *Why ERA Failed*.

26. Maureen, Poor Black Women, quoted in Polatnick, "Strategies," 119.

27. Smith, *Home Girls*; Moraga and Anzaldúa, *This Bridge Called My Back*.

28. Polling data in Rosen, *The World Split Open*, 337, 338.

Selected Bibliography

Repositories

JBE   Judith Brown Women's Liberation Leadership Endowment Project (Judith Brown Endowment), c/o Gainesville Women's Liberation, P.O. Box 2625, Gainesville, FL 32602.

JFPF   Jo Freeman, personal files.

RWLAA   Redstockings Women's Liberation Archives for Action, P.O. Box 744, Stuyvesant Station, New York, NY 10009. www.redstockings.org. A catalog of writings from the 1960s rebirth years of feminism, as well as more recent work, is available from the Redstockings Women's Liberation Archives for Action Distribution Project, P.O. Box 2625, Gainesville, FL 32602, or online at www.redstockings.org.

Works Consulted

Abbott, Sidney, and Barbara Love. *Sappho Was a Right-On Woman: A Liberated View of Lesbianism*. New York: Stein and Day, 1972.

Abramson, Michael, and Young Lords Party. *Palante: Young Lords Party*. New York: McGraw-Hill, 1971.

Abubakari, Dara. "The Black Woman Is Liberated in Her Own Mind." In Lerner, *Black Women in White America*, 585–87.

Alexander, Dolores. "Outlook '68—Women's Rights, Militants Uniting in a New Group." *Newsday* (Long Island, N.Y.), 4 January 1968.

Alexander, Shana. *Talking Woman*. New York: Delacorte, 1976.

Allen, Pamela. *Free Space: A Perspective on the Small Group in Women's Liberation*. New York: Times Change Press, 1970.

Altbach, Edith Hoshino, ed. *From Feminism to Liberation*. 2nd ed. Cambridge, Mass.: Schenkman, 1979.

Angelou, Maya. *I Know Why the Caged Bird Sings*. 1969. New York: Bantam, 1970.

Aptheker, Bettina. *Woman's Legacy: Essays on Race, Sex, and Class in American History*. Amherst: University of Massachusetts Press, 1982.

Atkinson, Ti-Grace. *Amazon Odyssey: The First Collection of Writings by the Political Pioneer of the Women's Movement*. New York: Links, 1974.

Atkinson, Ti-Grace, Florynce Kennedy, Susan Sherman, and Joan Hamilton. "The Crisis in Feminism." *Majority Report* (New York), 8 March 1975, 3.

Attica Brothers. *Fighting Back! Attica Memorial Book 1974*. Buffalo, N.Y.: Attica Brothers Legal Defense, 1974.

Babcock, Barbara Allen, Ann E. Freedman, Eleanor Holmes Norton, and Susan C. Ross. *Sex Discrimination and the Law: Causes and Remedies*. Boston: Little, Brown, 1975.

Babcox, Deborah, and Madeline Belkin, eds. *Liberation NOW: Writings from the Women's Liberation Movement*. New York: Dell, 1971.

Bair, Deirdre. *Simone de Beauvoir: A Biography*. New York: Summit, 1990.

Baker, Ella. "Developing Community Leadership." In Lerner, *Black Women in White America*, 345–52.

Balser, Diane. *Sisterhood & Solidarity: Feminism and Labor in Modern Times*. Boston: South End Press, 1987.

Banks, William H., Jr. "Women's Liberation: A New Cop-Out on the Black Struggle?" *Liberator* 10, no. 9 (September 1970): 5–9.

Baraka, Imamu Amiri. *Raise Race Rays Raze: Essays Since 1965*. New York: Random House, 1971.

Bates, Daisy. *The Long Shadow of Little Rock*. New York: David McKay, 1962.

Baxandall, Rosalyn. "The Question Seldom Asked: Women and the CPUSA." In *New Studies in the Politics and Culture of U.S. Communism*, edited by Michael E. Brown, Randy Martin, Frank Rosengarten, and George Snedeker, 141–61. New York: Monthly Review Press, 1993.

Baxandall, Rosalyn, and Linda Gordon. "Second-Wave Soundings." *Nation*, 3 July 2000, 28–32.

———, eds. *Dear Sisters: Dispatches from the Women's Liberation Movement*. New York: Basic Books, 2000.

Beal, Frances. "Double Jeopardy: To Be Black and Female." In Cade, *The Black Woman*, 90–100.

———. "Sisterhood Is Still Powerful: Speaking Up When Others Can't." *Crossroads*, no. 29 (March 1993): 4–5.

Beauvoir, Simone de. *The Second Sex*. Translated by H. M. Parshley. New York: Alfred A. Knopf, 1953.

———. *All Said and Done*. Translated by Patrick O'Brian. New York: Putnam, 1974.

———. *A Transatlantic Love Affair: Letters to Nelson Algren*. Edited by Sylvie Le Bon de Beauvoir. New York: New Press, 1998.

Benston, Margaret. "The Political Economy of Women's Liberation." *Monthly Review* 21, no. 4 (September 1969): 13–27.

Bernstein, Judi, Peggy Morton, Linda Seese, and Myrna Wood. *Sisters, Brothers, Lovers . . . Listen . . .* Toronto: New Left Committee, 1967.

Berry, Mary Frances. *Why ERA Failed: Politics, Women's Rights, and the Amending Process of the Constitution.* Bloomington: Indiana University Press, 1986.

Bierbaum, Martin A. "Free Acres: Bolton Hall's Single Tax Experimental Community." *New Jersey History* 102 (Spring–Summer 1984): 47.

Bird, Caroline. *Born Female: The High Cost of Keeping Women Down.* With Sara Ward Briller. New York: David McKay, 1968.

Bond, Jean Carey, and Patricia Peery. "Has the Black Male Been Castrated?" In Cade, *The Black Woman.* Reprinted from *Liberator* 9, no. 5 (May 1969): 4–8.

Booth, Heather, Sue Munaker, and Evelyn Goldfield. "Women in the Radical Movement." Mimeograph, 1968. RWLAA.

Boston Women's Health Course Collective. *Our Bodies, Ourselves: A Course by and for Women.* Boston: New England Free Press, 1971.

Bouchier, David. "The Deradicalization of Feminism: Ideology and Utopia in Action." *Journal of the British Sociological Association* 13, no. 3 (1979): 387–402.

———. *The Feminist Challenge: The Movement for Women's Liberation in Britain and the USA.* New York: Schocken, 1984.

Braden, Anne. *The Wall Between.* New York: Monthly Review Press, 1958.

———. "Southern Women Talk Freedom." *Southern Patriot* (Louisville), 1 March 1969, 3.

Bradley, Patricia. *Mass Media and the Shaping of American Feminism, 1963–1975.* Jackson: University Press of Mississippi, 2003.

Breines, Wini. "A Review Essay." Review of *Personal Politics*, by Sara Evans. *Feminist Studies* 5 (Fall 1979): 496.

———. *The Trouble Between Us: An Uneasy History of White and Black Women in the Feminist Movement.* New York: Oxford University Press, 2006.

Brown, Judith. "Freedom Day Last Monday in Quincy." *Gadsden County Free Press*, 1 August 1964. JBE.

———. "CORE Voter Registration Drive." In Judith Brown's notebook of the Big Bend Voter Education Project, Quincy, Fla., 1964. JBE.

———. Editoral. *Radical Therapist* (Minot, N.D.) 1, no. 3 (August–September 1970): 2. JBE.

———. *Origins of Consciousness-Raising in the South: Gainesville or Tampa?* Gainesville: Gainesville Women's Liberation, 1986. Pamphlet. RWLAA.

Brownmiller, Susan. "Everywoman's Abortions: The Oppressor Is Man." *Village Voice*, 27 March 1969.

———. "Sisterhood Is Powerful." *New York Times Magazine*, 15 March 1970.

———. *In Our Time: Memoir of a Revolution.* New York: Dial Press, 1999.

Buhle, Mari Jo, Paul Buhle, and Dan Georgakas. *Encyclopedia of the American Left.* 2nd ed. New York: Oxford University Press, 1998.

Cade, Toni, ed. *The Black Woman: An Anthology.* New York: New American Library, 1970.

Carabillo, Toni, Judith Meuli, and June Bundy Csida. *Feminist Chronicles: 1953–1993.* Los Angeles: Women's Graphic, 1993.

Carden, Maren Lockwood. *The New Feminist Movement.* New York: Russell Sage Foundation, 1974.

Carmichael, Stokely. *Stokely Speaks: Black Power Back to Pan-Africanism.* New York: Random House, 1971.

———. *Ready for Revolution: The Life and Struggles of Stokely Carmichael (Kwame Ture).* With Ekwueme Michael Thelwell. New York: Scribner, 2003.

Carson, Clayborne. *In Struggle: SNCC and the Black Awakening of the 1960s.* 1981. Cambridge, Mass.: Harvard University Press, 1995.

Chafe, William H. *The American Woman: Her Changing Social, Economic, and Political Roles, 1920–1970.* New York: Oxford University Press, 1972.

———. *The Paradox of Change: American Women in the 20th Century.* New York: Oxford University Press, 1991.

Chafe, William H., and Harvard Sitkoff, eds. *A History of Our Time: Readings on Postwar America.* 4th ed. New York: Oxford University Press, 1995.

Childress, Alice. *Like One of the Family: Conversations from a Domestic's Life.* 1956. Boston: Beacon Press, 1986.

Chisholm, Shirley. *Unbought and Unbossed.* Boston: Houghton Mifflin, 1970.

———. *The Good Fight.* New York: Harper and Row, 1973.

Chrisman, Robert, and Robert L. Allen, eds. *Court of Appeal: The Black Community Speaks Out on the Racial and Sexual Politics of Thomas vs. Hill.* New York: Ballantine, 1992.

Cisler, Lucinda. "On Abortion and Abortion Law: Abortion Law Repeal (Sort Of): A Warning to Women." In Firestone and Koedt, *Second Year,* 89–93.

Cleaver, Kathleen. "An Interview with Kathleen Cleaver." *Woman's World* 1, no. 4 (March–May 1972). Reprinted from Julia Herve, "*Black Scholar* Interviews Kathleen Cleaver," *Black Scholar* 3, no. 4 (December 1971): 54–59. RWLAA.

Cleaver, Kathleen, and George Katsiaficas, eds. *Liberation, Imagination, and the Black Panther Party.* New York: Routledge, 2001.

Cole, Johnnetta Betsch, and Beverly Guy-Sheftall. *Gender Talk: The Struggle for Women's Equality in African American Communities.* New York: Ballantine, 2003.

Collins, Patricia Hill. *Black Feminist Thought: Knowledge, Consciousness, and the Politics of Empowerment.* New York: Routledge, 1990.

Conrad, Earl. "I Bring You General Tubman." *Black Scholar* 1, nos. 3–4 (January–February 1970), 2–7.

Cooke, Joanne, Charlotte Bunch-Weeks, and Robin Morgan, eds. *The New Women: A Motive Anthology on Women's Liberation.* Indianapolis: Bobbs-Merrill, 1970.

Cooper, Anna Julia. "The Status of Woman in America." 1892. In Guy-Sheftall, *Words of Fire,* 44–49.

Cott, Nancy F. *The Grounding of Modern Feminism*. New Haven, Conn.: Yale University Press, 1987.

Crittenden, Ann. *The Price of Motherhood*. New York: Henry Holt, Metropolitan Books, 2001.

Curry, Constance, et al. *Deep in Our Hearts: Nine White Women in the Freedom Movement*. Athens: University of Georgia Press, 2000.

Cusac, Anne-Marie. "Tillie Olsen Interview." *Progressive*, November 1999. www.progressive.org/mag_intv1199.

Damned, The. *Lessons from the Damned: Class Struggle in the Black Community*. New York: Times Change Press, 1973.

Davis, Angela. "Reflections on the Black Woman's Role in the Community of Slaves." *Black Scholar* 3, no. 4(December 1971): 2–15.

———. *Angela Davis: An Autobiography*. New York: Random House, 1974. Reprinted by Bantam under the title *With My Mind on Freedom*.

Davis, Flora. *Moving the Mountain: The Women's Movement in America since 1960*. New York: Simon and Schuster, 1991.

Dittmer, John. *Local People: The Struggle for Civil Rights in Mississippi*. Urbana: University of Illinois Press, 1995.

Dixon, Marlene. "Where Are We Going?" In Altbach, *From Feminism to Liberation*, 33–43. Reprinted from *Radical America* 4, no. 2 (February 1970): 26–35.

Dobbins, Peggy Powell. *From Kin to Class*. 4th ed. Berkeley, Calif.: Signmaker Press, 1981.

Dudar, Helen. "Women's Lib: The War on 'Sexism.'" *Newsweek*, 23 March 1970, 71–78.

Due, Tananarive, and Patricia Stephens Due. *Freedom in the Family: A Mother-Daughter Memoir of the Fight for Civil Rights*. New York: Ballantine, 2003.

Dunbar-Ortiz, Roxanne. *Outlaw Woman: A Memoir of the War Years, 1960–1975*. San Francisco: City Lights, 2001.

DuPlessis, Rachel Blau, and Ann Snitow, eds. *The Feminist Memoir Project: Voices from Women's Liberation*. New York: Three Rivers Press, 1998.

Duster, Alfreda M., ed. *Crusade for Justice: The Autobiography of Ida B. Wells*. Chicago: University of Chicago Press, 1970.

Eberlein, Roxane. Diary entry, Bern, Switzerland, 16 March 1941. In *Treasures of the Little Cabin: A Free Acres Cabin Tells the Stories of Those Who Loved It and Sought Its Shelter*, edited by Laurel Hessing, 316. Free Acres, N.J., 1999.

Echols, Alice. *Daring to Be Bad: Radical Feminism in America, 1967–1975*. Minneapolis: University of Minnesota Press, 1989.

Edwards, Hodee. "Male Supremacy on the Left—Personal Encounters." *Meeting Ground*, no. 4 (March 1978). Available at www.carolhanisch.org/Purchase/CHpubsAvailable.html.

Ellis, Julie. *Revolt of the Second Sex*. New York: Lancer, 1971.

Engels, Friedrich. *The Origin of the Family, Private Property, and the State*. 1884. New York: International Publishers, 1971.

Equal Employment Opportunity Commission. *Second Annual Report*. Washington, D.C.: Government Printing Office, 1968.

Evans, Sara M. *Personal Politics: The Roots of Women's Liberation in the Civil Rights Movement and the New Left*. New York: Alfred A. Knopf, 1979.

———. *Tidal Wave: How Women Changed America at Century's End*. New York: Free Press, 2003.

Ezekiel, Judith, et al. Comments, "Hanisch on 'The Personal Is Political,'" 26 May–11 June 2006. "The 'Second Wave' and Beyond." scholar.alexanderstreet.com/pages/viewpage.action?pageId=1501&focusedCommentId=2789#comment-2789.

Faludi, Susan. *Backlash: The Undeclared War against American Women*. New York: Crown, 1991.

Fanon, Frantz. *The Wretched of the Earth*. New York: Grove Press, 1963.

———. *A Dying Colonialism*. New York: Grove Press, 1967.

Firestone, Shulamith, ed. *Notes from the First Year*. New York: New York Radical Women, 1968. RWLAA.

———. "Anticredentials." N.d. RWLAA.

———. *The Dialectic of Sex: The Case for Feminist Revolution*. New York: William Morrow, 1970.

———. *Airless Spaces*. New York: Semiotext, 1998.

Firestone, Shulamith, and Anne Koedt, eds. *Notes from the Second Year: Women's Liberation*. 1970. RWLAA.

Fleming, Cynthia Griggs. *Soon We Will Not Cry: The Liberation of Ruby Doris Smith Robinson*. Lanham, Md.: Rowman and Littlefield, 1998.

Florida Paper. *See* Jones, Beverly, and Judith Brown, "Toward a Female Liberation Movement."

Foner, Philip S., ed. *The Black Panthers Speak*. Philadelphia: Lippincott, 1970.

Forman, James. *The Making of Black Revolutionaries: A Personal Account*. 1972. Seattle: Open Hand, 1985.

Fosl, Catherine. *Subversive Southerner: Anne Braden and the Struggle for Racial Justice in the Cold War South*. New York: Palgrave Macmillan, 2002.

Fox-Genovese, Elizabeth. *Feminism Without Illusions: A Critique of Individualism*. Chapel Hill: University of North Carolina Press, 1992.

Free Acres Association. *Constitution of the Free Acres Association*. Free Acres, N.J., n.d. JBE.

Freeman, Jo. "The Genesis of the Women's Liberation Movement." Manuscript. Chicago, ca. February 1968. JFPF.

———[Joreen], ed. Voice of the Women's Liberation Movement (Chicago). 7 issues, March 1968–June 1969. RWLAA.

———. *The Politics of Women's Liberation*. New York: David McKay, 1975.

———. "On the Origins of the Women's Liberation Movement from a Strictly Personal Perspective." In DuPlessis and Snitow, *The Feminist Memoir Project*, 171–196.

Friedan, Betty. *The Feminine Mystique*. 1963. New York: Dell, 1964.

———. "No Gods, No Goddesses." *Saturday Review*, 14 June 1975, 16.

———. *It Changed My Life: Writings on the Women's Movement*. 1976. New York: Dell, 1977.

———. *Life So Far*. New York: Simon and Schuster, 2000.

Gainesville Women's Liberation. "Declaration of Continued Independence." Document 4 in *Selected Documents from Gainesville Women's Liberation History and Organizing*. JBE.

Gallo, Marcia M. *Different Daughters: A History of the Daughters of Bilitis and the Rise of the Lesbian Rights Movement*. New York: Carroll and Graf, 2006.

Gerassi, John. "Interview with Simone de Beauvoir." *Society* 13, no. 2 (January–February 1976): 79–85. At www.marxists.org/reference/subject/ethics/de-beauvoir/1976/interview.htm.

Giddings, Paula. *When and Where I Enter: The Impact of Black Women on Race and Sex in America*. New York: William Morrow, 1984.

Gilman, Charlotte Perkins. *Women and Economics*. 1898. New York: Harper and Row, 1966.

Gitlin, Todd. *The Sixties: Years of Hope, Days of Rage*. New York: Bantam, 1987.

Goldstein, Robert. *Political Repression in Modern America: From 1870–1976*. Urbana: University of Illinois Press, 2001.

Gornick, Vivian. "The Next Great Moment in History Is Theirs." *Village Voice*, 27 November 1969.

———. *The Romance of American Communism*. New York: Basic Books, 1977.

Gornick, Vivian, and Barbara K. Moran, eds. *Woman in Sexist Society: Studies in Power and Powerlessness*. New York: Basic Books, 1971.

Grant, Joanne. *Ella Baker: Freedom Bound*. New York: John Wiley, 1998.

Greenberg, Cheryl Lynn, ed. *A Circle of Trust: Remembering SNCC*. New Brunswick, N.J.: Rutgers University Press, 1998.

Greene, Christina. "'We'll Take Our Stand': Race, Class, and Gender in the Southern Student Organizing Committee, 1964–1969." In *Hidden Histories of Women in the New South*, edited by Virginia Bernhard et al., 173–203. Columbia: University of Missouri Press, 1994.

Greer, Germaine. *The Female Eunuch*. 1970. New York: Bantam, 1971.

Gregory, Yvonne. "Poet Demands Equality for Negro Womanhood." *Freedom* 1, no. 3 (September 1951): 7.

Guy-Sheftall, Beverly, ed. *Words of Fire: An Anthology of African-American Feminist Thought*. New York: New Press, 1995.

Halberstam, David. *The Children*. New York: Random House, 1998.

Hampton, Henry, and Steve Fayer, comp. *Voices of Freedom: An Oral History of the Civil Rights Movement from the 1950s through the 1980s*. New York: Bantam, 1991.

Hanisch, Carol. "The Personal Is Political." 1969. In Firestone and Koedt, *Second Year*, www.carolhanisch.org/CHwritings/PIP.html.

———. *Promise and Betrayal*. Port Ewen, N.Y.: TruthTeller Productions, 1995.

———. "Two Letters from the Women's Liberation Movement." In DuPlessis and Snitow, *The Feminist Memoir Project*, 197–207.

———. New introduction to "The Personal Is Political." January 2006. www.carol-hanisch.org/CHwritings/PIP.html.

Hansberry, Lorraine. "Simone de Beauvoir and *The Second Sex*: An American Commentary." In Guy-Sheftall, *Words of Fire*, 128–44.

Hansberry, Lorraine, and Robert Nemiroff, eds. *To Be Young, Gifted, and Black*. New York: Penguin, 1970.

Hayden, Casey. "Fields of Blue." In Curry, *Deep in Our Hearts*, 335–75.

Heath, G. Louis, ed. *Off the Pigs! The History and Literature of the Black Panther Party*. Metuchen, N.J.: Scarecrow Press, 1976.

Height, Dorothy I. "'We Wanted the Voice of a Woman to Be Heard': Black Women and the 1963 March on Washington." In *Sisters in the Struggle: African American Women in the Civil Rights–Black Power Movement*, edited by Bettye Collier-Thomas and V. P. Franklin, 83–91. New York: New York University Press, 2001.

Hennessey, Caroline. *I, B.I.T.C.H.* New York: Lancer, 1970.

Hews, Janet. "Sisters." *Lilith*, 2 December 1968. RWLAA.

Hill, Myrna. "Feminism and Black Nationalism." *Militant*, 2 April 1971.

———. "Zulu Woman: A Book Review." *Woman's World*, July–August 1971. RWLAA.

Hine, Darlene Clark, Elsa Barkley Brown, and Rosalyn Terborg-Penn, eds. *Black Women in America: An Historical Encyclopedia*. Bloomington: Indiana University Press, 1993.

Hinkle, Warren, and Marianne Hinkle. "A History of the Rise of the Unusual Movement for Woman Power in the United States, 1961–1968." *Ramparts*, February 1968, 22–43.

Hinton, William. *Fanshen: A Documentary of Revolution in a Chinese Village*. New York: Monthly Review Press, 1967.

Hole, Judith, and Ellen Levine. *Rebirth of Feminism*. New York: Quadrangle, 1971.

Horowitz, Daniel. *Betty Friedan and the Making of the Feminine Mystique: The American Left, the Cold War, and Modern Feminism*. Amherst: University of Massachusetts Press, 1998.

Howard, Pamela. "We Want to Be Free." *Florida Times Union* (Jacksonville), 3 May 1970.

Hymowitz, Carol, and Michaele Weissman. *A History of Women in America*. New York: Bantam, 1978.

Isserman, Maurice. *If I Had a Hammer: The Death of the Old Left and the Birth of the New Left*. New York: Basic Books, 1987.

Jackson, Esther Cooper, ed. *Freedomways Reader: Prophets in Their Own Country*. Boulder, Colo.: Westview Press, 2000.

Jaggar, Alison M. *Feminist Politics and Human Nature*. Totowa, N.J.: Rowman & Allanheld, 1983.

James, C. L. R. *The Black Jacobins*. 2nd ed. New York: Random House, 1963.

James, Tarah. "Sisters in Struggle: The Development of Black Feminism in SNCC." Master's thesis, Sarah Lawrence College, 2000.

Jones, Beverly, and Judith Brown. "Toward a Female Liberation Movement." Gainesville: Gainesville Women's Liberation, 1968. Reprinted in Tanner, *Voices from Women's Liberation*, 362–415; page numbers refer to this edition. Copies of the paper are available from RWLAA.

Jones, Marshall B. "Berkeley of the South: A History of the Student Movement at the University of Florida, 1963–1968." Manuscript, Gainesville, 1968. JBE.

Karenga, Maulana Ron. From *"The Quotable Karenga,"* in *The Black Power Revolt: A Collection of Essays*, edited by Floyd B. Barbour, 162–70. Boston: Porter Sargent, 1968.

Kelley, Robin D. G. *Hammer and Hoe: Alabama Communists During the Great Depression*. Chapel Hill: University of North Carolina Press, 1990.

Kennedy, Florynce. *Color Me Flo: My Hard Life and Good Times*. Engelwood Cliffs, N.J.: Prentice-Hall, 1976.

King, Mary. *Freedom Song: A Personal Story of the 1960s Civil Rights Movement*. New York: William Morrow, 1987.

Klagsbrun, Francine, ed. *The First Ms. Reader*. New York: Warner, 1973.

Klein, Ethel. *Gender Politics: From Consciousness to Mass Politics*. Cambridge, Mass.: Harvard University Press, 1984.

Komisar, Lucy. *The New Feminism*. New York: Franklin Watts, 1971.

Kramarae, Cheris, and Paula A. Treichler. *A Feminist Dictionary*. Boston: Pandora Press, 1985.

Lader, Lawrence. *Abortion*. Indianapolis: Bobbs-Merrill, 1966.

———. *Abortion II: Making the Revolution*. Boston: Beacon Press, 1973.

———. *Power on the Left: American Radical Movements Since 1946*. New York: W. W. Norton, 1979.

Lawson, Steven F. *Black Ballots: Voting Rights in the South, 1944–1969*. New York: Columbia University Press, 1976.

Leader, Alexandra. "Consciousness-Raising in the Women's Liberation Movement and the National Organization for Women: Theory and Practice." Undergraduate honors thesis, University of Florida, 1994. JBE.

Lear, Martha Weinman. "What Do These Women *Want*? The Second Feminist Wave." *New York Times Magazine*, 10 March 1968.

Lee, Chana Kai. *For Freedom's Sake: The Life of Fannie Lou Hamer*. Urbana: University of Illinois Press, 1999.

Lenin, V. I. "Communism." In *Collected Works*, vol. 31. Moscow: Progress Publishers, 1950.

Lerner, Gerda, ed. *Black Women in White America: A Documentary History*. New York: Pantheon, 1972.

———. *Fireweed: A Political Autobiography*. Philadelphia: Temple University Press, 2002.

Lester, Joan Steinau, with Eleanor Holmes Norton. *Fire in My Soul*. New York: Atria, 2003.

Lester, Julius. *Look Out Whitey! Black Power's Gon' Get Your Mama!* New York: Dial Press, 1968.

Lomax, Betty Frank. "Afro-American Woman: Growth Deferred," *Liberator* 6, no. 5 (May 1966): 18.

Luker, Kristin. *Abortion and the Politics of Motherhood*. Berkeley and Los Angeles: University of California Press, 1984.

Lumsden, Linda. "The *Chicago Defender* Rides the Second Wave: Coverage of the Women's Liberation Movement, 1968–1973." Paper presented to the Organization of American Historians, Minneapolis, March 2007.

Lynch, Gayle. "Black Women's Manifesto." In *Documents from the Women's Liberation Movement: An Online Archival Collection*. Special Collections Library, Duke University. scriptorium.lib.duke.edu/wlm/blkmanif.

Malcolm X. "At the Audubon." In *Malcolm X Speaks*, edited by George Breitman, 115–36. New York: Grove Press, 1966.

Mao Zedong. *On New Democracy; Talks at the Yenan Forum on Literature and Art; On the Correct Handling of Contradictions Among the People; Speech at the Chinese Communist Party's National Conference on Propaganda Work*. 4th ed., 2nd rev. trans. Peking: Foreign Languages Press, 1967.

Martelli, Jane. *The Mushroom Effect: A Directory of Women's Liberation*. Albany, Calif.: Mushroom Effect, 1970.

Martinez, Elizabeth Sutherland, ed. *Letters from Mississippi*. New York: McGraw-Hill, 1965.

———. " . . . because he was black and I was white." *Mademoiselle*, April 1967, 241–45.

———. "A View from New Mexico: Recollections of the *Movimiento* Left." *Monthly Review* 54, no. 3 (July–August 2002): 82.

May, Elaine Tyler. *Homeward Bound: American Families in the Cold War Era*. New York: Basic Books, 1988.

McAdam, Doug. *Freedom Summer*. New York: Oxford University Press, 1988.

Meier, August, and Elliott Rudwick. *CORE: A Study in the Civil Rights Movement, 1942–1968*. New York: Oxford University Press, 1973.

Meyerowitz, Joanne. "Beyond the Feminine Mystique: A Reassessment of the Postwar Mass Culture, 1946–1958." *Journal of American History* 79 (March 1993): 1455–82.

Michel, Gregg L. *Struggle for a Better South: The Southern Student Organizing Committee, 1964–1969*. New York: Palgrave Macmillan, 2004.

Miller, James. *Democracy Is in the Streets: From Port Huron to the Siege of Chicago*. New York: Simon and Schuster, 1987.

Millett, Kate. *Sexual Politics*. Garden City, N.Y.: Doubleday, 1970.

———. "Simone de Beauvoir . . . Autobiographer." Paper given at the Simone de Beauvoir Colloquium 3, New York, 4–6 April 1985. RWLAA.

Mills, Kay. *This Little Light of Mine: The Life of Fannie Lou Hamer*. New York: Dutton, 1993.

Mitchell, Juliet. *Women, the Longest Revolution*. Boston: New England Free Press, 1966.

Moore, Louise. "When Will the Real Black Man Stand Up?" *Liberator* 6, no. 5 (May 1966): 4–6.

———. "When a Black Man Stood Up." *Liberator* 6, no. 7 (July 1966): 7–9.

———. "Black Men vs. Black Women." *Liberator* 6, no. 8 (August 1966): 16–17.

Moraga, Cherrie, and Gloria Anzaldúa, eds. *This Bridge Called My Back: Writings by Radical Women of Color*. Watertown, Mass.: Persephone Press, 1981.

Morgan, Robin, ed. *Sisterhood Is Powerful: An Anthology of Writings from the Women's Liberation Movement*. New York: Random House, 1970.

———. "Goodbye to All That." In *Going Too Far*, 121–31. New York: Random House, 1977. First published in *Rat* 2, no. 27 (6–23 January 1970).

Morris, Aldon D. *The Origins of the Civil Rights Movement: Black Communities Organizing for Change*. New York: Free Press, 1984.

Moynihan, Daniel Patrick. *The Negro Family: The Case for National Action*. Washington, D.C.: Government Printing Office, 1965.

Murray, Pauli. *Pauli Murray: The Autobiography of a Black Activist, Feminist, Lawyer, Priest, and Poet*. Knoxville: University of Tennessee Press, 1989.

———. "The Liberation of Black Women." In Guy-Sheftall, *Words of Fire*, 186–97. First published in Thompson, *Voices of the New Feminism*.

Nabaraoui, Ceza. "African Women Seek Independence and Peace." *Freedomways* 1, no. 1 (Spring 1961): 102–6.

Nadasen, Premilla. *Welfare Warriors*. New York: Routledge, 2005.

National Organization for Women. *NOW Guidelines for Feminist Consciousness-Raising*. Washington, D.C.: National Organization for Women, 1982.

Newton, Huey P. "The Women's Liberation and Gay Liberation Movements: August 15, 1970." In *The Huey P. Newton Reader*, edited by David Hilliard and Donald Weise, 157–59. New York: Seven Stories Press, 2002. Reprinted from the *Black Panther* newspaper.

New York Commission on Human Rights. *Women's Role in Contemporary Society: The Report of the New York Commission on Human Rights, September 21–25, 1970*. New York: Discus, 1972.

New York Radical Women. "The Ten Points We Protest." In *No More Miss America!* pamphlet, 1968. www.uic.edu/orgs/cwluherstory/CWLUArchive/miss.html.

Norman, Martha Prescod. "Brightly Shining Lights: SNCC and the Woman Question." Paper presented at the 55th annual meeting of the Southern Historical Association, Lexington, Ky., 10 November 1989.

Norton, Eleanor Holmes. "A Memory of Fannie Lou Hamer." *Ms.*, July 1977, 51.

———. "I was Able to Participate in the Great Movements of My Time." Interview by Claudia Dreifus, October 2004. "Voices of Civil Rights." www.voicesofcivilrights.org/civil3.html.

O'Connor, Lynn. "The Monkey Paper." 1969. RWLAA.

———. "Defining Reality." *Tooth and Nail*, 1 October 1969. RWLAA.

Okely, Judith. *Simone de Beauvoir*. New York: Random House, 1986.

Olson, Lynne. *Freedom's Daughters: The Unsung Heroines of the Civil Rights Movement from 1830 to 1970*. New York: Scribner, 2001.

Papachristou, Judith, ed. *Women Together: A History in Documents of the Women's Movement in the United States*. New York: Alfred A. Knopf, 1976.

Patton, Gwen. "Black People and the Victorian Ethos." In Cade, *The Black Woman*, 143–48.

Payne, Charles M. *I've Got the Light of Freedom: The Organizing Tradition and the Mississippi Freedom Struggle*. Berkeley and Los Angeles: University of California Press, 1995.

Peck, James. *Freedom Ride*. New York: Simon and Schuster, 1962.

Piercy, Marge. "The Grand Coolie Damn." 1969. In Morgan, *Sisterhood Is Powerful*, 421–38. Also at www.cwluherstory.com/CWLUArchive/damn.html.

Polatnick, Margaret Rivka. "Strategies for Women's Liberation: A Study of a Black and a White Group of the 1960s." Ph.D. diss., University of California, 1985.

Pontecorvo, Gillo, director. *The Battle of Algiers*. Written with Franco Solinas. 1966.

Pouissant, Alvin F. "The Stresses of the White Female Worker in the Civil Rights Movement in the South." *American Journal of Psychiatry* 123, no. 4 (1966): 401–7.

Price, William A. "Behind the NCNP Meeting." *The Guardian*, 16 September 1967.

Rabby, Glenda Alice. *The Pain and the Promise: The Struggle for Civil Rights in Tallahassee, Florida*. Athens: University of Georgia Press, 1999.

Radicalesbians. "The Woman-Identified Woman." 1970. www.cwluherstory.com/CWLUArchive/womidwom.html.

Ransby, Barbara. *Ella Baker and the Black Freedom Movement: A Radical Democratic Vision*. Chapel Hill: University of North Carolina Press, 2003.

Redstockings. "Redstockings Manifesto." 7 July 1969. In *Redstockings' First Literature List and a Sampling of Its Materials*. New York: Redstockings Archives, 1969.

———. *Feminist Revolution*. 1975. 2nd ed., abridged and expanded. New York: Random House, 1978.

Reed, Evelyn. *Problems of Women's Liberation: A Marxist Approach*. New York: Merit, 1969.

Richardson, Beulah. "A Black Woman Speaks . . . of White Womanhood, of White Supremacy, of Peace." New York: American Women for Peace, 1951. RWLAA.

Robins, Joan. *Handbook of Women's Liberation*. North Hollywood, Calif.: NOW Library Press, 1970.

Robinson, Patricia. "Malcolm X, Our Revolutionary Son and Brother." In *Malcolm X: The Man and His Times*, edited by John Henrik Clarke with A. Peter Bailey and Earl Grant, 56–63. New York: Macmillan, 1969.

Robinson, Patricia, and Group. "On the Position of Poor Black Women in This Country." In Cade, *The Black Woman*, 194–97.

Robinson, Patricia, Patricia Harden, Sue Rudolph, Joyce Hoyt, Rita Van Lew, and Catherine Hoyt [Poor Black Women]. "The Sisters Reply." *Lilith*, December 1968. Widely anthologized, notably in Morgan, *Sisterhood Is Powerful*, 360–61, as "Statement on Birth Control" under the new name Black Women's Liberation Group, Mount Vernon, New York.

Robnett, Belinda. *How Long, How Long? African American Women in the Struggle for Civil Rights.* New York: Oxford University Press, 1997.

Rodgers, Evelyn. "Sisters—Stop Castrating the Black Man!" *Liberator* 6, no. 5 (May 1966): 21.

Rodrique, Jessie M. "The Black Community and the Birth Control Movement." In *Unequal Sisters,* edited by Ellen Carol DuBois and Vicki L. Ruiz, 333–44. New York: Routledge, 1990.

Rosen, Ruth. *The World Split Open: How the Modern Women's Movement Changed America.* New York: Viking, 2000.

Ross, Loretta J. "Understanding Reproductive Justice." SisterSong Women of Color Reproductive Health Collective. 2006. www.sistersong.net/publications_and_articles/Understanding_RJ.pdf.

Ross, Rosetta E. *Witnessing and Testifying: Black Women, Religion, and Civil Rights.* Minneapolis: Fortress, 2003.

Roszak, Betty, and Theodore Roszak, eds. *Masculine/Feminine: Readings in Sexual Mythology and the Liberation of Women.* New York: Harper and Row, 1969.

Roth, Benita. *Separate Roads to Feminism: Black, Chicana, and White Feminist Movements in America's Second Wave.* Cambridge: Cambridge University Press, 2004.

Rowbotham, Sheila. *Women Resistance and Revolution.* London: Allen Lane, 1972.

Sale, Kirkpatrick. *SDS.* New York: Random House, 1974.

Sarachild, Kathie. "Funeral Oration for the Burial of Traditional Womanhood." In Firestone, *First Year,* 20–22. Also at scriptorium.lib.duke.edu/wlm/notes/#funeral.

———. "The Power of History." In Redstockings, *Feminist Revolution,* 12–41.

———. "The Civil Rights Movement: Lessons for Women's Liberation." Speech given at "The Sixties Speak to the Eighties: A Conference for Activism and Social Change," University of Massachusetts, Amherst, 22 October 1983. RWLAA.

Sarachild, Kathie, Jenny Brown, and Amy Coenen, eds. *Women's Liberation and National Health Care: Confronting the Myth of America.* New York: Redstockings, 2001.

Scanlon, Jennifer, ed. *Significant Contemporary American Feminists.* Westport, Conn.: Greenwood Press, 1999.

Schneir, Miriam, ed. *Feminism in Our Time: The Essential Writings, World War II to the Present.* New York: Vintage, 1994.

Schulder, Diane, and Florynce Kennedy. *Abortion Rap.* New York: McGraw-Hill, 1971.

Schwarz, Judith. *Radical Feminists of Heterodoxy: Greenwich Village, 1912–1940.* Rev. ed. Norwich, Vt.: New Victoria, 1986.

Seale, Bobby. *Seize the Time: The Story of the Black Panther Party and Huey P. Newton.* New York: Random House, 1970.

Shreve, Anita. *Women Together, Women Alone: The Legacy of the Consciousness-Raising Movement.* New York: Viking, 1989.

Sicherman, Barbara, and Carol Hurd Green, eds. *Notable American Women: The Modern Period*. Cambridge, Mass.: Belknap Press, 1980.

Simmons, Gwendolyn Zoharah. "Mama Told Me Not to Go: Working with SNCC in Mississippi, Freedom Summer 1964." In Smith and Koster, *Time It Was*, 93–119.

Smith, Barbara, ed. *Home Girls: A Black Feminist Anthology*. New York: Kitchen Table–Women of Color Press, 1983.

Smith, Karen Manners, and Tim Koster, eds. *Time It Was: American Stories from the Sixties*. Upper Saddle River, N.J.: Pearson Prentice-Hall, 2008.

Springer, Kimberly, ed. *Still Lifting, Still Climbing: African American Women's Contemporary Activism*. New York: New York University Press, 1999.

——. *Living for the Revolution: Black Feminist Organizations, 1968–1980*. Durham, N.C.: Duke University Press, 2005.

Stambler, Sookie, ed. *Women's Liberation: Blueprint for the Future*. New York: Ace, 1970.

Stanton, Elizabeth Cady, Susan B. Anthony, and Matilda Joslyn Gage, eds. *The History of Woman Suffrage*. Vol. 1. Rochester, N.Y.: Charles Mann, 1889.

Steinem, Gloria. "After Black Power, Women's Liberation." *New York Magazine*, 7 April 1969.

Tanner, Leslie B., ed. *Voices from Women's Liberation*. New York: Signet, 1970.

Tate, Claudia, ed. *Black Women Writers at Work*. New York: Continuum, 1983.

Terborg-Penn, Rosalyn. *African American Women in the Struggle for the Vote, 1850–1920*. Bloomington: Indiana University Press, 1998.

Thompson, Mary Lou, ed. *Voices of the New Feminism*. Boston: Beacon Press, 1970.

U.S. Department of Labor. Women's Bureau. *Handbook on Women Workers*. Washington, D.C.: Government Printing Office, 1969.

——. *Trends in Educational Attainment of Women*. Washington, D.C.: Government Printing Office, 1969.

Valk, Anne M. *Radical Sisters: Second-Wave Feminism and Black Liberation in Washington, D.C.* Urbana: University of Illinois Press, 2008.

Ware, Cellestine. *Woman Power: The Movement for Women's Liberation*. New York: Tower, 1970.

Weathers, Mary Ann. "An Argument for Black Women's Liberation as a Revolutionary Force." In Guy-Sheftall, *Words of Fire*, 157–61. First published in Cell 16's journal *No More Fun and Games*, no. 2 (February 1969).

Webb, Marilyn. "Women, We Have a Common Enemy." *New Left Notes*, 10 June 1968, 15.

Weddington, Sarah. *A Question of Choice*. New York: Putnam, 1992.

Weigand, Kate. "Vanguards of Women's Liberation: The Old Left and the Continuity of the Women's Movement in the United States, 1945–1970." Ph.D. diss., Ohio State University, 1995.

——. *Red Feminism: American Communism and the Making of Women's Liberation*. Baltimore: Johns Hopkins University Press, 2000.

Wells, Ida B. *A Red Record*. Chicago: Donohue and Henneberry, 1895.

Williams, Juan. *Eyes on the Prize: America's Civil Rights Years, 1954–1965.* New York: Penguin, 1987.

Williams, Robert F. *Negroes with Guns.* 1962. Detroit: Wayne State University Press, 1998.

Willis, Ellen. "Up from Radicalism: A Feminist Journal." In *US: A Paperback Magazine #1,* edited by Richard Goldstein, 118–19. New York: Bantam, 1969.

———. *No More Nice Girls: Countercultural Essays.* Hanover, N.H.: University Press of New England, 1992.

Wolseley, Roland E. *The Black Press, U.S.A.* 2nd ed. Ames: Iowa State University Press, 1990.

Women's Caucus of the Radical Caucus of the American Psychiatric Association. "Resolution." May 1969. JBE.

Yaffe, Deborah Rachel. "The Second Sex: A Work in Progress." Master's thesis, University of Victoria, 1992.

Index

Abbott, Sidney, 221–22

Abolitionists: black feminists and, 29; use of "woman question" by, 246n9; First Wave feminism and, 35, 60; in families of WLM leaders, 59, 60

Abortion: legalization of, 2, 208, 209, 237; in 1950s, 16; relevance to black women, 17, 121; Giardina experience with, 18; as genocide, 49, 71; Flo Kennedy lawsuit on, 69; black feminists on, 71, 74, 79, 105, 208; Atkinson on, 77; WLM actions on, 96, 129, 204–10; Jane collective and, 96, 225; Young Lords on, 216; and NWRO, 220; Chisholm on, 232; public support for, 243

Abramowicz v. Lefkowitz, 69. *See also* abortion

Abubakari, Dara, 105, 208

Abzug, Bella, 239

Adams, Jane, 129, 169

Africa, 65, 104, 108, 114, 174, 224

African-American women. *See* black women

African People's Socialist Party, 211

Alexander, Shana, 199, 236

Algeria, 108, 264n46

Allen, Donna, 141

Allen, Pam: family background, 4, 59, 72; fought campus curfews, 22; Civil Rights experience, 51, 52; NYRW and, 71, 75, 131–32; and Patricia Robinson, 79, 203; on Black

Power, 124; spouse of, 159; on independent WLM debate, 162; *Guardian* article by, 169; on consciousness-raising, 182

Allen, Robert, 51, 159–60

Amatniek, Kathie. *See* Kathie Sarachild

Amazon Project (of SNCC), 32–33

Angelou, Maya, 232, 286n89

Anthony, Katharine, 67

Anticolonial struggles: Beal influenced by, 65; Baker steered SNCC towards, 101; Nkrumah on, 104; *Freedomways* on, 166; sexism in movements for, 174; WLM introduces women to, 189. *See also* Third World revolutions

Antiwar movement. *See* Vietnam War

Appearance issue: women college students and, 17; in *Second Sex*, 75; Cell 16 on, 78; and natural hair, 118; in Old Left, 148; beauty pageants and, 195–196; black women and, 196–197

Aptheker, Bettina, 68, 86, 91

Atkinson, Ti-Grace: and Beauvoir, 77–78; influence of, 79; radicalized by feminism, 187; exit from NOW of, 203; on lesbianism, 223; *Newsweek* interview of, 230; and Feminist Party, 239; as displaced WLM leader, 240

Attica Brothers, 246–47n17

Civil Rights Movement—*continued*
in, 20, 27, 28, 34, 36, 103; Norton on
connection to feminism, 35; women in
pulpit in, 38; violence against, 45, 46–47,
49; influence on WLM leaders, 51–52;
consciousness-raising and, 180, 182–83.
See also Black Freedom Movement;
Congress of Racial Equality; Southern
Christian Leadership Conference; Student
Nonviolent Coordinating Committee
Clark, Septima, 28
Class: race oppression compared to, 60; "sex
class" used, 76; black feminists on, 116–17;
Black Power advocates on, 119–20; ERAP
project and, 120; Sisterhood Is Powerful
and, 190; use of term, 275n7
Cleaver, Eldridge, 103, 113
Cleaver, Kathleen, 26, 112, 213–15
Cold War, 13
Cole, Johnnetta, 29, 180, 261n39
Collective struggle: insights from other
movements, 3, 52–53, 82; helped by Old
Left terms, 71; *Second Sex* on, 81–82;
proposed in Florida Paper, 94. *See also*
Sisterhood Is Powerful
College: women in, 16; black women in, 17;
sexist rules at, 17, 22, 24, 55, 69–70; lack
of female professors in, 18; sexism in, 37,
60; race segregation in, 100; WLM gains
at, 193, 194
Colon, Clara, 188
Colonialism. *See* anti-colonial struggles
Combahee River Collective, 243
Communist Manifesto, 69
Communist Party (CP): Patricia Robinson
and, 63; Beal's family and, 65; Davis and,
67; influence on Flo Kennedy, 68–69;
Carmichael and, 119; Olsen on feminism
in, 148; DuBois and, 163; writing on WLM
by, 188; use of "woman question" in 246n9;
during Depression, 284n44. *See also* Old
Left; red-diaper babies
Congress of Racial Equality (CORE):
Firestone and, 24; March on Washington
and, 27; Due leader in, 35; future WLM
leaders in, 37; Judith Brown's work in,

43–48; Weisstein and, 66; adopted Black
Power, 101
Congress to Unite Women, 221
Consciousness-raising: development
of, 128, 175–80, 275n15; explained at
Sandy Springs, 141; echoed Civil Rights
"testifying," 143; Olsen's work and, 148;
misunderstood, 152, 183, 184; distortions
of, 176, 241, 276–77n46; effects of, 181–82,
224; poster on, 184, 277n51; *Fanshen*
and, 184, 277n49; spread of, 185–86, 191;
debated at Lake Villa, 200; and abortion
advances, 204, 209; speak-outs evolve
from, 207–8; problems for black women
in, 210; promoted in feminist books,
234. *See also* Program for Feminist
Consciousness-raising
Consumerism, debate on, 127–28, 136–37
Contraception, 19, 58; Patricia Robinson's
family on, 4, 64; in 1950s, 16; men
oblivious to, 18; black feminists on, 30,
105; black community support for, 64;
Poor Black Women on, 79; SDS and, 96;
cultural nationalism and, 103. *See also*
abortion; sterilization, forced
Cooper, Anna Julia, 30
CORE. *See* Congress of Racial Equality
CP. *See* Communist Party
Crisis (magazine), 228
Cultural nationalism: in Chisholm's family,
70; women's roles and, 103; contraception
and, 105; vs. Black Power, 106; Malcolm
X's turn from, 114
Curfews for college women, 17, 22, 55,
69–70

Daughters of Bilitis (DOB), 223
Davis, Angela, 67–68; work in white Left,
26, 27; mother Sallye Davis, 29–30; on
WLM, 68; *Black Scholar* article by, 68; on
Moynihan Report, 90, 237; Chisholm and,
238, 240; trial of, 239; Communist Party
and, 287n3
Dawkins, Jack, 124
Day care. *See* childcare
De Beauvoir, Simone. *See* Beauvoir

Dee, Ruby, 135

Dell'Olio, Anselma, 181

Democratic centralism. *See* leadership question

Democratic National Convention (1964): challenge led by women, 35; Norton and, 50, 62; MFDP action at, 42–43; besieged by militant black women, 88. *See also* Mississippi Freedom Democratic Party

Democratic Party, 87–88, 239, 240

Denmark, Redstockings of, 224

Dennis, Gene, 119

Densmore, Dana, 141, 200

Dialectic of Sex (Firestone), 13, 76, 222–23, 233

Direct action, 42, 46–47, 61

Discrimination. *See* employment discrimination; racism; sexism

Divorce, 19, 237

Dixon, Marlene, 139, 200

Dobbins, Peggy, 128, 178, 198

Dohrn, Bernardine, 136

Domestic work, 17, 70, 218

Donaldson, Ivanhoe, 37

Double Jeopardy (Beal), 105

Douglass, Frederick, 227

Dress codes. *See* appearance issue

DuBois, W.E.B.: Clark and, 28; on contraception, 30, 64; Patricia Robinson and, 63, 64; Hansberry and, 74; support for feminism of, 163, 228

Dudar, Helen, 229–30

Due, Patricia Stephens: CORE leadership of, 35, 44–47; mentored Judith Brown, 43–44; used jail-in tactic, 44–45; Brown on militancy of, 138; and testifying in CORE, 182–83

Due, Tananarive, 196

Dunbar, Roxanne: and *Second Sex*, 78; influence of, 79; on Sandy Springs, 141–42; and SFRU, 225; *Newsweek* interview of, 230

Eberlein family, 57–59

Ebony (magazine), 89–90, 228

Echols, Alice, 7–8, 125, 128

Economic Research and Action Project (ERAP), 94, 120

EEOC. *See* Equal Employment Opportunity Commission

Egalitarian structure. *See* leadership question

Employment discrimination, 17, 20, 193–94, 220, 229

Engels, Friedrich, 187, 189

Equal Employment Opportunity Commission (EEOC), 20. *See also* Title VII

Equal pay, 121, 129

Equal Rights Amendment (ERA): Senate passage of, 220, 237; *Chicago Defender* on, 227; NOW's strategy for, 242

ERAP. *See* Economic Research and Action Project

Essence (magazine), 226, 230

Evans, Sara: contrasts Civil Rights and SDS, 3; on WLM founders, 7–8, 71; on WLM debt to Civil Rights, 9; on sexism as spur to WLM, 10; on WLM origins, 11, 157; WLM organizing by, 96; on SNCC staff sit-in, 31

Evers, Medgar, 49, 50

Fanon, Frantz, 65, 108

Fanshen (Hinton), 184, 277n49

Farmer, James, 40, 70, 238

FBI. *See* Federal Bureau of Investitation

Federal Bureau of Investigation (FBI): and Civil Rights, 50, 52; and Davis, 68; tracked MFDP, 88; and WLM, 281n88

Fellowship of Reconciliation, 62

Feminine Mystique (Friedan), 16, 55, 80, 93, 133

Feminism (term), 246n12, 251n48

Feminisms: as dilution of feminism, 25; debate on, 25–26, 29; concept opposed, 31

Feminist literary criticism, 79–80

Feminist Party, 239

Feminist Revolution (Redstockings), 75

Feminists (group), 77–78, 79, 203

Feminist Studies (journal), 8, 9

"Fight own oppressors," 11, 122, 123–24, 137. *See also* self-emancipation

Gordon, Linda, 9, 10
Grant, Joanne, 41
Greer, Germaine, 236
Guardian (newspaper), 156, 164, 168–69
Guatemala, 183
Guy-Sheftall, Beverly, 29, 180, 261n39
GWL. *See* Gainesville Women's Liberation

Hall Wynn, Prathia, 28
Hamer, Fannie Lou: leadership in MFDP
    challenge, 6–7, 89; SNCC leadership
    of, 35, 42–43; on feminism, 43; beaten
    in Winona, 49; Norton and, 61; media
    criticism of, 89; Malcolm X and, 114–15; on
    forced sterilization, 205–6
Hanisch, Carol: Rivil Rights experience of,
    11; background of, 23–24, 69–70; and "The
    Personal Is Political," 76; SCEF and, 128,
    143, 150–52; formation of NYRW and,
    131; Life Group and, 143; Martinez and,
    148; Bill Price and, 164; on consciousness-
    raising, 178, 184, 185, 275n15; Bitch Sisters
    Bitch poster and, 184; on WLM as Left,
    186; on privilege, 190; had Miss America
    Protest idea, 197, 198; on Lake Villa, 200;
    on participation of black women, 202; and
    GWL, 225
Hansberry, Lorraine, 3, 15, 74–75, 167; and
    Alice Childress, 147; confronted Robert
    Kennedy, 87, 89; death of, 75; editor
    for *Freedom*, 166; influences on, 163; on
    Second Sex, 74, 273n107;
Harlem YWCA circle, 29, 59–60
Harmeling, Dan, 45, 48
Harvard University, 22, 24, 52, 60, 15
Hawley, Nancy, 185
Hayden, Casey: family background, 21–22;
    and Baker, 23, 29, 41–42; wrote feminist
    SNCC memo, 26; recruited to Freedom
    Ride, 42; quoted Thoreau, 52; and "Sex
    and Caste," 53, 54, 91, 94; and *Second Sex*,
    80–81; and *SNCC Position Paper*, 83; on
    Carmichael's "prone" joke, 85; on class
    question, 120; welfare women and, 123;
    on Black Power, 125; spouse of, 159. See
    also "Sex and Caste"; "SNCC Position
    Paper"

Hayden, Tom, 159
Hayes, Curtis, 111
Hedgeman, Anna Arnold, 27, 29, 60
Height, Dorothy, 27, 29, 60, 217
Henry, Aaron, 43
Hernandez, Aileen, 27, 228, 242, 285n69
Heterodoxy (group), 67
Hews, Janet, 153
Hill, Myrna: family background of, 36–37;
    on cultural nationalism, 104, 263n31;
    on contraception, 105; on Black Power,
    120–21, 262n1; and Childress, 147; effect of
    consciousness-raising on, 181
Hinton, William, 184, 277n49
History of Woman Suffrage (Stanton et al.),
    235, 236
Holmes Norton, Eleanor. *See* Norton,
    Eleanor Holmes
House Un-American Activities Committee.
    See McCarthyism
Housework issue: in black families, 37; and
    SDS, 96; in West Side Group, 130; in Old
    Left, 66, 148; for Weills, 160; WLM code
    discussed on, 191
Howe, Irving, 79
Humphrey, Hubert, 88, 89

Illegal abortion. *See* abortion
Imperialism, 25
Incest, 232
Independent WLM debate, 133, 136; at Sandy
    Springs, 142; in Seattle, 153; in SDS caucus,
    162; in *New Left Notes*, 169; politicos on,
    174; Kathleen Cleaver on, 214; Greer on,
    236
Individual solutions, 18–19; Beauvoir
    and, 81–82; consciousness-raising and,
    176, 180–82; Hanisch on, 184. *See also*
    "Personal Is Political"; Sisterhood Is
    Powerful
Institute for Policy Studies (IPS), 160, 170
Integration and Black Power, 100–101
Internal democracy. *See* leadership question
International (Working) Women's Day,
    188–89
IPS. *See* Institute for Policy Studies
Irwin, Elizabeth, 67

Rush, Florence, 239
Rustin, Bayard, 39, 88

Salt of the Earth (film), 189
Salzman, Marilyn. *See* Marilyn Webb
Sanders, Beulah, 217–18, 221
Sandy Springs (Md.) meeting: Giardina's
    impressions of, 14, Brown and, 92;
    planning for, 140–41; attendance at, 141,
    269n76; debates at, 142, 175
Sanger, Margaret, 30, 58
Sarachild, Kathie (Amatniek), 66–67;
    on WLM origins in Civil Rights, 11;
    and sexism at school, 22; on SNCC,
    34–35, 52, 54–55; coined Sisterhood Is
    Powerful, 53, 132, 268n34; development
    of consciousness-raising by, 71, 178–79,
    180, 275n15–16, 276n18; on *Second Sex*,
    75; Program for Feminist Consciousness
    Raising by, 76; on Malcolm X, 115; on
    Carmichael, 122; and formation of
    NYRW, 131; Rankin Brigade speech,
    133; reaction to Florida Paper, 143; on
    Childress' feminism, 147; anti-war work
    of, 156; Bill Price and, 164, 171–72; on
    consciousness-raising in Civil Rights,
    182; and Bitch Sisters Bitch poster, 184; on
    Pro-Woman Line, 189; on privilege, 191; at
    Miss America Protest, 198; at Lake Villa,
    200; on participation of black women,
    202; at abortion hearing disruption, 207;
    and *Ladies Home Journal* sit-in, 224–25;
    on leadership question, 241; on dilution of
    WLM, 242; on primary sources, 248n43;
    interviewed in *Mademoiselle* 268n26; use
    of "class" by, 275n7
Sartre, Jean Paul, 78, 80
SCEF. *See* Southern Conference Education
    Fund
Scheer, Anne, 133, 160
Scheer, Robert, 160
Schmeerguntz (film), 197
Schulder, Diane, 236
Science and Society (journal), 68–69
SCLC. *See* Southern Christian Leadership
    Conference
SCUM Manifesto (Solanas), 77, 202

SDS. *See* Students for a Democratic Society
Seale, Bobby, 246n17
Seattle Radical Women, 153
Second Sex (Beauvoir), 73–82; seminal
    for WLM, 1; WLM understood male
    supremacy from, 3; effect on feminism's
    rebirth, 16; Sarachild and, 54, 66;
    term "women's liberation" used in, 73;
    introduced to Jones and Brown, 93; effect
    on Pappas, 133; Dunbar on, 141; taught
    by Richer, 165; Hansberry on, 191–92,
    273n107; on lesbianism, 222; Redstockings
    on, 245n2. *See also* Beauvoir, Simone de
Second Wave, 25–26, 274n142. *See also*
    Women's Liberation Movement
Seese, Linda, 284n39
Self-blame, 18, 180–82
Self-emancipation: WLM insight about, 2;
    Evans on, 3; recommended by Carmichael,
    11; Baker on, 41; resistances to, in SDS, 95,
    97; lesson from Black Power, 116; common
    to WLM and Civil Rights, 245–46n7. *See
    also* "fight own oppressors"
"Sex and Caste: A Kind of Memo" (Hayden,
    King), 53, 54; writing of, 91–92; cited in
    Florida study group, 93; Florida Paper
    authors and, 94; origin of, 94–95, 123;
    distributed by New Left, 161; published in
    Liberation, 168
Sex class, 76
Sexism, 1, 4, 8
Sex-race analogy. *See* race-sex analogy
Sexual harassment, 32
Shange, Ntozake, 211
Shelley, Martha, 221
Sherrod, Charles, 182
Silber, Irwin, 274n127
Simmons, Zoharah (Gwendolyn Robinson):
    confronted sexism, 6, 27, 48; SNCC
    leadership of, 6, 35, 251n62; and SNCC
    sexual harassment policy, 21, 31–32; led
    Amazon Project, 32; and "SNCC Position
    Paper," 84; and Jimmy Garrett, 95; and
    Black Power, 101–2; in SNCC's New
    York office, 112; and Forman, 162; on
    appearance issue, 196; assault of, in SNCC,
    251n64

on consciousness-raising in Guatemala, 183

Suffrage movement: and WLM founders' families, 4; black women's organizations in, 29–30; Judith Brown's family and, 58; in Pam Allen's family, 59; links to abolitionism, 60; and Women's Strike for Equality, 219; and Terrell, 249n22. *See also* First Wave

Sutherland, Elizabeth (Betita Martinez), 147, 178, 268n26

Sweden, 140

Tanner, Leslie, 231–32, 235

Terrell, Mary Church, 61, 249n22

Testifying, in Civil Rights Movement, 182

Third World revolutions, 107, 263n40. *See also* anticolonial struggles

Third World Women's Alliance (TWWA): international work of, 26; interactions with white feminists, 27; Norton and, 62 ; Beal and, 65; theory study in, 113; Forman and, 163; debated CP on "woman question," 188; origins of, 212; Women's Strike for Equality and, 219; publishes *Triple Jeopardy*, 224; on West Coast, 237; leadership question and, 282n96. *See also* Black Women's Alliance; SNCC Black Women's Liberation Committee; *Triple Jeopardy*

Tillinghast, Muriel, 84, 85

Title VII (Civil Rights Act, 1964), 20, 88

Tomboys: Baker as, 23; Bates as, 28; Beal as, 65; Hanisch as, 23

Toward a Female Liberation Movement (Jones, Brown). *See* Florida Paper

Traditional womanhood, burial of, 132–133

Triple Jeopardy (newspaper): use of term by Baker, 62; debated CP on "woman question," 188; viewpoint of, 212; publication of, 224; meaning of name, 284n51

Trivial, feminism as, 97

Truth, Sojourner, 29, 60

Tubman, Harriet, 29

Ture, Kwame. *See* Carmichael, Stokely

TWWA. *See* Third World Women's Alliance

Unemployment compensation, 17, 70

UNIA. *See* Universal Negro Improvement Association

Union WAGE (Women's Alliance to Gain Equality), 283n2

Unions. *See* Labor Movement

Universal Negro Improvement Association (UNIA), 30

University. *See* college

Unpaid labor, women's, 20

US Organization, 103, 112, 262n14

Vietnam, 107–8, 112, 263n41

Vietnam War: WLM organizers and, 4; Flo Kennedy opposed, 69; Gainesville (Fla.) organizing against, 93; contrasted to feminist demands, 97; Moynihan Report and, 106; Carmichael on draft resistance in, 119; Rankin Brigade march against, 131–32; effect of Tet Offensive, 134; Poor Black Women on, 135; Sarachild's work against, 156; Weisstein's work against, 157; Chisholm's opposition to, 238

Violence against Civil Rights Movement, 45, 46–47, 49, 52, 87–88; female leadership in face of, 35, 40; effect on Civil Rights workers, 35, 50–51; compared to feminist demands, 97

Voice of the Women's Liberation Movement (newsletter), 208, 268n37; origins of, 133; reviewed in *Guardian*, 168–69

Wages, women's, 16, 17, 121, 129, 218

Walker, Barbara, 51

Waller, Joe (Omali Yeshitela), 124, 211

Ware, Cellestine: work in white groups, 26; on black and white feminists, 121; on radical feminists, 127; and NYRF, 225; book publication by, 232; on consciousness-raising, 234; on "fight own oppressors," 265n96

Warner Communications, 241, 287n19

Warsoff, Louis, 70

Washington, Cynthia, 85

WBAI-FM (New York), 169

Weathers, Mary Ann, 107, 204, 233

Weaver, Claude, 66

Carol Giardina is a visiting assistant professor with a joint appointment in the Department of History and the Department of Women's Studies at Queen's College in New York. She contributed to *Making Waves* (UPF, 2003) and *The Human Tradition in the Civil Rights Movement*.